3-2012

W9-CDP-638

THE CONTENT AND STYLE

of an

ORAL LITERATURE

Clackamas Chinook Myths and Tales

THE
CONTENT AND STYLE
of an
ORAL LITERATURE

Clackamas Chinook Myths and Tales

MELVILLE JACOBS

THE UNIVERSITY OF CHICAGO PRESS
CHICAGO & LONDON

This volume has also been issued by the Wenner-Gren Foundation for Anthropological Research, Incorporated, as *Viking Foundation Publications in Anthropology Number 26,* in a limited, paper-bound edition for private distribution to scholars and institutions throughout the world. The publishers gratefully acknowledge the permission granted by the Foundation for the appearance of this edition.

International Standard Book Number: 0-226-38973-1
Library of Congress Catalog Card Number: 58-5617

THE UNIVERSITY OF CHICAGO PRESS, CHICAGO 60637
The University of Chicago Press, Ltd., London

PREFACE

D
URING about two months in the summer of 1929 and in another session of two
months, January–March, 1930, I recorded Clackamas Chinook myths, tales,
and ethnographic items in text and translation near Oregon City, Oregon.
I also obtained miscellaneous ethnographic notes in English and a collection of songs.
The informant, Mrs. Victoria Howard, was one of the last two, or at most three,
surviving speakers of the Clackamas dialect of Chinook. She spoke good English
and at all times co-operated with efficiency, speed, and delightful humor. The American Council of Learned Societies Committee on Research in American Indian Languages and the University of Washington provided equal funds for the research. In
the years from 1949 to 1953 I prepared *Clackamas Chinook Texts* from the field notebooks which contained Mrs. Howard's materials. The first segment of her texts appeared in April, 1958, as *Clackamas Chinook Texts: Part I* (Publication 8 of the In-
diana University Research Center in Anthropology, Folklore, and Linguistics). Upon
completion of the manuscripts of both parts of the texts, I proceeded to study the
content and style of the myths and tales. The Agnes Anderson Research Fund of
the Graduate School of the University of Washington thereupon supported the
services of a research assistant, Miss Sally Snyder, doctoral candidate in the Depart-
ment of Anthropology. She provided devoted labor and stimulating comments, for
she had lately returned from Salishan researches which had supplied her with notes
even more extensive than my Chinook files. My wife, Elizabeth D. Jacobs, who in
the 1930's secured quantities of linguistic, folkloristic, and ethnographic materials
from several western Oregon Indian peoples, supplied invaluable suggestions and
criticisms at all stages of the work. The publisher of *Clackamas Chinook Texts* has
graciously permitted reprinting the story translations of Part I.

I have used symbols currently employed by students of American Indian languages for the transcription of a few names which could not be translated. I promise
the reader that his mispronunciation of them, if he is unacquainted with transcrip-
tional symbols, will not adversely affect his reading of the method and theory which
this book presents.

MELVILLE JACOBS

1-1

TABLE OF CONTENTS

PART IIB. FEATURES OF STYLE

INTRODUCTION

THE history of developing realization of the complexities and values of non-Western social systems and their cultural expressions is a long one. Portions of such points of view can be traced back at least to Rousseau.

Although anthropology, which developed a century after Rousseau, has a great many descriptive treatments of technologically primitive societies' various cultural manifestations—religious ideology, music, and oral literature—the processes responsible for such creativity are little known because anthropology has not proceeded far toward a system of scientific theory. It has advanced little beyond sketchy description and orderly but untheoretical arrangement in its reports on the world's peoples. The many causes of cultural phenomena can be identified when the innumerable components of that which is created and maintained have been intensively sought out, properly arranged or structured, and their ties with everything else estimated. The initial task is to portray the basic structure and functioning of the socioeconomic system whose cultural products and projective expressions interest us. Analogous dissection, arrangement of parts, and weighings of the import of cultural expressions can follow. This book is concerned with a cultural expression; one of its principal objects is to present a method by which the impressive oral literature of a now extinct food-gathering people can be understood—in its inner content, its structurings and functions, and the probable causes, including projective mechanisms, for its forms and operations.

Except for the small band of professional folklorists, readers of non-Western oral literatures are, I suppose, about as rare as nuclear physicists who read Bulgarian poetry. A few reasons account for the absence of a world audience which enjoys exotic oral literatures in an equivalent of the manner in which Euroamerican audiences enjoy their own theater. One reason is that the content of an exotic literature is not often very intelligible to persons of other sociocultural heritages. Many of the themes are foreign. The manner of life of the people is strange and is left undescribed. The personalities of actors in the stories are unfamiliar. The humor feels bizarre. A second reason lies in the structuring and style of an oral literature: its narrators usually delivered relatively bare bones of their stories, while the native audience immediately filled in with many associations and feelings which a non-member of the group could not possibly have. An outline, no matter how excellently translated, is not likely to maintain a reader's curiosity because too much of the original, whether spoken or sensed, is missing.

Accordingly, I believe that except for texts and literal translations, which are primarily of value for linguistics and source documentation, publications of non-

1

Western oral literature must be written out in terms of the total literary event in the native setting, accompanied by all that needs to be said in order to reconstruct and explain that phenomenon to the outsider. In other words, publication of an exotic oral literature should comprise both the dictated version and the probable audience and community responses to it. The particular event should be set in its context. Until both the original version and the native responses to it are presented, we can know and appreciate little more of folklore than we know and appreciate of a conversation between two foreigners, only one of whose words are recorded. Furthermore, publication of such literatures should include discussions of socio-cultural features which tie in vitally with the literature itself.

One of the values in a work of this kind is that it may exhibit to the contemporary literature-reading public and to literary critics the complexity and worth of litera-tures which non-literate peoples transmitted. A collection of texts and translations of an oral literature may be unimpressive and unintelligible because the expressive content is hopelessly hidden or incomprehensible and the design strange. I believe, then, that non-Western oral literatures will become increasingly accepted as worthy forms of art, not in word or sentence translations, but in interpreted and annotated presentations. A principal problem for the author of a work of exegesis like this one, apart from the care which he must exert to be accurate and to deal with prob-abilities in his interpretations, is to present the stories more vividly and intelligibly than they would be in a bare translation.

His offering should attempt to do still more for the reader. He may be able to show how the literature's transmitters expressed, in a stylized way, their needs and feelings about themselves. He may find evidence, in the stories, that the natives often responded to life by means of humor, by examples of supposed predecessors who successfully utilized or leaned upon supernaturals, by displacement of feelings upon scapegoat actors, and by identification with actors who represented reality and values. The problem is to point to if not lay bare these and other mechanisms and to show how the society created them. I do not believe that I have gone far in doing these things for Clackamas Chinook literature and society because my ad-vent was so late that I was not able to learn enough about the people. Even if I have not exhibited much of the content, form, and functions of an oral literature because I studied one that was in a late stage of deterioration, I hope that I have shown how others may understand and appreciate a folklore. In fact, the paucity of knowledge about a Chinook people has been advantageous: my study could be completed more speedily and with less bewilderment consequent upon possession of quantities of information. But no sociocultural heritage is simple. No people is simple-minded. I am sure that many Chinooks were complicated, subtle, humor-ous, dignified, bravely realistic, foolish, ridiculous, and anxious. I think that we of modern Western civilization ought to be concerned as much about their arts and themselves as we are about the wealthy civilizations.

My study has had various motivations. One has been to explore in the direction of finding a more revealing procedure for presentation of an oral literature, so as to supplement the bare dictations which dominate the archives of folklore. A second motive has been to espy diverse components and processes in an oral literature. Another has been to offer a demonstration of what can and always should be done with exceptionally scanty oral literature materials, such as those which anthropologists obtain from a moribund society. But the primary interest has been to show that analysis of an oral literature, as of any portion of a society, should be undertaken with a multifaceted approach. This study has been premised on the assumption that factors of causation or process are plural. They are historical. cultural, psychological, linguistic, and aesthetic. They arise on various levels. They include features of societal structure and the many ways in which people relate to one another. In short, this book tries to show that there is a method by which an oral literature can be examined in a scientific spirit and that such examination will greatly enhance enjoyment of the literature's content and form. Multifactorial premises constitute the basis of the method and alone permit the integration of an oral literature's content and processes with the rest of the societal heritage.

Let us turn, then, from such general thoughts to an outline of the analysis ventured in this book. In it I present eight stories as illustrative samples of the procedure which I adopted in interpreting the sixty-four stories in the field notebooks from Mrs. Howard. The remaining fifty-six analyses will appear in a later publication which will bear the title *The People Are Coming Soon: Analyses of Clackamas Chinook Stories*. I have attempted to reconstruct for each story as much as I could of what I deduced was happening before, during, and after the narrator's recital. I have tried to "hear" the audience and the community as well as the raconteur, because of the conviction that everybody participated—at least in northwest states Indian groups. I have tried not to underplay that which the narrator devised, but I have been painstakingly attentive to what I felt must have been happening to her audience and in the community.

In *Clackamas Chinook Texts*, Part I of which has been published, the stories appear in the form in which they were dictated and in the traditional format that was set for folkloristic anthropologists by Dr. Franz Boas in the 1890's, when he, too, printed Chinook texts. The two dialects which he recorded were to the west of Clackamas, in Washington.[1]

Although the eight sample stories of this book are given in close translation, I have, on the contrary, attempted to follow a method of reconstruction and interpretation, to see the literature as it appeared to Chinooks, and to show the reciprocal processes between the stories and the culture, between the particular event and the people themselves. Part I discusses each of the eight stories in relative isolation from analyses of other Clackamas stories. In the analysis of each I have attempted to do at least the following things in the order indicated: A usable version, in translation, has been given initially. A freer version has been woven into the interpretation. Deductions have been made about interpersonal relationships and personalities which were present in the literature and the society or which were conceived of by the people. Suggestions have been made of what

I judge may have been the intent of the raconteur and the responses of the people. Choices of the storyteller and responses of the audience point, in many instances, to decisive and recurrent features of content and style. These are suggested. I regard content and form not as sharply distinguished but as contrasted extremes in an intergrading continuum of interacting features.[2] A very few features, such as introductory and closing formulas, are relatively formal in myths of the northwest states; such strongly stylized items lack meaningful content of moment.

Part II is a report of a later period of study, when it became possible to examine the collection as a unitary literature. Only a few more features are treated in Part II than are noted within the analyses of individual stories, but the intensity and detail with which these are examined is in many instances greater in Part II, which also applies simple quantification wherever it assists in revealing significant characteristics. Part II includes unified studies of titles, stylized introductions and closing sentences, humor, values, types of plays, formalized actions or plot expediters, and other traits of content and style which are cited only incidentally or occasionally in the analyses exemplified in Part I.

The problem of presentation here is to analyze each story in detail but to avoid an insufferably repetitive citation of items which recur in a number of the stories. Part II assembles, arranges, and discusses the important recurrent features, and these really characterize the literature. The consequence of placing in Part II those repetitive features which are basic is that individual story analyses are perforce sketchy for many of the characteristics which are central to the literature. An example of the exclusion of much of the analysis from the discussions of individual stories and its relegation to topical headings in Part II is in expressions of humor. Were every one of many hundreds of instances of the comic examined in the discrete analyses, these would be long and wearisome. Clackamas humor may be classified according to fifteen or more major types of stimuli. Need for efficient presentation results in their assignment to a section in Part II, where each kind of humor stimulus is documented by only a few citations of occurrences in the discussions of individual stories. In a sense, then, these discussions, which are meant to be read as if the literature had been a written one, constitute an introduction to the serious and dry business undertaken, with as much brevity as possible, in Part II. At present I am unable to envisage a more satisfactory form for close analysis of an oral literature if that analysis, or part of it, is to be read by anyone who is not fascinated by highly schematized forms of publication. The sample analyses of Part I show how I was thinking as I went along. Part II compactly offers the results of analyzing sixty-four stories. It spotlights a method.

The method involves the selection, identification, and interpretation of as many features of Clackamas literature as I can find, against the background of the rest of the literature and in the feeble light of what I have been able to ascertain about Clackamas society and culture. That heritage has been extinct since 1936 or 1937 and can be reported upon only in the fragments and petty items which were earlier noted from the two last usable informants in the group. The literary analysis suffers very much because of meager ethnographic information. Analysis would have been much lengthier, and certainly superior, had I arrived on the scene a few decades earlier, when a rich ethnographic picture could have been secured. A comprehensive study would have contained approaches in addition to those which I employed. But I have tried, after isolating every identifiable constituent in each story, to point to the ways in which these constituents fit together, both in the story and in the society.

It may be well to make brief note of a number of additional formulations upon which the analyses of stories are predicated. Each myth, and each phrase within a myth, functioned in a raconteur-audience-community relationship of shared participation, because literary creativity resided as much in the community as in the storyteller of the evening. That which was familiar to all was treated with an extreme of selectivity as well as with a special kind of stylization. Only a few features of a situation or actor were chosen for mention; they were worded succinctly and in traditional manner. The narrator's terse phrases were, in current terminology, coded signals. Audience members reacted by decoding, reconstructing, filling in, and by a variety of such other responses as identification and projection. These responses were at once ideational and emotional. The choices of what the narrator was to say resulted in a report of external behavior, almost never of feelings, although voice, gesture, and other devices for dramatic expression permitted a raconteur to act out the emotions of characters. The important thing to keep in mind is that the narrator did not verbalize actors' feelings. The absence of verbalized emotions was so complete that the scholar may only speculate about the actors' and audience's feelings, but he must not evade such theorization if there is to be any serious analysis of the literature.

Furthermore, the characters' personalities constituted one of the central literary interests. Such personalities may be revealed only by study of what they did, not by anything that the raconteur said in judgment or commentary—although, in a living native society, one might obtain such insights by direct questioning of members of the community. Although the personalities of story actors did not necessarily duplicate personalities of Clackamas Indians, components of the former undoubtedly represented components of the latter. Interpersonal relationships constituted another central interest; and, again, they may be deduced, although they were not formulated as such by a narrator. The various feelings of kinship and relationship which are represented in the literature include some of the most valuable insights about Clackamas life that can be gleaned from the stories. In fact, they may throw light on other sociocultural heritages of the Pacific Northwest.

Interpretation of most of the first myth and of other stories does not have the minuteness of analysis which was attempted for the first lines. However, when a personality, relationship, or other feature of content, or a trait of style, appears for the first time, it is sometimes examined with similar care instead of with the usual cursive interpretation. If such a feature appears a number of times, and most of them do, some repetitiousness may mar the discussions. But it may be better to repeat than to leave items unnoticed merely because similar ones had been commented upon earlier.

Reading of each story analysis may be done without examination of the translation which precedes it, because each analysis contains the essentials of the story. However, many readers may prefer to examine a translation in order to contrast it in all its starkness with the interpretive treatment. I hope that the almost literal offering will display sufficiently the bleakness—only to an outsider such as a Euroamerican reader—of the original version. Each translation seems to me to be so terse or obscure that I have added many explanatory words: such additions are in parentheses. *Clackamas Chinook Texts* also presents all stories which are referred to parenthetically by number.

One characteristic of the literature deserves underlining. I obtained definite responses from northwest states Indians when I asked, as I often did, a question such as What did Coyote look like in the Myth Age? or, What did Skunk look like then? or, What did Grizzly Woman look like? I always obtained a succinct reply. In every instance it amounted to, "He (or she) looked just like a person." For a long time I doubted that this answer could be literally true, because I knew that precultural actors often behaved like coyotes, skunks, or grizzlies. The problem was to find evidences that would throw additional light on the Indians' visual images of their myth actors. Earlier anthropological and folkloristic workers in the northwest states had not clarified this question. Not until I formulated, as I have in the following pages, something of the region's ideology of spirit-powers, did I comprehend that I must accept exactly what the Indians said about the physical appearance of myth actors. Actors who were given animal, fish, bird, or insect names sometimes differed in behavior, not in significant features of body structure, from actors who were avowedly human in temperament. From the Indians' viewpoint a Myth Era actor who was named Skunk was really a human-like being possessed of a supernatural which was both a skunk and human-like. At a later precultural time he metamorphosed into a skunk, to remain a skunk for all eras to come.

A modern Indian woman who had long before effected a relationship with a grizzly spirit-power might briefly and episodically mutate into grizzly garb when she was out in the woods. But she would revert to her normal human body before she returned to her hamlet. So, too, in the Myth Era the actor named Grizzly Woman was normally a woman, not a grizzly. She would change into her grizzly form when she was on a cannibal orgy. It was her inner nature to do that because of her grizzly spirit-power. The story analyses of Part I will be misunderstood if there is confusion about the manifest human appearance of most of the myth actors or if, like writers and illustrators of children's story books, we permit ourselves visual images or cartoon notions of animals or half-human, half-animal figures. Clackamas, like the Indians of neighboring societies, regarded most actors of their myths as human beings, but as humans who often had most distinctive or powerful supernatural relatives. The animal names of actors were consequent upon these actors' spirit-powers and correlated behavior, not upon their physical appearance.

I have been speaking of "actors" rather than "characters" in the stories; this is deliberate. Folklorists have tended to treat oral literatures of non-Western peoples as if their subject matter were analogous to novels, short stories, or poetry. I believe that stress upon Chinook literature as a kind of theater does better justice to its content, designs, and functions. Therefore emphases are upon actors, acts, scenes, epilogues, and the like, rather than upon plots, motifs, and episodes. The absence of psychological interpretation and notation of feelings in the native lines, the terse summarization of action, and the indications which we have that narrators gave dramatic renditions warrant the deduction that recitals of stories resembled plays more closely than other forms of Western literature. Since the lexicon of English reflects Euroamerican culture, terms which come from the theater of that culture offer fitting analogues for features of the literature of Chinooks.

Several considerations and decisions about the philosophy of art should be made explicit. First, Clackamas literature offers no evidence to support either protagonists of art for art's sake or supporters of instrumentalism in art. The literature obviously served needs and was intrinsically pleasurable. It would not have been maintained had it not served and pleased. The analysis therefore points to aesthetic pleasures and various other services provided by the stories. Second, the literature contains few if any wholly self-contained stories which can be interpreted or properly appreciated in isolation from other stories or from the culture. Therefore, close textual reading and interpretation of each story is combined with or related to customary feelings, relationships, and ideological features of Clackamas. There is nothing new in a procedure of literary criticism which utilizes close reading. But a many-sided approach of that kind has, I think, never been applied to the literature of a people who lacked a technique of writing, although careful analyses and interpretations of special aspects of oral literatures are already familiar in technical folkloristic publications.

Literary criticism has so often accepted the viewpoint that linguistic factors are important in literary expression that it is proper to anticipate and evaluate such factors at the start. Phonological factors in Clackamas literature involved principally two processes. But neither was distinctive for literature. They appeared as frequently and in the same ways in everyday conversation, as far as I know. One process was the employment of onomatopoetic morphemes. The other was the use of regular consonantal changes to express so-called diminutive and augmentative nuances of meaning. The only special morphological factor which might be identified is the use of the remote past tense verb prefix, but it was also used in ordinary conversation to indicate remote past time. Its especially frequent employment in stories reflects only their placement in bygone eras. Lexicographic or semantic factors in the literature may include a few morphemes which were archaic. I find no syntactic forms that were peculiar to the literature. If distinctive frequencies of such forms are present, we cannot ascertain the fact because we lack text materials in everyday speech. In summary, my conviction is that linguistic factors exhibited in the text data which we have were so negligible, if contrasted with factors of content and style, that the present study could properly ignore them. Vocal mannerisms and melodic patterns must have been important in the literature, but they cannot be identified because of the lack of mechanical or electric recordings of Clackamas utterances.

A comparative-historical approach has been omitted, too. Its pursuit would take a number of years of additional research. Studies of that kind are exemplified in Boas' monumental *Tsimshian Mythology* and Reichard's *Coeur d'Alene Myths*.[3] Since I identify and deal with many items in addition to the plot and motif features which those authors studied, the time which would have to be spent in preparation of a similar type of comparative research would be several times greater than they invested.

A normative or evaluative approach has been largely avoided because I believe that at present any non-Chinook lacks sufficient Chinookan cultural background, as well as the necessary heritage of Chinookan aesthetic values. Subjection of the stories to critical judgments would therefore be premature and culture bound.

In spite of these and other omissions, the study is, I hope, a useful although only partial demonstration of how one might proceed toward comprehension and appreciation of an oral literature. What I have done may not have gone far toward a full interpretation. But if my attempt has shown a way of placing flesh upon the bones of translated dictations that were given by one of the last informed survivors of a virtually extinct heritage, and if the procedure has revealed pitfalls for others, it has been worthwhile. Further study may prove both feasible and rewarding when other oral literatures have been analyzed and when comparative study has increased our insights and sharpened our analytic tools.

Before the analysis of stories, a background sketch of the sources and nature of our information about the sociocultural heritage is needed. We know that people who spoke Chinook languages lived on both sides of the lower Columbia River. Their riverbank hamlets were close to the coast near the estuary of the river; they were along the river up to the large Wasco and Wishram villages, the most easterly of the Chinook communities, a few miles beyond the modern city of The Dalles, Oregon. Many explorers and travelers, from Lewis and Clark in 1805 and on through several decades, reported odds and ends of externals of Chinook life. About 1890 Dr. Franz Boas obtained texts and a very few ethnographic notes on a coastal Chinook people of southwestern Washington—he called them Lower Chinook—and he briefly visited Clatsop Chinook survivors who lived in the vicinity of Astoria, a modern city on the Columbia at the northwestern corner of Oregon. He also recorded texts in the Kathlamet dialect—it was intelligible to Clackamas—which was spoken along the Columbia in Washington hamlets some tens of miles east of Astoria.

In the 1930's Dr. Verne F. Ray secured a few additional notes on southwestern Washington Chinook customs. In 1905 Edward Sapir, then aged twenty, recorded

Wishram texts, and in the 1920's Dr. Leslie Spier gleaned ethnographic items from Wishram and Wasco survivors. In 1930 Walter Dyk studied Wishram grammar, and in recent years Drs. David and Katherine French have obtained further materials on Wishram and Wasco customs. Knowledge of Clackamas people, who lived halfway between the coastal or near-coastal Chinooks and the Wishram-Wasco peoples, the latter almost two hundred miles up the river, was unavailable until my research with Mrs. Howard in 1929 and 1930. Philip Drucker briefly supplemented it in a few days of interviews with John Watcheeno in the middle 1930's. Except for the well-structured grammatical analysis of Wishram by Dyk, which has not been published, every report on a Chinook group has constituted a listing of fragments. The cluster of hamlets and villages which spoke the Clackamas dialect is about as poorly known as other Chinook groups, and it is much too late to add to our crumbs of information, except for the upriver informants who are available today to Drs. David and Katherine French. Clackamas settlements were along the lower Willamette River from Portland to Oregon City and up the Clackamas River, which empties into the Willamette between those modern cities. Clackamas had a society and culture which cannot now be distinguished from other Chinooks, except for items of linguistic and folkloristic kinds.

I therefore note the pittances which have been procured about all the Chinooks, in order to present the probable essentials of Clackamas life, custom, and belief. Similar gleanings—largely my own—about contiguous but non-Chinookan peoples help to fill in the sketch.

The ribbon of coastal and river Chinook settlements may have numbered over one hundred. The central district, where the Clackamas dialect was spoken, may have been especially densely populated and may have numbered twenty or more hamlets and one or two villages, the villages at the Willamette River falls at Oregon City. There many hundreds of persons dwelt in a few score houses.

During most months of the year, and according to the season, groups of men left the settlements to hunt or fish, perhaps more often the latter; women departed in spring and summer to gather roots, sprouts, or berries. Produce of food parties was shared. Individuals who went out alone kept the food they obtained. Smoke-drying of deer and elk meat and of fish, and various means of drying and preserving berries and roots, usually guaranteed surpluses of foods for later winter months when people had to stay at home. In the most inclement parts of the winter, men remained in the houses making or repairing weapons and equipment, while the women labored at garments, baskets, and mats, either inside the houses or at menstrual-and-women's-work huts nearby. On winter evenings everyone attended recitals of myths or participated in spirit-power singing and dancing in the larger houses which belonged to well-do-to families.

Such families lived in rectangular hewn plank houses; poorer families perhaps had inferior structures whose walls were chunks of fir or cedar bark. Slaves lived in their well-to-do masters' homes.

Toddlers and older children very likely spent the day playing in the woods or clearings near the village and returned at sundown. Older children took care of the younger ones at such playgrounds, and the older ones occasionally accompanied the adults of their sex, helping in food production and preservation, receiving plaudits for their successes, and identifying as early as possible with adults.

From six or seven years of age until puberty, youngsters practiced and gradually mastered the handicraft, food-producing, and other skills customarily assigned to their sex. Before puberty, older persons, not parents, inculcated values and lore and received payments for their pedagogy.

At the time of her first menstruation a girl's father gave her an expensive puberty ceremonial and feast, attended by everyone. Its important details are largely unknown. Subsequently, the girl was closely chaperoned by older females, lest she be disgraced by a pregnancy and thereby diminish the purchase price that her father would otherwise receive for her as an unsullied bride.

At puberty and after, adolescent boys were directed to known sites beside lakes or in the hills where spirit-powers were customarily about. There a youngster remained for days, fasted, bathed, performed arduous tasks, and faced the terrors of dark nights, until a spirit-power instructed him and gave him one or more songs, perhaps dances too. When the youth returned and signified to his father that he had "found" a supernatural, his parent at once arranged and incurred the considerable monetary cost of five nights of spirit-power singing and dancing, with accompanying feasting and gifts for those who attended. During such sessions, people who already had "found" supernaturals also sang and danced in terms of their own spirit-powers.

Older persons went away too, in order to effect relationships with new spirit-powers, so that over the years an individual might amass a number of non-visible kin, each conferring distinctive abilities, immunities, songs, and dances. A few men acquired supernaturals which accounted for their becoming specialists at woodwork, hunting, or fishing, but we do not know whether women also became specialists at some type of woman's work. Occasionally an older person who had encountered a spirit-power granting one or another kind of doctoring ability became a curing shaman and received fees from the sick or their relatives. Like many practitioners of the healing arts, shamans were jealously protective of their supernaturals, skills, and fee-charging; sometimes they offered competitive public demonstrations of shamanistic power. Some shamans accepted fees to "poison" people; others only cured the sick or controlled the weather. Everybody sought to acquire spirit-power kin, but there was overweening respect for and tension about persons whose supernaturals could affect other persons' lives.

Rules exacting village exogamy, and exogamy where there was known kinship, were rigorous. In well-to-do families resident in different villages, the fathers anticipated the marriage of their offspring by exchanging valuables—sea-shell money, furs, and perhaps other commodities. In this manner fathers progressively cemented a marital relationship-to-be between their postpubescent offspring and, in effect, their families. Child betrothals occurred between the wealthiest families.

Although adultery before marriage made a girl valueless and disgraced her relatives, an unmarried youth was expected to travel from village to village, to "see the world," and to sow his wild oats by raping unchaperoned adolescent girls and younger women who were out alone. If caught, he might be killed by his victim's relatives. On the highly ceremonialized marriage day, after the girl's parents and family retinue had escorted her to her new husband's settlement, the father of the youth, who was often a few years older than the bride, bought his son's wife with an especially large final payment. Arranged marriages, a formal bride "purchase" on the day of the marriage, and elaborate later gift exchanges between in-law families were standard, but minimal sums were expended by poor families. Married couples visited their families sometimes as often as annually, always with much exchanging of garments and other gifts, in order to exhibit wealth and thereby status.

Leaders of well-to-do families, especially headmen, owned important productive property such as fishing stations and captured or purchased slaves. Headmen and their wives also possessed many money sea shells. Headmen were particularly wealthy and secure in status because of their money, their property in slaves, and the percentage they withheld when they collected a fine imposed on a malefactor of the hamlet; they also had the valuable help of the younger men who continued to reside in their household, who assisted them in food production, and who produced for them the equipment for which they had special spirit-powers and handicraft skill. In addition, headmen were wealthy because of their plural wives—possibly never more than four or five—and their larger supply of maritally purchasable daughters.

Every family pooled its resources to give feasts and spirit-power dances, which were concluded with feasting and gifts, to make a deep impression, competitively, upon other families. In all likelihood the society was profoundly, indeed bitterly, competitive; families vied more or less hostilely for status, well-do-to sought to avoid sinking in community regard, and poor people struggled, usually vainly, to ascend into the ranks of the well-to-do. The social structure was stratified in nominal terms of headmen, well-to-do, poor, and the slaves who belonged to the headmen and the well-to-do. Except for slaves, tensions must have been extreme because of the potential to ascend or descend the social ladder. However, open hostility was usually displaced upon families resident in other villages.

A headman was the core of executive power. He was maintained in his role by community respect for him because he was the oldest son of the previous headman, because he was wealthy and owned slaves and had various followers living in his house, because he was polygamous and his wives came from fine families of other communities, and because he was more likely than other men, excepting only shamans, to have a number of strong spirit-power allies. His supporters and assistants, whom he housed, fed, and aided in many ways, were also his faithful police or soldiery. If a headman lacked a son, his daughter might become *de facto* head of the community. A headman dispensed justice in intravillage trouble situations, fined offenders, and served as a guardian and adviser to his villagers.

He held councils with the male leaders of the village's well-to-do families, whose opinions he did not disregard, if he was wise. People spoke of him as a good man, primarily because of his wealth in money and slaves, his hereditary and high status, and his executive role. If he was unjust, unwise, or insufferably authoritarian and pompous, they had little opportunity to strike out at him with anything more potent than humor behind his back. However, social slights caused extreme rancor and might result in "poisoning" or terrifying feuding.

Females, who were married off by their fathers as soon as possible after the first menstruation and the puberty rites, remained purchased commodities and operated within severely confined domestic limits until the climacteric; that is, they did not travel alone or take initiative in community affairs. In a wealthy household which was polygamous, the first wife dominated her co-wives. Their function as the property of their husband and husband's family metamorphosed after the menopause. Doors of opportunity then opened. Wives and widows could then become shamans, artists, or controllers of all the young people of the house. Feelings about older women were therefore mixed with respect and resentment, to a degree that the mythology contains many projections of how they were actually regarded.

Slaves and their offspring remained slaves. The certainties about their status, and the securities arising from the conviction that they were least often benefited by acquisition of potent supernatural allies, were such that captive or inherited slaves infreqeuntly received projection into myths. One did not compete with or really fear a slave. He performed menial services and had little chance of successfully returning to a natal community and freedom. Flight through hundreds of miles of strange communities was almost impossible because such peoples would also enslave a fugitive who had been a slave before.

The important people of a hamlet or village were the hereditary headman, his immediate kin, and the few well-to-do. Their anxieties lest they lose status, wealth, and power, and everyone else's suppressed feelings about them, were vital factors in their dominance as actors in myths. I presume that if their position in society had been more secure, they might have figured less importantly in the literature.

A few headmen, abetted by their young male assistants and household followers, raided and massacred peoples far to the south, to return to the Columbia with valuables and bound younger captives who henceforth were slaves. Chinook headmen who engaged in such raiding and in the marketing of slaves probably were outstanding factors in the perpetually turbulent social ranking of well-to-do and headman families, and they were also the principal participants in intervillage economic exchanges. The few large Chinook villages, such as the two Clackamas communities at Oregon City, functioned as informal market centers. Visitors from other peoples entered a market village, received hospitality in a headman's slave-serviced house, and there exchanged commodities, whether slaves, dried foodstuffs, or artifacts, at the same time that dancing and competitive games were enjoyed.

The basis of religion was in the animistic ideology of innumerable spirit-powers, sometimes translated as dream powers—a vast population of projection figures in the form of animals, birds, fish, insects, and various other beings. They "slept" here and there far from the hamlet and usually waited for a clean suppliant to come to them. Then they awoke and aided that person all through his life. Although the dominant means of "finding" a spirit-power was to go to a site at a distance where such animistic gentry were resting and waiting, close contact with elders and dreams were also ways by which some persons "found" supernaturals. A person obeyed his new kin's instructions, sang and danced the songs and dances which the spirit-power had given him, but never revealed, except by indirection and symbolic expression in songs, dances, and perhaps dance regalia, the details which characterized his non-material kin. A person sought not one but many such supernatural relatives. Wealth, status, health, abilities, and long life—which everyone wanted but was never certain he could depend upon—rested upon both biological lineages of ordinary humans and the wholly private supernaturals. A person dreamed about the latter, and he intensified and validated his relationship to them in the public winter spirit-power dances which were given by richer men of the community.

In addition to the indispensable security which each person received in his individual ties with supernaturals, religion provided public security in rites for the first salmon, first berries, and first roots. Clackamas literature cited only the supernaturals, not the public rites; it thereby shows where Clackamas were unsure of themselves, for they did not need to project into myth the ceremonials which a hamlet conducted with efficiency.

The land of ghosts of the recently deceased was neither a heaven or hell, by analogy with Western civilization's concepts. It was a dismal country beyond a river, where the recently deceased persons' soul-ghosts tarried for about a decade. Persons long since dead had vanished entirely. The land of dead persons was of less concern than ghosts which were still close by, because such ghosts were persons who had died in very recent years. Corpses were placed in shallow graves apart from the village, in charnel houses of planks, constructed on river islands, or in canoes placed on branches of trees. People kept far from such decomposing bodies and at a funeral encouraged the ghost to go away, lest it entice survivors to die and accompany it. Connections between religion and death had little to do with an ideology about the uninteresting land beyond, where one stayed for only a short term of years before disappearing eternally. A person's ethical worth had no relationship to his fate: everyone went to the land of dead people, and there the valuables which were placed at the grave gave him some sort of status, but nothing like his ranking in the land of the living. The principal relationship between religion and annihilation anxiety was in the process of securing and reinforcing ties with the almost tangible spirit-powers, who aided only the living. The ghosts in the land of the dead had no spirit-power allies.

Doctoring was religious in ideological content: a shaman employed his supernaturals in various therapeutic ways. He was able—for a considerable fee—to remove and "kill" potentially lethal "poisons" inserted by another shaman, or he could send out his supernatural to find and return a dying person's ghost-soul. His dramatic ministrations continued for many nights, in the presence of many adult residents of the community. Shamans functioned as therapists principally for high fevers and protracted conditions which seemed likely to kill, because the theory was that anything which was causing a person to die came from others' spirit-powers or from loss of one's own. Northwest Indians treated in a different way another important category of ailments which were not yet obviously lethal: these ranged from colds to muscular aches, and included some quick fevers. An individual took a twenty- to twenty-five-minute "sweat bath" in a small beehive-shaped hut beside a stream; after steaming—using water poured over hot pebbles—he dashed into the stream, then returned to the house. He sang his own or special spirit-power songs during his stay in the hut, and so he connected his self-therapy with supernatural aid. A third category of ailments, including cuts, infections, burns, and broken bones, was largely or entirely unconnected with supernaturals: poultices, herbs, and splints were among the wholly substantial methods used.

The oral literature reveals next to nothing about people's involvements in such plastic and graphic arts as woodwork, basketry, matting, woven fiber headbands and packstraps, and fringed hide garments. The literature also fails to give significant information about the functions of the large repertoires of songs and dances. It offers little more than its own art form. It supplies no insights into oratory, the formal utterances of headmen, councilmen, and emissaries, or the poetic phrasings in seasonal, marital, or girls' puberty rites. Nevertheless, artistry of many kinds constituted a central interest and served many vital social functions.

Clackamas ethics can be deduced solely from the recorded tales and myths. So too, the cosmology, logic, and other cultural traits of a philosophical kind are visible, if at all, only in the lines of the oral literature. The range of personality features and the processes of emotional and mental maturation, indeed almost all psychological aspects of Clackamas life, are unknown except for the small harvest of items collected in the course of analysis of the literature; in spite of omissions of reference to some main themes of Clackamas life and an absence of most of the descriptive detail which an outsider would like to have, these stories present far more about the Clackamas world than all the information which travelers and ethnographers have collected.

PART I

Analyses of Eight Stories

CHAPTER I

COYOTE AND SKUNK. HE TIED HIS MUSK SAC

OYOTE and Skunk lived there (at an undisclosed location). They would look for (hunt) something, they would eat it. I do not know how long they did like that. Then he (Coyote) said to him, "Younger brother. Supposing I tie you (your anus), and then I summon everyone, they will come to see you." "Oh no!" (in a pained tone). I do not know how many times he spoke to him (urging him), before he permitted him to. Then he (Coyote) went outside, he hallooed and hallooed,

"Who will come?
Our younger brother might die (because of) his stomach."

Pretty soon a Doe came. (She cried out as she approached,) "Oh dear! my older brother! oh dear! my older brother!" She came, she got to there. There Skunk lay. He was saying, "It is coming out! Hurry! it is coming out!" "Yes. Yes. You see him now. His spirit-power is getting ready to go out of him now (and when it does he will be dead). Some shaman or other did like that to him" (said Coyote to Doe). "Indeed." He said to her, "Let us move him from there." "All right," she said to him. He said to her, "Hold his legs toward you, he is light on that side." She took hold of him, while Coyote (held) his head. They moved him. He untied him (Skunk's anus). He broke wind. Doe fell there. Coyote (and Skunk) had killed her. Now then Skunk's breath had all gone out of him there (and he lay unconscious for some time).

Coyote butchered her, he roasted her (on spits), he ate her, he ate her all up. Some little pieces of bones remained lying there.

Skunk came to. There was absolutely nothing left (to eat) in their house. He (Coyote) told him, "Here are a few small things (left for you). (Not just) one person got here, lots of them got to us." He (Skunk) took and ate the bones. Now again they were living there. They looked for (hunted) various things, (and) that is what they ate.

After quite a while now again he (Coyote) said to him, "Younger brother. We are hungry. I will tie you again." "Oh dear no!" (in a pained voice). Then he said to him again, "There is nothing now for us to eat." "Oh no!" (pained voice again). So many times (Coyote urged him), and then he (Skunk) permitted him. He tied him (his anus). He lay down. He (Coyote) went outside, he hallooed,

"Who will come?
Our younger brother might die (on account of) his stomach."

I do not know how long, and then Buck came along. (As he approached he cried out,) "Oh dear! my younger brother! Oh dear! my younger brother!" He got to them there. He (Coyote) said to him, "Observe what our younger brother is saying. I do not know where he has been going around, (and now) that is what some shaman has done to him." Now Skunk himself (said), "It is coming out! Hurry! it is coming out!" "Indeed" (Buck said). (Coyote said,) "Now that is his spirit-power speaking. Will you please help me?" "Yes," he (Buck)

From *Clackamas Chinook Texts*, 1.

said to him. "You take hold of him toward his legs, I by his head." They took hold of him, they moved him, he (Coyote) untied it, he broke wind at him. Buck fell back there (unconscious), Coyote killed him. He butchered him, he roasted him, he ate him, he finished eating all of him.

Only some few small pieces remained. Soon now Skunk came to. He looked around. (There was) nothing at all, only bones were there. He (Skunk) said to him, "Where is something for me?" He (Coyote) said to him, "Oh dear oh dear. People got to us. They took away absolutely all the meat" (and I had to share it with these guests). Skunk got up, he took the bones, he gnawed on them.

Now again they lived on (there). Coyote would go away, he would bring back some mice. That is what they would eat. As for Skunk, he would dig out yellowjackets, he would bring them back. They would eat them.

After a while then he (Coyote) again said to him, "Younger brother. Now there is nothing for us to eat." "Oh no!" (in a pained voice). After a while he (Coyote) spoke to him again. "Oh no! (pained voice). Something (bad) might come to us" (said in fear). He (Coyote) said to him, "No. Now I will (for safety sake) shut our house." After some time he (Skunk) said to him, "All right." So now he tied him again. He went outside, and he hallooed,

> "Who will come?
> Our younger brother might die (because of) his stomach."

Even as he was hallooing, then along came a big Horned Buck. He came along, he got there. Then Skunk was saying, "It is coming out! Hurry! it is coming out!" "Yes yes yes yes! (said Coyote). Do you hear him? Now the spirit-power is leaving him (and he will die). I do not know where he was going about, (and then) some shaman did that to him." "It is going out!" (Skunk howled again). "Assist me (said Coyote). Let us take him close to the door." "All right," he (Horned Buck) said to him. They took hold of him, and then while they were taking him, he (Coyote) untied him. There Buck fell back (unconscious), he (Coyote) killed him too. He butchered him, he roasted him, he ate him, he ate him all up.

Shortly Skunk revived. He (Skunk) said to him, "What have you saved for me?" He said to him, "I was outside, people got to us, (and because they were guests) they took everything (all the leftover food) away." He (Skunk) said to him, "So! You are not going to tie me again." "No no younger brother! I have saved lots of (i.e., some) things (food) for you." "Hm! It is nothing." (But) he took the bones, those are what he chewed on.

The next day Skunk went somewhere or other to look for things (to eat). In the evening they came back. He (Coyote) said to him, "Younger brother. Now there are no more mice where I go." He (Skunk) paid no heed. They lived on for a while, and then again he said to him, "Dear oh dear. Younger brother. We have nothing to eat now." He paid absolutely no heed. Skunk thought, "There is nothing (to eat) now. (But) I will not let him tie me." I do not know when it was, but it was a long time before he let him tie him (again). Coyote went outside, he hallooed,

> "Who will come?
> Our younger brother might die (because of) his stomach."

After some time now an Elk came along, he was weeping. He was saying, "Oh dear! my younger brother!" He got there. Skunk now was nearly dead (from waiting and from being tied for so long). He (Coyote) said to him (to Elk), "Come closer! come sit down! Now it (the spirit-power) is getting ready, the spirit-power is going to leave him." "Indeed" (said Elk). Now Skunk was dying (to all appearances). He was saying, "It is going out! Hurry! it is going out!" "To be sure. To be sure. Listen to him. Wherever he was going about, there some shaman did like that to him. Do assist me. We will lay him by the doorway." They took hold of him, they dragged him. He (Coyote) said to him, "Hold him by the legs." Coyote took hold of him, he untied him, he broke wind, Elk fell back there (unconscious). Coyote made haste, he killed him, he butchered him, he roasted him, he ate him.

Shortly then Skunk revived. He (Coyote) said to him, "Younger brother. I saved a lot of things for you." Skunk got up, he picked up bones and sinew and things, he ate them.

The fifth time, now I do not know what came. Maybe Grizzly, maybe something or other. It killed Coyote, but I think not Skunk. I recall only that much of it now.

It told Skunk, "Your flatus will not kill people (after the Indians enter this land). You will just scare them somewhere or other by rotten logs. Then you will break wind, (and) they will only smell your vile odor. You will not kill people."

The words in which my informant, Mrs. Howard, phrased this myth, which appears to have a continuous distribution in the groups around Clackamas territory, do not appear to a literate Euroamerican to offer a notably interesting narration. It lacks the copious content of many other stories of the collection and therefore may seem trivial. Nevertheless, like the several Indian groups of the northwest states who told it, Clackamas doubtless enjoyed it. I present it here because in form and subject matter it is so simple that it can serve as an elementary example of the premises and procedures I have used in all the discussions of stories.

It would be possible to discuss in minute detail every step of every story, but such a treatment would require an astronomical number of pages and would quickly become unreadable. It is necessary to present compact interpretations and commentaries, but a detailed analysis of only the first lines of this first story will display the wealth of component parts in every story.

The title of each myth or tale was originally given by Mrs. Howard in her own words, usually at the end of her dictation and translation. I suppose that a narrator rarely if ever announced a title to an audience at a formal winter oral literature session. I believe that titles were quick references to myths or tales when they were being commented upon informally.

As in other myths, the first words announce the names and location of actors who appear in the first scene. Clackamas literature lacked a stage, acts, and scenes, but such analogies with European drama display structural characteristics of the literature. Mrs. Howard commenced her recital of the myth by saying, "Coyote and Skunk lived there." A Clackamas audience would not have repeated these introductory words, although complete repetitions did occur among some or all of the Sahaptin Indians who lived adjacent to Chinooks. A Clackamas audience responded, instead, with a choral $a^{n}\cdots$ to each phrase of the narrator.

The initial words are frustratingly uninformative to a Euroamerican, but so stark an introduction was not unrevealing to a Clackamas audience. They demanded a stylized preface which at once placed the first actors and named them. Clackamas auditors also automatically saw a Coyote and a Skunk as masculine, not merely because, in Chinook dialects, masculine prefixes (i-) attach to the morphemes for these words. Every Clackamas already knew that Coyote and Skunk were adult male actors of the Myth Age and that a number of Coyote Men and Skunk Men lived in that era.

Furthermore, when the narrator said that the two "lived there," a European's reaction might be, Where? How? In what kind of dwelling or camp? At what point in the lives of the actors? Did they live in a single abode or in adjacent structures? Were they bachelors or married? Such queries reflect interests of a very different cultural heritage; in a Clackamas recital such questions would not occur to anyone. The first phrase, with its citation of well-known precultural personalities, presented a kind of signal to an audience. The immediate response was that this was the familiar play about the incompetent and preposterous hunters, Coyote and Skunk, who lived together or near each other. They shared food gained from their hunting. Their houses were on an embankment or bluff above a stream. A comment about the actors' residence would have been an esthetic irrelevance because emphasis was upon the behavior of Coyote and Skunk and their relationship, not upon architecture and site.

The second and third phrases, "they would look for something, they would eat it"—a linguist would describe them as in equational predication—express the fact of a hunting and eating partnership. In languages of the northwest states, to look for or seek something connotes, in the present context, hunting or collecting of foods. (In other contexts it means a spirit-power quest.) Kinds of foods did not need to be cited, nor manner of hunting or collecting. Everyone knew that this Coyote, probably like other Coyote Men of the Myth Age, subsisted on rodents, not deer and elk. Methods of preparing the foods for eating receive no reference because they, too, are irrelevant. The first three phrases function, then, to present formally two familiar actors in a relationship which is like that of male kin, perhaps brothers, who produce food together and share what they have hunted. Actually, the recitalist has so far indicated overtly nothing more than a brotherly sharing, but her spoken words and emphasis on a sibling-like relationship do not comprise the totality which she has communicated to her audience.

In order to detail the elements of content of this literature and to exhibit in addition their forms, functions, and processes of development and change, it is necessary to reconstruct everything that we can about the narrator's phrases. We must ascertain what stirred in the people who responded in stylized or spontaneous manner to her words and who actively joined her and one another in the dramatic experience. I suggest that at this point in the rendition each auditor quickened to memory associations and feelings of identification with the familiar personalities of the play's precultural actors, Coyote and Skunk, and sensed their distinctive relationships to other personalities of early epochs. Since the psychological makeup of the two men and their relationships to people become progressively revealed during discussions of other myths in which they played roles, it is sufficient to observe that an audience responded with immediacy, fulness of imagery, and richness of feelings to the recitalist's announcement that Coyote and Skunk were on the stage. No European could possibly react with such images and feelings, nor could he have comparable responses of identification with the actors. The amplitude of audience response therefore contrasts with the tasteful parsimony of the narrator's phrases. Their brevity is neither bleakness nor simplicity, nor is it symbolism. The phrases deftly trigger the varied reactivity and imaginative creativity of the audience, and these audience responses, which folkloristic science must ascertain, are central to style, stability, and change in the art form. It is a pity that we cannot return to interview Mrs. Howard or any other Clackamas raconteur, but it is reasonable to suppose that each knew what he was stirring, what the listeners were filling in, and what the spare statements really projected.

Mrs. Howard's next phrase, "I do not know how long they did like that," is a recurrent stylized expression in her rendition of Clackamas literature. It provided a transition from the first three phrases, which present two actors, their relationship, and their most stressed feature of behavior—shared hunting and eating. It carried the audience along to the next idea, a fresh plan conceived by Coyote to ease his and his associate's food problem, and it suggested that the actors had had an unsatisfactory method of hunting for a long time. An enumeration in terms of months or years is stylistically impermissible. Only a long duration is mentioned. Possibly a progressive development of hunger is indicated too: the audience filled in the background of a long, long time during which the inept actors had become increasingly dissatisfied with their skimpy diet.

The next sentence, "he said to him," does not reveal the speaker. But the vocative word which follows, "younger brother," shows that the speaker has been Coyote. Everyone knew that a Coyote was a headman in other myths, a man who would call the male villagers and his followers or dependents "younger brothers." Not a single myth has a Coyote address another man as older brother, and Skunk is never well-to-do, never a headman.

From the Clackamas point of view, the next words give the essence of Coyote's scheme to obtain more and better foods. The narrator's words are a kind of coded and terse message which signals the fact that Coyote broaches his plan; the audience remembers from earlier myth recitals particulars of the stratagem. In an oral literature where reactivity and recall follow each statement of the raconteur—if they do not precede it—it would be ridiculous to verbalize things which are well known to the audience. Artistry, then, is in selection of apt words and neat phrases, those which say least and project most; artistry effects a minimum of structure and detail in order to allow the audience the maximum of imaginative creativity. Accordingly, Coyote tells Skunk in three compact utterances: "Let me tie you. I shall summon various people. They will come to visit you." The indication that Coyote wants to fasten Skunk's rectum to prevent him from prematurely spraying musk at a visitor implies that Skunk is compulsive and not too bright, that he might explode at the wrong moment. The binding permits Coyote to determine the instant when Skunk will discharge. The audience is amused at Skunk's subservience, his inability to express violence by means other than anal sadism, and the socially superior man's assumption of the right to turn Skunk on and off like a faucet.

Since the plan is the older man's, who is superior to Skunk if not actually a headman in this myth, he assumes responsibility for summoning the sorrowing visitors. Because Skunk is to feign mortal illness, Coyote says that the people will come to see Skunk before he dies. Auditors know that Skunk is not close to death, for there are no surprising turns of plot in this kind of literature, and the excitation of the audience is only to generate humor. Coyote's phrases express his role as malicious controller of the situation, the villain of the play: he will temporarily apply the fastening to his comrade's rectum, and he will call out to the unsuspecting people. He has devised the scheme for killing people easily, and he manages its operation by using his loyal companion as a dupe and tool. All that he seems to need is assurance that his worried follower will allow himself to be tied and carried outside, since Skunk can hardly restrain himself in any case from spraying the visitor. Coyote pressures for co-operation. Everyone knows that Skunk is unhappy about giving it, but, like actors in other myths, he cannot long negate urgings of a fellow villager, surely not one who is well-to-do. His first reply of "Oh no!"—no doubt rendered dramatically by the raconteur—expresses anticipation of suffering, timorousness, dislike of being forced to retain and then discharge musk because the effort nearly kills him, and resentment against being used as the handy implement of the older and more affluent brother. But Skunk is trapped in relationships that shackled Clackamas themselves: one could not say "no" indefinitely, least of all to a man of wealth.

The discussion has now proceeded as far, perhaps, as is needed to suggest the manifold possibilities in an interpretive treatment which attempts to present most items of identifiable content. A compact analysis of the rest of the myth follows.

Upon five successive occasions Coyote urges his reluctant companion to co-operate in the device to obtain food without the frustrations and exertions of hunting. When Skunk capitulates, Coyote ties Skunk's rectum, Skunk lies down to pretend a fatal spirit-power illness, and Coyote goes outside to call to one of the forest's kindly animal-people to come because Skunk may be dying of stomach trouble caused by a malevolent shaman. The animal-persons understand that Skunk's spirit-power is about to depart from his body and that soon he will die. In the Clackamas version of the comedy, persons who visit include Doe, Buck, Large Horned Buck, Elk, and a fifth whose name Mrs. Howard failed to remember. Each comes alone. Each aids Coyote, who holds Skunk's head. The unsuspicious helper takes Skunk's feet and the seemingly unconscious fraud is carried outside. Skunk releases musk undoubtedly at the moment when Coyote furtively unties the fastening. Skunk then really faints, whereupon Coyote kills the visitor who is unconscious from the fumes. Four persons are murdered in this way. In each instance Coyote at once gorges on the victim's flesh and leaves only some bones for Skunk to gnaw when he recovers consciousness and his breath, which he lost because of his explosive exertion. The fifth and unnamed person summoned kills Coyote, not Skunk, and announces Skunk's future role, which will be only to cause a bad odor, not to kill people.

An item of plot content which is wholly on the surface and so obvious to a native audience that it may be noted as a manifest trait of the culture is the identity of a Coyote. In this myth, as in others, Coyote represents an upper-class person (as

among other peoples of the northwest states). Although a Coyote possesses unexampled supernatural powers at certain times in his career, he is here an incompetent hunter and is therefore also impoverished, which is shameful. He pretends,
like many a headman, that he is a fine provider. In fact, Coyote actors of other
Clackamas myths never manage to catch anything larger than mice for food, except
where a Coyote plays a deity-like role—as in later scenes of the long epic myth
which recounts one Coyote's great upriver journey (9).[4] In this first story a Coyote
dupes and exploits his brother or the villager who is the homologue of a brother.
Skunk is both foolish and loyal, like many villagers. He co-operates, although with
misgivings and ultimately with much anguish.

The selfishness ascribed to the older brother suggests both hostility to such a
kinsman and distrust of wealthy gentlemen. The sibling relationship in the play
includes exploitation of a younger by an older brother and therefore suspicion of the
decency of the older brother's motivation. Other Clackamas accounts of a Coyote
supply the supporting notion that every Coyote is so narcissistic, when he is not a
deity-like figure, that he is hostile to everyone except his daughter. The comedy also
tells about naïve visitors who get killed and eaten in spite of their kindliness. This
is another way of expressing feeling that neighboring villages may be dangerous;
perhaps, too, it indicates the presence of tension or distrust about in-laws.

In addition, the play allows the audience, like other Indian audiences of the northwest states, to enjoy vicarious sadism—the tying of Skunk's rectum, the killing of
people by a lethal flatus, and Skunk's exhaustion—that is, any poor man's—from
the violence of his flatus. The diffusion of the myth may even have been expedited
by these enjoyable motifs. But in no long time the practiced hands of literary masters
and well-informed citizenry could refurbish and realign the comedy. While Clackamas heartily enjoyed the myth's anality, they could shift their major interest in
the plot and still retain its anal aspects.

Versions of the play recorded among neighboring peoples make evident the essentials in the Clackamas version and thereby enhance understanding of Clackamas
society and sentiments about social relationships. In myths of Sahaptin-speaking
villagers who lived about a hundred miles away and directly to the east of Clackamas, Coyote is another kind of gentleman. He does not deceive or make selfish use of
Skunk—which may mean that in Sahaptin villages a leader did not manipulate and
humiliate his fellow villagers and younger brothers. Sahaptins' Skunk comes off less
well than Coyote in the fifth scene, since he is impaled and carried away on antlers,
and Coyote even weeps at his brother's fate. Furthermore, in each earlier Sahaptin
scene Coyote and Skunk share their meals of persons that Skunk has gassed. The
Clackamas Coyote can easily gorge himself and deceive Skunk by saying that other
people came, because guests always receive leftovers and take home whatever they
are unable to consume at the meal. But the Sahaptin Skunk is not in the least sub-
missive; he is a voluntary and equal partner in a crooked enterprise. On the other
hand, the Clackamas Skunk nearly kills himself when he releases his gas, and so he
serves a controlling older brother who in return does less than nothing for him. He

is weak and subservient, and he lacks self-respect; he fears the pain and exhaustion of gassing people but lets himself be argued into doing it. And he is not much of a hunter himself, since he can find only yellowjackets to share with Coyote.

Why is Coyote the greedy and mean older brother in the Clackamas comedy, the sharing brother or friend in Sahaptin versions? Some pertinent sociocultural factor may have brought about the difference in sibling relationships described by generations of narrators, and that factor may be the domineering role of wealthy Chinook villagers in relation to members of their own family—especially their younger brothers—and to other villagers. The contrasting tepidity or absence of such dominance and subservience in nearby Sahaptin bands would account for the different relationship of Coyote and Skunk in their myths. In the wealthier river and coastal communities of Chinooks, the portrayal of Coyote as a chieflike person who uses and deceives his closest relatives, as well as the rest of the people, suggests that Chinooks felt their headmen might be like Coyote. In the interior where Sahaptins lived there may have been less adverse feeling toward outstanding persons and less pressure to depict Coyote as narcissistic and cruel precisely because he was in a position of power. To be sure, Sahaptins' Coyote plays mean tricks and is malicious. But neither to his kin nor to members of the band. Sahaptin raconteurs would hardly have imagined, nor would they have sensed, that leaders or older brothers made cruel use of fellow villagers or near relatives. Such recitalists would have been less likely than Chinooks to project onto their Coyote feelings against a headman and an older brother.

While the Clackamas expression of roles appears to tie in with the kind of leadership found in a relatively wealthy trading and slaving group, versions of the myth published for two other Chinook groups, Wishram and Kathlamet, unexpectedly resemble the Sahaptin account. The Wishram version, which comes from about a hundred miles east of Clackamas, in a district which was in daily contact with Sahaptins, treats several of the five episodes rather sparely.[5] Probably it is a poorly recounted text. But enough appears in it to indicate that in attitude and motivation the theme is Sahaptin, not Clackamas, in temper. Skunk is not ordered to fake sickness. He happens to become ill. Coyote stuffs pitch in his brother's rectum—an anal reference which should be compared with Bear's fatal plastering of pitch on his wife's anus in a Clackamas myth (14). When the Wishram Coyote pulls out the pitch, the deer, antelope, and other persons who come to help carry Skunk are gassed and die—this in contrast to the Clackamas myth in which the people are merely gassed and Coyote, the arch villain, kills them. The Wishram Coyote and Skunk share the deer. Coyote takes the fat ones, Skunk the lean, and this is just, because their respective ancestors liked fat and lean meat. The Wishram relationship is therefore essentially an equal sharing of spoils. At the climax neither Coyote nor Skunk dies. Henceforth other forest people are fearful, and they refuse to heed further fraudulent summonses. The Wishram play treats Coyote and Skunk so equally that it patently relates to a tradition different from Clackamas.

Kathlamet Chinooks lived a few score miles west of Clackamas. The one published version of their play, which seems to have been well told to Franz Boas,[6] agrees surprisingly with the more distant Sahaptin and Wishram, rather than with the nearby Clackamas, in its phrasing of the relationship between the two brothers. Coyote and Skunk's (or Badger's, if Dr. Boas' translation is correct) prey in the Kathlamet myth are Sturgeon, Beaver, Seal, Porpoise, and Sea Lion—obviously coastal personnel, but perhaps of no additional significance. Musk kills these gentry directly, as in the Wishram version. And the people learn that Coyote and his brother are killing persons and refuse to respond to further summonses. The feature of distinctive interest in the Kathlamet myth is the sharing in the relationship of the brothers in the famine and gassing scenes, coinciding with the Sahaptin and Wishram versions. It contrasts with the Clackamas role of Coyote as the man of wealth who uses his weaker brother, offers him leftovers, and is finally punished by death. Unlike the other accounts, the Kathlamet myth goes on to an act wherein the principals exchange buttocks, anuses, or rectums at Coyote's suggestion, because he is a poorer hunter than his brother. This added component of the Kathlamet play may be historically related to Coyote's borrowing of Skunk's resounding organ in a Clackamas myth (9).

In the light of the several versions, a problem arises: Why did a Clackamas group located midway between Kathlamet and Wishram differ from them, as well as from Sahaptin, by portraying a relationship of abuser and abused? The other groups offer a comedy about two equals. If Clackamas at some time changed the play to fit the social relationships which we are confident that all Chinooks had, why had not Kathlamet and Wishram changed the lines, too? The trouble with formulating an answer is that knowledge of Kathlamet ethnography is almost nil. Furthermore, Dr. Boas' informant was as much a coastal Chinook as a Columbia River Kathlamet. The similarity in Wishram and Sahaptin accounts is more easily explained; various Sahaptin bands had probably long enveloped the Wishram people, and there were consequent relationships, including intermarriages. The Wishram play therefore would not closely reflect their social structure of traders and well-to-do slavers because of their participation in Sahaptin ways of thinking. Perhaps Kathlamet and some other Chinook village clusters also had intimate relationships with simply structured hunting societies in their vicinity.

Indeed, some bits of ethnographic evidence which I have about Clackamas suggest much contact with structurally simple hunting peoples like Kalapuya and Molale in northwestern Oregon, but propinquity in these instances may have intensified Clackamas pride in trade, wealth, slaves, chieftainship, and numbers. If such considerations are accurate and relevant, the unique slanting of the Clackamas myth seems explicable.

Personality portrayal as such is definitely present and important in this comedy, but it is not the uppermost interest in the Clackamas version. Skunk is primarily a symbol, without detail or incisive strokes, of a domineered, mistreated, and weak younger brother or villager. Apart from the several Clackamas myths in which a Coyote is given fuller description, that worthy is a symbol of a controlling and brutal older brother. And he is as selfish and dishonest as some well-to-do men or headmen.

The Clackamas play is also distinctive, if not notable, in its denotation of a younger brother who is less competent than the older one. Except for Skunk, younger Myth Era children, whether male or female, are usually framed in the terms of the "youngest-smartest" motif: they are smarter, fiercer, possessed of superior spirit-power, or more successful than their older brothers and sisters. So there is an additional interpretive problem in this myth: how to account for the exceptional offering of a younger sibling who is a simpleton. Clackamas perhaps continued to call Skunk "younger brother" because neighboring peoples agreed in so naming him; at the same time Clackamas themselves came to feel that the essence of the sibling relationship was that the older brother was wealthier and that he accordingly used or managed people. Skunk therefore had a special place for Clackamas. He was a symbol of ordinary people of a village, people who worked so hard that it nearly killed them, only to find that the very food they had produced was stolen by their headman or oldest brother. When a Clackamas audience laughed at Skunk—poor people break wind explosively; wealthy ones do not—poor men could air their feelings of resentment at the pitiable situation they were in. Older brothers or well-to-do men might not mind a bit of projecting of their own superiority and the ridiculousness of other persons. For both wealthy and poor, abusers and abused, the recital permitted enjoyable ventilation of feelings about relationships which produced tensions in Clackamas society.

CHAPTER II

BADGER AND COYOTE WERE NEIGHBORS

Coyote and his five children lived there (at an undisclosed location), four males, one female. Badger was a neighbor there, he had five children, all males. Each day they (all ten children) would go here and there. They came back in the evening. And the next day they would go again. Now that is the way they were doing. They would go all over, they traveled about.

Now they reached a village, they stayed up above there, they looked down below at it, they saw where they (the villagers) were playing ball. And as they stayed there and watched, the people (of the village beneath) saw them now. They went to the place there where they played ball. Now they (the villagers) played. When they threw the ball it (that ball) was just like the sun. Now they stayed (above) there, they watched them playing. Sometimes it (the ball) would drop close by them. Now they quit (playing). Then they (the ten children who were watching) went back home, they went to their houses.

The next day then they did not go anywhere. All day long they chatted about that ball (and schemed about stealing it). They discussed it. Now their father Badger heard them. He said to his sons, "What is it that you are discussing?" So they told their father. "Yes," they said to him, "we got to a village, and they were playing ball. When the ball went it was just like the sun. We thought that we would go get it." Now then he said to his children, "What do you think (about talking this over with Coyote too)?" So then they said to Coyote, "What do you think?" He said, "My children should be the first ones (to run with the ball), if they bring the ball." Badger said, "No. My children should be the first ones to do it (run with the stolen ball)." Coyote said, "No. My children have long bodies, their legs are long. They can run (faster than your children). Your children have short legs." So then he replied to him (to Coyote), "Very well then."

Now the next day they got ready, and they went. They reached there. At that place one of them (the oldest son of Coyote) went immediately to the spot where the ball might drop. He covered (buried) himself at that place (on the playing field). Then another (the next oldest son) buried himself farther on, and another one (the third in age) still farther away. All four (sons of Coyote) covered themselves (with soil on the field). The last one farther on at the end (was) their younger sister. Now the (five) children of Badger merely remained (on the hill above the field), they watched.

Soon afterwards then the people (of that village) came to there, they came to play ball. Now they threw the ball to where it fell close by him (Coyote's oldest son). He seized it. They looked for it, they said, (because they knew that) "Coyote's son is hiding it!" He let it go, and they took it, and they played more. Now it dropped close by him there once again. So then he took it, and he ran. The people turned and looked, they saw him running, he was taking the ball. Now they ran in pursuit, they got close to him, he got close to his younger brother (the second in age), he threw the ball to him. He said to him, "We are dying (going to be killed) because of the ball. Give a large chunk of it to our father." (His pursuers now caught up to and killed him.) Then the other (the second) one took it, and he ran too. The people pursued him, he got close to his young brother (Coyote's third son). Now they seized him (the second son),

From *Clackamas Chinook Texts*, 10.

and he threw it to his younger brother. They killed all four of them. Now only their younger sister held the ball, she ran, she ran and ran, she left them quite a distance (behind because she was the fastest runner of them all). She got close to the Badgers. Now as they (the villagers who pursued) seized her she threw the ball to them (to the five Badger children), she said to them, "Give the biggest portion to our father (to Coyote). We have died because of the ball."

The Badgers took the ball. He (the first and oldest Badger child) dropped it when he picked it up. Another (the next to the oldest) took it, he also dropped it when he picked it up. They (the pursuers) got to there, and the people stood there (watching the Badger children fumbling the ball). They said, they told them, "So those are the ones who would be taking away the ball!" They laughed at them (at the seemingly clumsy Badger children). They said, "Let it be a little later before we kill them!" Soon now they (the Badgers) kicked at the ground, and wind blew (and) dust (and) darkness stood there. Dust covered (everything), and the wind blew. Now the Badgers ran, they ran away with the ball. And those people pursued them. They got tired, they got thirsty (from wind and dust), they (the pursuers) turned back to their home.

On the other hand those others (the Badgers) lay down (because of exhaustion) right there when they had gotten close (to their own home). And there they sat (and rested). Now they hallooed, they said to their father, "Badger! we left your children far back there!" Now they hallooed again, they went and told Coyote, "Back yonder we left your children." That is the way they did to them (they first deceived Badger and Coyote). Now Badger went outside, he said to his children, "Now really why did you do like that? You have been teasing and paining him (Coyote)." Then they (the Badger children) went downhill (and entered the village), it was only Badger's children (who returned). They brought the ball with them.

Now Coyote tried in vain to drown himself. He did not die. Then he built a fire, he made a big fire, he leaped into it there. He did not burn, he did not die. He took a rope, he tied it, he tied it on his throat, he pulled himself up, once more he did not die. He took a knife, he cut his throat, (again) he did not die. He did every sort of thing that he intended for killing himself. He gave up. I do not know how many days he was doing like that (trying one or another means of committing suicide). Now he quit it, and he merely wept all the day long. (After a while) he gave that up (too).

Then Badger said to his children, "He has quit (mourning) now. So then cut up the ball for him. Give him half." And they did that for him, they gave him half. He took it, and he went here and there at the place where his children used to play. There he now mashed (into many pieces) that ball, at the place where they used to play. That was where he took it, he mashed it up, the ball was entirely gone (now).

Then they continued to live there, and Coyote was all alone. Now he went to work, he made a loose big pack basket. Then it was getting to be springtime, and when the leaves were coming out, now he got ready, and he went to the place there where they had killed his children. He got to the (grave of the) first one (his oldest son). He picked ferns, he lined his pack basket with them. He got to the place where they had killed the first of his sons, he collected his bones, he put them into it (into the basket), he laid them in it neatly. Then he got more ferns, he picked the leaves, he covered (the bones of) his son. Now he went a little farther, and he again got to bones (of his second son). Then he also put them into it (into the basket), and that is the way he did again. He collected the bones of all five of his children.

Now he went on, he proceeded very very slowly, he went only a short distance. Then he camped overnight. The next day he proceeded again, also very slowly like that. On the fifth day, then he heard them (talking to one another in the basket). They said, "You are lying upon me. Move a little." Then he went along all the more slowly. Now he kept going, he went just a short distance, and then he picked more leaves, he covered it all (with utmost care and constant replenishing with fresh leaves). And that is the way he did as he went along.

She (perhaps a centipede) would run across his path, she would say to him, "Sniff sniff sniff!

(because of the bad odor of decaying flesh) Coyote is taking dead persons along!" He paid no heed to her. Now she ran repeatedly and all the more in front of him, again she would speak like that to him, "Sniff! Coyote is carrying dead persons along!" He laid his basket down very very slowly (with utmost care), he got a stick, he ran after her. I do not know where she went and hid.

Then he packed his carrying basket on his back again, and now he went very very slowly, and he heard his children. Now they were chatting, they were saying, "Move around slowly and carefully! we are making our father tired." Then he was glad, and he went along even more slowly and cautiously. (He walked so very slowly that) he saw his (previous night's) campfire, and then he again camped overnight.

He went on again the next morning, and then that thing (the bug) ran back and forth across his path right there by his feet. Now he became angry. He placed his basket down, and again he chased it. I do not know where it hid.

On the fifth day then he heard them laughing. So he went along even more painstakingly. Now that thing went still more back and forth in front of him by his feet. He forgot (in his great irritation and tension), he (much too abruptly) loosened and let go his pack basket. "Oh oh oh" his children sounded (and at once died from the shock of the sudden movement of the basket). All done, he finished, and he again put back his basket on himself. When he went along now he did not hear them talking at all. He went along then. They were dead now when he uncovered his basket. Only bones were inside it. He reached his house. The following day then they buried them. He finished (with that effort). He wept for five days.

Then he said, "Indeed I myself did like that (and lost my children because of my doing). The people (who will populate this country) are coming and close by now. Only in that one manner shall it be, when persons die. In that one way had I brought my children back, then the people would be like that (in later eras). When they died in summertime wintertime or toward springtime, after the leaves (came on the trees) they (all the dead) would have come back to life, and such persons would have revived on the fifth day (following a ritual like the one I attempted). But now his (any mourner's) sorrow departs from him after ten days (of formal mourning). Then he can go to anywhere where something (entertaining) is happening or they are gambling (and) he may (then shed his mourning and) watch on at it."

Let us examine this plot and its form in detail. The narrator did not say which one of the Myth Age men who were named Coyote has four sons and a youngest and favorite child who is a female, nor did she indicate the names of the sons. Older storytellers would have recalled and noted both. However, Mrs. Howard did give the daughter's name, literally translated as "good runner" or "fast runner." This daughter has a spirit-power for foot-racing, somewhat as in another myth (*Clackamas Chinook Texts*, 7) where a Coyote's daughter, also a favorite child, has a spirit-power —this time for fatty foods.

The fact that the fifth, youngest, and most fleet-footed of Coyote's children is a daughter is not central to this myth, although it serves to identify the Coyote actor who is the tragic parent of the drama. The daughter's presence also reminded an audience about the exceptional regard in which several Coyotes held their feminine offspring. Such affection is of interest in a social system where females occupied a lower status and where projections of females in the Myth Age were often unflattering. Since the literature also presents the younger child as the smartest, the play barely hints at an Oedipal theme: it is really ignored in the plot and is not evinced again even at a deeper level of awareness.

The Coyote of this myth is to a degree consistent with the familiar Columbia River Valley composite of a more or less entertaining narcissist (this aspect of him usually placed in the earlier portion of the play) and an adult, mature, and deity-like man. Usually the second part of the composite completes the myth. The structuring of such a personality in a plot which also has two parts—the first Id-dominated, the second reality-oriented—connects with the native conceptualization of genetic developments in the personality of a man.

Actually, the myth provides no significant increment to the inventory of Myth Age personalities or to knowledge of Clackamas concepts of personality characterization. Since Badger is a plot expediter—he stands for any father who has a number of sons—and his children represent any village youngsters who are sensible because they are well reared, a recitalist suppresses citation of other traits of their personalities.

When Coyote's five children and his neighbor Badger's five are at play, they wander about, like any northwest states group of children. They emerge from the woods and see a nearby village where people are playing a game with a marvelous ball. "It shines like the sun" is a literal translation of words which are very likely a poetic way of indicating that the ball is a remarkably good one and that the visiting children would like to have it. Unfortunately, the ball suggests something about which ethnographic and myth materials offer no really satisfactory clues. Perhaps the ball is just a shinny ball of wood (Indians of western Oregon played this game). Perhaps the myth implies, instead, something which is admirable and therefore referred to metaphorically as an object as bright as—that is, as impressive or excellent as—the sun. The logical ethnographic deduction would seem to be that youngsters of one hamlet might roam to another hamlet and conduct a raid to obtain valuables from it. It would appear that danger accompanied such excursions and that there was tension between children as well as adults of different settlements.

The next day the ten children, who continually play together, devise a scheme to steal the ball. Badger's children tell him about the plan. He suggests that they discuss it with Coyote, and they do so, perhaps in the spirit in which children shared desires and plans with respected elders of the household and with the village headman. Coyote persuades Badger that his own Coyote children should take the ball first because they have longer legs and bodies than the Badger children. This passage is primarily a petty item of naturalist biology which accounts for the anatomy of badgers, but it may also imply that Coyote is expressing pride, as a northwest coast man might, in his children. He is therefore also speaking, in characteristic northwest coast temper, with hurtful detraction of his friend's children. Since Coyotes are headmen, it is fitting that he speak as such worthies would have spoken.

So on the next day, the Coyote children steal the ball. The feature of style which I call "youngest-smartest" requires that the oldest carry the ball first. He sprints with it to the next in age, and so on to the fifth, who is the speediest although she is female. She passes the ball to the Badger children. By the time they have acquired it the villagers have pursued and killed all five of Coyote's children. The Badger children are smarter than the reckless Coyotes. The Badgers stand and pick up and drop the ball as if they were fumbling it, and the pursuing villagers pause to ridicule the seemingly clumsy Badgers. When the villagers are all around, the Badgers kick at the soil, a wind comes up, and the place becomes dusty and dark. The villagers cannot peer through the dust to see what the Badgers are doing. Now they are free to run away at their own moderate speed with less danger of capture and death. The intelligent subterfuge of the children who know their limitation allows them to escape with their lives and with the ball.

When the Badger children near their home, they at once try an extremely cruel deception on their father. They call to him as if they were the young Coyotes returning. They tell him that his children have been killed. When Mrs. Howard was translating, she added the comment that Coyote then tells Badger that the Badger children "could not do anything," which is hardly a sympathetic way of addressing a parent thrown into sudden shock and grief. Coyote is thereby portrayed as lacking in warmth of feeling for his friend. The storyteller does not resort to a verb or statement which offers a single lineament of Badger's feelings. The raconteur presents solely some facts of external behavior—the return of the Badger children, their misrepresentation of themselves, and Coyote's disparaging observation about Badger's children. These are the two or three cues which the audience receives. Individuals might respond according to the identification which each has for children, Coyote, or the shocked Badger father, and in terms of a northwest Indian's perception of such a situation and the relationships in it.

I think that Badger's response, whatever it is or whatever each member of the audience feels empathically for him, is not necessarily the principal expressive feature of this scene. The sentiments of the grieved and tricked parent would perhaps be thought central by a Euroamerican raconteur because of his concern for control of children by a father and because of a Euroamerican father's feelings about his progeny. Speculation about audience identification with the shocked Badger should not be burdened by the typical Euroamerican manner of involvement in the needs of a father. I believe that Clackamas witnessed as much if not more of identification with the children who so mercilessly deceived their parent, and with Coyote, who in typical northwest coast fashion decries the young Badgers although he supposes that they have just died. I have no doubt that his ungracious observation was amusing to Clackamas. He was more interested in cutting down to size the young Badgers, even after their death, than he was concerned about being supportive to their anguished sire, his neighbor and friend.

Some members of the audience may have identified with the bereaved father, others with the sadistic actors. But the point is that stimulation of audience response to the scene is unguided—the raconteur did nothing to structure audience reaction. She presented only an outline of a situation, and her sketchy depiction left each person free to respond according to his leanings. The audience knew that Badger would quickly feel better because it was Coyote who would shortly learn about the fate of his own children. Therefore the audience need not long identify with Badger, if it did so at all. In Western literatures a reader does not know what is going to happen. Since most of the oral literature audience already know, their response of identification with one or another actor is determined by foreknowledge.

Now the Badger children come closer, speak to Coyote, and reveal the truth about his frightful loss. When they near their father and Coyote they can no longer maintain the imposture. Coyote is obviously overwhelmed, although the story-teller does not employ such a descriptive verb. Mrs. Howard subsequently informed me, and a more practiced narrator probably said, that Coyote falls down, rolls on the ground in agony, and cries out in the intensity of his dismay and grief. Badger's behavior is limned with similar brevity and externality. It is clear that he has more kindliness than Coyote because he scolds his children for their deception which fooled both him and Coyote and which only augments Coyote's tragedy.

Over a period of days the sorrowing father attempts to commit suicide. He tries to drown himself, but he cannot. He tries to leap into a big fire, to hang himself, and to cut his throat—perhaps he tries other devices, too. But he lives. One wonders whether his ineptitude or his strength of will to remain alive are greater than his wish to destroy himself. At last Coyote gives up the abortive efforts at self-destruction; then he weeps for some days. Finally he returns to normal behavior and manner of living.

Badger, who is consistently benevolent, has his children cut the ball and give half of it to Coyote, because of the equal share in it that the five Coyote children established with their five Badger colleagues in thievery. The division of spoils probably reflects native custom wherein plunder is shared within the raiding party. (It is also of interest, apropos of native evaluations, that the two parents never advised their children against undertaking the foray.) Now Coyote takes his half of the ball, chops it into small pieces, and leaves them at the playground where his deceased children lie. To all appearances he does not want to see or possess the reminder of his children's sad fate and his loss; perhaps, too, his action parallels the customary burying or disposing of a deceased individual's personal effects so that they are not close to his home.

So far the plot centers upon a tragedy wherein a parent is so crushed by the death of his children that he strives, at least consciously, to destroy himself. The grieving parent's attempts fail for reasons which the raconteur neither reveals nor needs to divulge but which can be deduced from our knowledge of the personality of a Coyote and from general knowledge of causes of failure at suicide. Presumably everybody, in every society, has mixed feelings about his extinction. Coyote's inability to succeed in self-destruction is also consistent with the literature's delineation of a Coyote: whenever that actor responds to a wholly internal stimulus or need, he is a bungler. When something entirely outside himself challenges, something much more important than himself, his responses are powerful, adult, even deity-like. In the first part of this myth, Coyote is perhaps felt to be the trickster who is so absorbed in himself—and his children are an extension of himself—that he has only a modicum of hostility toward the outside world. The energy in his hostility is feeble, and he directs it, in the form of a slight antagonism, against Badger. His urge to kill himself is not reinforced by a need to strike at Badger or anyone else. Clackamas probably laughed at his successive ventures at suicide and commented about his ineptitude. They also laughed, I think, because they identified with him and were relieved when he remained alive. Of course, since they recalled the story, they knew that he would not kill himself, and so they were released to laugh at fumblings at the same time that they felt pity for him.

However, we should not read in too much about the psychology of suicide among Clackamas. Nowhere else is suicide noted in their myths, and the region's ethnographic notations of instances of suicide are virtually nil. Stylized procedures for suicide must have been present, but evidences of them, except for this myth, are lacking. Field data which can be utilized for formulations concerning social relationships and central features of personality are so fragmentary that we must be especially cautious in inferences about the causation or manifestations of any infrequent or pathological behavior like suicide.

During the following winter Coyote, who now lives by himself, is obviously continuing to think of his children. He therefore makes a loose pack basket, with a singular purpose in mind. In the springtime he goes to the playground where his children lie buried in shallow graves dug by their executioners. He lines his pack basket with fresh ferns, carefully lays the bones of his children in it, and cushions each skeleton with fronds. Since he appropriates nothing which really belongs to the village, the removal of bones from the graves causes no opposition in the residents.

Now Coyote proceeds homeward with the precious pack on his back. He walks with extreme slowness and caution so as to avoid jarring the bones and "killing" the children for all time. Although the walk from his home to the graves near the other village takes only some hours, the return requires five days because of his measured steps. He must never jar the bones. It is very likely on the fourth day, when he is close to home, that he hears or believes that he hears the children talking in the basket behind his head. At once he walks still more slowly and carefully. He constantly adds fresh fronds to the basket, perhaps in the belief that they will help in curing the children. There is drama and pathos in this adding of curative greens, in this at once hopeful and sad experiment designed to change decomposing flesh into healthy living matter.

Now a horrible centipede-like bug crosses back and forth in front of him, calling to him, "Coyote is carrying dead people!" and sniffing in a manner which indicates that the contents of the basket smell like decomposing corpses. Coyote is annoyed. He lays down the basket with utmost care and he pursues the bug with a stick. But she is so fast that he cannot find her (a prefixed morpheme for gender notes her sex). When he resumes his slow walk, the children in the pack talk again. Or he supposes that they are talking. Then the bug reappears and distracts him again; he chases it as before but cannot kill it. While he walks along, he senses that the children are shifting positions in the basket in order to make each other more comfortable. That is, he feels that they are alive or virtually alive. Now his hope mounts to its highest pitch, and the audience can identify with the parent who feels that lost ones are about to be delivered living and well.

The next and last day, when Coyote is proceeding at a pace no faster than creeping and home is in sight, the bug once again runs back and forth in front of him. It annoys him to a point where he lets down his basket abruptly, and the children die immediately because of the suddenness of his movement. He realizes what he has done to his children when he no longer feels or hears them as he walks, but he does not examine the contents of the basket until he reaches home. Then he finds only lifeless bones.

The drama says simply that Badger and Coyote give the remains a final burial, in a manner which may have reminded Clackamas of neighboring peoples, such as Tillamooks, who practiced ceremonial reburial. When the story succinctly adds that Coyote weeps again for five days, it implies that now his grief is under control and that he mourns in a stylized manner. Again, canons of literary form bar any mention of feelings. The storyteller remarks solely about facts of the burial and Coyote's subsequent five days of weeping. Selection of these two items provides the stimuli to spur the audience' reaction. It is as if, in terms of current communication theory, an elaborate body of information was transmitted in two neatly coded signals. Every member of the audience would automatically decode and comprehend. Today, because of the deaths of employable native informants, a scholar can only speculate about the details of such comprehension.

In the scene which follows, Coyote assumes his role of announcer of things to come. He says humbly that if he had done otherwise, all dead persons would be revived in springtime after the first fresh leaves were opened. But, he proclaims, people will henceforth die and remain dead, even as his children have died; furthermore, a male mourner's formal expression of sorrow, even a parent's, will last no more than ten days. The myth ignores mention of the much longer period of mourning that was assigned to females.

The principal stress in this drama is patently upon the problem of death, but it is not wholly of the kind that folklorists caption "The Origin of Death." Its theme is not so much causation of death as the tragedy and sorrow of a bereaved father. Although a mother's experience of such sorrow is not suggested, one wonders whether women responded to the drama much as men, and therefore whether omission of a mother is stylistic parsimony rather than a meaningful feature of expressive content. Although the words of the play deal with fathers, their children, and death, it may not be a man's rather than a woman's story, because it really treats of broad problems of death, immortality, and the feelings of any grieved parent. Parents may be symbolized, with characteristic northwest coast antifeminism, by fathers.

Audience identification with Coyote flows partly from the deep wishes in everyone to circumvent the outrage and horror of decomposition and permanent death for kin and for one's self. Coyote's nearly successful rescue of his beloved children and his almost triumphant resuscitation of them are imaginative projections of a wish that people might return unscathed from a terrible death, perhaps long after burial and decay. The play is by the same token a projection of a wish that one's deceased children might return to life and that one might be indestructible himself!

This is not all. Latent features of the myth, that is, audience responses at deeper levels of awareness, are perhaps not so few or simple; yet further speculation about them may be worth venturing. The recitalist portrays Coyote as a father who almost manages to do the impossible for his children (it was at least possible in the remote era of myths), and Coyote appears to be succeeding because he hears the children speaking, and he feels their movements. Success is almost achieved when at the crucial moment he no longer can control the fury, the outrage, stirred in him by a tormenter who is overtly only a nasty bug but who covertly may represent feelings that are much more basic than those initiated by a mere bug.

The centipede mocks Coyote until his poise and his care in walking disintegrate. Who could remain well co-ordinated in the decisive moments before one's five children escape from everlasting death into eternal life? The fast-moving bug's reiterated taunts unnerve Coyote in the infinitely anxious and ultimate minutes of the victory which he feels is virtually his. The creature's sniffs tell him that the children are more than dead: they are putrid, even as he shall be some day. An unbearably tragic reality confronts Coyote in spite of his wishes. And there is a sound dramatic touch as well as psychological insight in the selection of a centipede as the symbol of nagging reality. It is a hideous bug who says to Coyote, in effect, that he is deceiving himself in supposing that any dead and disgustingly putrescent person can be revived. The bug develops in Coyote both frenzy and a flickering attention to reality; his anger grows with increasing fear and doubt that movements he feels and voices he hears in the pack basket are really the living children. He is in mounting terror that they may remain bones and decaying flesh in spite of his supernatural power and his care. And so in his final agony of uncertainty and frustration, he strikes out at that which symbolizes reality.

Finally he has to look at the lifeless bones and flesh which, with the bug, constitute another facet of this drama's symbolization of reality. Coyote must accept reality even though it is extreme tragedy for him. Reality is corpses. It is only when Coyote achieves final acceptance that he announces the manner in which reality will operate for future people, as for himself. No one will ever be able to return from death or to effect the return of others.

When Coyote fails, it is as if he suddenly matures—in a manner which northwest Indians point up by his transition to a godlike enunciator of the future. As with us, a person who suffers deeply and is humiliated by his error may thereupon urge others not to act as ill-advisedly. Still more, acceptance of a cruel reality is mature and wise. Now Coyote reacts not as a mere human being who is unable to succeed and who lashes about in frenzy. He becomes the herald of the future, a role which ordinary human beings never play, and he no longer seeks suicide. Now he and all other males will mourn only during a ritually limited period of five or ten days. The death of loved kin will be resolved not in a self-destructive response or in irate striking-out but in the culture's formalized manner and time for expression of grief. After the tenth day, people will cease overt and stylized expressions of sorrow. Social participations, even gambling, may follow.

The myth which deals in this dramatic manner with the universal challenge of death also appears, as do a number of other myths, to put deities in their place in this culture which never accorded omnipotence or omniscience to a projection figure. The myth appears to say that even the most deity-like personage was circumscribed in what he could do. He was unable to defeat decomposition, that is, an inevitable and eternal death. There is a reality which the most potent of persons cannot control, and a more specialized group in a wealthier society than the Clackamas might have formulated in words the fact of such a reality.

Nor did Coyote's inability to conquer death arise solely from the nature of living things; it came also from a human failure to control his aggressive impulses. It would therefore appear that here, as elsewhere, Clackamas hardly ventured upon a distinction between nature and man. To Clackamas, that which is tragic is consequent upon man's nature, and his capacities and qualities are due to the nature of his human-like predecessors in the Myth Age. Coyote lacked self-control—anger rose in him to such a pitch that it shattered him. Again, the drama documents the conviction that there has never been a perfect or godlike person, one who could handle with poise every situation, no matter how grim. No one, certainly not Coyote, has ever been all-wise, all-powerful, or perfect. That is why no person of the modern period may live forever.

A philosophically more sophisticated recitalist might have said, "That which our predecessors in this Clackamas land experienced because of their human limitations correlates as cause of our happinesses and tragedies." No god intervenes in the destiny of human beings, and there never was a god. Only the human-like actors of the myths played a role in fashioning the world. Thus the myth offers important evidence of the Clackamas world view. Coyote puts in words that which must be for all time regarding death.

CHAPTER III

FIRE AND HIS SON'S SON

THEY lived there, Fire, his son's son, (and) his (the grandson's) two wives. The first one of his wives gave birth, then the other one. I do not know how soon (it was that) each of his wives gave birth to a boy. They continued to stay (and live there). The woman (the second wife) thought, "I shall go back" (to my parents' home). She made ready, she went back home to her village. She had left her small son. Now she reached her village.

Meantime those (others back there) now were living there. Just the one woman (the first wife) took care of the two children. They became bigger. They played outside all day long. Now he (the grandson of Fire) said (to his loyal first wife), "I am going to go to where she (my second wife) has gone. I am going to look for (and find) her." "All right," his wife replied to him. So then she beaded (put decorative and valuable shells on) his garments, (and on) his moccasins, she beaded everything (that he wore, in order to indicate his great wealth). Then he got a feather, he tied it to there (to the bed-platform where they slept). He said to her, "If blood comes out from this feather, then they have killed me. No blood, then I am living."

Now he went, he kept on going, I do not know how far (or) how long a time, (and then) he saw a village. He got to there. He sat down, he looked at the village (below him). "Lots of people! One house at the very end (of the village)," he thought, "I shall go in to that (house) there." So he went down the hillside, he went along, he got to the (end) house. He stood there (at the door). Whereupon two old women were jumping at one another, they were fighting. He stood by watching them. When one of them was pinned underneath, she would defecate. He said to them, "Dear me! old women! I was thinking I would enter. And that is the way you are doing!" "Oh oh, is it really you?" They cleaned it there, they made it quite clean there. They poured sand over it (all over the floor), they stretched out a bed (mat) for him. They told him, "Now come sit here." He went inside, he sat down. While he was sitting there he said to them, "Don't they (the people of this village) play games of any kind?" "Oh yes, when someone comes here our chief is extremely bad. His name is *Hə'naqɪdway*. When we name him here, he is sneezing immediately. When we inform you of this, then they will already be coming after you." "Indeed," he responded to them. He remained there.

The next day a boy (Chub) came to there, he said, "Our chief sent me. I have come to tell you to come gamble the disk game." "All right," he replied to him. "I will be going shortly." They (the two old women) told him, "Oh dear, look out! Oh dear, look out! He (the village chief) is bad! He is bad! When a person gets to him, when they gamble (and) they are defeated (by our chief), everything, even his head hair he will cut off. He will place it all on his smoke hole." "Indeed," he replied to them.

So then he went. He went on (through the village), he got to there (to the chief's house). He entered. Now people were already seated there, they were awaiting him. He turned and looked, he saw his (own) wife. He went, he sat down. He (the chief) said to him, "Be seated now! What more are you waiting for?" He sat, and then they two played (gambled at the disk game). Now he (the grandson of Fire) defeated him. All done. Then after that the man (the chief) said, "How and when now did your village turn?"

Now something (Crawfish) came out (to help the chief gamble). And he (the grandson of

From *Clackamas Chinook Texts*, 13.

Fire) noted him. He (Crawfish) went to there (to where they were gambling), he took the disks, he played (and as he played Crawfish sang),

"I have taken hold of it ha!
I have pinched it ha!"

He (Crawfish) began to cheat. He (Fire's grandson) noted it. Back to the rear in there an old woman (his second wife's mother) said to her daughter, "Oh dear, oh dear! daughter! Possibly this man came here for your sake." "Humph, when could I have had some husband for myself?" So then they two (the chief and Fire's grandson, with Crawfish assisting the chief) played (gambled) some more. Now he (the chief) defeated him, he won back all his things. And what he (the grandson of Fire) had on, everything he wore, he (the chief) won from him.

He (Fire's grandson) said to him, "Now you have won everything from me, but not our head hair." So they played further. Over there the old woman (his mother-in-law) would not quit talking, she kept on saying, "Dear, oh dear! daughter! he is a fine man! Your older brother will kill him!" She shoved her mother (away). All done. He (the chief) defeated him. The man (the chief) stood up, he cut his (Fire's grandson's) hair off, and even his ears. He seized him, he took him, he hung him up by the smoke vent where the smoke went out (in order to torture and eventually kill him). Then they quit.

Yonder at his house, while Fire sat there, then the feather bled. They (Fire and his grandson's first wife) screamed, they wept. Fire spoke, he said to her, "Stop that now! The (two) children might hear us." They quit, they washed their faces (to prevent their distress from being apparent). He said to her, "They (the children) might notice us. Do not act every which way (in an unusual manner)." They just stayed there.

Now the children (both boys) became larger. He (Fire) made them a bow (and) arrow. Now all day long they (the two boys) would go all over, they killed various small things (game). They would get back in the evening, they would say nothing whatever. The next day they would go again, they would go all over the entire day long. And they would bring back a young doe. (Because they returned with the doe early in the day) they saw that their mother appeared as if she had wept. They said nothing to her. They went (apart from her). He (the younger brother) said to his older brother, "What do you think? Looks like our mother has been crying." "Yes. Perhaps." Then still not minding (not yet noting her weeping), they went, they went here and there, they got back home in the evening. Their mother was (now) going about quietly (no longer apparently in tears), (also) their great-grandfather. He said to his younger brother, "Maybe she was just some (inconsequential) way or other (and was not weeping about something of importance)." The next day then they two went again. When they went, then she would look (to see if they were far away), (indeed they were) gone. She would go inside, she would say to him (to Fire), "(They are) gone now, they have already gone." Then she would weep all the day long. That is the way they were. (When) the sun (was) far over to one side (in the middle to late afternoon), then they washed their faces, and they ceased (weeping). Then she would (get busy and) fix something or other. They (the boys) would return in the evening. They would observe the eyes of their mother and their great-grandfather. Looked like they two had been weeping. The next day they (the boys) went away (again). He said to his older brother, "What do you suppose? Maybe our mother (and) our father's father's father have been weeping continually?" "Yes," he replied to him, "that is what I think." He said to his older brother, "Let us hide ourselves from them." After quite a while (and) when they had returned, they saw their (elders') eyes were swollen. They (the boys) brought back a deer.

Now they (the boys) were becoming big. He said to his older brother, "Now let us hide from them tomorrow." They went off the next day, they (only) circled around the house. They went up onto the top of the house, they looked down inside at where the smoke vent (was). Soon then their mother stood up, she went outside, she looked around, she went inside, she said to Fire, "They are long since gone now." "Indeed." Then they wept. He said to his older brother, "That is what I have been supposing. There is something amiss. Why have they not told us about it? Now you aim (an arrow) at him, I will aim at our mother. We will tell them that they must inform us why they have been weeping." They descended (from the roof), they circled round the house, they entered. He went at once to his father's father's father (and) he aimed at him, the other one at his mother. They said to them, "Tell us why it is that you have been weeping here." That is the way they did to them. Now their father's father's father told them, "Yes! son's son's son! We only supposed that you (two) were still (too) small before I could tell you about it. But now I shall tell you. Your father left in the first place because your mother (his second wife) left you when you were small. Just your older brother's mother raised you both. Then your father went in that direction to the place where they have been killing him. If you think that you are strong (within yourselves so that you can acquire spirit-powers), I will make fire for you (a 'slow match' to light your way when you travel at night)." "Yes indeed," they replied to him, "we are sufficiently strong (to acquire spirit-powers) now." "Very well then," he replied to them. Then he made a fire for them, its name is slow match. He made it for the younger one, he made another for the older one. Then he told him, "Go (you two) now!"

They got ready the next day, then the next day they went. They kept on going, I do not know where to (in order to find spirit-powers). They came back. The younger had used up all of his fire (his slow match). The older one brought back half of his fire. "Indeed," he said to him (actually, to the two youths), "that is fine." The next day then he made still more fire for them, now two fires for each of them. They went, I do not know where all over. I do not know how long before they then got back again. The younger had used up all of his (two) fires, but the older one brought back a half of (one of) his (two) fires. "Well," he said to them, "that is fine." The next day he again made three fires (now) for each of them. They went away, I do not know how long a time, it was a pretty long while before they got back. Now the younger was (already sort of) different (in demeanor and appearance). He had finished all of his fires. The older one brought back a half of his (three) fires. "Well, well," he said to him (them), "that is good." Now that is the way they (two) were doing (in order to acquire supernaturals). As for their mother, now she was fixing up their garments, she put beads on their moccasins, she put beads on everything (that they wore). Every day she was working on them (on their garments). Now the fourth time they went he had given four fires to each of them. Then they did not come back for a long long time (perhaps as long as seven to ten days). Then at length they returned. Now the younger one was different (because he had matured visibly). He had used up all his (four) fires. As for the other one, he brought back half (a fire because he had used up only three and a half slow matches). They stayed there all day. The next day then their father's father's father said to them, "Now this is the time to go. And whenever it is (that you return) then show yourselves (your newly acquired supernatural strengths) to me." So then they went away. He had made five fires for each of them. They went. Now I do not know where (they went and sought more spirit-power help) for a long long time. Then they got back. The younger one had used up all his (five) fires. As for the older one he brought back half a fire (because he had used up only four and a half slow matches). "Well, well! great-grandson!" he said to him. "Show me tomorrow how strong (in spirit-powers) you have become." The next day then they showed themselves (their new supernaturals) to him. He said to him, "First you." The younger one turned and looked, he sort of glanced, it burned across over there. He turned and looked, everything burned (in that other direction). Where he looked, there it burned. "All right," he said to him. As for the older one, his (spirit-power) strength was not quite so much. He tried but it burned (where he glanced) only a little. He had gotten about half as much (supernatural strength) from his father's father's father. "Apparently you (the younger brother) have finished now (and your supernatural strength is sufficient for your purposes). The other (and) older one's (spirit-power) strength is not as much." They (two) said, "We want to hasten at once. We will go to where our father went." "Very well."

The next day then they made ready. Their mother gave them various things, all of them fine things (such as richly beaded garments of great value). He (Fire) said to him, "You (two) go. At the first of the mountains that you arrive at, you should halloo to your great-grandfather Grizzly. You should tell him, 'We have come for (in order to borrow) your ground that you track (that is, your back-of-neck hairs).' You will borrow them (those neck hairs) from all five of them (from five Grizzlies), before you proceed (to the village where your father is dying)." "Very well," they replied to him.

They went away. The younger one covered his own head, his face stuck out only a little (lest he start conflagrations when he looked at things). So then they went along. They got to the (first of the) mountains at the place where their great-grandfather had told them. They stood still and hallooed. The second time, then omm he did (in the angry growl of a grizzly). "Omm. I was turned down. Who is waking me?" He came out (from his den, growling angrily) omm omm. He came toward them, he got close to them. He (the younger boy) said to him, "Oh, we came merely to borrow (a neck hair) from you." Ow ow (more angry growls). (But then) he (Grizzly) went up to them, he bent down his head, he (the younger youth bravely) pulled one of his hairs from his neck. He put it inside underneath (next to his chest). They left him.

They went on. They got to the second mountain, and they again hallooed. Then again (they heard the angry Grizzly growling) "Omm omm. I have been turned down. Who is shaking and awakening me?" He went toward them, close by, (and then) he (the younger brother) said to him, "Yes, we merely came to borrow (two neck hairs) from you." "Very well! my great-grandchildren!" He turned and moved (and lowered his head for the youth). He (the younger brother) pulled out two of his (the second Grizzly's) hairs from his neck. He placed it (the hairs) underneath (inside his garment). They left him.

They went on, they came to the third mountain. There they stood, and again they called out. The third time (that they hallooed), then he (a third Grizzly) emerged. He was furious. Omm omm, he went toward them, he got close to them. He (the younger brother) said to him, "Goodness! we merely came to borrow from you." "All right!" He (this third Grizzly) lowered his head, he (the younger brother) pulled out three of his hairs. He put it underneath (inside his garment). They left him.

They went on. They got to the (fourth) mountain, they stood there. He called out (three calls), and upon the fourth one then he (a fourth Grizzly) emerged. "Omm omm, I was turned down. Who awakened me? Omm!" He was angry, he was pawing the ground there. He went toward them, he turned around (his back toward them and still pawing the ground). His older brother retreated. He said to him (to his older brother), "Stop!" He (the angry Grizzly) kept going toward him. He (the younger brother) said to him, "Oh, we merely came to borrow from you." "Indeed is it you?" He lowered his head, he pulled four of his hairs, he put it underneath (inside his garment). They left him.

They went on. Now they got to the fifth (mountain). They stood there. He hallooed, upon the fifth (call), omm omm, and then he came out (from his den). Omm, he was angry, he was throwing up soil, he was clawing away at it. He was going toward them. The older one fled in the other direction. He said to his older brother, "Stop!" Then way over there he (the fifth Grizzly) was just going along threateningly. "So here you are!" He said to him, "So here you are!" "We came merely to borrow from you." "Indeed is that you?" He went toward them, he lowered his head. He pulled out five of his (neck) hairs, he put them away (inside his garment). Then they went on.

They kept going along, they reached a village. They sat there (on the trail above the village), they looked at it below, they saw one house at the end there. He said to his younger brother, "Let us go inside there." Whereupon they went, they went along, they got to the (end) house. He sort of looked inside there, two old women were there. They leaped at each other, they fought each other. When one of them was on top of the other, she (the woman pinned underneath) would defecate.

After a while he said to them, "Hi! old women! We are thinking of coming inside to you." "Indeed. So it is you." They cleaned the place, they made it clean there, they poured on sand. They fixed a place for them there. They told them, "Enter now!" They went inside to them, they sat down. Shortly then the older one said to them, "Do they not gamble at something or other?" "Yes, yes," they replied to him. "He is a bad one." "What is his name?" "Oh don't! One should not name him." "Oh do indeed name what his name is." "Oh dear, oh dear! The man's name is Hə'naqɫdwaya. Indeed (since) I have named him here, he sneezed immediately. Soon now they (Chub) will come to tell you. That is the way it was with your father. He came here to us. Now he is virtually dead, and only bones (he is reduced to skin and bones now). They (Swallows) have been taking water to him (because only they can fly into rafters and smoke vents). As for her (Bat) only she has been giving him smoke (to eat because he has a fire spirit-power). We hired them (to do this and so save his life)."

Now pretty soon a boy (Chub) got to them and said (to the older brother), "Our chief sent me. I came to tell you to (come and) gamble (at) the disk game." He (the younger brother who sat there with covered head) looked at him (at Chub), he merely turned and glanced just a little at him, he looked at him, "Ow ow ow ow (and Chub slapped at his burned lips), oh oh, my mouth!" He ran out, his mouth got puckered and drawn, it became red. He had burned him. He ran, he ran back, he said (reporting to the headman), "Some different sort of person (a stranger to our village) merely looked at me, he burned me." "Aha," they said to him. "Where did you stand? close by the fire?"

They said to Blue Jay, "You go too." Blue Jay went, he got there, he went inside. He said to them (to the older brother), "Our chief sent me (to tell) you to gamble at the disk game." "Indeed. We will go shortly." He (the younger brother with covered head) merely turned and looked (at Blue Jay), ash ash ash ash (cries denoting torture), he ran outside. He had burned his eyes, they became turned (cross-eyed). He ran, he got back, he said, "Soon some different kind of (two) persons will be coming. One of them is covered over."

Soon then they (two) went. (But first) then they told the two defecators, "Now be gone somewhere else at quite a distance. All these people (all the villagers except you two women) will be no more (because we are going to kill them)." So they (the two old women) went away. I do not know where they went.

He (the younger brother) was (still) covered over. They (two) went, they got there (to the chief's house). They went inside, they sat down. The old woman there said, "Oh dear, oh dear! my daughter! this person's face is just like you (the younger brother resembles you)." (The daughter retorted) "Where do you suppose (that I could have had) a child of my own?" "Oh dear, oh dear, my daughter!" She (the daughter) paid no attention to her mother.

They (two) sat down, and then they (all the men) gambled. They (the two youths) defeated him completely. Now he (the headman) said, "When now did your village turn?" Whereupon something (Crawfish) came out from a bed, he went, he took disks. They (two) watched him, he began to cheat at the disks. He (the younger brother) looked at him (at Crawfish), his eyes became red (from the flame), they popped out. He went groping away. They (the people) said, "Holy mackerel! (an expletive indicating fright). Now our chief has encountered something (that can match his spirit-power)!"

Then they gambled again. They turned and looked, he (the younger brother) had let go a pup (a young grizzly metamorphosed from a hair of a grizzly). Blue Jay ran (to the grizzly pup), "Mm (nice little) puppy!" He (Blue Jay) did it to his finger (moistened it), he poked it at the pup, (but) he bit his (Blue Jay's) finger clear off. "Ow," he (Blue Jay) said, "there is something different about this! Ouch ouch ouch, I am hurt! The little pup bit me."

They gambled. They (the two boys) defeated him. Now they (the chief and his followers) said to them the (two), "Now that is all (let us cease gambling)." "Hm," they replied to him, (let us gamble now) "for our head hair." (The old woman wailed) "Oh dear, oh dear. Over there, oh dear, oh dear, daughter! oh dear, oh dear, daughter! That person there has your entire face (he resembles you)! Oh dear, oh dear, daughter!" She paid no heed to her. They (the two youths) defeated him. He (the younger youth) stood up, he went to him (to the vanquished headman), he cut off (one side of) his head hair and his (one) ear (down to the bone). He (the younger youth) went across to the other side, and (because he insisted) they gambled further. He (the headman) said to him in vain, "Now enough of that (let us quit gambling)." They (the youths) replied to him, "Oh no. You still have hair on the other side (of your head)." They played. Pretty soon they defeated him. He (the younger brother) arose, he uncovered (his own face), he went to him, he cut it (the remainder of the chief's scalp) off, and also his ear and all (to the bone).

(Now his mother wailed) "My son! your poor poor father's brother!" He turned (toward her), he kicked her away. He turned aside, he released his pups (the small grizzlies which he produced from grizzly hairs). They (the doomed villagers) turned and looked (at the grizzlies). His mother shrieked, she leaped on him (in order to stop his slaughter of the villagers), she said to him, "My son! (he is) your poor poor father's brother!" He threw her aside. Now they were already (large) grizzlies (and) they went about in the village. He himself went, in whatever direction he glanced it flamed there. He looked in some (other) direction, that place also burned. The entire place burned. As for those grizzlies they ate up the people.

They (the two youths) went, they took off their father (from where he hung above in the smoke vent), and now (almost) only bones (he was virtually skin and bones), they took him with them, they brought him back to their house. Their (the older youth's) mother washed him all over. Then the old man (Fire) himself massaged his body all over, they caused him to come to.

Now they lived there. He himself (Fire) did nothing. Only the youths hunted. After some time then they said to their mother, "There are now no deer where we have been going (when we hunt)." "Indeed," she replied to them. "Do not go in that other direction. It is a bad place there." "Very well," they replied to her. So then they would sometimes go (in their usual hunting area), they would bring back only a single deer.

Then they said, "Why did our mother tell us not to go in that other direction?" They went in that (ill-advised) direction. They went a little way, they killed two deer. They went back home. The next day they went again, they went further on, they saw a village (below). They lay down (in order to watch it). After a while then they saw a person (a girl) go directly to their menstrual-and-women's-work hut. Shortly afterwards then another one. Two of them had gone. They (the youths) lay there, they kept watching them. They said, "Shortly now when it gets dark let us go to the place there where those two (young) women are." They kept lying there. It became evening. When it was dark then they went, they went along, they got to there. At that place one (youth) lay with her. The other (youth) lay with the other one (who was his mother's sister although he did not know it). They remained there (during the night), they lay with them. I do not know who saw them (after sunrise). The next day then the people (of that village) killed them (the youths).

They used to say, Myth Age people lacked sense, (because) she (the older youth's mother) had nowhere told her son, "Your relatives are yonder there. One of them is your mother's sister."

They lay them aside (the bodies). They said, "This one person (youth) here is just like our own child in appearance." As for them yonder, their mother and their father spoke. She said, "Now they are at the village (where I warned them not to go)." That feather was always fastened up there. Shortly now it dripped blood. She (the older youth's mother) wept. She said, "They have killed them now." She got ready, and she went. She went directly to the village. She got to there. The people were crowded about, they came to see the (dead) youths.

She went at once, she was weeping, she took her boys. The people said, "We said it was so. He looked just like her." Those people right (there now fought one another).

They used to say they had fire as their strength, grizzlies for their spirit-powers. They had killed people, (and in turn) they killed them (the youths). They (the youths) just did not know (that in spite of all their supernaturals they would be easily killed themselves). Now they (the people of that village) fought one another. (Then) they ceased (fighting). Now they were ended and became this and that (animal, bird, fish, or other creature). As for her (her name was Sun) she took her boys away with her. She said, "If they should kill some person who has a big name (because of his great wealth), they will see both my sons (as stars at dawn or dusk near me). (If) they should kill merely some person (who is not well-to-do), they will see only one of my sons (as a single star near me). I will bring him out."

Now story story.

Let us retrace and examine the drama in order to lay bare, as well as we can, the various responses which Chinook people may have had to it. As in any Chinook community, an older man is living in his grandson's house. The elder's name, and in fact one of his spirit-powers, is Fire. But Clackamas rarely or never referred to a person by a supernatural which he had acquired. Personal names and nicknames were of other kinds, and I think the former usually were names of long-deceased kin. The use of a supernatural's name, such as Fire, may therefore have been restricted to a myth recital.

Fire's grandson has two wives, each with a son. Obviously this is a well-to-do family because it is polygynous. When the second wife returns to her parental village, ostensibly for a visit of a customary and accepted kind, she leaves her son in the temporary care of the first wife. But she never goes back to her child and husband. Her desertion is culturally disapproved because it amounts to denial of her marriage and refusal to function as wife and mother in the household which purchased her, and her family is reprehensible because they do not make the customary return payment to her husband in order to compensate him for what he lost and for his expenditure when he bought her. Her action is also viewed with disfavor because she has abandoned her child. Although her conduct is nowhere motivated in the lines of the recitalist, she may reflect feelings of a plural spouse who is not the first and preferred wife.

The prevailing omission of phrasing of emotional reactions is apparent in the first scene. The consistent negative feature of the literary styles of the northwest states, that is, lack of explicit notations of feelings, interrelates with the paucity, in that region's many languages, of morphemes or combinations of morphemes that describe feelings; and this same lack of explicit feelings contrasts with the richness of morpheme inventories for expressing other kinds of actions.

The first wife correctly signifies approval when her husband announces that he is going to see what has happened to his long-absent second wife, who is still his property because he has received no recompense for her. His trip to her village is at once warranted and perilous. Before the journey the first wife sews valuables on his garments in order that his wealth and high status may be evident to those whom he meets. But he anticipates mortal danger to himself in his second wife's village, in spite of uneasiness that might be felt by an antagonist observing the visitor's obvious wealth. He ties a feather to his bed and says that if it should bleed he may be dead or nearly dead. The same folkloristic motif of a feather signal, bleeding or otherwise, appears in another myth (26). The husband's concern lest he be killed when he arrives in his second wife's village suggests that the raconteur's design is to indicate covertly the husband's awareness of the reason, which is not phrased in the myth, for the woman's desertion. Her decampment and his preparations before the trip, especially the feather signal but later happenings as well, reflect trepidation about in-laws and the potential for difficulties with them. There is also the possibility that a polygynous wife's family was likely to be a source of friction because of its involvement in co-wives' jockeying for position.

When he arrives at his second wife's village, the husband enters a house which lies at the periphery of the community, that is, a house of persons who are not well-to-do. Possibly it was etiquette for a visitor to a strange village to enter such a house first, in order to orient himself to the village's leading family and the chief. Perhaps too the visitor customarily went into an end house in order to permit the moneyed family some time for preparation of hospitality. The episode at the end house is a theatrical interlude rather than a development of plot essentials. It also may express upper-class depreciation of persons of lower class who inhabit end houses. When the visitor looks inside the house of poorer people, he observes two old women who are fighting. The woman who is pinned down defecates.

The raconteur offered a curious and maybe perspicacious footnote: she laughed when she suggested that the women fought and that the woman who was below defecated at the moment when they saw someone coming or watching. They did it, she said, "only to show off." Psychiatrists have suggested that exhibitionistic defecation or defecation for purposes other than to relieve the bowels is regressive behavior of the kind frequently displayed by psychotics. But the little that this myth reveals about the two fighting women is that they are not psychotic except if we assess their wrestling and defecation as psychotic symptoms. In fact, the women are so generous and adult in relationships with newcomers to the village that a deduction of psychosis is insupportable. The narrator's amusement concerning the seeming aggression in the wrestlers also tends to support the view that their behavior was a kind of clowning by excellent persons of lower class. In other words, conduct which in Western civilization would never constitute permissible buffoonery and which would warrant disapproval, segregation, and perhaps hospitalization provoked only amusement in a Clackamas audience. Further amusement arises from the names of the two women—the translation is "defecate all over."

A factor of cultural difference is decisive here, a difference which applies to audience feelings elicited by defecation. Clackamas probably suffered little disgust when they heard about defecation as an expression of aggression to which the loser resorted. Ethnographic as well as mythologic items from the northwest states suggest that, like their neighbors, Clackamas were less rejecting of overt anality than are most persons of European heritage. Either less of psychosis is implied in the women's behavior, or Clackamas enjoyed a permissiveness and even a pleasure about psychotic manifestations which many Europeans would not accept as funny. We may also note insight in the description of defecation as a final aggressive recourse by a person who is pinned down and defeated. The principal entertaining feature about such a response may be that defecation as a resolution of the fight is itself insoluble. It is a means of fighting, and of ending the contest, which virtually negates the winner's victory.

Although wrestling occurred as sport among modern Indians of northwest states areas, I doubt that anal accompaniment was present. Miss Sally Snyder has suggested to me that, in the light of her recent ethnographic researches among northern Puget Sound and Skagit River Indians, the Defecators' indecorousness and dirtiness before the upper-class visitor arrives may express poor persons' uncleanness and unpreparedness for hospitality. A village headman was more likely to have a house with fresh mats and dusted furnishing. Unmannerly goings-on might not so often be observed in his hostel.

Cultural disapproval of excrements inside a house is expressed by the women's immediate tidying of the interior. Their goodness is indicated by their hospitality: they stretch out a mat on the cleaned floor, so that the visitor may sit comfortably, and they thereby express respect for him. They are evidently neither fearful nor defensive about their headman, who is the brother of the visitor's second wife, but they warn the stranger that the headman is murderous. He wreaks frightful reprisals upon visitors who gamble with him and lose.

Far away in the end house the mere mention of the headman's name is a signal to him that an outsider has come to the village. Utterance of his name in the other house causes him to sneeze. Sneezing is not noted elsewhere in this collection, nor is there another marvelous and automatic indicator of a visitor's approach. Features of interest, then, are the preternatural signaling power of the personal name of one man of great wealth and spirit-power and, second, the nature of his response, which is a sneeze. There is no reason to assume that a taboo on employment of the chief's name was felt beyond the myth village. Since we lack relevant information, we are in the dark about the native notion of the meaning of sneezing; but one may suggest that a certain kind of spirit-power connects with pronunciation of a name of a very wealthy and supernaturally powerful man, and with his sneezing. It may be that the headman would not have reacted in exactly the same manner had a woman rather than a man entered the village.

The headman next dispatches an emissary, Chub, to invite the new arrival to come to play the disk game. Chub receives no delineation. He is merely a messenger who symbolizes the male follower and loyal dependent attached voluntarily to a headman's household.

Fire's grandson anticipates adventure and danger in the game at the chief's house. But when he responds to the invitation and enters the dignitary's abode, he is distracted by the sight of his second wife, seated among villagers who are assembled to watch the game. The words of the myth lack explicitness, but it appears that he is so startled or perturbed by her presence that he does not sit down at once. Therefore the headman, who is a hating brother-in-law, takes unfair advantage by gibing hurriedly, ill-humoredly, and hostilely. He says bluntly or harshly, "What are you waiting for?" That is, "Let us proceed with the game, and do not continue staring at my sister!" In this manner at least some of the motivation for the chief's opposition is suggested. Because of the affectional tie to his sister, the chief resents another man who is interested in her. Possibly the recitalist was conscious of special feelings in actors who are siblings of opposite sex. She did not phrase the fact or nature of such feelings because of the literary style's censuring of that kind of expression.

Fire's grandson wins the first game. Crawfish, like Chub an ally and dependent of the headman, joins in the next game, sings his gambling spirit-power song, and cheats as he plays. The Crawfish episode is mostly theater, of a kind which Clackamas enjoyed because they played the same game with the help of spirit-powers and duplicity, too. Citation of cheating perhaps reflects the hostility which modern villagers had toward a headman, especially one whose honesty was in question.

At the same time the audience hears about the mother of the second wife. This older woman has observed the breasts of her lately returned daughter and has at once suggested that they indicate nursing of a baby. But the younger woman denies that she has returned from residence with a husband or that she has ever had an infant. A response of such a kind is precultural. In the modern society no mother would have remained uninformed about a daughter's marriage and motherhood. Now, during the gambling the persistent older woman suggests obliquely that the visitor came solely because of his interest in her daughter. Again the younger woman denies that she could ever have had a husband. She implies that Fire's grandson has never had anything to do with her.

These asides of wife and wife's mother during the gambling reinforce other indications that raconteurs provide, without explicitly saying so, that Fire's grandson's wife cruelly rejects both husband and child. She is devoid of affection for anyone except her murderous and wealthy brother. She hates her mother and her husband but loves her brother who may also represent her father. She lies to her mother about the marriage, which she keeps secret so that the mother will not force her to return to her husband. Fire's grandson's in-laws are thereby revealed as divided in feelings. The older woman's two children, that is, the murderous village headman and his sister, are dishonest, relentless, and maybe incestuous. Their affectional tie and malevolence toward other people are culturally impermissible. On the other hand, Fire's grandson's mother-in-law does not share the ill nature of her children. She represents a good and just in-law. Therefore the theme of in-law tension is not oversimplified.

In fact, the raconteur is at pains to note various kinds of in-laws, covillagers, and followers of in-laws. Some persons in the other village may be good at the same time that others are maleficent. Even in the dangerous village of the in-laws three ethical older women, the mother-in-law and the amusing Defecators, are present. The headman's allies are unethical, although their characters are evinced only by their function as followers. The narrator therefore skilfully avoids ingenuous treatment of the themes of in-law antipathy and Oedipal feelings. Additions of minor actors, although each lesser individual is delineated briefly or not at all, make for variability of feelings and personalities.

When Crawfish assists and cheats at the game, the chief wins everything that the grandson of Fire wears. Every such traveler carries valuables, most if not all of which are sewed on his garments. When the men play another game and gamble their scalps, the mother-in-law of the visitor expostulates with his wife, saying that the headman will kill him. The wife "shoves her mother aside." Again hatred of husband and mother are succinctly indicated in a stroke which makes note only of physical behavior.

The woman's violence against her mother provides a suitable point at which to pause for further comment on the Oedipal component in this scene. First, it includes an oblique suggestion of a mother's vain attempt to manage a daughter's marital career and to expel the younger woman from home and village by means of a polygynous marriage. Such a marriage implies greater wealth and therefore enhances the older woman's social status. Second, the rejected daughter's love for her older brother, who I feel is a substitute father to her, is such that she forsakes her husband in order to return to her brother's household. Third, there is no suggestion that this brother has a wife or child, although his wealth must be such that normally he too would be polygynous. The omission of suggestion that he is married is very likely a studied one. It underlines his love for his younger sister and hers for him, without transgressing cultural dislike for manifest expression of a thought that he remained unmarried because of incestuous regard for her. Since he is both a chief and an older brother, his feelings toward his sister are, again, those of the Oedipal father. In the fourth place, his savage treatment of his sister's husband fits in with the Oedipal patterning, and interpretation of the developments of the most gruesome portions of the drama may therefore follow.

When the ill-fated grandson loses to his wife's older brother, that ruthless leader scalps his brother-in-law and also severs his ears. Washington coastal Chinooks cut off the ears of a runaway slave, and they did the same to an adulterous wife.[7] The mutilations constituted an extreme in precultural punishment and abasement, but we cannot deduce that the modern Clackamas duplicated such treatment. Next, the chief hangs his wretched visitor and in-law from a rafter near the smoke vent, so that he may suffer a slow death by torture and suffocation. Possibly a similar handling of enemies occurred in the modern period, but ethnographic evidences from the entire Chinook area are also a blank on this matter.

Now the responsive feather bleeds, whereupon Old Man Fire and his grandson's loyal wife cry aloud. In another myth (26) a feather of Blue Jay displays a unique sensitivity and signaling power when it signifies a safe arrival home, but the notation of a feather bleeding as a sign of mortal danger or death is largely different. The only common feature of feather items in various myths is the notion of long-distance signaling power. Bleeding of a feather seems an obvious indication of dying or death. The problem is less in interpreting bleeding than in explaining the use of a feather as the medium for production of blood or as a kind of indicator of a significant event which transpires at a distance.

Soon Old Man Fire says that they must not weep lest the two children notice them, and the elders wash their faces in order to erase visible evidence of a grief which combines sincere feeling and stylized mourning. When the boys approach, the elders try to act as if nothing unusual has occurred. When the boys are away all day, their mother and great-grandfather weep. They attempt when the boys return to appear and behave normally.

The scene exhibits nicely the manner in which some Clackamas treated with dignity and discretion the security needs of their children. The mother and great-grandfather avoid burdening the boys with news of the tragedy that befell their father. An audience must have had empathy for the feelings of elders who maintained the emotional security of children by sedulous repression of melancholy sentiments. Not until the boys are far from the house do these admirable adults vent feelings of sorrow by weeping. They cry all day. Knowledge of length of periods of audible wailing or visible weeping is largely dependent upon early reports of travelers, but whatever these may suggest, surely few if any natives cried and wailed all day. Probably there were formalized shorter intervals such as in the morning and evening, when a mourner expressed his culturally required grief in sight or hearing of others. Therefore when the narrator said that the afflicted elders cried all day long, interpretation must be that the duration of stylized grief is a theatrical exaggeration which applies to a headman's relatives in a precultural epoch, symbolizes especial profundity of sorrow, and expresses cultural judgment of a headman's outstanding worth and social status.

Fire now makes weapons for his great-grandsons. The boys hunt all day long. And they grow up. The orphan whose mother deserted him supposes that he is the son of the first wife, who has nurtured him and acted as if she were his mother. Again we observe evidence that Clackamas met parental and security needs of orphan children by caring for them as if they were their "own" children. Foster parents did not reveal the fact of orphan status until the children had grown to a point, not indicated in this myth or in ethnographic notes, where they could receive the information with adult-like acknowledgment.

When the boys return from hunting, they note indications that their mother has been weeping, but at first they are not concerned because they are uncertain that their deduction is correct. Here the raconteur does several things. She indicates that a woman's tears or feelings of grief are more visible than a man's, because nothing is said about the countenance of Fire. The storyteller also indicates covertly, and in another way, that Clackamas knew that children may share the feelings of their elders and be grieved when their parents sorrow. Boys are woeful if they observe the sadness of their mother. The older boy restrains his suspicions and incipient grief and protects his brother, as an older sibling should, by remarking that perhaps their mother was crying about some matter of comparative unimportance. Not only do elders meet the security needs of children. The older boy helps the younger at the same time that he keeps up his own chin.

At length the boys only pretend a departure to hunt, because they have become alarmed to a point where they must determine whether the elders are truly sorrowing. The boys hide on the roof, peer inside at the smoke vent, and witness audible and visible grief below. At once they discuss what to do. They re-enter the house, aim weapons at the elders, and demand the reason for the weeping. The show of violence may amount to a bluff, but it does make it easier for the great-grandfather to reveal a truth which he has been unable to tell before. He explains that the facts have been long withheld because the two of them were small. He tells the orphaned younger boy about the frightful circumstance of his mother's desertion. He promises to give both boys his fire spirit-power, which means that he will give himself, because he himself is a spirit-power. He will confer it if they believe that they are now sufficiently old and strong to receive it. They reply affirmatively. That is, they bravely assert their manhood. Then they leave in order to gain and subsequently strengthen their relationship with the spirit-power of Fire, maybe other spirit-powers too.

Incidentally, the informant had never heard of a fire spirit-power apart from this myth, although she knew about analogous spirit-powers which connected with lightning and smoke. On the other hand, the concept of a fire spirit-power seems consistent with Clackamas theology. Possibly the period of the informant's lifetime, with its few survivors and their rapid acculturation, accounts for her lack of knowledge of a spirit-power that earlier nineteenth-century Indians possessed.

When the youths threaten to shoot if left uninformed, they act symbolically, not in a fashion which a pugnacious modern youth would have resorted to in order to obtain information from close relatives. After all, this is a drama of precultural people who resort to extremes which must be impermissible in later times. The symbolism amounts to an announcement by the boys that they are no longer children. They speak and act so as to give evidence of graduation from childhood. It is as if they say, "Now we are prepared to endure the rigors, dangers, and responsibilities of life as adults." Furthermore, no one tells them that they have become adult or demands that now they act in grown-up ways. Their sponsor, the great-grandfather, does not proclaim that they are adults. Transition to adulthood was therefore very likely effected, in native theory, by a youth's aspiration to achieve adult status, a resolve which was supported or pressured by the supervision, preaching, encouragement, and example of older persons. But the youth and no one else announced the time when he would behave as an adult. The vivid manner in which he proclaimed it was to go away alone, in order to seek a spirit-power. It is hardly necessary to suggest that every member of a Clackamas audience had empathy for the sentiments of youths who were passing through so vital a transition and who showed not by words so much as by actions their will and readiness to live as mature citizens rather than as dependent children.

A person who went to the hills to obtain or strengthen a spirit-power relationship usually if not always carried a rolled and compacted foot-long stick of bark, translated as "slow match." It was ignited upon departure from the village and burned slowly for a day or more. It allowed easy building of a fire for warmth during the night out. Each time the youths return, Fire makes more "slow matches" for them to carry on their next wandering in the mountains.

In this segment of the drama the stylization is considerable. The older youth is portrayed as acquiring fire spirit-power of somewhat less strength than the younger and orphaned youth: the bark brands of the older youth do not burn completely; those of the younger are always used up by the time of his return. In this literature the youngest sibling is almost always outstanding. His capacity for excelling, conse-quent upon being younger, is reinforced in this play by the dolorous fact that he is an orphan. The brands and their duration of burning express the potency of the supernatural power which the youths acquire.

During the weeks that the youths are strengthening their bonds to supernaturals the mother sews money beads and other valuables on their garments. Perhaps she does so in order that her sons may appear and be received as the wealthy and upper-class persons which they are. They will also wear these impressive clothes when they have completed work on their spirit-powers and are supernaturally prepared to travel and brave the spirit-powers of residents of other villages.

The fact that the youths strengthen their spirit-power ties together rather than in solitary journeys may not be Clackamas custom. A modern Clackamas in search of a spirit-power relationship or in process of increasing its vigor perhaps always went alone to the wilderness. I do not know why the myth describes joint rather than solitary wanderings of half-brothers, unless it is to stress the intensity of their feel-ing of kinship and the excellence of sibling relationship, to emphasize the fact that they acquire the very same fire spirit-power, or to suggest by indirection that the power of the villainous chief is so great that the youths' dual strength is demanded for victory.

The myth also describes the youths' gradual change in physical appearance and demeanor when they come back from spirit-power trips. As in the modern society, elders note pleasurably and comment approvingly upon such progress in the direc-tion of adulthood. Great-grandfather Fire at length asks the youths to give specific evidence of control of their new spirit-power, of which he is the donor. The younger sibling exhibits what he has acquired by looking in one or another direction and burning every object there as if he were employing a twentieth-century flame-thrower. The older sibling's new flame-throwing spirit-power is not as strong.

The younger one's spirit-power is patently great, and the older's, although weaker, is sufficiently lethal for purposes of the vengeance they seek. The great-grandfather does not tell them to proceed forthwith in order to obtain that revenge. He asserts only that the younger youth appears to have completed his control over the spirit-power. Then the youths themselves announce that they will travel to the village where their father met disaster.

Before they depart the great-grandfather tells them about another spirit-power which they ought to acquire along the way, as a supplement to their fire supernatural. It is the grizzly spirit-power of their unfortunate father. The great-grand-father summarily informs the youths that they should borrow back-of-neck hairs from five successive grizzlies. The audience must have understood at once that the gallant procurer and potent possessor of such a hair could metamorphose it at will into a raging grizzly.

Now the myth describes a second session of spirit-power acquisition, wherein the youths successively encounter five sleeping grizzlies who wake up when the approaching youths call out. The notation that these grizzlies are sleeping is consistent with belief that spirit-powers rest and wait for suppliants to approach and awaken them. Each grizzly allows the valiant younger boy to pull out and keep neck hairs, one hair from the first grizzly, two from the second, and so on to five hairs from the fifth. Demands of literary style account for such arithmetical progression. The grizzlies are successively more angry, in other words, more supernaturally powerful. The fifth is so terrifying in his fury at being awakened that the older youth retreats. Clackamas thought of spirit-power beings as wanting people, giving themselves to people, in a kind of kinship symbiosis, but the first meeting with supernaturals might provoke them to emotional outbursts.

Now the youths are fortified with fire and grizzly spirit-powers. They are prepared to defeat the potent adversary who is the uncle of the younger half-brother. The failure of the narrative to reveal whether the older brother also acquires grizzly spirit-power is in keeping with the stylistic feature of "youngest-smartest."

When the youths enter the nefarious headman's village, they enjoy the same experience that their father had at the end house, where the women fight and the one who is pinioned defecates. The Defecators promptly cease the droll exhibition, clean the floor of their home, accord hospitality to the visiting youths, warn them about the chief, and tell them that their father is almost dead. They also say that they have paid Swallows to fly into the rafters to bring the wretched victim a little water and Bat to fly up and feed him smoke. The smoke nourishes him because he too has a fire spirit-power, presumably by infectious inheritance from his grandfather Fire. Clackamas might have felt that one or another spirit-power had kept the pitiable man alive. Of course, he is unaware of the advent of his sons. He cannot know that rescue as well as vengeance are soon to occur.

The version contains no additional words that offer information about the Swallows or Bat. Like Crawfish and Chub, these minor actors function as theater devices, accounting for the survival of the unfortunate man. One may suppose that Clackamas thought of them as spirit-powers of the Defecators.

When the chief's emissary, Chub, arrives to invite the youths to gamble, the younger brother scorches Chub's mouth with a brief glance—hence the kind of mouth now had by chubs. A narrator is not expected to phrase or even hint at the torture from fire, consternation, dishonor, or other feelings of Chub, or the satisfied feelings of the flame-throwing young man. The audience, as always, is given an almost completely unstructured presentation, and each individual empathizes in terms of his makeup.

When Chub reports back about the throwing of flame, the headman and his retinue cannot believe the tidings. They order Blue Jay to invite the youths. Flame from the younger brother's glance burns Blue Jay's eyes, which become "turned," whatever that translation of the native verb signifies. The chief and his following are convinced when Blue Jay returns with visible corroboration of Chub's misadventure. Again the emotions of each of the actors are left to members of the audience to create.

Before the youths proceed to the chief's house, they tell their amusing and gracious hostesses to go far from the village because soon its people "will be no more." The motivation is patently to spare residents who are good persons and who have been helpful allies.

When the youths sit down in the chief's house, the bad wife's mother cries out that the younger youth has a face like her daughter. But the daughter denies that she ever bore an infant. Once more she rejects both husband and child. Her mother expresses concern either over the ethics or likely consequence of such insistence, but the daughter pays no more attention to her mother.

In the initial game of gambling with disks the youths defeat the chief and his followers. When Crawfish joins the game and cheats as before, the younger youth sears his eyes. They protrude, and he gropes his way out. Again, this is an explanation of why crawfish now have such eyes. The chief's people express alarm at the additional evidence of the spirit-power strength of the youthful visitors. When the gambling continues, the younger sibling turns a grizzly hair into a grizzly pup. Blue Jay offers a moistened finger to the pup, merely in play; but the tiny grizzly bites off the finger, and Blue Jay cries out in pain. The audience probably enjoyed this incident in which the clown character, who wants to play with or tease the little grizzly, is again hurt. Here the clown is the ally of the villain, and it is satisfying to witness punishment of evildoers. Citation of Blue Jay and the severance of his finger serves as a brief and entertaining pause in the awful advance toward the gory climax.

When the youths again defeat the chief and his adherents, the latter suggest a halt to gambling. Their feelings about continuing are not indicated. The youths insist on another game, with scalps as stakes—a climactic challenge which expresses their trust in ability to win and need of a most painful degradation for the relentless opponent. Again the mother of the chief cries out apprehensively to her daughter, but the daughter pays no heed. Now when the youths win, the younger sibling scalps half the head of the chief and also severs one ear. The youths insist on still another game. The chief pleads in vain that they quit gambling. The narrator again says nothing about the dismal feelings of the blackguard. Upon victory the younger sibling scalps the second half of the chief's head and cuts off the remaining ear. The raconteur asserted that she had never heard of severance of an ear as payment in gambling. She made no statement about a scalp as a gambling payment, but possibly scalps were stakes upon rare occasions.

Now the younger sibling's mother wails in anguish at his extreme exactions. Finally she confesses that he is her son. She says simply, "My son! your poor, poor uncle!" The youth turns upon her and kicks her away, justly so in the light of cultural standards, because she had indicated sharply her love for her vicious brother and rejection of husband and child.

The ethnographic notes themselves offer no evidence regarding Clackamas values in a specific case where a mother deserted her son. His violence, when he kicks her, probably excited approval in an audience whose Draconian standards of wifely dependability, maternal responsibility, and family loyalty were outraged. Very likely she went much too far to justify a jot of forgiveness or filial loyalty.

At once the younger youth transforms all remaining fourteen grizzly hairs into tiny grizzlies which become large with miraculous swiftness. Again his mother resorts to the sole device that might even yet arrest his extreme vengeance. She shrieks about his kinship; she leaps at him in order to restrain him. She repeats, "My son! your poor, poor uncle!" And with utmost brevity the raconteur describes the youth's culturally approved response. "He threw her aside." Then he proceeds with the just and frightful punishment. He burns every house with the flame that comes from his eyes. His fifteen grizzlies devour every villager, including his mother, her brother, and their mother. And as ever the narrator offers not a word about the feelings of actors. The stimulus presented to the audience is only external reporting of the repulsive finale of fires and devourings on the one hand, triumphant retribution on the other. The audience reacted in its several ways to this partially structured account, which connected with everyone's memory of descriptions or observations of actual intervillage warfare.

When the conflagrations and slaughter are ended, the siblings bring home their debilitated father. His good first wife washes him, in the folkloristically familiar motif of therapeutic water. His grandfather Fire massages him, another culturally correct expression of approval, pity, and healing. These devices restore him speedily to health, because it is the Myth Age, not modern times. Precultural people never endured a prolonged convalescence; they got well almost immediately, although they sometimes underwent long sufferings, as in this drama.

The victory of right over evil, which is uniquely alarming when malignity is incorporated in a parent and in-laws, is not the whole story. So far the youths have acted justly, at the ghastly but necessary price of killing the younger boy's mother, grandmother, and a whole village community with its chief. In order to do so indispensable and so terribly difficult a thing, they had had to acquire potent spirit-powers. Clackamas accepted the concept of acquisition of a spirit-power as the consequence of intimate familial relationship and daily living with its earlier possessor; therefore, such acquisition may be termed a special kind of inheritance of spirit-power by heredity and infection due to propinquity. The deduction that spirit-powers are kin is supported by the explicit citation here of a relative who is a spirit-power.

The drama now builds toward an anticlimax somewhat in the manner of another play (40). It shows how reality works out harshly even against the great, that is, those of most formidable spirit-power allies. The narrative proceeds to show how the most powerful persons must die notwithstanding all the things they may long have possessed and done. The tragic epilogue is developed in its details differently from the myth (40) where the hero at length is humbled and succumbs because he eats bones of dead persons. In the present drama the heroic youths fail to heed their mother's warning that they should never go hunting in a specific district which she points out to them. The clear implication is that persons who have acquired an enormously strong spirit-power, especially youths, may suppose that they are indestructible. Therefore they ignore advice or precautions which everyone should observe in a world whose dangers involve potencies exceeding those of the most powerful individuals. Accordingly, the play points a moral. No person is so righteous or durable that he can afford to ignore advice or to disregard dangers. The formidable hero of the other myth referred to was not at all seraphic. He lacked admirable qualities except those which came from his relationships to special kinds of spirit-powers; thus he believed that he could not be slain. The youths of the present myth perhaps felt that they were virtuous, and indeed they were. The myth therefore may have a moral component besides that of the other myth: nature and reality do not necessarily protect or reward the deserving during an indefinite period, any more than they guarantee everlasting survival for the person who has obtained the greatest spirit-power.

In the final act the half-brothers become so baffled by scarcity of deer in districts where they have been hunting daily that they hunt in the very territory which their mother has cautioned them not to enter. Such disobedience or nullifying of a parental admonition is a frequent motif in northwest states literatures, and invariably the culture's conscience intervenes to punish the youth who has shown disrespect toward a parental trustee of standards.

At first the youths' hunting in the forbidden area is more successful, as elsewhere in the region's literatures. Then the youths observe a village and descry two unmarried girls at a menstrual hut. The girls are unchaperoned by an older and married female and so are fair game for male prowlers. In modern Chinook communities a chaperone was perhaps not often lacking. In the myth the youths have sexual relations with the unguarded girls, one of whom is a sister of the mother who had been killed in the village slaughter. The escapade therefore also involves the detestable crime of incest with no less a person than a maternal aunt.

From the point of view of Chinooks, the youths have in a single act committed at least five offenses: severe damage to valuable family property, namely, purchasable girls; illicit sexual intercourse; intercourse with an unmarried and high-priced virgin; intercourse with a menstruating female; and incestuous intercourse, one of the most frightful of all offenses. The participants had no suspicion of the last crime; but the crime, not the intent, is decisive. After dawn the villagers kill the youths who are lying with the virgins. Although incest is the blackest of deeds, the deaths are also deserved because a pregnant girl's monetary worth in subsequent marriage payments was slight. Nevertheless, the recitalist did not hint at the fate of the females; she added only a few words which suggest that overt feeling about the rightness of the punishment of death was that incest was far more heinous than simple extramarital intercourse.

The youngsters are so much in the wrong that their flame and grizzly spirit-powers cannot now save them. Perhaps, too, their supernaturals are temporarily enfeebled or impotent because of sexual activity. A connection of incestuous sexuality or any sexuality with loss of "power" is plausible here, a connection which operated in the context of the distinctive values of Clackamas culture. Contact with a menstruating woman was additionally crippling. The youths are so weakened by their sexual adventure that they are killed with an ease that allows the storyteller to omit indication of how it is done. Probably most if not all male Indians of the northwest states followed a policy of sexual abstinence and avoidance of contact with menstruating women or foods prepared by such women for a day or two before hunting, fishing, or fighting.

The parents of the youths again observe the feather dripping blood and deduce that the boys have been killed. The weeping mother journeys to the fateful village and sees the bodies, and fighting of a kind which is not indicated ensues between her relatives and the villagers who killed the youths. Most likely such intravillage fighting, whatever it comprised, would also have occurred in the modern period if monetary payments were not quickly guaranteed or paid to the dead youths' relatives. The narrative here seems extremely compacted, but perhaps a raconteur did not provide further details of a situation of this kind. The audience filled in with memories because of its knowledge of analogous instances of feuding where causation, course of the struggle, and resolution were similar.

Not until the finale is the name of the youths' mother mentioned. She is Sun. She takes to the sky the bodies of the boys, and, deity-like, she announces that whenever a very well-to-do person is killed, her boys will be visible at dawn or dusk as stars close to the sun. If a person who is not of notable wealth is killed, only one boy (that is, one star) will be visible.

The raconteur added to this astronomical lore the thought that some members of the avenging village argue that the youths were killed with undue haste. The people should first have ascertained who the youths were. The ethnographic point is that Clackamas wanted at all costs to avoid intravillage fighting. Members of the village who are chagrined because the youths are their kin fight covillagers who justly killed the youths. A modern Chinook village possibly acted less hastily. I suspect that it would have spared the lives of the youths in order to resolve with large monetary payments any feelings regarding violation of virgins.

The raconteur also noted that Sun and her sons as celestial bodies suggest a person different from the Sun Woman of another myth (46). Mrs. Howard smiled at the possibility of narratives that were in conflict. She did not venture to reconcile the contradiction, if there was one, perhaps because she was not as well versed in cosmology as older Indians would have been.

Detailed delineations of characters do not appear in this myth, in spite of its length and abundance of expressive content. The characters are almost all mere types. Chub is here and in the other myth where he appears (8) a symbol of a headman's follower, and his characterization is slight. Fire represents a well-to-do elder who hands on his spirit-power to descendants, to all of whom he relates without enmity. His grandson typifies the well-to-do polygynous man whose spirit-power is taken over by sons. He also does what he can to force the return of the wife who has deserted him and her baby. He exemplifies an excellent father and husband who nearly loses his life because of hazards that arise in polygyny and connected in-law problems. His first wife is a typical good wife and mother, as well as an accepting stepmother, in a polygynous household. Apart from her Oedipal and incestuous responses, his second wife appears to be a projection of the fear that such a wife may express anger and abasement because of her lesser status in a well-to-do household and that she may do things so terrible as to cause fighting between in-law groups. The youths exemplify scions of a well-to-do family: they acquire great spirit-powers, rescue their father, punish evildoers, and enjoy spectacular careers. They stand for the aspirations of every Clackamas male. The malevolent chief is a projection of fears about well-to-do male heads of in-law lineages. Other characters are also largely types that function as theatrical props. For example, the Defecators serve as props and as means of relieving the somberness of the play; they share general characteristics—notably kindliness and an entertaining anality—with the Crow Women of other myths. They may have been meant to be Crow people.

The plot comprises so many themes that it bears comparison with the novel of European literature. One theme celebrates great spirit-power by indicating circumstances in which such support is acquired and used. A second theme expresses conflict between familial loyalty and disloyalty, especially concerning marital obligations and care of children. A third expresses fears of in-law friction and intervillage, even intravillage, antagonisms. A fourth focuses upon an exciting gambling game in which the stakes are scalps, ears, and life itself. A fifth points the same moral that is expressed elsewhere (40), that great supernatural power does not confer indestructibility. A sixth, which is also a moral, displays consequences of illicit intercourse of an incestuous kind with menstruating virgins of well-to-do station. And certainly not least in importance are the myth's Oedipal themes.

CHAPTER IV

GRIZZLY AND BLACK BEAR RAN AWAY
WITH THE TWO GIRLS

THEY (many families) were living there, in their large village. Two (marriageable) girls all the time went swimming in the river. I do not know how long a time, again they went, they swam. They did not look back (to the river bank). They said, "Now let us go ashore." They swam, (but) they did not go to the shore, (because) they saw two men seated on their clothes. Grizzly was seated on the older one's clothes. Black Bear sat on the younger one's clothes. They (the girls) said, "What (term of address) should we say to them?" They sat in the water (to cover their nakedness), they said to them, "Oh grandfathers! our clothes!" They (the men) paid no heed to them. Then again they (the girls) said, "What (else) might we say to them?" One (girl) said, "Oh dear! father's brothers! our clothes!" No (reply). They (the men) paid no heed to them. One (girl) said, "Older brothers! our clothes!" No. They paid no attention to them. One (girl) said, "Mother's brother! our clothes!" They paid no heed to them, they just sat there. "Oh me, oh my! What should we say to them? Grandfather's father!" They did not heed them. "What shall we say to them?" One (girl) said, "I am getting cold now. And it is evening. Hey! Brother's sons!" No. They paid no heed to them, they just grinned and grinned as they sat there. "Oh dear! What can we say to them?" One (girl) said, "Well then, old men (our husbands)!" Grizzly laughed. "Had you said that long ago, we would have given you back your clothes." So then they gave them to them. Grizzly took the one who was the older one, Bear took the younger one. They carried them on their shoulders. Grizzly took her to his house, while Bear took her (the younger girl) to where his house was. They lived there then.

It became winter. Bear plastered pitch on her anus, and then she died.

Grizzly himself (and his wife) lived there. She became pregnant, she gave birth to a girl. He said to her, "What did you give birth to?" She told him, "A girl." "Look at me!" She looked at him, he swallowed her eye, and then she had only one eye.

They lived there (Grizzly and his mutilated wife and their baby). Now she would go root-digging, she would take her daughter along. I do not know how long a time, and then she was again pregnant. She gave birth to a male. He said to her, "What did you give birth to?" She replied to him, "A male." "Look at me!" No. She would not look at him. She thought, "If I look at him he might gulp down another eye of mine again." He said to her in vain, "Look at me!" No. She feared him (wrongly, upon this occasion). He left her alone (and did not harm her). Had she looked at him, he would have given her eye back to her.

So they lived there then. He (the son) was his (Grizzly's) boy. The next (each successive) day she would go root-digging, she would take her daughter along. I do not know how long a time after, while she was digging she (the little girl) said to her, "Mother! Now let us go back home." She replied to her, "Oh dear. Pretty soon now." She (the daughter) said to her, "Let us go now! Let us go! Let us go back home! Make haste!" She replied to her, "Pretty soon now." After some time then the girl went away yonder, she sat down, she was angry. She said to her daughter, "Now let us go back." She replied to her (in anger), "Why? Go dig roots!" She (the mother) said to her, "We shall be going now." They went, they returned.

From *Clackamas Chinook Texts*, 14.

(When mother and daughter reached home) the boy (young Grizzly) was running about. She (his older sister) got her root-digger, she struck her younger brother (with it). She (the mother) said to her, "Oh dear! What are you doing to your younger brother?" She (the girl) said nothing, she (thereupon) left him alone. She went, she lay down (and sulked). Her mother said to her in vain, "What is the matter with you?" She (the girl) paid no heed (to her mother's query).

The next day then they (mother and daughter) again went, they went to dig roots. I do not know how long after, and then again she said to her, "Mother! Hurry! Let us go back home!" "No. In a little while." She would (repeatedly) say to her, "Hurry! Do hurry (and) let us go back home!" "Oh dear! What are you in a hurry about?" "Yes (I insist)," she said to her. "Hurry (and) let us go back home!" "Pretty soon!" After some time then she (the girl) went over there (at a distance from her mother), she sat down, she wept. She (her mother) said to her, "Why are you doing that?" She would not say anything (in reply).

After some time then they went back home. They got to there. The boy was running about. She (his sister) took her root-digger, and again she whipped him (with it). She (her mother) said to her, "Why is it that you are doing that to your poor younger brother?" She did not reply at all to her. She (the girl) went, she lay down (to sulk again).

The next day then they again went, they went root-digging. I do not know how long a time after, and then again she (the girl) said to her, "Now let us go, let us go back home. Hurry!" She snatched her mother's root-digger. "Oh all right," her mother replied to her. "We will go in a while." "No. Let us go now!" After some time then she (the angry daughter) went again, she sat down, she cried. Then she (the mother) said to her, "Very well, now let us go back home." They went.

The boy was running around, with something in his mouth. She (the girl) took her root-digger, she whipped him. He swallowed whatever was in his mouth.

I do not know how many days they did not go root-digging, and then they went again. They got to there (to the root patch). Soon after that she again said to her, "Mother! Hurry! Let us go now. Mind you listen to me now!" "Oh dear!" she replied to her. "(It was) a short time ago we got here." She (the girl) said to her, "Never mind!" She took away (forcibly) her (mother's) root-digger, she said to her, "Let us go! Let us go back home!" "Dear, oh dear!" she replied to her. "We will be bringing nothing (no roots) back." "It makes no difference." They went (at once then), they got back.

He (the son) was still eating something. She (the girl) took her root-digger, she whipped him. Their father (Grizzly Man) just lay there (and said nothing). (Presently) he said (to his daughter), "Oh dear! girl! (and you do that) to your poor younger brother!" "Oh yeh! the poor fellow!" (Now) she hit him all the more (and) on his mouth. Whereupon it (something which he was munching) popped out from his mouth. She took it, she threw it to her mother. She (the girl) said to her, "Look at this, (it is) your younger brother's (my uncle's) big toe. And it is the last one (the last bit left of my murdered uncles). Now they (father Grizzly and my Grizzly Boy brother) killed him (as well as my four other uncles), they ate him (after they killed and also ate my other four uncles)." "Oh oh oh!" (Now) she (the mother) wept. She (the girl) said to her, "Why cry? I kept telling you (in vain), Now let us go back home. No. You would not heed me." "Oh oh oh," she replied to her.

(The daughter now explained to her mother:) "It was that very first one of your younger brothers (my uncles) who got here. They (my father and my brother) killed him, they ate him. They did to the second one that same way too, they killed him, they ate him. When we got (back) here (from our root-digging) that is what I whipped him for." "Indeed," she replied to her. (The girl continued:) "Now this one (my fifth uncle) was the last of them, they ate him (too)." "Indeed," her mother said to her. (The daughter said:) "Now we must kill them. That younger brother of mine was worse (than my father). He was telling his father, Hurry! Now we will eat them up." (So then her mother agreed to the proposal and said:) "Very well."

Now it became winter. She (the mother) brought dry grass, she stuffed (the cracks in the walls of) their house. She got pitch, and there where she had stuffed in the grass, there she put in pitch (too). He (Grizzly Man) said to her (to his wife), "Why are you bringing grass?" "Surely. It will be getting cold soon." "Yes indeed." But that boy said (repeatedly) to his father, "She is just deceiving you." He replied to him, "Why no! It will get cold soon." "Well then (it is useless arguing with you)."

I do not know how long after, and then she said to her daughter, "Now tonight I will burn them up." "Very well indeed," she (the daughter) replied to her. She (the mother) tied them (her husband and son) together (while they slept). They (the mother and daughter) went outside. She (the mother) set fire to the pitch. It burned, grass and all. They (mother and daughter) sat outside. Then soon afterwards he (Grizzly Man) called out. He said, "Oh oh! old woman (wife)! We are burning." "Oh dear, oh dear" (she said) from outside where she sat (and speaking as if she were inside and in order to deceive him). The boy said to his father, "You suppose that they are really (inside with us), (but) they are outside. They have caused us to burn. I told you long ago to hurry and eat them." Now he (Grizzly Man) hallooed again. "Oh old woman! We are burning our children." They burned up there.

The next day then they (mother and daughter) went (away). She said to her mother, "Let us go now to where your village (is)." "Very well," she replied to her. They went by canoe. (As they were paddling along) she would look at her mother, she would think, "Maybe at the place (village) where we get to, they will laugh at us, (because) my mother has only one eye. Oh dear," she thought, "perhaps I will throw her away somewhere." They kept on going. I do not know where, she (the girl) saw a high rock bluff, she took her, she threw her mother far over yonder, she got stuck up high above on the rocks.

Then she (the daughter) went on (alone). She did not see her (mother's) hat. She went ashore, she spruced herself up. Shortly thereafter as she was sitting, now an old woman got to her. She (the old woman) said to her, "Let us go (together), dearest!" She (the young woman) thought, "I shall throw her into the fire." She threw her into the fire. She did not see her (the old woman's) hat, it fell at a distance. Her mother's heart was actually in that thing (hat) there.

Now she went on, she got to children. She said to them, "Where is the house of your headman?" "Yes. Way over there in the middle (of the village)." "Very well." She went, she went inside (the headman's house), she sat down. The people said, "Aha. A woman has come to our headman (to be his new wife)." They went to see her. Pretty soon an old woman (her mother) entered, she sat down, she peered at everything (with her hand at her brow). She said, "I have come to see the woman who has come to your headman. Oh! That is her! It is Half Grizzly Foot. Now while your bodies are still light (while you are alive yet), go somewhere else (and flee Half Grizzly Foot)!" She (the daughter) thought, "Hm! (a growl expressing anger). She is shaming me." She (the Grizzly daughter) stood, she went out, she went away.

(The myth recital repeats three occasions when Half Grizzly Foot pretties herself at a fire which she builds along the trail, is confronted by an inquisitive old woman, actually her mother's heart in the hat, and throws her but not the hat into the fire. Then, each time the young woman enters a village which is of her mother's kin, goes to the headman's house as if to marry him, and is confronted by the same old woman who warns the villagers to flee Half Grizzly Foot. The young woman is thereby revealed as before, and decamps.)

I do not know where she proceeded. As she went (on this fifth occasion), then she stepped on (on a leg of) Meadow Lark Woman. She (Meadow Lark) said to her, "Ouch ouch ouch ouch ouch! I am not the one who is following you! But nevertheless you broke my leg!" She said to her (to Meadow Lark), "Ah old woman! Tell me about it! I am taking along all sorts of (valuable) things (and I shall give you a gift in return for information). I shall (also) wrap up your (injured) leg." She said to her, "All right. When you have thrown away your mother, her hat dropped. That is where she placed her heart. These are all her villages that you have been coming to here. Now when she gets to you, (and) you seize her (and) burn her, you should look around. You will see the hat. Burn it. Then you will have killed your mother. She is the one who has been following you." "So that is it!"

She (Half Grizzly Foot) went on, she saw a village close by there. She thought, "I shall stop right here." She made a fire. While she built a fire, now already the old woman was coming along. She got there. She (the daughter) seized her forthwith, she threw her into the fire. She looked around, she saw the hat, it was lying way back yonder there. She got it, she burned it, it burned all up. She groomed herself, and then she went on.

Soon now as she proceeded (toward the fifth and last village), she got to a person. She said to him, "Where is the house of your headman?" "Yes. Over there!" She went, she went in, she sat down. Soon then they were saying, "Gee! a nice woman has come to our headman." They went to see her. She thought, "Soon again she (my mother) will be coming." But not at all! It became night. Not at all. Her mother did not come. She thought, "I have killed her now."

So then she stayed. She became married (to the headman). I do not know how long a time before she was pregnant. She gave birth to a boy. He became big. Then (she bore) another boy also.Whatever they would eat, she would put away the bones (for herself, to use or eat furtively). I do not know how long a time, (and then) she would go to their little house (to the women's menstrual-and-work hut). When she was there, she would be working (at basketry or other tasks). Actually then it was fingernails she was making (when no one was observing her). She was doing that for quite some time.

She thought, "Now let me try myself out (with my new grizzly claws)." There she was in their menstrual-and-work hut. Her (two) sons were playing (in the village). I do not know where her husband had gone. The (two) children went to see their mother. They saw her. "Oh dear, oh dear! It is a (supernaturally) dangerous being swinging and turning from side to side." They screamed in terror. The people stood up, they said, "What is the matter?" The (two) children said, "Our mother has become a dangerous being!" Their father went, he saw her, she was (merely) whipping reed mats (in order to clean them). He said to her, "What (is the matter) again? You frightened the children." "Not at all! I was merely whipping (cleaning) some of these things here." "Indeed."

Now then they lived (there, as before). (But now) wherever she would go (when she was at a distance from the village), then she would become a dangerous being. When hunters got back, they would say, "Dear, oh dear! Something (bad) is going about. We got to its tracks. Looks just like a grizzly." She herself (when at home) would say that. "Oh dear me, oh dear me!" And so they (the villagers) were afraid (about the grizzly in the vicinity). The next day (every day now) she would go off somewhere all day long. She would get back in the evening. When they went to bed at night, he (her husband) would smell her when she was asleep. The next day he would say to her, "Where have you been?" "No. (I was) just somewhere or other."

Then they continued to live (there). That was what she was doing. I do not know how long a time, and then quite a while after that they (the two sons) had become big. Now again she stayed in their menstrual hut (in her grizzly garb). Soon now they (the villagers) said, "Oh dear! What has come to us now?" (Now they realized that she was a grizzly-like being). They took their bows, they shot at her (in vain). She ate all of them (in that fifth village). She ate them up. She went back to those villages there that she had (earlier) passed through, she ate all of them (those villagers too). She had become a dangerous being. Now I do not know where she went to. That is all now. Story story.

What unphrased things did this drama express for its recitalist and audience? The story commences with two unwed damsels who are not named in the play. They are bathing or swimming in a river out of sight of their village. A man named Bear comes by and sits on the younger girl's garments. His companion, Grizzly, sits on the older one's. The embarrassed girls do not want to emerge naked, probably because females after about eight or ten years of age never appeared without a pubic cover and a skirt of some kind, in the presence of males. Therefore the girls remain in the water and ask for their garments while they futilely address the men with a series of kinship appellations. The men smile at the terms but do not accept them. Bear and Grizzly do not allow the girls to put on the garments until addressed as "old men," that is, husbands. When the girls have dressed, the men take them away to be wives. Apparently in the Myth Era such girls have no alternative to accompanying men whom they have addressed and therefore accepted verbally as husbands. The more attractive man, Bear, acquires the girl who is preferable because she is younger.

Modern Clackamas disallowed seizure of females with the exception of slaves. This first scene therefore appears to concretize a most pleasant wish fulfilment, projected onto the screen of the precultural past, by a society which debarred capture of freewomen. Monetary outlays, competitive and aggressive feelings, and a variety of anxious sentiments normally accompanied marriage arrangements. But the two furry gentlemen of the Myth Age, if they were really conceived as cloaked in fur, obtain wives by direct rather than involved negotiations. Throughout the episode there is an indescribably comfortable absence of relatives, expenses, and strains of any other kind. Not least, the females are completely at the mercy of their captors.

So simple and perhaps wholly happy a fantasy, which effects discharge of feelings about the essential relationship between the sexes, is not likely to be long maintained when untold generations discuss its implications apart from story recitals. And so the drama proceeds to elaborate qualifications about the successful and dominant men.

During the next winter Bear, who is stupid, plasters pitch over his wife's anus in order that the house be made less dirty by her defecation during hibernation. His misguided effort to keep the winter habitation clean kills his wife. In the myth we hear no more of Bear, whose own uncleanness is not set forth. It is the wife who soils the house. Her death may be a projection consequent upon apprehension of constipation. Nowhere else is constipation referred to, although myths frequently mention diarrhea. A Freudian hypothesis that Bear's conscious wish to be neat is a defense against an impulse to penetrate his wife anally cannot be subjected to corroboration from the data which we have.

Grizzly is a "better man than Bear," in the informant's words. That is, he is not so stupid because he does not block his wife's rectum with pitch; he is also innocent of anality, if a Freudian hypothesis is relevant. Bear's aggression is criminal, but it also seems to be funnier to Clackamas than to many Euroamericans. Various circumstances that arise in Northwest communities account for such merriment: the death involves destruction of valuable property which a wife constitutes. Again, the killing is droll, like Blue Jay's ridiculous cutting-up of his wife (in myth 26), where the clown supposes that her carcass may provide a repast for his guest. These wife-killings are additionally diverting because they express feelings toward the purchasable sex.

Later Grizzly's wife gives birth to a female infant who is only partially a Grizzly.

When she tells her Grizzly husband the sex of his child, he orders her to look at him. When she does so, he gouges out and swallows one of her eyes. The raconteur accounted for his action by saying only, "He was just mean." Such an observation is a typical expression of Northwest natives when they venture to describe and account for feelings. Its succinctness is as significant as its superficiality. We cannot often expect to find a more revealing analysis of motives by people whose security needs are such that they evade recognition of the profound animosities that occur in their society. Mrs. Howard added that Grizzly's wife now has only one eye and certainly does not like that, but she can do nothing about it. The wife of a man, especially so "mean" a man as Grizzly, does not often dare to leave him or to exact some milder reprisal. She has to endure a certain amount of bad treatment. Undoubtedly in the modern villages a man who deliberately, maybe even adventitiously, gouged out his wife's eye would be subjected to severe penalty. Besides, his own relatives would not uphold him. Mrs. Howard frequently commented on the lack of resourcefulness or self-respect in some precultural people like the hapless wife of Grizzly. The motif reflects the property status of a wife who can do little to counter her husband's sadistic control of her: a precultural wife could not retaliate even if she was blinded by her husband.

Later she gives birth to a male infant who is wholly a Grizzly. Now when Grizzly asks her the sex of his second baby and she tells him, he again orders her to look at him. She refuses because she fears that he will swallow her remaining eye. But this time he would have returned her gouged-out eye had she looked at him! (With characteristic sketchiness the myth does not say where he was keeping it after he swallowed it.) Because of her distrust of her husband's motivation, she remains one-eyed. Perhaps, too, she refuses to accept his evaluation of a male baby as superior to a female infant, but if this is a part of her feeling the myth lines do not reveal it. Interpretation of the eye-swallowing and eye-returning is handicapped by a lack of ethnographical, comparative mythological, and other materials. The swallowing subsequent to the birth of a female infant who is only half a Grizzly appears to express the man's wrath at his wife for having borne a female rather than a male child and for having an infant which is his wife's rather than his own offspring, in the light of judgments regarding heredity that are, I think, ascribed only to the Myth Age. The myth says explicitly that subsequently Grizzly would have returned her eye upon birth of a son whom Clackamas genetic theory, applied to the precultural era, would judge as wholly Grizzly's. But his wife is so resentful—no doubt rightly from the culture's viewpoint—and also so terrorized that she no longer dares to glance at him. She cannot now express, by looking directly at him, warmth toward a husband who has exhibited so much meanness and inhumanity.

The essential feature of this scene appears to be not the eye-swallowing but the expression of latent emotions in a domestic relationship. The plot symbolizes one husband's feelings about his wife and offspring. Another component in the drama is the wife's indignation at a spouse who punishes her when she bears his daughter, and who apparently prefers a son. The myth does not say that she knows he will return

the eye if she reveals that she has borne a son; it indicates that she lacks foreknowledge that he will ever return her eye. The implication is that she has become panicked, so that she supposes that her husband will add insult to injury by swallowing
her remaining eye, even though the second child is a male and thus a full-blood
Grizzly. Perhaps, then, the raconteur wishes to convey the thought that the wife is
so frightened that she supposes that her husband is psychotic, that he is likely to
blind her. Masochism of the wife, and of Clackamas wives, is evident. Cultural policy
is to endure and even to tolerate extremes of evil in males of the household. It never
occurs to the precultural wife to leave Grizzly or to do anything to control her Grizzly son. Such an extremity of masochism might not be often tolerated in the modern
society, but its expression in a myth points to important attitudes.

In the light of the behavior which this drama limns for Grizzly Man, his is a
psychotic personality with peculiarly archaic responses. He reacts sadistically by
destroying or returning a cardinal organ which is bound up with his helpmate's
self-identity. The manner in which her masochism fits in with his sadism resembles
the sado-masochistic partnership which clinicians frequently encounter in Western
civilization.

The ethnography gives no information about the incidence of blindness among
Clackamas. The few and unsatisfactory evidences about its cultural functions come
from myths (especially 46) where it is a consequence of excessive weeping. No other
Clackamas myth makes note of eye-gouging, much less eye-swallowing. It seems
profitless to pursue an orthodox Freudian hypothesis that the eye motif involves
phallic and castration components at deep psychological levels, because evidences
that might be brought to bear are meager or absent in the ethnographic and literary
materials and the possibility of working with Clackamas informants who are psychologically Indian has passed. On the other hand, if one surrenders a Freudian-like
pursuit of origins in a person's dread of body injury or mutilation, the eye motif can
be accepted as exemplification of what one may term a mutilation complex, that is, a
universal kind of anxiety. In Northwest Indians a strong component of humiliation
must have been interwoven with mutilation anxiety, because mutilation was resorted to for extreme offenses.

In the next scenes Grizzly's one-eyed wife takes her half-Grizzly daughter to the
root patch on five, that is, many, successive occasions. Each day the daughter presently urges the mother to hurry back home. The mother responds, "Pretty soon,"
but continues to dig roots for quite a while. Then the daughter sits down at a short
distance and in obvious anger. Sometimes she also weeps. The girl does not explain
her actions or feelings, nor is the audience told the reason why the youngster has
knowledge of happenings which justify a speedy return. It is sufficient to note here,
as for many analogous precultural situations, that a younger person possesses insights and foreknowledge which an elder lacks.

At length when the industrious mother suggests returning, her daughter replies
bitterly, "Why should we go now? Keep on with your root-digging!" She is really
saying, "It's too late now, so why return at all? After all, you have let me down and

your kin too!" From the daughter's point of view the mother has procrastinated, snubbed her, and endangered other relatives. When the females get back, the daughter at once clubs her younger brother with a root-digger. When scolded for her treatment of him, she makes no reply. She lies down again in patent ill-humor. She continues to say nothing when her mother inquires what is the matter with her. Her silence expresses exasperation. Muteness is the culture's stylized way of handling asperity to parents or relatives. Upon the fourth occasion the younger brother has something in his mouth when the sister returns and beats him with a root-digger. He swallows whatever is in his mouth.

The girl's insistence that they make a hasty return from the root site is still greater upon the fifth occasion. She seizes her mother's root-digger in order to impress upon her that she should halt digging in order to return, although at a cost of having gotten no roots whatsoever. When they arrive home and the daughter again cudgels the brother, even on his face, a big toe which he has been chewing pops out of his mouth. The daughter exhibits it and explains that it is the remaining part of the body of the last of her mother's four younger brothers, whom Grizzly and Grizzly Boy have been killing and eating during the absence of the females. The daughter explains that her younger brother is more bent upon killing and cannibalism than is his Grizzly father. When the daughter asserts that the two Grizzlies must be killed, the mother agrees because it is her brothers who have been killed and eaten. In accordance with the style of the literature, the mother's feelings are left to the audience to deduce. It appreciated that murders of relatives as close as siblings are insupportable.

The myth is not explicit, but it suggests that the masochistic mother is in certain respects so weak that she resorts to severe justice only when her daughter forces such a choice upon her. When the daughter can show objective evidence, the toe, the mother can resist no longer. Her character is streaked with corrupt features: she is unable to respond with respect to her child's awarenesses; she is unable to do what a good wife and mother should when her husband brutally attacks and maims her; she cannot control, much less stand up against, viciousness of males of her household; she resolves her masochism and incompetence at home by compulsive work away from home in toil so protracted that her brothers are killed. Her responses offer cumulative evidences of defectiveness in character.

As the daughter grows up, the warpings in her mother constitute some of the triggering for the daughter's descent into hate and cannibalism, a developmental course which is the dominant theme of the remainder of the drama. Grizzly's killing and eating of his wife's younger brothers, and Grizzly Boy's abetting of such cruelty and voracity, are of less interest than dramatic portrayal of the daughter's life.

When winter approaches, the mother stuffs dry grass and pitch in the cracks of the house, ostensibly to keep out cold. She does it at a time when Grizzly father and son find such action plausible. However, like daughter, so Grizzly son. He is as perspicacious as younger persons always are in Clackamas literature. He vainly warns his father that the mother's explanation for the combustible grass and pitch is a deception. When Grizzly and Grizzly Boy are asleep at night, the mother ties them together and the females set fire to the dwelling. The males wake up but cannot escape because they are tied. In the last moments the boy scolds his father and says, "I told you long ago to hurry and eat them," that is, to eat his mother and older sister. The son is as revolting a murderer as his father. There is an effective employment of irony in the way the narrator balances the daughter's inability to sway her mother in time with the son's incapacity to convince the father.

Following the demise of Grizzly and Grizzly Boy, the plot narrows and intensifies in interest because of dominance of subtle suggestions of developments in a single personality, the daughter's.

In the next act mother and daughter proceed by canoe in order to live in the mother's home village; in a modern community the death of hunters would also have obliged female survivors to leave for the maternal home. En route the daughter quickly exhibits deterioration of an incipiently psychotic kind when she expresses to herself concern lest people deride her and her mother because the latter is one-eyed. The girl thereupon seizes her mother and expresses violently her rejection of the woman by casting her high above, as in another myth (5), onto a rock bluff. Then the girl paddles along, goes ashore, and spruces up before entering the village. In other words, she turns unexpectedly and with utmost aggression upon her mother not only in order to achieve vengeance against the cause of her uncles' deaths. She spurns her mother for being one-eyed and thereby, she feels, a butt of ridicule. The girl is developing or intensifying wishes that are getting out of control, becoming too angry and murderous to be held in leash. Her standards weaken as she attempts to carry on alone.

Now it appears that her mother has a heart which she keeps not in her body but in her hat. The hat lies in the canoe. Accordingly, while the daughter is seated on the shore, supposing that she has gotten rid of her mother and can proceed alone to the village, an old woman approaches. This woman is the mother's heart-in-the-hat, which has speedily metamorphosed into an old woman who wears a hat. Possibly in native theory the heart connects with spirit-power. The latter may invade a thing which belongs to a person. Now the older woman says, "Let us go along together, my dear!" The girl is as violent and unrestrained as she had been when she hurled her mother onto the bluff. At once she throws the older woman into the fire, apparently to burn and die. But the hat has fallen elsewhere. The old woman is therefore unharmed, although the girl does not know this. Nor does she suspect that the old woman is the creation of the heart of her mother.

The girl also does not know that the village at which she now arrives is peopled by her mother's kin. Children direct the girl to the headman's house, where she sits down as if come to marry him. Villagers enter in order to take a look at her, since her arrival signifies, in narratives of the Myth Era, the voluntary coming of another wife to the headman's polygynous household. Shortly an old woman, who is the reincarnation from the heart-in-a-hat, enters also and peers under her hands as if her eyesight is failing. The aged woman pretends that she too has entered in order to observe the attractive arrival, the headman's latest bride, but she quickly calls out something which meant to Clackamas, "That's half-grizzly-foot!" That is, this girl is part grizzly or, in effect, a part Grizzly Ogress! The old woman goes on to warn the villagers inside the headman's house, "While you are yet alive, flee! flee before she eats all of you!" At once the daughter growls to herself and thinks, "She is shaming—or ridiculing—me!" She walks away from the village.

One function of the aged woman is symbolic. The old woman plagues the girl or follows her closely, just as a person's conscience stays with one and causes a response of shame when vicious behavior is driving to control. The old woman is at once internalized mother and anthropomorphized voice of conscience which humiliates and forces the girl to leave before her drive to murder takes over.

The girl travels alone. She halts along the trail, builds a fire, and washes her face in order to appear attractive in the next village. A decrepit woman, again her heart-in-hat mother, comes up to her, sits on the opposite side of the fire, and says anew, "Let us go along together, my dear!" These words amount to, "Take along your conscience so as to keep your part-grizzly nature under control." Once more the girl responds with anger. She throws the exasperating old woman into the fire. But she fails to note that a hat has fallen away from the embers. The girl proceeds, arrives at another village, and as in the earlier episode enters the headman's house.

The raconteur cites five such villages at which the part-Grizzly arrives, and to which also comes an unidentified aged woman who is really her mother. The mother has five villages, which is a stylized way of saying that her relatives reside in many villages. She endeavors to protect their populations from her cannibal daughter and is successful for the time being. She shames the girl away from each village by calling her by name, by intense gazing at her with hands raised to brows, by warning people that the girl will eat them, and by calling out to flee while they are still alive. The old woman also encounters the girl five times, that is, many times, along the trail, sits on the opposite side of the fire, and peers at her, hands raised to brows. These adroit descriptive touches are projections of conscience. Each time the daughter throws the old woman, that is, conscience and values, into the fire. Upon ten occasions, along five trails and in five villages, the aged anthropomorphization of conscience looks intently at the girl, who is infuriated and shamed. Five times when no one else is around the anger-driven girl casts conscience into the fire. Five times when villagers are watching inside a headman's house she does not yet dare to throw conscience into the fire and therefore beats a shamed retreat. Each time that the girl is ready to perpetrate a frightful cannibalistic aggression upon villagers who are her mother's relatives, the mother reappears and temporarily holds the killer in line.

When the girl heaves her mother into the fire along the last trail, she is so infuriated by the recurring visitations that she stirs up the fire so as to burn more completely the remains of the old woman and of conscience. Of course she does not kill the elder because the hat is lying nearby. At the last headman's house the girl does not wait for the old woman to enter. No sooner does the girl enter and sit down than she hears shouts outside. She knows that the villagers are calling out about an old woman who is approaching the village. The girl flees this last house and village before the woman can enter, look intently at her, and reveal her identity. The girl decamps because she still has some conscience. She is in more violent conflict than ever between the grizzly part of her which has been reinforced by identification with the father and the mother whom she once accepted as representative of the culture.

Now when the girl is walking along, she steps on Meadow Lark and breaks that ever-helpful old woman's leg. Whenever a person who has accidentally broken her leg takes care of the damaged member, Lark explains what has been happening and what should be done. Lark informs the girl about the hat, the heart in it, the need to burn the heart-hat in order to kill the mother, the fact that the villages are the mother's kin's villages, and each other item in the situation. Lark sets up no standards. She is ethically neutral. She gives mechanically perfect responses of an informative kind in return for repair of the injured leg.

When the girl, who remembers Lark's information, halts on the trail, builds a fire, and the old woman arrives as usual, she casts woman and heart-hat into the flames, in accordance with Lark's prior explanation. At last the girl has killed her mother and discarded conscience. After she tidies herself, she enters the next village, remains, marries the headman after the fashion of Grizzly Women whom headmen cannot reject in marriage, and later bears two sons.

Many years pass. She lives outwardly like other well-dispositioned wives. However, her inner nature eventually comes through the disguise of conventionality which she has long used. She sets aside deer bones which her boys had eaten the meat from. She takes the bones to the menstrual and work hut and sharpens them so that they may serve as her grizzly claws. One day her sons, who are playing nearby, observe animal-like movements as she is trying on the claws. The boys are terrified perhaps not so much at the wearing of claws as at their mother's grizzly-like posturing. When they scream, she quickly halts her movements, removes her grizzly accouterments, and resumes ordinary feminine work. When her husband investigates, he finds her merely whipping and cleaning reed mats.

Now whenever she travels alone, she transforms into a grizzly. Hunters return and report tracks of a grizzly nearby. And at night the husband who lies beside her smells blood on her. He does not yet realize that she is the one who has been eating people during her daytime journeyings. In fact, her biography is so exclusively the preoccupation of narrator and audience that her headman husband remains undepicted.

At length when her boys are older, perhaps about puberty, villagers themselves see her in her grizzly garb at the menstrual hut. They shoot at the grizzly in vain. The raconteur said that forthwith she eats every villager, but I am uncertain about the implication that she also eats husband and sons. When she has annihilated the village, she returns to the other four villages of her long-deceased mother and devours their occupants too.

Clackamas perhaps sensed that it is not until her sons' developing masculinity threatens her that she is goaded to slaughter all the villagers and kin. Full explosion of her psychosis is triggered by the youths' puberty. A Clackamas probably would never offer such a hypothesis, which involves facing Oedipal hence denied feelings; a storyteller evaded such recognition of emotions by pointing instead to the circumstance that villagers for the first time see her as she really is, a grizzly and therefore a murderess, but concurrence in time of that perception and the boys' puberty indicates that Clackamas and their storytellers apprehended that the mother's change of appearance and disposition was a partial consequence of her sons' maturation.

A crucial turning point in the drama is the ascendancy of the girl's murder drive in its long conflict with village respectability and social conscience. This victory actually occurs at a deep level years before the sons reach puberty. And the cause is accidental although a *deus ex machina*, Lark, is resorted to in order to turn the tables at that time. Because of the chance stepping on Lark's leg, that informant innocently makes it possible for the girl to wipe out her remainder of control by conscience. The girl can spurn values once she has consumed her mother's heart in the flames. A fortuitous encounter with an automaton who stands for a newly acquired supernatural is presented as a major precipitating factor in the history of the girl's psychosis. When the girl's mother has been eliminated, all that is left is a residual conscience in a scheming murderess. To be sure, the girl waits more than ten years, until her sons have reached manhood, before another psychotic break is triggered. Then she wreaks a mad vengeance against her long-deceased mother and the mother's kin. It is as if for more than ten years she is in remission because long before she had been enabled to vent wrath, get rid of conscience, and minimize inner conflict. She goes wild again at the point when her boys reach puberty and her unresolved Oedipal conflict is reactivated.

Why did Clackamas preserve this myth? What did the life history of a madwoman mean to them? Very likely the myth, like others in which Grizzly actors appear, is partly motivated by terror of those most dangerous animals and by a correlated fear of persons who acquired a grizzly spirit-power. However, another level of behavior may involve the mechanism of projection, by way of anthropomorphization of the lethal hatred which women in this culture sometimes felt toward others, coupled with protracted planning and scheming preceding consummations, murderous ones no doubt when women secretly hired shamans to do the dirty work. Such a projection is Grizzly Woman. The drama also functions as a kind of explanation of why some persons who are haters or killers have gotten to be that way: the woman has a grizzly spirit-power. That is, the story describes the Clackamas notion of how a person who has such a supernatural metamorphoses into its physical appearance and behaves like it; psychosis is neatly explained in the terms and processes of supernaturalism.

The leading actor displays specific features which are necessary for the development of the drama. Initially she behaves like a good girl. For a long time she acts like a human being, keeping in control the hereditary component which comes from her Grizzly father. She is able to effect control because of partial identification with her weak but principled mother. But since that unfortunate woman lacks an eye, the daughter who as a younger child has identified with her suffers reiterated humiliations from comments that villagers level at her mother. Then the mother's industry and responsibility about securing a good supply of roots result in further humiliation because of refusal to accept the daughter's worth, that is, to heed the warning that they should hurry home. Humiliation generates anger.

Hostility to the mother appears more than justified when the mother's brothers are murdered; the mother has ignored admonishings which should have opened her eyes to her Grizzly husband and son. The girl is rightly furious that her mother's deafness to pleas to return amounts to condoning savage liberties taken by the males at home, and she sees her mother's conscience as corrupt. The grizzly component and spirit-power which is as yet a buried part of the girl's nature resents the freedom granted by her mother to cannibalistic urges of father and brother. Her mother appears to allow the males to kill and eat people, while the daughter must remain human. When she develops envy of freely aggressive males, she begins a process of identification with the men rather than the mother; she feels that her mother rejects her, that her understanding is limited, her values inconsistent since they do not extend to males, and she is shockingly unattractive and a source of shame because of a gouged-out eye. So begins the process of becoming freer to be aggressive, that is, to be like the cannibalistic and conscienceless males of her family. At the same time her grizzly spirit-power is strengthening within her. She identifies with it more and more.

The girl is finally overwhelmed with mourning for her devoured uncles, whose deaths are due to their sister's stupidly compulsive industry or moronic procrastination at the root site. A girl can turn only against her mother in order to avenge those unnecessary deaths. She has already helped her mother dispose of the father and younger brother, and she cannot wreak further aggression against these murderers. She purged her hostility toward them when she burned them alive. She has not only a hereditary component, which implies a supernatural, too, from her Grizzly father; she has an identification with him that has been increased by jealousy of his greater ability to vent aggression. Was it not he who extracted the eye of her hated mother? She is not wholly swayed any longer by a conscience which puts limits upon female and not male behavior, so now she struggles, along five trails and in five villages, with her grizzly drive to kill and eat people. On the other hand, she has to control vestigial shame at exposure of this drive, shame pricked by the portion of conscience which long since originated from identification with the mother. The myth not only utilizes the mother as a symbol of conscience; it symbolizes the virtual indestructibility of conscience in its representation of the life of the mother as preserved in the heart-hat.

The myth also shows how circumstance may supply the stimulus, the extra push, that tips the beam so that a conscience which has kept a person more or less human is at last overwhelmed by the reinforced drive to hate and kill. The girl finally destroys every person whom she was not quite able to kill in her travels from village to village during earlier years. The human being completes the course of deterioration to a Grizzly. The same human being completes the change to a psychotic who is projected as the most dangerous of animals. Finally, she becomes identical with her grizzly spirit-power: the main themes of this tragedy are delineations of personalities and a history of personality change.

CHAPTER V

GRIZZLY WOMAN KILLED PEOPLE

T HEY lived there in their village. Their headman's house was in the center (of the village). After a while then a woman came to him. They (the village residents) said, "Some woman has come to our headman (to be his wife)." Now they lived there (and she remained as his wife). When it got toward springtime she went to I do not know where. She returned in the evening. Oh dear, she brought back camas with her. She shared it about. They said to her, "Where did you get them?" She replied to them, "Indeed I got to a burned-over place. The camas were just standing thickly there." They replied to her, "Goodness, whenever you go again let us follow you." "Yes," she said to them, "perhaps tomorrow." "Indeed. Let us follow you." "All right," she replied to them.

The next day then they (only women) went. I do not know how many canoes went. They got to there, they went ashore. They dug (camas). It became evening, and they camped over-night. They said, "It will be tomorrow before (we return to the village, because the camas digging is so good here)." In the evening they went to sleep. Toward dawn she got an arrow-like spear, she went through the camp, she broke (pierced) their hearts. She killed them all. Now it became morning, and then she carried them away, she laid them down, she hid the paddles. She thought, "I shall go now. I shall go back home." She took along those camas of the (murdered) people. She reached the village. She said to them (to women at the village), "They (the women who accompanied me to the root patch) sent this (the camas) to you." At another house (to which) she went, she took along their camas to them (to the women at that house). She told them, "It will be till tomorrow before I go fetch them (the women who have remained overnight at the root patch)." They said to her, "Let us follow you too." "All right," she replied to them.

The next day then they (the second group of women) got ready, and then they went, three canoes. They went along, they arrived, they (their murdered predecessors) had tied up the canoes there, so they too tied up their canoes at the place. They went ashore. She told them, "Dear me, I guess they went yonder. There are even lots more camas over there. But stay here first. Let it be tomorrow before we go in that direction (where the first group of women went)." "Very well," they replied to her. They dug. It became evening. They turned away from there, they made fires. Shortly then Grizzly Woman got to them, she said to them, "Goodness, now they (the women of the first group) have lots of camas. They said to me, Per-haps we will cook them right here." "Indeed," they replied to her. Then they ate. They fin-ished (their camp meal). Grizzly was gone.

Shortly now they heard singing. They said, "Goodness! singing! Listen!" They listened. Shortly afterward she got back. She said to them, "Why are you silent? They are singing yonder." "To be sure!" they replied to her. "We heard them." They said, "Let us sing too." So then they began to sing. They quit (singing, after a while), they went to sleep. Toward sunrise then she again went through the camp, she caused them (with her spirit-power) to sleep. Then she again took her arrow-spear, she broke (pierced) their hearts. She killed all of them. The next day then she again carried them away, she laid them there where she had laid those first ones. She collected their camas, she put it in (her camas bag), and she went back.

From *Clackamas Chinook Texts*, 17.

She got there. Now again she informed them in the same way, "They are not going to come, it will be a while (tomorrow) before they will come back," she said to them. "Indeed," they replied.

Now others (of the remaining women at the village) said, "Let us go too." The next day then they got ready, they went. She took them along (to the root patch) also. They arrived, they went ashore. They became somehow or other (they felt something was amiss). She said to them, "This is the place where they (first) stopped. Possibly they moved yonder to where there are much more camas." "To be sure," they replied. They dug (camas). One (of this group of women) said, "What do you think? Looks like a long, long time since they were digging (at this site)." "Yes," they replied, "we noticed that." They stopped (digging). In the evening they made their camp there. They said, "It is not good. Something is some way or other (wrong)."

Shortly afterward then Grizzly arrived. She said to them, "Why are you silent? Yonder they are singing, they are giggling, they are laughing—those who came first. And they baked their camas over there." "Indeed," they replied to her. "We merely got to feeling queer." "Oh dear, oh dear!" she said to them, "why? Soon they will be dancing again (yonder). Suppose I go see them again." She went. Soon afterward as they sat there they heard singing. They said, "It is indeed so. They are singing now. Listen." "Yes," they said. They sat there. Now she got back to them, she said to them, "You sing too!" "All right," they replied to her. They tried to sing, but no, they quit, they lay down to sleep. Now Grizzly arose, she caused sleep in them. She got her arrow-spear, and she went among them, she broke their hearts (with the dart), she killed all of them. The next day then she again carried them to the place where she had laid those earlier ones. All done. Then she loaded up (her canoe) with their camas, and she went back (to the village). She arrived. Now she told them the same way again, "They sent these (roots) to you." "Very good," they replied. "The first ones who went (to the root patch), now they are baking them (the camas they dug) there." "Goodness! Let us go tomorrow too." "All right," she replied.

They got ready then the next day, they went, they got there, they went ashore. They got to the place where their fire had been. One of them began crying. They said to her, "Why are you making a bad sign for yourself?" She replied, "No. Something is amiss. It (must have) happened to our people at the place where you see." "Why no! Their fire is from a very long time ago, and now it is gone there," they said to her. "Never mind! say nothing to her (to Grizzly)!" They went to dig, they dug. That one (woman) attempted to quit (digging), for then she would be crying again (involuntarily). In the evening they stopped (digging roots), they went to their camp there, they sat. They said, "We will not build a fire (because we are uneasy about the danger we sense)." Shortly afterward then Grizzly came too. She said to them, "What is the matter with you?" They replied to her, "This one here is ill." "Indeed. She will quit (feeling like that) soon." Now they also lay down to sleep.

She got back to them, she said to them, "Goodness! Have you already laid down to sleep?" They replied, "Yes. It will be tomorrow when we (rise and) dig." "To be sure," she replied to them. "I will go inform them (the earlier arrivals whom Grizzly had indicated as camped at a distance)." They paid no attention to her there. She went away, pretty soon they heard, "Goodness! they (the women yonder) are singing." They said, "Listen! they are singing." One of them said, she said, "Do you suppose that it is really so?" They quit (discussing their doubts). Now she came to them again, she said to them, "They were going to come but I told them that they (you women) had long ago lain down to sleep. So let it be. Now I shall lie down too." Then she lay down. They went to sleep.

Now she again made sleep sleep sleep for them. Then she arose, she got her arrow-spear, and again she went among them, she broke (pierced) their hearts. Again then in the morning she carried them away. All done. She quit (carrying away corpses and hiding evidence). She loaded up with their camas, (only) a very few (had been dug by them). Now she went home.

She got there. She shared their camas around. She told them (at the village), "They became lazy. They dug only a few. They said, It will be tomorrow before (we dig plenty)." "Very well," they (the remaining village women) replied.

Now the others (the remaining women) also said, "We will go too in the morning." Her (Grizzly's) sister-in-law also said, "I will go tomorrow too." At once her (that woman's) little younger sister said, "I will go too, older sister!" She (Grizzly) said to her (to the girl), "So you too already! Now really why should you accompany us?" She (the girl) said, "I will merely follow my older sister." "No!" she (Grizzly) replied to her. "You must not go." She (the girl) said, "I will go!" She (Grizzly) said to her, "No!" "I will go." Her older sister said to her (to Grizzly), "Oh she is merely saying that to you (and so you need not be concerned about her presence). We will go in the morning."

The following day then they got ready. The very first one was (the little girl named) Water Bug. She went, she hid in the canoe. They went to the river, they got into their canoes, they went along. Grizzly turned and looked, she saw her (the girl). She said to her, "Goodness! I told you not to come." She (Water Bug) paid no attention to her there. They went along, they arrived. They went ashore. Grizzly forgot (about Water Bug). She forgot, she did not take the older sister's paddles. Water Bug took them, she went, she hid them. She ran about, she got (discovered) all those paddles (which Grizzly had hidden), she moved them away.

Then she went ashore, she got to her older sister, she said to her, "All the dead people are lying right here. Let us go (see them)!" So the two of them went, they got to them (the corpses). Dear oh dear, the dead persons lay there. The two of them sat, they wept. She said to her older sister, "Wash your face. She (Grizzly) might get suspicious." They got (back) there, they told them (the other women) about it. They wept. They quit (crying). They washed their faces. Water Bug said to them, "Say nothing. If she should tell us, Sing, do that. But be very careful! She will be coming soon now." (When Grizzly arrived) she nudged her older sister, she nudged her, she said, "She will be talking (lying) to us now!"

She (Grizzly) said to them, "What are you being quiet about? You have lied to the people about something or other, Water Bug!" She (the girl) paid no heed. She (Grizzly) said to them, "Goodness! Now they (the women who are yonder) are drying their cooked camas." She (Water Bug) nudged her older sister. She (Grizzly) quit, and then she left them.

Again then Water Bug informed them, she said, "Watch carefully!" "Yes," they replied. (Water Bug continued,) "You will not be first. I will be first. She plans to kill me (first)." She told them everything (that they had to do to survive). She said to them, "When she has fallen asleep, then we will leave her." "All right," they said to her. She went to the river, she picked up shells, she brought them to her older sister. Now it became nighttime, they went to bed (as if they were going to sleep).

She (Grizzly) got to them. "Humph!" she said (to Water Bug). "Now you lied about something to them." She paid no heed, she said nothing whatever. They had gone to bed. Grizzly said, "Now I shall go to bed too then." Water Bug picked up a lot of firewood. She (Grizzly) said to her, "Why are you going to build up the fire? So that is why you came (only in order to be a nuisance). You are supposing some youth may get to your older sister (during the night)!" She (Water Bug) ignored her. (Grizzly observed,) "They are sleepy. They will be getting up (very early) in the morning to dig (and so you should let the fire die down)." She paid no attention to her. She (the girl) lay down. She put those shells over her eyes.

Shortly afterward the fire went down. Grizzly arose slowly and silently. She (the girl) noticed her, she nudged her older sister, they saw her. She (Grizzly) went to them, she looked at Water Bug. She (the girl) was watching her. "Oh dear me!" she (Grizzly) said to her, "Are you not going to go to sleep? (You are very likely supposing that) youths are going about." "Aha!" Water Bug responded (pretending fright at being awakened). She (the girl) got up, she fixed the fire, she put large pieces of firewood on the fire. "Ah," she (Grizzly) said to her, "indeed why are you building the fire?" She did not reply at all, she lay down again.

Shortly afterward the fire became low. Now Grizzly got up again, she approached stealthily, she (the girl) heard (Grizzly saying) sleep sleep sleep. "Aha!" retorted Water Bug (as if she had been awakened). "Oh dear me! Have you not been asleep?" (Grizzly asked her). (The girl replied,) "Oh I was dreaming. I saw an arrow-spear with blood on it." "Goodness! Now she is lying to them. Leave them alone. They are sleeping." Then she (Grizzly) lay down again. Water Bug got up, again she put additional wood on the fire. She (Grizzly) said to her, "So that is why you came (in order to be a pest)! so you might awaken the people all through the night." Water Bug lay down.

Now it was getting close to dawn, and Grizzly became sleepy, she nodded off to sleep. She woke up, she arose stealthily so as to look at Water Bug. She (the girl) was keeping watch on her. Then she (Grizzly) lay down again. Soon afterward then it dawned, and Grizzly fell asleep. Water Bug arose, and she made sleep sleep sleep for her (for Grizzly). She slept.

She (Water Bug) said to them, "Hurry! get up!" They arose, they hurried, they went down to their canoes, they got onto them. She went, she fetched the paddles, she put all of them in (the canoes). Her older sister's paddles had holes in them (in the blades). Now they went away. They were going (paddling) along, they turned and looked, and now she (Grizzly) was already following them (in her canoe). She was pursuing Water Bug. "So that is why you came! You lied to the people." She got close to them. She took her nasal mucus, she hurled it at them. It broke their paddles. She followed them, she got close to them. She blew her nose, she threw her nasal mucus at them. Their (reserve) paddles became broken, all those paddles that they had taken along with them, they were all broken. Now they had gotten close (to their village), and she (the girl) took out her (older sister's) paddles (which were the only ones remaining unbroken). She (Grizzly now) threw her nasal mucus to no avail at them, it went right through them there (through the holes in the blades of the unique paddles). (Now) they went along.

The people (the men at the village) said, "Something is amiss. A canoe is approaching in a hurry." They (the men) went out (from their houses), they said, "Looks like our headman's wife is following (pursuing) them." They took hold of their bows and arrows. They (the women who were fleeing Grizzly) arrived. Water Bug went, she told their older brother (the headman), "She murdered the people. She took along so many of them, she killed all of them. She is pursuing us." Now they waited for her (for Grizzly). Pretty soon she came ashore, and then they shot at her. She (was unhurt and) said to him (to her headman husband), "Oh dear, oh dear! Why does Water Bug just lie and lie to you?" They shot at her as she went (from the shore up the trail to the houses on the bluff). Her husband sat on top of the house, he shot at her. When she got close to their house, now he had only one arrow (left). He thought, "Oh well, let it be! (she will kill us all)." He threw it at her (he shot his last arrow despairingly), he shot her small finger, it split, she fell there. He had killed her. It was just right there that she had put her heart, on her small finger. Now they burned her, they took (and) completely ground up her bones, they blew her (ashes) away.

Then they went, they went to gather up the dead persons. They got to there, they went ashore at that place. They took Water Bug along with them, she showed them the place there. They got to there where the first ones (who had been murdered) where now black (and) rotting. They took them all to the canoes, and they took them with them to their graveyard. They buried them all. They finished. All done. Story story.

When they were finished with everything (and had completed a myth recital), then they (raconteurs) would say, "Now let us (the Myth Age actors) separate (and go our respective ways to the rivers, mountains, or into the air)." And they would do just that then. Some of them would become birds, some of them animals of the forests, some of them (became the creatures) in the river, some of them (especially the larger animals) in the mountains, all sorts of things (they would metamorphose into).

When Mrs. Howard dictated this myth she began with the familiar motif of an unmarried woman who takes a culturally inadmissible initiative by turning up alone in a village, ensconcing herself in the headman's house, and marrying him. Although she is more than sinister because she has identified with a grizzly supernatural, neither her husband nor the villagers are represented as having the least suspicion. That is the way the Myth Era people were. They lacked sense. But the recitalist did not say this, nor did she yet phrase the fact that the new arrival was an ogress. Indeed, the audience already knew it. Presumably it also knew the woman's approximate age, but a recitalist never verbalized age in the manner of Western literature. A Chinook storyteller only implied, and an audience seems to have been content to understand, that a female is marriageable whether she is sixteen or twenty years older.

The raconteur proceeds, without a single additional descriptive touch, to tell that the newcomer returns from so successful a day at a camas patch that the village women ask to be taken there. They follow her lead the next day, dig camas at the patch, and sleep at an overnight camp before the return on the following day. Toward dawn the headman's Grizzly wife pierces their hearts with an arrow-like dart. After dawn she hides the paddles. She also kills the members of four successive parties of women who accompany her to the patch, and upon each occasion she sets the corpses and paddles aside and returns with all the camas produced by the murdered women. The quantity of roots that she brings encourages additional women to follow her to a site where digging is good. The camas also allow her to explain why women who went with her have not returned, obviously because digging is excellent and they wish to work and camp there for a number of days. When each group reaches the site, Grizzly accounts for the absence of earlier arrivals by suggesting, reasonably, that they wandered to a better patch. When the group that accompanies Grizzly finishes the evening repast, the women suppose they hear those who preceded singing yonder. Soon Grizzly, whose spirit-power in this one drama is such that she can sound like a number of women singing, appears and encourages the newly arrived group to sing too, before they turn in for the night. Obviously a group which is singing feels better, safer, than one which is silent. Grizzly is Machiavellian in her staging. Then she goes among them and magically causes each to fall into a deep sleep before she pierces every heart with her dart. She places the bodies out of sight so that the next party will not observe the fate of their predecessors, hides the paddles, and goes home with another load of camas in order to persuade a fresh group of victims that they ought to come out the next day with her to the patch.

The third and fourth groups become suspicious and anxious but not about any specific thing. They feel uneasy about something which they cannot identify. An especially poignant stroke is the weeping of one member of the third group. Artistry appears in the handling of suggestions of developing concern and of Grizzly's counterassertions, which quell such feeling. Interplay of this kind between Grizzly and her victims becomes more of a source of tension with each group, as Grizzly continues to conduct her risky deception. She works harder each time in order to prevent outright panic among progressively more apprehensive women.

Grizzly's husband's sister plans to join the fifth group of village women that will journey to the patch. The sister-in-law's small younger sister speaks up sharply and says that she will go too. This girl functions in the stylized role of "youngest-smartest" and hence is the individual who defeats the ogress. To me the treatment of this girl's personality is one of the most interesting sketchings of a character in the mythology. Her name, probably only a nickname, may be rendered as Water Bug. Although it is normally quiet, this bug bites sometimes, and the simile of a biting bug with a type of girl may not be farfetched. If a Clackamas girl was especially alert and perceptive, older people might nickname her approvingly and affectionately "Water Bug."

When Grizzly hears this girl announce her intention of going to the camas-digging, she reproves the youngster, calls her "Smarty" with obvious hatred and dismay, and tells her that she cannot accompany the women. The youngster's older sister halts a bitter argument between Grizzly and the girl by sponsoring the girl's coming. Grizzly is trapped because she must now tolerate the presence of Water Bug, and she fears what so bright a girl may do to reveal the situation to the more trustful women. Clackamas appear to have comprehended with simple clarity the manner in which a murderess would be so single-minded that, as she approaches an emotional peak which in this story is extermination of the fifth and last group of women, she becomes unable to deal with more frustrating features of the situation. Grizzly has never considered the likelihood that some individual among her intended victims could be bright enough to watch her closely. She blots out unwanted portions of reality which a more objective planner would take into account. Her anxiety becomes so great that she cannot control the additional worry about the smart girl who observes every step that Grizzly takes. The uninvited entry of the girl into the fifth group therefore exhibits the way in which planning of a massacre by a madwoman would omit the item whose inclusion is vital for success of her scheme. Clackamas apparently believed—the belief caused a glimmer of hope—that a murderer is insane or monomaniacal enough to slip up at one point which another person might anticipate.

When the members of the fifth group, led by Grizzly, depart for the camas patch, Water Bug proceeds with a series of moves that are enjoyable because they invade the smooth operation of Grizzly's design for murder. The girl is first to step into a canoe. Her awareness of Grizzly's especial hostility to and trepidation about her is such that she hides in the canoe and is not observed by Grizzly until the boats are on their way. Grizzly is then so alarmed that she cannot contain herself. She says pithily to Water Bug, "I told you not to come along." Water Bug wisely ignores her, because a response may do no good and silence may lessen Grizzly's self-control. Grizzly is now so upset, and so partially in contact with reality because of the intensity of her compulsion to kill, that presently she forgets about Water Bug. In order to persist in her course, she must erase cognition of the girl's presence.

When the canoes reach the camas grounds, Water Bug at once finds and collects paddles that were hidden by Grizzly after the massacres of previous days, and the girl thereby shows that she foresees use of many paddles for the subsequent flight from Grizzly.

Next Water Bug finds the bodies of the slain and discloses them to her older sister. The youngest female is so superior to the women in her comprehension of Grizzly that she advises first her older sister, then the other women, that they wash their faces in order to hide from Grizzly the evidences of their weeping for the dead. Such lamentation, which is due to intense affection for and identification with covillagers who have died, is not mere formal mourning. It is sincere and deeply felt in a village because of these people's fervent feelings of relatedness one to another.

Now Water Bug advises the camp of women to sing if Grizzly should tell them to, because for a time they must veil their mood. The madwoman senses that Water Bug is up to something and turns violently upon the girl. She accuses her of telling lies to the women. Again the girl wisely ignores Grizzly's observation and in the latter's presence preserves an absolute quiet that is broken only when she silently nudges her older sister. The girl then tells the women that she will be the first whom Grizzly will attempt to kill.

Water Bug now describes to them measures by which they may foil Grizzly and escape. She obtains shells in order to place them over her eyes—so as to appear to be asleep. During the night she rises from time to time in order to place more fuel on the campfire. Grizzly protests at the maintenance of so bright a fire. She accuses Water Bug of keeping the fire high so that her older sister may not be approached by some prowling male. The accusation is ridiculous, to be sure. Grizzly must apprehend that Water Bug is keeping the fire bright in order to forestall murder. Grizzly also must recognize that youths are unlikely to be present in the vicinity of a root patch. Her hypothetical prowler is of interest because Grizzly displays an insulting insight: you, Water Bug, are jealous of your older sister who is more attractive than you; your older sister is therefore likely to be a magnet tonight for some young fellow.

Another factor may be present in Grizzly's assertion that Water Bug's older sister has male friends. Grizzly thereby may be saying that the older sister is a philanderer; she is untrustworthy; she is therefore more than capable of shaming her brother, the headman, and she is planning an illicit affair to shame him by her misbehavior. Still more may be found in Grizzly's claim. Grizzly's headman husband undoubtedly stands in a loving father relationship to his sisters. Accordingly, Grizzly is also expressing an Oedipally determined sibling rivalry toward the two sisters, especially the older one who is nubile.

Perhaps Grizzly, who is after all a madwoman at the peak of her rampage, is confused in her perceptions and interpretations. The raconteur may have utilized Grizzly's explanation of the reason for the girl's maintaining the fire as a device to indicate bewilderment and inability to handle the additional anxiety that would have been generated in her had she faced the fact that Water Bug was putting wood on the fire solely in order to confound a murderess. Accordingly, the raconteur resorts, with insight, to description of a combination of displacement and projection: Grizzly cannot face the threat of the firewood and Water Bug's efficient hostility. Therefore Grizzly, who is also sure that men lust for her, displaces by asserting that the brightness of the fire is a threat to the sexual success of the older sister. Grizzly at the same time projects. She accuses Water Bug of keeping the fire high because of animosity to her older sister.

Grizzly tries another tack in order to halt the periodic placing of fresh fuel on the embers. She appeals to Water Bug to stop it because the other women are sleepy and will be wanting to rise early for the day's root-digging. Water Bug's policy of silence only intensifies Grizzly's frustration. Water bug also continues to wear shells on her eyes in order to appear to sleep. When Grizzly rises, she observes that the little nuisance is awake, and upon this occasion Grizzly shifts her attack by accusing the girl of a personal interest in prowling youths. Whereupon Water Bug pretends that Grizzly has awakened her. The girl rises and puts an especially large amount of fuel on the fire, says nothing, and lies down again. Now when Grizzly rises and uses magic to put Water Bug into a deep sleep, the girl responds as if startled. She says pointedly to Grizzly, "I was dreaming about a bloody dart." The narrator does not say that the girl's words throw Grizzly into acute alarm. The raconteur says, with subtle understatement, that Grizzly asserts to the reclining women that the girl is lying. Grizzly naïvely wishes to think, and to indicate to the women, that no such dream was possible. That is, she hopes to abate their mounting suspicion. She does not want them to deduce that the dream comprises a message and a warning to them. Actually, Grizzly is so poorly oriented that her very protest about the lie serves to enhance the meaning of the dream to the women. And dreams were serious matters because spirit-powers played vital roles in dreams.

Grizzly forlornly adds a plea that the girl leave the women alone because they are sleeping. When Grizzly lies down again, Water Bug once more rises and places additional fuel on the fire. Grizzly can do no more than protest feebly that the girl came only in order to be a nuisance and to keep the women awake all night long.

Later in the night Grizzly approaches Water Bug stealthily. Again the ogress must retreat because the girl is obviously awake, and at dawn Grizzly is so worn out that she herself falls asleep. Water Bug deepens the sleep of the ogress with slumber magic which, like Grizzly's utilization of such a resource, remains undescribed in the drama or the ethnography but which may have consisted of employment of a special spirit-power. The girl then summons the women, they secure the paddles, and they flee homeward in the canoes as Act I with its five scenes closes.

In this act, Water Bug parallels the regional ascription in literary characterizations of special ability and perceptivity in the youngest of a number of siblings; in this myth the youngest one's insight is into the personality of Grizzly. Here we may have an awareness, in Clackamas and other people of the region, that a younger child tends to have more empathy than older persons for the "primary" or "unconscious" drives of adults. Accordingly, Water Bug is more perceptive than the others, all of whom are older. Water Bug alone is young enough to sense the hidden feelings and intent of a psychotic.

Nor may we neglect the other side of the coin. The storyteller indicates that Grizzly herself senses, as a murderous psychotic might, the child's understanding. Clackamas seem to have known in some deep way that there was a special fulness or profundity of communication of feelings between a child and a psychotic. Indeed, a principal feature of the artistry of plot development and character delineation in this myth is the representation of the relationship between the child who is acutely perceptive of a psychotic's needs and the psychotic who is unnerved by the child's capacity to observe the drive that is hiding under a mask of pretense. Awareness of a child's empathy for deeper levels of feeling became a feature of literary style in the northwest states as well as a central portion of the plot in this myth.

The second and last act deals with Grizzly's pursuit of the women who are fleeing in canoes in an attempt to reach the village. As Grizzly's canoe draws ever closer and audience tension increases, her fury continues to be leveled primarily at Water Bug. Grizzly again calls out to the women in the canoes ahead that the girl came to the camas patch in order to lie to them. These words indicate that the ogress has not perceived the reality of her situation because she is unable to. She is unaware that the women collected paddles which she had covered over and that the women saw corpses which she had dragged aside. She cannot comprehend that they witnessed evidences of her massacres; otherwise she would not still be calling out to the girl, with almost pathetic disorientation, "You came only in order to tell lies about me!" Her very pursuit of the women heightens appreciation of the extremity of her incomprehension. Were she not stark mad she would not be both following women in order to murder them and claiming innocence of murder.

When the distance between her and the fugitives lessens sufficiently, she blows her nose several times and hurls the nasal mucus toward them. It does not strike the women, but it breaks all the paddles they are using. When the women are no longer able to propel their craft, Water Bug brings forth reserve paddles in the bottom of her canoe. These paddles have holes in the blades. Now when Grizzly casts more nasal mucus it goes harmlessly through the holes in the blades!

The first problem in this remarkable motif of nasal mucus which shatters ordinary paddles is to account for the prescience of Water Bug in holding in reserve certain kinds of invulnerable paddles. Unfortunately the narrator tells no more than that such paddles belong to Water Bug's older sister. We do not know why they are made or by whom, or why only the older sister owns such specially designed equipment. Of course exaggeration and extremes are attributes of precultural eras. The precultural girl is so farseeing that at the very start she takes along paddles which can survive the battering of perfectly aimed nasal mucus! A matter-of-fact explanation for a concept of Myth Age paddles that would not be vulnerable to mucus propelled at them may be derived from the possibility that Chinooks made holes in blades of paddles that were the property of a person who had died, but the fragmentary ethnographic notes which Dr. Philip Drucker and I obtained on Clackamas contain no support for this possibility. A surrender of explanation, such as a notion that paddles with holes are a literary *deus ex machina*, avoids the need to account for the concept of such paddles. One needs also to find a reason for the failure to use another resolution of the problem of why the fugitives succeed in reaching their village.

The next problem is to account for Grizzly's propulsion of nasal mucus rather than some other means of demolishing paddles. Nasal mucus probably should be distinguished sharply from expectoration. Nasal mucus may equate with pus, which revolts people because it awakens fear of grave mutilation or death. For example, Mucus Boy (23) horrifies people because of his body sores and nasal discharge. On the other hand, expectoration may be conceived of as an entirely different body product. It may symbolize something such as seminal fluid. In the northwest states expectoration serves in myths as a substance which effects oral impregnations, and natives may therefore have reacted to expectoration without anxiety or disgust. In Clackamas literature oral impregnation appears in three myths (23, 28, 30) and in each instance is unaccompanied by an aura of anxiety or disagreeableness.

Grizzly's final recourse to one of the most horrifying of substances now becomes intelligible. The raconteur's task is to symbolize inhumanity, cruelty, and awfulness—hence the insight which is expressed in Grizzly's final frenzy, wherein she uses a most disgusting and threatening substance. The violence of her feelings is symbolized by her hurling of the horrifying material, her accuracy of aim, and the consequent breaking of paddles. That which is hurled is revolting and powerful; that is, her anger and murderous hatred are revolting and powerful. Perhaps the special paddles which remain unbroken meant that only a non-material counterpart of paddles, a dead person's paddles, could survive such battering. The hurled mucus then symbolizes an extreme of violence, range, frustration, wish to kill, and disgusting behavior which is associated with death. Nothing that Grizzly possesses and can throw is so expressive of her climactic frustration as her use of a most fearful body discharge. Her earlier recourse to darts and later resort to nasal discharge are indicative of generations of cumulative insight into progressive stages of fury and frustration correlated with progressive horror in substances used.

Furthermore, Grizzly's inordinate frustration and ferocity are also expressed in her casting a substance which itself neither kills nor injures. She is now so angry that she resorts to torture rather than gentle sleep and arrow-like darts. She throws a weapon which prolongs the terror of the women: the loss of their paddles will only slow up their death, because a creature who can fling a substance which destroys paddles can surely toss something which destroys people. The women are therefore subjected to additional torture to continue to try to get away. As long as they live and have a chance of safe arrival, suspense increases; horror augments by the device of breaking the paddles. Direct shooting would be less horrible and would not cause suspense.

When the women reach the village, Water Bug, not her older sister, is first to inform the headman about the Grizzly who is shortly to arrive. The words used by

Water Bug are not given, nor is the headman's verbal, emotional, or other response. The audience must fill in details of mood, action, and executive decisions as the narrator goes swiftly on to say that men of the village shoot at Grizzly. Probably they do so as she ascends the path from beach to village, trying even yet to maintain her masquerade. The narrator stresses the monomania of the ogress by reporting that she calls out to her headman husband, "Why does Water Bug continue lying about me to you?" The rhetorical question shows that Grizzly is consistent in one area in spite of her confusion, disorientation, and panic. She still believes that she can persuade people that she is harmless. As before, she displaces the falsehood onto her principal frustration, Water Bug. She reiterates what she hopes is a still plausible theme because it is addressed to a man who has not yet learned about events of the past five days.

The raconteur now resorts to a literary device. Grizzly's husband, who has shot a number of arrows at her, has only one remaining. He is so resigned to death that he shoots his last arrow almost wildly, that is, not directly at her heart. The arrow hits her small finger, splits it, and she dies immediately because she does not have a heart that is located in the normal place. Hers is an external heart, on the very finger which his arrow strikes. In order to assure that she will not revive, the villagers cremate her, grind the bones in mortars, and blow the ashes away. Now she will never return to life. The feared and hated creature is not merely buried or tossed away to rot. Her flesh must be burned, her bones ground to powder, and as if such thoroughgoing measures were not yet sufficient to satisfy the hatred and anger of the people, every remaining fleck of powder must be carried away by the wind. If it is not strong enough, the people must blow away the powder. No other method could banish hatred or purge anger more completely. By contrast, Coyote and other myth characters merely kill bad precultural creatures and depart nonchalantly. But Grizzly Ogresses (although not Grizzly Men) are so unconditionally terrible that people can exorcise them only by the technique of incineration, grinding to powder, and blowing away. Could so exhaustive a procedure express deep feelings of many Clackamas toward supernaturally powerful older women, maybe even mothers?

Incineration of a dangerous being and blowing away every bit of ash produced from the charred and ground bones may express fulfilment of several wishes and ventilate feelings about older females. One wish is to exterminate grizzlies as such. Another is to destroy those modern human beings who exhibit comparable inhumanity. Still another may be rooted in Chinookan feelings about any older women. The means resorted to in precultural times in order to get rid of Grizzly and guarantee that so dangerous a being would never return contrasts with modern Chinookan customs, wherein dead were buried, placed in punctured canoes on limbs of trees and perhaps on some sort of scaffolding, or put on shelves in crypts. Mortal remains were perhaps never handled subsequent to such disposal, nor were they cremated, as in a few groups of central Oregon.

Significance of the motif of the headman shooting at his wife in her one vulnerable spot, her external heart, may reside both on a stylistic level and on one of expression of content. This motif may include, too, some reflection of cultural feeling of propriety that he be the man to protect and save the villagers. Ideally the headman ought to be the strongest villager in physical and supernatural power. He should be ablest among the citizenry.

His accidental and despairing shooting of his wife's Achilles heel, after he has expended arrows that were directed at her heart, may also signify something: Although Grizzly is female, she resorts to unexampled aggression and violence; she has tremendous physical strength; she is almost invulnerable. Freudian thinkers might suggest that such attributes are masculine rather than feminine. They might suppose that the little finger which contains the heart of this one Grizzly symbolizes her weakest feature. Her little finger, is, then, indicative of femininity. Before an explanation of this kind be rejected as farfetched, observe that in the long Coyote myth (9) a precultural female who is not otherwise characterized becomes pregnant in her little finger. One may therefore inquire whether these two instances of possible connection of femininity with the little finger carry weight, especially if additional support be found, in nearby cultures, in favor of a hypothesis that masculinity was conceived of as strong or nearly invulnerable by contrast with femininity, which is weak and vulnerable. A corollary is that Clackamas may have felt an especial aptness in citing a husband as the very one who could hit his wife's weakest and most feminine spot. He does so in the myth—in a hopeless mood, to be sure—but he permits a cessation of tragedy by penetrating the very place where he can hurt his wife most.

The concept of an external heart also appears in the notion of a heart in a woman's hat (14), where its externality renders the woman invulnerable for a time. However, the heart in a hat is really a symbol not of femininity but of indestructibility of values. Perhaps in the present myth the concept of a heart which is not in the usual and vulnerable place also connects in some manner with the notion of a spirit-power relative who is more or less external although his bond to a person is a kind of symbiosis.

There is no unusual significance, I think, in the final scene of transportation of bodies of murdered women back to the village burial ground. Such behavior is very likely a modern custom.

This myth resembles a story about Bear Woman and Grizzly Woman (16) in its integration of two features of content. One is the sketching of a few personalities; the other is a theme of increasing frightfulness. In the first place, the drama expresses fascination with grizzlies; therefore raconteurs present in some detail the personality and deeds of a Grizzly Woman. Additional details about a compulsive Grizzly murderess appear in the myth above—recitalists selected for mention only some aspects of her personality when they told a story in which she figured. Wherever a personality such as Grizzly Woman appeared, differences in details of delineation were such that reflective natives reminded themselves that myth times witnessed a goodly number of Grizzly Women. Clackamas presumed that there were a number of Coyote Men and a number of Grizzly Men too, and their conviction was substantiated by the differing literary treatments of those personages. But all Grizzly Women are fundamentally the same. So are the Coyote and Grizzly Men. Differences from Coyote to Coyote, for example, may have developed as different plots and situations pressured successive generations of members of the community to fashion each myth in the most effective way. A native deduction that several Grizzly Women and plural Coyotes lived may therefore have been a secondary development.

As a foil to the Grizzly ogress in this myth, the narrators develop another personality, the smart but very young girl who alone has insight into the mentality of the murderess. The plot centers upon the Grizzly characterization, but treatment of the personality of Water Bug serves to relieve augmenting tension and to express respect for the worth of very young persons, even girls. The culture must have been peculiarly guilty about them because of the manner in which they were purchased in marriage and circumscribed in participations until post-menopause years. Integral with portrayals of two personalities who are polar opposites is the theme of progressive horror and terror and the resolution, thanks to Water Bug, by elimination of the cause of terror.

CHAPTER VI

FLINT AND HIS SON'S SON

PEOPLE lived there (in a village). In the center was their headman Panther's house. They (youngsters of the village) played (shinny) all day long. When it became evening the children were still playing. They (the villagers) told them in vain, "Quit (playing) now. It is night now." They did not listen. They played only the more. They said to them, "It might happen that you scare out something (some dangerous supernatural) there (if you do not go inside at dusk)."

Now to be sure their headman had gone off (hunting). Then they (the disobedient children) scared out something (a Flint ogre), (he was) small (dwarf size), five hairs tied together on his (otherwise bald) head. His (right) hand remained also there (pressed against his right ear). The thing (Flint) began to run about, he said to them (to the children), "Let us play together." He followed them about. They took sticks, and they hit him, they clubbed him. He said futilely to them, "Don't do that! Let us play together." They clubbed him only the more.

Now that thing (Flint) became infuriated, he said, "Hm." And then he commenced to hit them about, he hit at them. Where he hit them, he cut them there. He hit absolutely all those people, he cut them into halves. They died. Then he went to the house of their headman there, and he stayed there.

Pretty soon Panther who was hunting, he broke his bow. Then he wondered, "Something (bad) must have happened to my people." So then he went back home, he got back, he looked over toward his village (as he approached on the trail). No. He did not see them playing. He reached there, he saw halves of his people lying there. Then he thought, "Something is wrong." However he saw smoke coming up from his house. He went, he got to there, he stood at his door. The thing (inside) said, "Hm. I might hit you." He said to him, "Why? This is I who have returned." "Oh, son's son!" he replied to him, said that thing (Flint) there. Then Panther went inside, he sat down. His heart was wrong (felt badly) about it. Now he (Flint) told him about it. He said to him, "If they had left me alone, I would not have done like that to them. They injured me, they clubbed me, and I did like that to them on account of that."

Now (the following morning) Panther went, he dug (a large grave) in the ground, and then he carried those corpses (to it). And that thing (Flint) assisted him. They threw them all into just that one (grave that) he dug in the ground. They covered them over. Now the two of them lived there. He set fire to them, he burned their houses. Now he (Panther) again went hunting, every day (as before).

Now then he saw tarweeds. He got back and told him (Flint), "Supposing you go gather tarweeds." He replied to him, "Yes. I shall go tomorrow." And indeed he went, he brought them back, he roasted them, he pounded them. He merely broke them (but he failed to grind them into a fine flour). Panther got back. He (Flint) said to him, "Here it is." Then he saw it, he said to him (to Flint), "Goodness, if you mashed it some more, it would be good." He said to him, "Oh yes. It will be a little while longer now before I have learned how."

From *Clackamas Chinook Texts*, 18.

So then they lived there, that is the way they were. When he (the hunter) got back he would drop his pack, he would go inside, he would tell him, "Bring it inside now." And he did so. Then he himself (Panther) would go get his pipe. He would say to him, "Do not look at me. I am going to smoke now." Then that thing (Flint) would cover himself (so as not to see Panther). When he was all through his smoking, then he did various things. He would butcher, he would hang up his meat (in strips), he would smoke-dry it. Some (pieces) he would roast on spits. When they were done (roasted), then they would eat. That is the way they were (living together there).

Now they (people of another village) chatted about the news that had gotten to there. (Of) five girls (there) the one who was their youngest sister said, "I am going to go tomorrow (to find a husband)." Then she went. She went along (and) on the fifth one of the mountains she saw smoke (rising from a house yonder). She thought, "I guess that is the place where I go." She went on, she arrived there, she stood by the door. Something or other sitting (inside) there said, "Hm, you are a different sort of thing! I might hit (and cut) you!" He began to hit and slash around in the house. She got scared, she said to him, "Ah you old man (that is, my husband)!" "Yes," he replied (satisfied by the way she named him), "is that you? is that you? my wife?" He said to her, "Come inside." She went inside. He said to her, "Sit right here (beside me, like a proper wife). Across over there (on the opposite side of the house) is our slave's bed-platform." As soon as she sat down, he jumped at her, he did it to (had intercourse with) her. He got through with her, and then he served food to her. She ate. He told her, "Our slave will be back shortly. If when he comes he should smoke, do not look at him. I shall hide you from him." They sat there, and then he told her, "I shall hide you now." Then he hid her, he spread a mat there (in front of her). Now she sat there (behind the mat screen).

Soon afterward then he had already come. She heard goo (the noise of a pack dropping when) he took off his pack. He entered, he said to him (to Flint), "Bring it inside now." And he did so. He (Panther) put away his bow (and) various things. He (Panther) said to him, "Now be still! I am going to smoke." He got his pipe, he smoked. Now he choked from the smoke. He (Panther) said to him, "Why did you look at me again?" He (Flint) said to him, "Yes. I just sort of turned and looked (glanced)." He (Flint) thought, "She looked at him." Actually she had moved the mat, she looked at the person who was smoking. Now that was why the smoke choked him. He finished (smoking), and then they (Panther and Flint) again butchered, they smoke-dried their meat. That is what they did.

The next day he (Panther) went away (to hunt as usual). As soon as he had gone outside, then that thing (Flint) ran outside, he looked around, no, he (Panther) was already gone. He (Flint) ran inside, he said to her, "Wife! come out now! Our slave is gone now." She emerged, she sat there, and then he again jumped on her, he did it to her (raped her). He finished with her, and then he served her food. She ate, she finished eating. He said to her, "I told you yesterday, do not look at him when he smokes. You looked at him anyhow."

Then he told her, "I shall go now." He said to her, "Now I am going for tarweeds." And he ran off, he said (as he ran along), "Oh my wifey! my wife! Oh my wifey! my wife!" That is what he kept saying as he went (and) as he ran on. He got to the place there where he picked it (tarweeds). Now he picked it, he did it hurriedly, he kept saying like that, "Oh my wifey! my wife!" He filled his pack basket (with tarweeds), and he ran along, he went back, he got there. He went inside, he said to her, "Are you there? my wife?" "Yes," she replied to him. He jumped on her immediately, he did it to her again. He finished with her, and then he told her, "You grind these tarweeds for our slave. Do not grind them (too finely), just break them coarsely, merely carelessly."

Then she sat, she pounded them, she put it into it. She ground it finer, she put it (the finely ground flour) underneath. She put the merely coarsely broken ones on top (so that her work appeared to be) as he had told her. He turned and looked, he said to her, "Yes.

You have done that nicely like that." Now they remained there all day, and then he said to her again, "It is soon now. Our slave will be getting here now." So then he hid her again (behind the screen).

Panther arrived, he took off his pack, he went inside. He (Panther) said to him, "Bring it inside now." He (Flint) brought it in. He (Panther) said to him, "Now do not look at me. I am going to smoke now." He got his pipe, he smoked. Now he again did like that, he choked from smoke. All done (when he ceased choking) he (Panther) said to him, "Why did you do that to me?" He replied to him, "I do not know why I did it. I looked the other way, (and then) my eyes went toward you." Now he paid no heed to him, he fixed various things, they ate, they finished eating, they went to bed.

The next day when it became light he went away again. He went hunting. Now the same way again he (Flint) said to her, "Come out now!" She emerged, she sat down. Just as soon as she sat, then he again leaped on her, he did it to her, he finished doing it. Then he served food to her, she ate.

When she was through, he said to her again, "Now I am going to pick tarweeds." "Very well," she replied to him. He got his pack basket, and he ran off. Now he spoke (again) in that manner (as he raced along), "Oh my wifey! my wife! Oh my wifey! my wife!" He got to the place there where he picked tarweeds. He picked them, he made haste, he filled his pack basket, and he went back home. He ran along, he got there. He said to her, "Are you there, my wife?" She replied to him, "Here I am." He did like that to her (he raped her) again.

He said to her, "Now grind the tarweeds." She ground them. Then she ground (some of them) finer, she put them underneath. She pulled out one of her head hairs, she put it in with them. On top she put what she broke coarsely, because he had told her (to grind all of it) like that. She showed it to him, he said to her, "Yes. That is the way you should do it for him." He set it aside for him. They (Flint and the woman) remained there all day. When the sun was getting turned more (setting), then he said to her, "Now our slave will be getting here soon. Now I shall hide you." Then he hid her.

And soon afterward he got to there, he unpacked (several) deer. He (Panther) said to him, "Bring it in." And he did so, he brought it in. He said to him, "Be still now. I am going to smoke." Then he smoked. Then he again did that, he choked from smoke. Now he thought that something was amiss. "He never did like that to me before." But he said nothing to him, and they did (their evening chores) again like that. They butchered, they roasted it, it got done, they ate, they finished eating.

He gave him his tarweeds, he ate it, while eating it he got to where it was finely ground. He (Panther) said to him, "Well well well! Now you are learning! Now you have ground it real fine!" Then that thing (Flint) thought, "I told her, you should not grind it fine for him. Nonetheless she did grind it fine for him!" As he ate, then he felt something in his mouth. He sort of moved it (around in his mouth), it was a head hair in his mouth. He pulled out a very long head hair. He looked at his (Flint's) head, he had only so many (five) head hairs tied together. He (Panther) rolled up the hair, he did not show it to him. Then he went to bed, and he began to think it over. "Something is amiss. For this long a time we have been living here, (and) for so long a time he did not do like that to me."

The next day (was) the third time (Mrs. Howard should have said fourth), he was gone all day. And he did not feel good about it, and that is the way he was (uneasy) then.

Now on the fifth day, then he went, he got to the outside, he (merely) went around the house, he went above by the smoke vent. He lay there, he looked down below (into the interior of his house). Very soon now that thing ran outside, he said, "I am going to go look for our slave." He went inside, he said to her, "Come out now! my wife!" She emerged and sat down. Then again he leaped on her, he did it to her, he finished it. Panther was watching, Panther saw it all. He thought, "So that is the way that that thing must have been doing."

He (Flint) served food to her, she ate, she finished eating, and then he said to her, "I shall go again now for tarweeds."

Now he ran off, he dashed along, again he did (cried out ecstatically) "Oh my wifey! my wife! Oh my wifey! my wife!"

Then Panther descended stealthily. She was there. He entered, he said to her, "Now then. Where has your husband gone now?" She did not look at him at all. After some time then she said to him, "He said he went for tarweeds." "Indeed," he replied to her. "Since how long now have you been right here? from where did you come?" She said to him, "It was quite a while ago that I came here." "Oh," he said to her. They went to bed all day long. He joined days, five days, five nights. That is what he did. He (with the aid of his spirit-power) made a hole in that thing's (Flint's) pack basket, (so that) he (Flint) put things (tarweeds) into it in vain, he was unable to fill it (and so his return with a full container was delayed).

Then those two arose and they got ready. He (Panther) said to her, "Let us go away. Did you ever suppose that he was a person? He was only the one who killed my people. He slashed around at them, he cut them in two." He informed her about it all. Now they went away. They went along to the fifth mountain. Then he said to her, "Now let us stay right here. Your husband (Flint) will get to us pretty soon." He made it (with the help of his spirit-power) there, he shut off (walled off with rocks) a flood. He made another (a second rock wall). And again he made (a barrier of) rocks, he shut them (the waters) in. He made a flood, five of them (with) rocks he shut in, he made (five) floods (and five rock dams). They remained at that place (and waited for Flint to pursue them to it).

He told her, "Now when he gets right here, he will cut me (in two). You should then say to him, Now you have killed our slave! Then lay me well. Cover me (and) my arrows (and) my bow. Lay them well (with care) beside me. Be very careful when you (accompanied by Flint) reach your parents. Tell your father that he should do various (harmful) things to him. Be in a hurry, (lest) things might eat me (in my shallow grave)." Now they were lying together there. Then he said to her, "He (Flint) is searching for us now." A little while later he said to her, "Now he has reached the place where the first (wall of) rocks are." Shortly afterward he told her, "Now he has come through there. He made a hole (through the barrier)." Shortly afterward then he again said to her, "He has reached another (dam) now. He is hitting and hitting at it. Now he has broken through it." He got to the third (wall of) rocks, and he hit and hit at them for quite a while before he broke through. He got to the fourth, and he hit and hit at it a long time before he broke through. He said to her, "Only one more now, and then he will reach here." They lay there, they were there for quite some time before he broke through.

He (Flint) said "Oh my wifey! my wife! I wondered where you went?" He ran, he got to them, he hit him, he cut him into halves. She said to him, "Now you have killed our slave!" "Oh yes, my wife!" She stood up, she prepared the ground, she laid his body well, she put it (the halves) together. That thing assisted her. They covered him over, they laid on top of him such things as bark (and tree) limbs (to keep animals away). Now they left him.

They went along, they got to a river. She hallooed, her younger sisters came out (from their house on the opposite bank), they said, "Looks like our older sister, and her dog." "Hurry!" her mother said. "Hurry! Go fetch your older sister!" They went across, they went to fetch her. They saw something, but actually it was not a dog. They said nothing (about Flint) to their older sister. They went (back) across, they got to their house.

She informed them (when Flint was apart), "This is not my husband. He (Flint) killed him. We left him there. He had told me, Be quick! You should do all sorts of (harmful) things to him (to kill him)."

So then the father-in-law said to him, "I have no more wood. Let us go gather it." "All right," he replied to him, "let us go." They went, they went and collected it. He (the father) took limbs, two and a half limbs. That thing thought, "They are too few." He picked up another (limb). Then he threw them (the three and a half limbs) on himself, he took them along (and carried all the fuel while his father-in-law carried nothing). Now they were (transformed by the father-in-law into) actually three and a half entire trees. They (the firs) lay heavily on him, he was underneath. "Ow (said in a falsetto)," he sounded. "I am Flint! I am Flint!" he uttered. He kept going along, he carried the big logs along, he went on, he got back with them. Then they said, "What can we do to him?"

So the next day he again told his son-in-law, "Let us go by canoe now. We shall collect it (more fuel)." "All right," he replied to him. They went, they got to the place there where they loaded their canoe. They filled it completely (and in fact they overloaded it). Then they went back, as they were going along he (the father-in-law) tipped it over, they were spilled into the water. Flint went down (and to all appearances drowned). His father-in-law went back, he returned. His daughter said to him, "He will get here shortly. Lie down!" He lay down, she poured water on him (so that he would appear to have nearly drowned). Soon afterward then he (Flint) went along, as he went (he was saying in anger) hm hm. He was angry. He was hitting (slashing) at everything, he hit their house too. His wife said to him, "You were not the only one who went in (and nearly drowned). Actually both of you (did). Look at your father-in-law. He got all wet." "Oh yes, my wife!"

Now they continued to live there. Then she said to her father, "Make haste! make haste! Be doing (lethal) things to him!" And he said, "I really do not know what to. Possibly I shall make (prepare) a sweathouse tomorrow." So the next day then they made a fire (for the hot rocks), and the people (the village men) got together, and they covered over the sweathouse (to produce maximal heat inside). When all done (with these preparations), then they went inside it. They at once went right through and out of it (on the other side and therefore unobserved by Flint), and the thing himself entered, he sat in it, they said to him, "Well now! how is it?" He said, "Rather cold." So then they poured water on it (on the hot rocks). They waited for some time, and again they said to him, "Well how is it?" "Rather cool." So then they again poured on water. Now he became uneasy (because it was already extremely hot inside). Now shortly afterward while they were by there, then they heard him. Now he had begun to hit and slash at the sweathouse. At a place where he hit, they put more rocks there. Now the sun was low down (in the late afternoon after Flint had been inside the superheated hut all day long), and then they heard something explode, they heard something like shahl (noise of glass breaking). They listened, they (now) heard nothing at all. Then they said, "Just let it be! Let him remain there until tomorrow before we open it." They passed the night, and the next morning they went, they opened it. Goodness! flint was scattered about there. Now they had killed him. Then they went back to their houses. Now then they had killed him.

Then she herself became quite pregnant. Now she got ill (labor pains began), she gave birth. Those children (her five Flint babies) immediately began running about. But the son of Panther on the other hand they put aside (because he was helpless and a normal human baby), they took (good) care of him. The old man (the babies' grandfather) seized them (the five tiny Flints), he threw the (Flint) children into the water. They came right out of the water, they said, "Our mother's father threw us into the water!" They came out of the water. "Oh," he said. He opened up (the red coals of) a fire, he put them in it to bake, they came out of it, they said, "Our mother's father baked us!" They ran here and there (shrieking) "Our grandpa baked us!" He said, "Oh yes. Tomorrow I shall make a sweathouse (ready) for them." So the next day he made the sweathouse, and he put them into it there, he shut them inside it. He waited there, and then he heard shl (a noise of glass shattering). Soon afterward then another like that also (sounded) shl. Something exploded. He counted all five of them. Then he thought, "Now they all died. But (it will be) tomorrow before

I shall open it up." When it became light the next morning he went, he opened it, only flints were scattered about. Then he went back, and he returned, and he told them about it.

Now they lived there. Meantime then she said, "Let us go look for him (my husband Panther). Possibly at that place they (animals) have long since scattered everything there (at his grave)." Now she went, she took her (young Panther) son with her. They went, they got to that place there. Nothing whatever (was left). I do not know where he went. And so she remained there. Now I recall only that far, no more.

(A day or two later, Mrs. Howard changed the ending and dictated the following sentences.) There she was. A little later then she saw smoke far away there. She thought, "Where shall I stay overnight? I shall go, I shall stay there overnight." So she went, she got there, to be sure her husband was there! She had found him. Now then they continued to live at that place with their son. That is as far now as I recall.

The preceding drama about a murderess is somewhat paralleled by this myth of a murderer, Flint. Let us return to the beginning of the plot in order to perceive as fully as possible what was going on in a Clackamas audience when the myth was recited.

In a village whose wealthy leader is a man named Panther—Panther people were respected persons in Myth Times—the children continue to play shinny after sundown in spite of adults' persistent warnings. In a modern community children were probably required to be inside before dark, and admonitions of precultural adult actors duplicated modern belief and behavior. Precultural and modern people feared that children might scare up a dangerous being. In the myth a diminutive ogre, a Flint man, appears suddenly. He has only five head hairs, tied together. His right hand is as if glued to his right ear. He at once asks the children to let him play with them. Instead they belabor him with sticks. He pleads to be freed from their attacks so that he can play with them, but they continue cudgeling him. Then he slashes about and cuts to death every adult and child in the village. The recitalist never pauses to phrase motivations, and so we are not told why the children hit at Flint, much less why he wants to play with children and then kills everybody in response to their treatment of him. Speculations about these matters follow shortly.

The chief, Panther, is away hunting. When his bow breaks in the familiar precultural omen of disaster at home, he rushes back and finds only parts of bodies lying about—the literature's stylized way of putting it is to refer to halves of bodies. Not one word reports his feelings, which the audience reconstructed by its identification with such a headman and tragic hero. He enters his house. The still angry ogre is inside but is at once mollified by a seemingly friendly greeting. (A good headman would act like that no matter how unprepossessing the visitor.) Flint explains to Panther that he killed all the people because the children struck at him. The next day he assists Panther in burying the dead! Subsequently Flint stays at home doing domestic chores when Panther is away hunting. Someone must do the housework, and in the absence of a female an older man serves willingly. Flint's labor, such as grinding tarweed seeds, is conscientious but lacks the skill of an experienced woman. Each evening when Panther returns and smokes his pipe, for which he has a special spirit-power, Flint must not stare at Panther lest the latter choke on the smoke.

Ethnographic notes do not contain an indication that the possessor of a spirit-power for smoking would choke as Panther did in the Myth Age.

At another village the youngest of five sisters decides to go to Panther, in the familiar precultural approach of a young woman to a prospective husband whom she selects and who has neither foreknowledge of her existence or, as yet, an interest in purchasing her as his wife. She enters while Panther is away hunting, an unfortunate circumstance. It is necessary for the plot. Flint at once slashes about, and in her terror she calls him the Clackamas equivalent of "My husband!" Flint speedily quiets down, with entire friendliness tells her to be seated on his slave's (that is, Panther's) bed-platform, makes a leap at her, and rapes her. Then he serves food to her. He hides her before Panther's return. After Panther enters, Flint assists the man of the house, as usual. Panther chokes during after-dinner smoking. Flint admits that he glanced at the discomfited smoker. Actually, the girl had done so from behind a mat screen. In this manner the storyteller shows that the girl deliberately causes Panther to choke in order to initiate a suspicion in him that something is amiss. Flint asserts his own guilt so as to lessen a chance that Panther deduce the presence of a third person.

As soon as Panther leaves the following morning and is out of sight, Flint announces to the girl that his slave is gone and that she may emerge from hiding. He leaps at her and has sexual intercourse. His postponement of sex until the "slave" has left the house may be especially plausible if it was custom—we do not know whether it was—to refrain from sexual behavior in the presence of a slave. Then he serves breakfast to her. He chides her for looking at Panther when that man was smoking last evening.

Flint then leaves to collect tarweed seeds. He runs rather than walks, saying without letup, "Oh my wifey! my wife! Oh my wifey! my wife! Oh my wifey! my wife!" The faster he runs, the faster he says these adoring words. He gathers tarweeds in haste and runs back breathlessly to his darling saying, "Oh my wifey! my wife!" continually. He dashes into the house, jumps at her, and enjoys sexual intercourse again. Then he has her grind the seeds he brought, and he admonishes her to grind them coarsely, not finely. But she deceives him by putting finer ground meal underneath in order to indicate to Panther that someone besides Flint has been preparing the seeds. The second evening that Panther returns he again chokes while smoking. Flint again confesses that an accidental glance by him caused it. As soon as Panther is out of sight the next morning, Flint leaps at the girl, has sexual intercourse, serves her breakfast, and dashes off to the patch of tarweeds saying all the way, going and coming, "Oh my wifey! my wife! Oh my wifey! my wife! Oh my wifey! my wife!" faster and faster as he runs. Later in the day, when he dashes into the house with his tarweed seeds, he at once has sexual intercourse with her. Then he orders her to grind the tarweeds.

Now she hides one of her head hairs below in the more finely ground meal. The motif of a woman's hair hidden in the bowl of food occurs widely in mythologies of the Northwest. Panther enters, eats, smokes, and chokes again. When Panther eats the seeds, he observes how nicely they are ground—an indication of presence of a competent wife. Presently Panther chews on a long hair and notices that Flint's absurd clump of five hairs is still five. So the hair in the seeds must have come from someone else. He thinks about it.

At last, instead of going away to hunt on the fifth day, Panther furtively climbs to the roof, looks down inside, watches Flint's preprandial explosive amorousness, and re-enters after Flint dashes away to the tarweed fields. Panther confronts the girl, who feels shame. Then Panther employs his spirit-power to join together five days and nights. With the same or another supernatural he makes a hole in Flint's tarweed basket so that Flint is delayed in filling the basket and unaware of how very long a time he is away from his beloved. Panther incidentally has time to become acquainted with the girl and to discuss with her their perilous situation. The narrator does not cite a single detail of their consultation and one can no more than wonder about the manner and extent of Clackamas speculation about the couple's behavior. All that appears in the words of the play is that Panther and the girl leave the house and go to the mountains. With his spirit-power he makes five flood waters and five rock barriers. While some of the audience may have taken the numeral five literally, five may also be translated without arithmetical specificity; that is, it means only a number of walls and bodies of water. Then Panther describes to her what will happen when Flint pursues, what she should do to kill Flint, and what to do to his dismembered body so that he may come back to life after Flint has been eliminated.

Flint pursues. He breaks through each rock wall calling out, "Oh my wifey! my wife! Oh my wifey! my wife!" He cuts Panther to pieces. The wife receives Flint circumspectly with a mere chiding that he should not have killed their slave. These judicious words reassure Flint that the girl really wishes to continue to relate to him, and so his agitation abates, and presently he even helps her bury the pieces of Panther. Then the couple proceed to her parents' village, where she is able to tell her family what to do about the tiny ogre. In a scene which amounts to the familiar motif of father-in-law testing new son-in-law, her father asks Flint to help carry firewood home. The old man employs his supernatural to enlarge some fir limbs into three and a half giant Douglas firs. But Flint is so sturdy that he can carry them without being crushed. As he staggers along under them, he croaks rhythmically and comically, "I am Flint! I am Flint! I am Flint! I am Flint!" The big canoe is overloaded, and the old man helps out by tipping over the canoe. But Flint does not drown. Later he returns and slashes about in rage. His beloved appeases him by pointing to her father who is also soaking wet. The next day the girl's father invites Flint into the reinforced sweathouse. The other village men at once slip out of the structure and Flint sweats inside alone. When it gets too hot for him, he hits and slashes around, trying to get out, and after many hours he explodes into fragments and dies. Only hot steam can kill a Flint.

The girl gives birth to five Flint Boys who at once run around like the nasty little rascals they are. Each has five head hairs and right hand glued to right ear, exactly like their late unlamented parent. She also gives birth to a normal baby which is

Panther's. The old man throws the five ridiculous and hyperactive Flint Boys into the water, but they emerge yowling. He throws them into the fire, but they dash out unscathed and protesting. Then he succeeds in exploding and killing them by shutting them inside a hot sweathouse. Now the wife seeks her Panther husband's grave: the first version says that she cannot find it, but the other reports that he puts his severed parts together, builds a house nearby, and waits for his wife to rejoin him.

Let us return to the first scene for the purpose of hypothetical interpretation. Why did raconteurs have refractory children who stay out after dark and club the preposterous little Flint Man who wants only to play with them? The answer may be that in this myth some children are represented as inclined to sadistic mischief and perverse disobedience with resultant stirring-up, as if out of the ground, of something awful which kills people. The myth starts out, then, with a convincing illustration, to children, of frightful consequences, to everybody, of laxness in obedience. Clackamas therefore may have had the idea that some children are by nature more than mischievous. They are so mean, in the colloquial connotation of that word, that they may do things that effect awful and irretrievable consequences to the community.

Next, what is latent in the myth's sketching of the personality of the ogre? His dwarf size, bald head, silly clump of five head hairs, and right hand permanently fastened to right ear appear to be means of representing abstractly or as in a cartoon the opposite of an attractive man who has normal height, adequate limbs, and thick long head hair. Reaction to dwarf size and hand cemented to ear may have been mixed amusement and horror at an incapacitating congenital deformity. At the same time, Flint may constitute a cartoon of a fetalized creature. He also serves as contrast to the physically attractive, virile, and well-to-do hunter who is pitiable because of the deaths of all his people. No more tragic fate could befall anyone than disappearance of kin and covillagers.

The episodes which effect delineation of Flint's personality start with a scene which highlights a stupid but friendly cripple who is unfairly cudgeled by children. They respond sadistically to his comical diminutiveness and almost fetal head. Flint is also a fantasy projection of hostile impulses of short time span. These do not come wholly from within him but are set off by provocation from outside. He is at once completely uninhibited and violent to an extreme. His sexual drive is subject to similar triggering from outside. When he sees his beloved and no one else is present, he is sexually as unrestrained as an animal. As the myth says, he leaps at her, which is a statement that Clackamas would interpret as indicative of absence of culturally standard sexual preliminaries. Flint behaves sexually like a beast, not a person. His siring of five little Flints, a litter like puppies, adds to the aura of bestiality.

The sketchings of a Grizzly Ogress offer an instructive contrast. Each Grizzly Woman also has an ever-present urge to kill. She too is smart only to a limited degree. But unlike Flint she postpones action; she is intermittently inhibited. She awaits more favorable opportunities to kill, but she never needs outside provocation. It is her constant inner nature to kill and kill, although she does so only when she supposes that she can get away with it. The remainder of the time she never ceases scheming and arranging opportunities, even when she is pretending successfully to be just like other wives. Flint never schemes.

The personalities of Flint and the Grizzly Ogress are, I suggest, projections of comprehension, such as it was, of contrasted extremes in certain facets of personality. Grizzly Woman may be regarded, in our terms, as a psychotic with unwavering hatred of everyone and inner need to kill them all. Flint is stupider and simpler. He has short-lived but most violent psychotic episodes of a homicidal kind. His sanguinary explosions are responses to maltreatment or humiliations, and at the same time he is too simple-minded to nurse a grudge.

Here as in other interpretations it is necessary to stress the significance of indications that Clackamas literature depicts women in a less attractive light than men. Women of the Myth Age are often relatively subtle and chronic haters. Flint, a male, is only a spasmodic hater and is never crafty. He is less smart than some clumsy women. After a wild outburst he forthwith forgives those who have hurt him. He becomes humble and even friendly. When his aggression is spent, he is meek, co-operative, and helpful. He therefore helps Panther bury the murdered villagers. And near the end of the myth he helps his beloved bury the segments of her husband. In addition he assists his father-in-law in bringing in the wood, although he groans under its weight.

But a Grizzly Ogress never ceases hating and therefore must never be trusted. The naïve male who cannot handle his detonations of violent temper should merely not be provoked; if Flint is not nettled he will wreak little or no harm because he is only ingenuous. He is so artless that he never says that he is sorry, nor does he mourn after committing a murder. He has only terse and honest comments which justify his violence and admit his devastating destructiveness. He tells rather reasonably who angered him and why he became angry. But a Grizzly Ogress never discusses her feelings or guilt. Nor does she—nor can she—account for the inner provocation that goads her into a murder rampage. In her case there is only a favorable situation, never provocation from without.

Entirely apart from his culturally disapproved sexual behavior, Flint is so unsuspecting, so surprised at ill will toward him, so humble and obliging after his episodic misbehavior, and also so preposterous physically, that he must be an amusing figure first and a terror figure second. No Grizzly Ogress is ever comical. She is altogether a figure of terror and horror.

Flint's sexual behavior was probably uproariously funny to Clackamas. Twice-a-day rapings before breakfast and dinner; breathless, panting rhythmical chanting of "Oh my wifey! my wife!"; crescendo of passionate and outspoken wanting of a woman even while journeying—all these particularize traits of a personality which is droll because it has accepted few restraints upon inner urges. In psychoanalytic terminology, Flint has a potent Id which is coupled with a feeble Ego. He is completely devoid of Superego control.

The scanty ethnographical evidences suggest that an ideal marital relationship in the lower Columbia River area featured, by contrast with average behavior in

Western civilization, extreme slowness and gentleness of sexual approach and prolonged play by the husband or both mates. Little Flint Man is at the opposite extreme from this ideal. We could not have deduced the contrast or understood how funny the ogre is had we lacked the important ethnographic intimation that we are fortunate to possess. Panther's joining together of five days and nights therefore probably meant that he was the ideal and truly virile lover, the one who takes his time and establishes a desired kind of marital relationship. The five-day romance whose length alone was phrased by the raconteur may also constitute an expression, as it does in another myth, of how much in love true lovers can be. It indicates their need to spend long hours together. Five days and nights are as one to persons so amorous. The long night is an oblique but serviceable indication of recognition of a desirable relationship in marriage, antithetical to Flint's grossly sexual and almost bestial behavior. The contrast in relationships suggests, in the first instance, a concept of a gentle, accepting, adult affinity and, in the second, a concept of an outrageous relationship which is little more than physical.

Flint is so obsessed with sex that he runs to and from work. He is so one-track in his lust and in such haste to return to the sexual object, as well as so simple in his responses, that he does not even observe the hole that Panther has made in the tarweed basket. Clackamas laughed comfortably, or a little guiltily, at an inadequate male and ridiculous husband like Flint. Very likely all peoples enjoy lampooning an oversexed husband.

But Clackamas could only suffer at the spectacle of Grizzly Ogresses who because of their inner nature had chronic hostility to everyone. They lacked capacity to relate decently to other persons. It may follow from reflection upon such ogresses that Clackamas women repressed aggressive feelings more than men did. All Clackamas must have suspected that many women concealed a raging torrent beneath modest demeanor. Such a presumption may have afforded one of the bases and reinforcements for projections such as the Basket Ogress (46) who stole and ate people's children and the several Grizzly Ogresses who devoured entire villages.

Flint and Panther, on the other hand, if added to other precultural males, give evidence of less stereotypy about men. These two actors are almost at polar extremes in personality structure. Flint is lust and self-abasement without the redeeming cleverness, amusing mischief, ineptitude, generosity, and creativity of a Coyote Man. Panther symbolizes the best from the Clackamas point of view: a fine man, perfect lover, and good hunter who suffers much although he is blameless. Indeed, in both myths in which a Panther appears he is a heroic representative of community values (vide myth 6). His fate is tragic because his wife is forced to submit to indignities by hypersexed villains, Coyote (6) and Flint. The two plots revolve around the resolution of such familial triangles. Panther's strength, skill, wisdom, courage, and sibling loyalty to Coon are emphasized in the other myth; his gentleness and perfection as a lover receive stress in the present story. His severe punishment of the unfaithful wife of the Coyote myth agrees with the Draconian customs of Clackamas. In both stories he is the perfect man whose life is marred by injustice.

The comparatively indistinct delineation of the woman in this myth is of interest. Although she comes because she wants a well-to-do man, she experiences Flint's bestiality without a direct stroke to indicate how she feels about it, other than acceptance of a later opportunity to go with the better man. She does a few things that are good and right: she survives by cajoling Flint; discerningly and cautiously she lets Panther know that she is in the house; her discretion is such that Flint is not provoked into turning madly upon her; she buries Panther so that later he can come to; and she suggests to her father just enough so that he resorts to measures that are necessary to destroy Flint. But at no point is she more than shrewd or competent. And one suspects, although this may be a Euroamerican rather than a Clackamas response, that she is as compliant as she is opportunistic or helpless. The vagueness of her characterization, a haziness in delineation which may be demanded of a storyteller but which involves omission of mention of her feelings, allows such an attitude to intrude.

The supposition, then, is that Clackamas who identified strongly with Panther or who, if women, knew what they would have done were they in the position of Flint's "wife" felt that she was wise and sexually no Puritan. Did she not submit to Flint in the first place? Until she ground tarweeds skilfully and put a telltale hair in the meal, was it not possible to look upon her as a woman capable of duplicity and lacking in loyalty to the hero? The key to the answer would have been given if responses could have been obtained from native informants. Without such testimony one has to make a deduction upon the basis of evidences which we have for Clackamas distrust of women, upon indications that Clackamas ratified personal survival effected even by cold-blooded opportunism, and upon the happy outcome which the wife's maneuvers made possible. Therefore, from a Clackamas point of view her actions add up to one of the better sketchings that the literature offers in personality depiction of an attractive woman. On the other hand, Clackamas were able to paint with much more insight and detail some hideous females like Grizzly Ogresses.

Finally, the story is a romantic play. The personality of the bestial Flint is responsible for the development of the plot, which in one version moves toward a happy resolution because husband and wife find each other. Both versions conclude with elimination of the villain and reconstitution of the family, and fun is provided by the ludicrous physique and sexual behavior of Flint. The narrator engages in three important delineations—the lecherous and impulsive Flint, the virile man and superlative lover, and the unnamed wife who maneuvers as a woman should.

CHAPTER VII

AWL AND HER SON'S SON

A MAN lived (alone) there. He hunted all the time. The following day he would go again. That is the way he was. I do not know how long a time he lived there. One day he thought, "I will not go today. I will stay and patch my moccasins." And so he did. He sewed all day long. After a while then he broke his (bone) awl. He thought, "Oh me oh my! my poor awl!" He took it, he threw it underneath his bed-platform. "I wish you would turn into a person!" Now he continued to live there. The next day then he went to hunt again. That is what he did.

I do not know how long after, he got back, his (hearth) fire was burning, he saw footprints of small feet (inside his house). He thought, "Where could a person have come from to me?" The next day then he made a bow (and) arrows, he laid them close by the fire. He thought, "If it is a male, then he will take hold of it" (and I will see that it has been moved).

Now he went away, he hunted. He returned in the evening. Again his fire was burning. Someone had fixed his things nicely indeed for him. The arrows (and) the bow just lay there (untouched). He thought, "Oh it is no male. Apparently it is a female."

So the next day he made a camas root-digger. He stood it in the ground close by the fire. Now he went away again. He got back at night. The root-digger was gone, it was standing far over there. He thought, "Indeed that must be a female." And again that was how she had covered (put away) nicely all his things.

So again the next day he went. And he went along, he hunted. He got back in the evening. Now she had swept his house quite clean, his fire was burning. He thought, "Maybe she just went somewhere a short while ago." He went to bed, and then he began to think it over. "Wonder where this person has been coming from? Now tomorrow I shall hide from her."

It became the next day. He finished eating, he got ready, he went outside, he forthwith went around the house. He went up above, he lay on his stomach on the roof, he looked down inside. Pretty soon then someone ran out (from hiding). She said, "Now I guess that my son's son has gone. Suppose I go look." She ran outside. "Oh yes now my son's son has long since gone on." She went inside. "Very well. Now I shall wash and clean up everything." And so she did.

But he himself descended (from the roof) slowly and cautiously now, he went all around the house, he entered, he spoke harshly to her. "Who are you? What people are you from?" She merely sat there. She said absolutely nothing to him. "Why have you come here and disturbed everything?" Now she replied to him, "Yes, but that was what you thought in your heart. You yourself said, I wish that you would turn into a person. That's me here." "Oh oh, I merely said that (unseriously) to you."

Now they lived there, he and his father's mother. She would say to him, "Son's son!" And so they lived on there. He served food to her, and then she said, "No! my son's son! Had you not broken me (the point at the tip of the bone awl), then I would be able to eat. But because you broke me, I cannot eat now." She did not ever eat. He would bring a deer, she would merely assist him. They would smoke-dry it.

Now it became summertime, and some blackberries became ripe. He had gotten there (to

From *Clackamas Chinook Texts*, 27.

a blackberry patch), he got back, he told his father's mother, "Father's mother! Perhaps you can pick berries. Some are commencing to ripen now." "Yes. I shall go tomorrow." He showed her the place where. And to be sure the following day then she went, she went to pick berries. She picked both green ones and red ones, with their stems on. She brought them back. He returned in the evening. She placed it (the basket of berries) before him. "Indeed," he said to her. "You found it (the berry patch)." "Yes," she replied to him. He selected ripe ones, he ate them.

Now they (people at a nearby village) were gossiping, they were discussing Awl and her son's son. "They live luxuriously." At once one unmarried girl said, "I am going to go tomorrow (to them)." So the next day the girl got ready (she dressed in her finest and carried all her valuables with her), she went away, she sought them. She went along, she reached a spring. She thought, "I shall wash my face right here." She sat, and she washed her face, she combed her hair, she put on her face paint. All done. Then she proceeded.

Presently while she was going along, she now reached the (patch of) blackberries. "Oh dear me, they are mixed red and black now (they are already ripening)." So then she picked them. Pretty soon now it became dark (because Awl made a storm with her spirit-power). She (the girl) thought, "Oh too bad! It will rain, I shall get wet."

Shortly after that then she heard someone hallooing, "Whooooo went through my patch? they have been pulled unripe! they have been trampled! Hm!" she sounded (angry). She (Awl) commenced stabbing at the woods. At the place where she (the girl) was hiding (to escape the stabs of the awl), right close by there she stabbed at her (in order to frighten, not to kill her). She (the girl) said to her, "Hey! old woman! You nearly picked at (stabbed) me." "Indeed. Is that you? my son's son's wife?" Now she (the girl) began to help her, they picked blackberries. She (Awl) said to her, "Don't pick the ones that are too black (overripe), pick all kinds." "All right." They filled her (Awl's) berry basket. Then they went home, she took her with her. They went along.

She (Awl) said to her, "Sit here. This is the bed of my son's son." She served her food, she ate, she finished eating all of it. Then she said to her, "Wash your head, son's son's wife. (Then) I shall look and see how you are." So then she washed her head. When all done she said to her, "Comb your hair. Stand over there. Let your hair down (over your eyes)." So that is what she did. Now Awl stood there, she said,

> "I am going to stab you, son's son's wife!
> Put your hair down! son's son's wife!
> I am going to stab you.
> Put your hair down! son's son's wife!"

Now she pierced her right to her heart. Her heart burst, she fell, and then she died. Now she dragged her to the rear of the house, she laid her down, she piled things on top of her.

Pretty soon afterward then he returned. He went inside. His father's mother (Awl) just sat there. "So you are sitting here!" "Yes indeed! son's son!" Whereupon she set food before him, he ate it. Then she set blackberries in front of him, he ate them. He said to her, "Oh dear me! father's mother! You are learning now." "Yes," she said to him. She thought, "I said to her, Do not pick the ones that are too black."

Then another one (the second oldest of the five girls) also said, "Our older sister perhaps found them. I shall go also." She got ready, and she went. She was going along, she got to a spring. She saw her (older sister's) tracks. Face paint was scattered around (on the ground). "Indeed," she thought. "Right here is where she must have been." She sat there too (and prepared herself as the older girl had done. The second girl's experience duplicates the first in almost identical words. A third girl then journeys, and the act is again the same, except that in the woods the girl almost weeps because of a premonition of danger. The day after her murder the fourth girl departs, and in the woods she weeps profusely in her anticipation of an unknown peril—she knows that her involuntary tears are a bad omen. The fifth and last girl's experience after the murders of her four older sisters, and the remainder of the myth, are in the following words).

Over yonder now there was only one (girl remaining). She thought, "I shall go too." She said to their (the five girls') parents, "I am going to go too. I am going to try to find where my older sisters went." "Very well." She got ready, and then she went away. As she was going along she wept (involuntarily). She thought, "Why am I doing like that?" She quit doing it. She kept on, she got to a spring. She saw their footprints where her older sisters had sat. She wept. In vain did she stop it. Now she wept still more. She thought, "Why am I weeping like that?" She did not wash her face, she did not comb her hair. Now she went on.

Presently as she was going along, now she heard, "Ouch ouch ouch ouch ouch my leg! and that is not my name, (nor) have I been killing your older sisters. You broke my leg." "Really," she said to her (to the injured Meadow Lark Woman). "Indeed tell me the truth. I am carrying along everything (that I possess that is valuable and I shall give you these valuables in return for information)." She took her valuables. She wrapped her (Lark's broken) leg, she chewed up a money-dentalium, she chewed it, she spit it over her (Lark's) leg. All done (the leg was repaired and the payment made).

Now she (Lark) gave her the information. She said to her, "To be sure, when the first of your older sisters came, she got to the place where Awl's berry patch is. At that place she (your older sister) assisted her. They filled up her berry basket. She (Awl) took her along with her to her house. She said to her, Wash your head! Comb your hair! Stand over there! That is what she (your older sister) did. She said (chanted) to her,

Undo your hair! son's son's wife!
I am going to stab you! son's son's wife!

She pierced her. Her heart burst. She killed her. She dragged her around to the rear of the house. She did like that to all (four) of them. Your older sisters are lying behind the house."

She (Lark) said to her, "Let us go together. Take me with you. Let us go together. When we get to where her berry patch is, she will come to us at that place. You will help her. You will pick blackberries. You should fill it (the berry basket). Then she will say to you, "Let us go now. I shall take you to my son's son's and my house. You will say to her, Yes. Go along. She will take you to there, she will give you food. All done (eating), and then she will say to you, Wash your head! Comb your hair! She will say to you, Stand over there! Put your hair down over your face. You will stand there. Then when she says to you (and chants),

Put your hair down over your face!

Then turn and move your hair, look (peering through it) at her. Then when she says to you,

I am going to stab you!

Watch out! Then she might pierce you. Turn and move (aside)! She will miss you, and then you will kill her. Let us be going! Take me along with you!"

They went along, and she placed her upon her shoulder. As they were going along, they got to blackberries. Now she (Lark) said to her, "This place is where she picks berries." Soon now it became dark (because of Awl's spirit-power to make it so). She (Lark) told her, "She is coming now. She is coming now. It will not rain, it is merely her doing that." Soon then they heard someone hallooing. She said, "Whooo has gone through my berry patch? They are being picked there! It is being trampled there!" She (Lark) said to her, "That is her now." Then she started to stab at the woods. She nearly stabbed them. She (Lark) said to her, "Speak to her!" When she (Lark) sat there (on the girl's shoulder), whatever she might have to say to her, she would nudge her, she would pinch her (with her beak).

She (the girl) stood, she said to her (to Awl), "Hey! old woman! You almost pierced me."

"Indeed! son's son's wife! is that actually you?" "Yes," she replied to her. She assisted her (picking blackberries). They picked blackberries. They filled her berry basket. She (Awl) said to her, "Let us go now. I shall take you along to my son's son's and my house."

So they went, they got there, she (Awl) served food to her. She (Awl) did not eat. She got through (eating). She (Awl) said to her, "Wash your head now." She finished doing it. "Comb your hair! Stand over there! Put your hair down!" She went, she stood there. She did the very way that she (Awl) told her. The old woman did (chanted),

> "Put down your hair! son's son's wife!
> I am going to stab you!"

She saw her, she moved and looked at her, she (Awl) stabbed at her. She missed her. She pierced the house (wall). There (stuck in the wall and howling in pain) "Ouch ouch ouch! ouch ouch ouch! ouch ouch ouch!"

Meadow Lark came out from there (because she had hid somewhere), she said to her, "You have killed her now. Now I shall take you to where your older sisters are." They went outside, they went around the house, they opened (uncovered) them where they were lying. She sat there, she wept and wept. She (Lark) said to her, "The man will get back pretty soon."

Presently he himself, while he was hunting, now he broke his bow. He thought, "Oh dear! my poor poor father's mother!" Something (bad) has happened to my father's mother!" He went back, he saw his house, smoke was rising (as always) from it. He went on, he entered, he saw the (young) woman seated there. He said nothing. No father's mother (was present). He sat down.

She told him, "Probably what is missing in your heart (is your grandmother), (but the fact is that) I killed your father's mother. Look over there!" He turned and looked, he saw his awl stuck there (in the wall). "Oh," he thought. "Indeed now," he said to her.

She told him, "The first of my older sisters came, another one of them came, all four of them. Then I myself came here too. I found all of them dead. She had killed them. Had I not found her here (my Lark helper), she would have killed me too." "Yes," he replied to her. Then they went, they uncovered them. They were becoming black now. "Indeed," he said to her.

(He proceeded to explain,) "To be sure, she was not actually my father's mother. I was merely sewing my moccasins. I broke my awl. I liked it. I threw it under my bed. Then it became this person (Awl) here." "Indeed."

The next day then they buried them. They worked all day long, they buried them. They wrapped them up in everything (of monetary value which) he had. And as for her she put her very own valuables on her older sisters (too).

Story story.

The recital commences with a hunter who is pathetic because he is unmarried and lonely and who wishfully anthropomorphizes his valuable awl. In the Myth Age it is an easy step for the wish which has generated a fantasy to transmute the fantasy into a reality. The awl therefore turns into a person, Awl Woman, who can function like a valued tool for domestic chores and can employ an awl herself.

The hunter does not wish that his awl become a person until he breaks it. Straightway he is sorry both for it and for himself, as if it were a relative whom he had gravely injured. He is frustrated because need for it, as for kin, is great in his sociocultural world, and his aloneness is intensified by the breaking of the cherished and indispensable implement. He therefore discharges new energies because of reinforcement of his urge for help, companionship, and relationship. At the point of exhausting frustration he blurts out the wish for a housemate. The pressure of his feeling of aloneness, which was undoubtedly much more agonizing and pitiable than a comparable individual isolation in modern Euroamerican society, must be a central theme. Loneliness and kinlessness, which initiate the play, are so intolerable that the force of the wish for a companion is sufficiently strong to create one.

After Old Woman Awl's arrival we need to account for her preliminary failure to confront her "grandson" at the time of her entry to do his household tasks. The myth does not suggest that the old woman is either so shy or frightened that she does not appear in person. And the motif of having to spy upon the magically created and non-visible housekeeper appears in the myth of Stick Drum Gambler, who has also been actualized by the intense wish of a man who lives alone (29). Therefore the sex of Awl has nothing to do with this portion of the plot. She is female simply because an awl is usually used by women. She is the important instrument of a woman. The initial hiding or non-visibility of the magically created housekeeper thus seems to constitute a subtle expression, by Clackamas discussants and artistic raconteurs, of awareness that creating reality out of daydreams and wishes is difficult. At first it is only as if a person had been there. Later the wish-person becomes reality, as need continues.

A similar mechanism appears in paranoias. The process includes frustration, loneliness, intensified needs, magical wishes, their projections into the outside world, and hallucinatory fulfilment by way of projections becoming apparent reality. Accordingly, a notably interesting feature of this myth, one which I think displays psychological sophistication, is the initial postponement of outright appearance of the housekeeper and the passing of a number of days before she is seen by her "grandson." If the suggested analogy with a paranoid process is warrantable, the story displays exemplary comprehension, on a deep level, of the development of a hallucination.

The young man's need to spy upon his lurking housekeeper in order to reveal her is also paranoid-like. It is psychologically sound in the myth context of wishful and magical creation of Awl Woman by a frustrated and lonely person. His ascent to the roof in order to peer at the woman appears to be no more than a device which has a history of literary stylization: this is the way in which various myth actors (vide 29, 47) look secretly into a house in order to observe its occupants. On the other hand, the hunter's spying by climbing onto his roof to look inside is again consistent with paranoia, because a paranoid person always seeks furtively for evidence that will document his wishes.

Earlier, when the hunter leaves both a male's and a female's implements in the house, he resorts to this means of determining the sex of the invisible housekeeper. His procedure is very likely of no importance beyond its service as a theater device, which appears elsewhere too (29). However, there may be psychological significance in the fact that the hunter displays curiosity rather than anxiety about the sex of his housekeeper. He wants to know whether his companion will give a male or female kind of assistance. He does seem uninterested in a mate and indifferent to sex, a stroke of characterization which may serve to maintain simplicity in the plot or may allow it to center, without distractions, about a housekeeper, helper, and companion.

The introductory description of Awl Woman reveals her as tenderly responsible for her "grandson's" housework. Nevertheless, when he descends from the smoke vent and first confronts her, he speaks harshly rather than gratefully and gently. He asks suspiciously, "Who are you? What group of people do you come from? Why have you come here and disturbed everything?" Again, his queries are sufficiently pugnacious and sharp to be consistent with the suggestion of a paranoid mechanism, although not a full-fledged paranoid system. His questions also exhibit a selection of features which serve literary purposes, especially the requirement of laconicism.

Awl Woman's reply mollifies him because it expresses exactly what would constitute an efficient means of calming paranoid agitation. She tells him, in effect, "I am here only because of what occurred deeply within your own heart! You alone caused me to appear!" She does not attempt to explain why she has "disturbed everything" in the house, nor does she meet his query directly. She ignores an unjustifiable and irritatingly hostile accusation and meets him at once, with brevity and cogency, on his real ground—in other words, within the confining premises of his paranoid-like thinking. She uses his private language. She has recourse to phrasings which are closest to his deepest feelings: "You were very, very lonely. You wished intensely for me. You created me. I am yours. I do not come from somewhere or somebody else." His reaction therefore is to relax, almost to apologize, because he immediately recognizes the truth of what she says. He replies, however, "Oh I merely said hostile words to you, but I was not serious about them." Of course he is lying. He was quite serious in his unfriendly querying because he was suspicious of her, in spite of the housework which she had been doing. He had not recognized that his own wish had created her, because, with probably characteristic Northwest misgiving about persons who came from other villages, he thought only that she had come from an antipathetic place and people. He accepts her comfortably when she reassures him, with utmost therapeutic skill, that she came from himself, not from anyone else. In short, the hypothesis of a paranoid-like lonely hunter is consistent with each successive item of description and discourse.

But now that something of the hunter's personality is sketched, and Awl is accepted and established in the home as a maternal figure, interest in the hunter, as well as any interest in his episodically aberrant mentality, wanes. The drama accordingly enters the second act. Its subject matter is at once directed to the personality and behavior of a typical grandmother who works for her grandson and provides him affection and companionship. He is no longer lonely and frustrated and hostile; he achieves emotional relaxation and is ready to become a normal man, a conventional provider for a family. To all intents and purposes his emotional disturbance vanishes. That is why he loses interest and distinctiveness; that is why the second act no more than implies his presence. He is the absent man of the house, and the spotlight is on his grandmother.

But every Clackamas knew, in one or another way, that older women who have reared children, and not least the women who are functioning overtly as grand-mothers, possess swirling emotional depths. It is therefore correct psychology and good theater to fashion the next portion of the narrative around such a woman. With a sure touch the raconteur at once reports concisely that "they live together" and that she calls him grandson. These simple phrases supply enough background, in a literary style which is characterized by an ultimate of terseness and abstraction, to point up the essentials of the household relationship of older woman and virile young man which constitutes a central theme of the remainder of the play.

Awl is unable to eat. Her explanation of her inability may appear an intrusive literary addition consistent with other myths in which a thing or animal which has transformed into a person has been permanently injured by some prior accident. It was a dramatic necessity that the awl be fractured in the first place, in order to symbolize the hunter's extremity of bafflement, his plight, and the strength of his wish. The breaking of the awl and concomitant permanent injury of Awl may appear to have no further importance for development of the plot. But we must shortly return to Awl's crippled condition, because it does have significance.

Another facet of the problem of accounting for Awl's appearance and personality arises from the ideology of spirit-powers. Exactly as in the myth (29) where Stick Drum Gambler is a spirit-power who anthropomorphizes and comes to live with the hunter in answer to his wish, so Awl Woman must have been plausible as a spirit-power who comes to reside with the lonely man who needs her and therefore wishes for her. Her later envy and murderousness are certainly traits which a spirit-power may possess. Nor is a spirit-power in the least depreciated because it behaves malevolently, like some people. In other words, the religious ideology reinforces, but to an indeterminable degree, the account of the coming and characteristics of Awl. Overtly, she is at once a grandmother and a spirit-power; covertly she is still other things.

Now that the hunter possesses a helpful houseworker who is also his serviceable spirit-power, he becomes so well off that, as in many Clackamas myths, an unmarried girl assumes a culturally unacceptable initiative to go to marry him. On the trail to his house the hopeful candidate for his hand in marriage pauses to pick black-berries at the very patch which Awl regards as her own.

The psychological soundness of the drama continues in a series of symbolic situations and utterances. Awl sees a potential mate journeying to the grandson whom she has been serving devotedly. The girl at once perpetrates insult in addition to injury; she infuriates Awl the more by picking berries in Awl's otherwise private patch. The approaching nubile maiden generates mordant anxiety and explosive anger in the older woman who is so crippled that she cannot even eat like people. Her advanced age is in fact symbolized by her physical handicap: she cannot eat foods of younger people. She magically makes darkness and a rainstorm which pos-sibly express her mood; at least she causes discomfort for the oncoming rival or uses the squall to drive the girl away from the patch and into woods.

When the downpour forces the girl to seek forest shelter, Awl transforms into an awl and stabs about wildly, nearly but not quite piercing the panicked girl. Probably Awl intends to terrorize her young competitor, for the sake of sadistic satisfaction. Very likely Awl may not mean to injure the girl; she may be saving that supreme pleasure for a later moment. Such postponement is a sound dramatic touch, and it was, I believe, developed by some bygone raconteur or discussant who understood that Awl's almost paroxysmal stabbing relieved her feelings so that she could proceed with a more refined design for torture.

When the terrified girl in the woods calls out in protest at the stabbing, Awl stops and at once names her "My grandson's wife," a frank verbal acceptance of a most distasteful fact, a venomous acknowledgment of a bitter reality. The concession costs Awl nothing, since she will shortly eliminate her rival.

The girl remains undescribed, as do the four sisters who follow her, and females tend to come off second best in Clackamas feelings. But since these girls are only plot expediters, they really need not be delineated; the audience can add imaginatively whatever it needs to about them. The only significant characteristics of these girls are youth, nubility, and certainty of superseding Awl if they live. Awl's Oedipal hatred of such girls, maybe of all girls, is the greater because of the domestic service which she has provided for her grandson and the companionship, security, and emotional health that her presence has guaranteed him. But the very health and wealth which her partnership with him has effected result in inevitable displacement by young things. Is this not the tragedy of older people?

Awl's fury against almost certain victors—assured victors if they live—is such that it cannot be resolved satisfyingly with precautionary murders out in the woods before the girls reach the house. Awl must enjoy terrorizing them because they cause terror in her. Then too, she must enjoy controlling their marriage preparations, in the fulness of knowledge that presently she will kill them. Only then is she released to pierce their hearts and throw the corpses aside.

Mrs. Howard's footnotes to the myth recital offer an interesting native contrasting of reality with the kind of reality experienced by precultural people. Although Mrs. Howard asserted that the girls insisted foolishly on proceeding to their doom and that Awl would have failed to destroy them had they fled in time, the point does not lie in Mrs. Howard's thought that girls of the Myth Age act stupidly. The girls are after all only theatrical props. They function so as to permit expression of an older woman's drive to panic and then eliminate the younger woman who threatens an established nuclear-family relationship with son, grandson, or husband. The older woman really expresses the envy and hate of any woman married to a husband who is bound to take another and younger wife. It is the fierce wrath of an older married woman or other older woman of the household who is certain to be set aside.

The myth does not once suggest a polygynous household. But the Clackamas conscience may not have allowed raconteurs to describe the envious and murderous woman in terms of fulminating emotions of the first wife of a well-to-do man or headman. So realistic a description of polygyny would have shaken a cornerstone of the society. And so raconteurs term Awl a grandmother, not a polygynous wife. But

Clackamas deeply distrusted the feelings of their grandmothers and older women in general, even as they did the wives of a polygynous chief; therefore, comprehension of feelings of one kind of woman was easily extended to other older women.

Each girl assists and accompanies the older woman, as younger women did in the society, in picking blackberries. When the two females reach the house, Awl enjoys vengeful moments when she hypocritically seats the girl on her grandson's bed and when she sanctimoniously serves food to the girl. Possibly these gestures are like marriage formalities; they are meant to be cruel token expressions because each girl must respond happily to such testimonial acts of welcome by in-laws. The process of killing each of the girls has to occupy a stretch of time for the sake of heightening suspense, and it also expresses the drawn-out manner in which a hating woman caters to a younger woman and tortures her before she deals the lethal blow. The cat plays with the mouse.

The last period of each girl's drama before the tragic finale consists of Awl's orders for the girl to wash her head, to comb her hair, and to let her hair down over her eyes. These orders sound like specific injunctions of a kind that a grandmother, mother, or mother-in-law, perhaps even a senior wife, might give to a girl during her puberty or marriage ceremony. If ethnographic notes about the one or the other ceremony had been detailed, we could determine what Awl is really doing. The point in any case is that the woman who is about to be displaced has her last pleasurable opportunities to control the younger woman, to tell her what cultural sanction demands that she do. Conceivably, again, the sequence of services and directions is also symbolic of a wedding, but without the throng of pleased relatives and villagers and with tragedy lurking. Perhaps the mother-in-law's or senior wife's assumption of authority is symbolized in the commands. Awl's sadism consists in her deliberately putting each ill-fated girl through formalities which under other and happier circumstances would have constituted official acceptance, an emotional truce, and fulfilment for the young bride. The horror of her situation is that she is about to be murdered, not married.

Piercings of hearts serve, then, as a means of representing the way women often feel about young brides of their own men. It makes no difference that in this drama the older woman is termed a grandmother and that she has been functioning as a kind of mother and wife all in one. The possibility must be urged that the myth stresses, in greater disguise, feelings of the first wife in a wealthy polygynous household when the husband purchases and adds a younger wife. The important thing in interpretation of feelings awakened in the audience is not to stress "grandmother," "mother," or "first wife" as such. The narrator manipulated relationships in the scene in such a manner that members of the audience identified with or expressed distaste for whatever actor their individual needs directed. The audience remained free to regard the nominal grandmother as a mother or older wife. Each member of the audience filled in individually while the public recital proceeded in its characteristically synoptic way.

Responses of women may have depended on their generation level and relationships toward members of the household. Surely each woman reacted according to her involvements. Any woman who looked forward to surrendering or had already relinquished to some younger woman a place of importance and affection in a man's life must have identified with older polygynous wives, grandmothers, or mother figures. On the other hand, any woman who in her day had been brought or was yet to be taken to a man's home where his mother, grandmother, or first and older wife also lived must have participated in the girls' terror and in the horror of their untimely destruction, although the narrator does not once employ a word which represents the feelings of such girls. Indeed, almost every female in the audience was involved in past, present, or future relationships symbolized in the myth. It was only overtly about Awl's crimes. Covertly it was about every woman's feelings. It treated a "universal theme" for Clackamas woman; it was really an Oedipal story from the woman's position.

This and other myths—for example, the one which describes a second wife's desertion and denial of husband and child (13)—reveal some of the responses of anxiety, tension, and hostility had by women in intrafamilial relationships. These feelings occasionally approached a point where they were almost unendurable; nonetheless, they had to be repressed. Recital of the present myth therefore permitted a moment of catharsis to older and younger women alike.

Perhaps this may be termed a woman's rather than a man's myth because it did not function as well for men as for women. Men presumably suffered more anxiety and guilt than release during the recital of Awl's behavior. Maybe no single and lonely man in the audience felt much satisfaction at the predicament into which Awl's grandson had gotten, although such a man felt strongly the desolate aloneness and frustration of the hunter at the commencement of the play.

The tragedy of the four successive terrorizations and murders is resolved in the stylized manner of many Northwest myths. Only a *deus ex machina* can halt the nightmare. The youngest of the five sisters accidentally steps on the leg of the informant, old Meadow Lark Woman. She wraps some of her money—dentalium shells —around Lark's broken leg, and she also chews one of the dentalia and spits it over the leg. In return for such contributions, Lark describes the journeys and deaths of the girl's older sisters and the means by which the girl can eliminate Awl. It is easy for a girl to be smart when she has an informant who is plentifully endowed with supernatural power! It is obvious in the light of the spirit-power ideology that, as in all myths where Lark is introduced, she symbolizes a spirit-power whom a person encounters and makes a relationship with, especially during a personal crisis.

This is the sole Clackamas myth in which Lark asks to be taken along by the person who has injured her. Why should a spirit-power not accompany its kin in a physical way? I see little significance in the dramatic stroke which places the bird on the girl's shoulder, beyond the trite deduction that Clackamas, like most or all peoples, tamed birds: other peoples of the region have informed ethnographers that certain birds were tamed. Any tamed bird might ride on the shoulder of a person, and certainly in the community's discussions of myth plots someone sooner or later expressed the thought that Meadow Lark behaved like other birds which rode on persons' shoulders.

Awl's manner of death follows from the specific instructions that Lark gives the fifth girl. Awl's drive to hate and kill is so violent that when the girl dodges, Awl becomes stuck, as an awl, in the wall of the house. She cannot then extricate herself and transform into a woman again. And the younger woman has, rather simply, not permitted herself to be stabbed. Perhaps the symbolism, if there be such, is that the girl escapes the violence directed at her heart and life by means of an unstudied evasion. Her behavior is realistic and mature from the point of view of Clackamas, because she does exactly what her spirit-power has told her to do. Therefore she survives. She has allowed the other woman's hate to penetrate something that cannot feel it. She has directed the force where it will be exhausted and harm nothing. Awl can live for as long as her hatred can reach a person's heart, but when no human target of vengeance is in line of aim, fury spends itself.

The narrator seems to have been saying that if a younger woman is able to keep out of the way of an older woman's anger, she may not be hurt; but if she is unsuspicious and compliant, she may be injured terribly. When she perceives hostility, the thing to do is to sidestep, not remain immobile or counterattack. If I have deduced the culture's preferred response, it is partially compliant, evasive, and pacifistic even in the presence of murderous violence. The girl's response is intended to represent intelligent and desirable behavior, correct behavior, because the recipient of hatred has at no point been subjected to depreciation and shame. Only a deliberate humiliation warrants opposition and violent response.

The drama thereby concludes with evidence that a principal villain, the person who in myths must be punished or eliminated, is the older woman. Younger people must be allowed happiness and fulfilment in the nuclear family, no matter what the feelings of its older members may be. Here as elsewhere, Clackamas myths offer indications of anxiety toward older women who may become controlling, possessive, sadistic, or murderous; and nowhere in myths is the older person allowed to win in the end. The inevitability of triumph by the younger person is anticipated by the older person, who is accordingly reinforced in feelings of anger toward the young. Perhaps, too, there is a little male guilt expressed obliquely in the beginning of the myth: is it not a man's very wishes which create, in part, the relationship with an older woman?

In the last scene the hunter appears again. He returns from hunting—because of the usual stylized device of a broken bow indicating trouble—and sees only a maiden, not his realized fantasy of grandmother Awl. His concern for the vanished old woman is for the moment such that, according to correct etiquette, he remains silent. (Mourning custom also prescribes such restraint.) Mention of his silence is the literary means by which the raconteur phrases succinctly the hunter's perturbation about what has happened to his companion and kin, but the implication is that he relaxes when, with the help of the real girl, he perceives a mere awl. The presence of such a girl is truly preferable to ministrations of a fantasy. He no longer need content himself with a wish that has somehow been realized. When fate gives him a more advantageous companion, he need no longer abide with an illusion. In other words, a person may live without the comfort and aid of spirit-power kin, but no one can long survive without human beings of flesh and blood.

The hunter and the girl uncover the four corpses, which have decomposed beyond a point which would permit returning them to the living. Clackamas myths contrast with Sahaptin in the way in which dead or murdered persons—more often women than men—stay dead. The bodies of the four girls are now turned black, and it is therefore too late for a precultural Clackamas to resuscitate them. They can only be buried. One may wonder whether Clackamas' frequent acceptance of deaths of murdered precultural actors and Sahaptins' magical revival of the dead by stepping five times over the corpse reflect different interpersonal relationships in the two societies. It might be inferred that for some reason Sahaptins were less able to accept utter extinction and therefore brought any and all dead back to life no matter what the degree of decomposition.

When the hunter explains to the fifth girl the manner in which he happened to create Awl, he is in essence explaining a number of things. He is informing her about his earlier lack of realism. He may also be reassuring her that with her help—as his wife—he can now accept reality and that she enables him to eliminate from his heart the fantasy which served him for a time. He is telling her, although not in so many words, that as a mature man he prefers a wife to a hating mother figure. Maybe he is also explaining the most unusual circumstance of his entrapment in a bad spirit-power relationship from which he was able to extricate himself only because of her coming. Nor is this change in his character inconsistent. Since there are no ethnographic accounts of successful riddance of a spirit-power which had become bad for its possessor, the myth may express wishful thinking that a person could break away from such a relationship and effect the banishment or death of the malign spirit-power. Again, since spirit-powers and kin are only distinct facets of relationships in general, another level of expressive content in the plot may represent death wishes which people have toward unwanted relatives.

The play contains two leading personalities: one is the man who changes from bachelor loneliness, suspicion, and hostility to normal masculinity and family living; the main personality is the older woman, murderously envious of younger women who are certain to displace her.

The plot themes, which are more important than particularized persons, give expression to a family drama of the triangular kind that must have been ever present in Clackamas feelings: the husband, any older female of his household, and the younger woman who is bound to take over the satisfactions of an older woman in her relationship to the virile man of the house. An Oedipal-like theme treats of the horror of successive episodes which begin with sadism and terminate with murder of a young woman by a maternal figure. The several themes are woven so as to effect a stylistically standard short myth of the type of a sequence of five siblings, the last and youngest of whom vanquishes the ogre.

The play has the kind of unity of time, place, form, and content that constitutes the most frequent structuring which we find in Clackamas literature. It is a perfect example of a regionally widespread stylistic type which repeats a difficulty four times with four siblings who are progressively younger. The climax is reached when the fifth and youngest is enabled to resolve the problem, after a chance encounter with a bird informant and supernatural. Almost identical stylistic frames characterize two other myths (29, 36), and stylistic cognates of varying kinds appear in nine other stories (4, 5, 6, 10, 22, 40, 46, 48, 49). Further examples of the five-episodes type could be cited for perhaps every literature for which we have a score or more stories, in an area composed of most of Oregon and Washington.

CHAPTER VIII

IDYA'BIX̣ᵂAŠX̣ᵂAŠ

THEY (many people of a Chinook village) lived there. The man's (the headman's) name was *Idya'biẋᵂašẋᵂaš* (and he was about eight or ten feet tall). His house was full of his slaves. He never walked. Wherever he went they would carry him, they would take him with them. He would simply purchase (a wife) at any place (village) that he would hear there was a fine girl. That is where he would go and buy her. That is the way he did. At the place where he bought the girl, they (her kin) would make a return gift only with blood (of animals). He would take it (and) drink it, no matter how much of it, he would drink all of it.

His house was full of his wives. When a wife of his would give birth, he would ask them, "What did she bear?" When they told him a male, he would say to his slaves, "Kill it!" They killed it. But if a female, on the other hand, he would tell them, "Take good care of the baby." And that is what they did.

On one night they would carry him, they would lay him beside some wife of his. On the following day they would lay him beside another one of them. That is the way he was, he would make the rounds of his wives.

Now then he heard them say, "Oh goodness! a fine girl! Her hair is right to the ground, it is yellow-brown." He told his slaves, "Take me tomorrow. I am going to buy her." "Very well."

On the following day they got ready, they took him along, they laid him upon his canoe, they went, they got to the place where the girl's village was. They (the residents of that village) said, "They are bringing *Idya'biẋᵂašẋᵂaš* to come buy the girl." The next day then he purchased her. They went back. He took the girl along.

They (her kin) said, "Where shall we find something that has lots of blood? That is the sole thing they give as a return present to him, blood." So then they sought it somewhere or other, perhaps near the sea they found something. They burned it, they hit it (in order to make the blood come out). They said, "Now we shall put the blood in containers." They put it in containers, they filled all of those things. Still so much blood was left over (because they lacked sufficient containers). They said, "Oh never mind what is left there."

Now they got ready. They went the next day, they took it for a return gift to *Idya'biẋᵂašẋᵂaš*. They arrived. They brought the blood to him. He drank it, he drank up all that they had put in a container. He set that thing beside him, he drank. He looked at it, there was that much blood left. Then he drank more. He thought, "I shall drink it up." No. He could not drink it up. He lay down. "Hu!" he said. "I am full now. Red Hair has filled me up!" That is the way he named his wife from then on. They (her relatives) remained there so many days, and then the people went back home. As for him, they (his slaves) just carried him (and) took him places (as before).

One of his wives gave birth. The slaves and the wives said (agreed), "If it is a male, do not inform him. He will say to us, What is it? We shall say to him (that it is) a female." "Yes," they said. She gave birth. He said to them, "What is it?" They told him, "A female."

From *Clackamas Chinook Texts*, 38.

"Very well." She had borne a male child. They simply deceived him, they said to him, "A female."

Five days afterward she bathed. She told him, "I am going away. I am going back home. She will have become bigger before I return." "All right," he replied to her. But she merely went to hide her son. She went back home. She remained there. Now her son got big. His feet were very long, long ones just like his father. I do not know how long a time after. Then she told him (her son) about it. She said to him, "We are not staying here just for nothing. I came to hide you from your father. If they had informed him that you were a male, he would have killed you." "Indeed," he replied to her.

In the evening then they (the giant headman's slaves) poured sand, they poured it around his house (in order to reveal the footprints of men who were prowling around his harem). The following day then he would say to his slaves, "Look for footprints." They would go outside. None at all. They saw no footprints. They would go inside, they would say to him, "No." "Very well."

Then he would say to her (to his favorite, Red Hair), "Now unloosen your hair (braids). Walk about for me to see you, Red Hair!" And that is what she would do. She would loosen her hair, and she would walk about. "Oh," he would say to her. "Now then!" he would say to his slaves. "Take me yonder!" They would take hold of him, they would carry him, they would move him from there.

Now he asked them, "I wonder where my (other) wife went (long ago)? What did she take with her? a female or a male?" (In order to allay his suspicion) they told him, "A female, and now it is a maiden." "Indeed!" Now that is the way they named her (his favorite wife) Red Hair.

Now his son (at the other village) thought, "Supposing I go see him." He went. He saw one of the slaves there. He asked him, "Where will he be sleeping tonight?" "Yes," he (a slave) replied to him. "Tonight he will sleep at Red Hair's place (on her bed-platform)." "Indeed."

He (the son) stayed somewhere there. Then in the evening he went, he entered (the house of his father) very slowly and cautiously. He went directly to the place where Red Hair lay, he lay with her. He arose the next morning, he went outside, he went back home. In the evening he went again, he got to her forthwith. He said to her, "How long before he will be getting to you?" She replied to him, "Dear oh dear. He is going right here shortly. (It will not be) until he has gone clear around (the circle of all) his wives, before he will get back to me. Sometimes he lies here (with me) two or three times, before they move him again (to another wife)." "Indeed," he said to her. Now that is the way they (his favorite wife and his son) were doing. He would go to her each night, in the morning he would go back home.

Pretty soon but I do not know how long afterward, then he made his footprints (visible, for the first time). He thought, "Now he will see them." He said to one of the slaves, "Show him my tracks tomorrow." "Very well." And that is what they did. They saw his tracks, they informed *Idya'bix*ʷ*ašx*ʷ*aš*. "Indeed," he said to them. "Take me. I shall go see them (the footprints)." They took him, he saw it, he stood in a footprint. It was somewhat longer than his own foot. He said, "That is what I supposed she took when she went back home."

He said to his slaves, "Go! Go see what she took when she went away long ago." Five slaves went. They reached the place where the son of *Idya'bix*ʷ*ašx*ʷ*aš* was. He (the son) said to them, "Do not go back home! Remain here!"

On the following day he (the headman) then said to another five slaves, "You go too! Go see where they went to and did not return from." "Very well," they replied to him. They went, they arrived, they saw the others (the first five slaves). He (the son) said to them, "Remain right here! Do not go back home!"

He said to just one of them (to one slave), "Only you go! He will question you. You will tell him that I have kept all the (nine) slaves." "Very well," he replied to him. He (the one slave) went, he got to there. He questioned him, "Where did they go?" "Yes. They arrived. Your son himself kept them at that place." "Really. That is just what I was thinking."

Then he said to his people (his still loyal retinue), "We shall go tomorrow. We shall fight." They made preparations (for fighting). The next day then they took him, they carried him, they laid him on his canoe, and then they proceeded. They went along. They (the people at the son's village) said, "Now *Idya'biẋʷaṡ̌ẋʷaṡ̌* is on his way here." "That is right." They got to there, they went ashore, they just carried him. He said (when he called out to the villagers upon the bluff), "Give me back the slaves." They said to him, "Your son said no. He will not give them to you."

So then they warred. They fought. His people fled, some others of them took his (the son's) side, they did nothing (refused to fight for the old headman). They deserted *Idya'biẋʷaṡ̌ẋʷaṡ̌*. Presently then he was standing there (alone). His son went after him, he shot at him, clear to his canoe. He said to him (to his son), "Sure enough! you are my son! Now you may take everything, my name (and all). I will not be like that any more now."

So from then on he became just like his father. Now *Idya'biẋʷaṡ̌ẋʷaṡ̌* himself had no such wives, no such slaves any more. He gave everything to his son. Now he walked about, no more did they carry him around. Now I do not know where he went to.

Then those people lived there, his son was their headman, his wife was Red Hair herself. He had taken her away from his father. He said to the others (his sire's other wives), "If you choose you may go back (to my father to remain married to him)." Now that is what they did, some of the women went back (to live with the former headman).

I do not know what happened then. Now I remember only so much of it. I do not know what became of them anywhere. Story story.

In the light of Greek mythology and drama, together with the modern theories of the psychoanalysts, this is a classical Oedipal myth because it resembles, more so than over a score of other Clackamas myths which contain Oedipus motifs, the ancient play which Freudians have found instructive.

The dramatic recital commences with the headman whose name is unfortunately not translated. My informant thought that the chief was between eight and ten feet in height. His many male slaves carry him everywhere so that he walks little if at all, and he purchases many wives. At the time of each marriage his new in-laws present him with quantities of animal blood or some bloodlike fluid, all of which he drinks at once. Perhaps the understanding is that he has a spirit-power which requires that he drink quantities of such "blood." Each evening the slaves pour fresh sand around the house in order to reveal footprints of prowlers who are interested in his many wives. At the birth of each of his children, female slaves inform him of its sex, and he orders them to kill a male infant but to take good care of a female baby. Slaves carry him to another wife's bed-platform each night.

At one time when he hears people speak of a marriageable girl with beautiful long brownish or slightly reddish hair—not black hair like most Indians have—he purchases her. Her kin and villagers make him a marital return-gift of a bloodlike juice which they put in all the containers they have. But he is unable to drink it all. In addition to his new wife's special beauty of hair, her relatives are the first in-laws who have supplied more "blood" than he can drink. Does the headman's inability, for the first time, to ingest all the liquid that is presented to him imply the beginning of decline of his virility and armory of spirit-powers? or does it point to the superior-

ity of his new wife's family? In any case, his inevitable defeat seems foreshadowed
in the opening lines.

In order to stress the attractiveness of Red Hair, the recitalist says that each day
the headman has her walk about with her hair flowing so that he can admire her.
She is at once his preferred wife. Then another wife, whose worth is never indicated,
gives birth to a male. Upon this occasion the wives and slave women agree to
deceive the redoubtable father. They tell him that the baby is a female. It is his
first male offspring to escape the customary decision that a son must not grow up
to confront him for his wives. The mother returns to her village with the infant,
ostensibly for a brief visit to her kin, actually in order to remain there and save the
child.

When the boy grows he develops big feet like his father, that is, he is to be like
him in size. When the child grows up to be a youth, his mother tells him about his
paternity. He goes to his father's village and finds out from a slave that on that very
night his father will sleep with the most admired wife; the next nights the youth
stealthily enters and himself sleeps with her. He returns to his village for the daytime intervening. Perhaps the son, and only a scion of the headman, has spirit-power
to make footprints that are invisible in the sand put around the house.

Later the young man deliberately makes his footprints apparent, because now
his supernatural power allows him to challenge his sire. When his father observes
the footprints and finds that they are larger than his own, he knows that they must
be from the child of the wife who had deserted him. Thereupon he dispatches five
male slaves, then another five, to her village in order to get the son. (Observe the
stylization which changes "many slaves" to two groups of five each.) The son persuades the slaves to remain and not return to their owner. He orders one of them
to tell the headman-father that the son is keeping the slaves. The father now has no
recourse short of fighting. He therefore assembles followers, they carry him, they go
by canoe, and when they reach the young fellow's village, the headman calls to the
villagers to return the slaves. This demand seems to constitute some degree of retreat because it does not include insistence that they surrender the son too. The
villagers refuse to hand over the slaves. Fighting ensues. A cultural factor is responsible for the displacement of emphasis upon the fight as a struggle consequent upon
theft of valuable slaves, not a struggle by father and son based on hatred and fear
of each other and competitiveness over Red Hair.

Now some of the father's men flee, others refuse to fight, and others join the
son's people. Clackamas seem to have needed to suppress a suggestion that a single
fighter is so much as scratched. The father shoots arrows at his son and the son
shoots at his father. Neither hits the mark. When the father lacks followers because
of desertions, the son keeps shooting at his father, who retreats to the canoe. There
the elder capitulates. He says that his son may now have his wealth, his wives, and
even his name. The father now walks about like other people because he no longer
has chieftain position or slaves to carry him. The son is now the chief, and he duly
takes Red Hair for his wife, not because he has to or because she asks him to but

because he wants to. He stipulates that the other wives may do as they wish, and some remain with his father.

The myth characterizes an outstandingly wealthy polygynous headman by means of exaggeration and selections of a few traits. He has so gigantic a body, and such spirit-power, that he can drink more blood than all the in-laws of a new marital relationship can collect; his nightly enjoyment of a wife stresses his vast physique and sexual potency. In other words, the myth includes a paean of praise for a great headman of enormous physical, sexual, and supernatural capacity.

But this headman cannot tolerate competition of sons. If they were to grow to adulthood they might, by the Clackamas theory of heredity, inherit his size, virility, and spirit-powers. They also might desire his wives. He must kill possible competitors because he fears this prospect. The narrator does not indicate the manner of killing, and one wonders, for a society in which infanticide was absent, whether the audience was clear about it. The headman spares male infants of other villagers because their sons cannot possibly become as potent sexually or otherwise, in the light of native genetics; however, he permits no male freemen to penetrate his house at night, thanks to his nightly spreading of fresh sand which will reveal footprints. Not a word in the myth, or in any myth, suggests concern about a headman's male slaves, their interest in his wives, or the wives' possible interest in slaves. Unfortunately the region's ethnographic notations, which do refer to sexual interest of wealthy men in their female slaves, fail to include evidence concerning freewomen's extent of or repression of interest in male slaves. Apparently many male ethnographers who studied Northwest Indians had an inactive interest in feelings of women, even those of upper class.

The recital describes the favorite wife, Red Hair, only in terms of hair and of excellence of kin who can collect more blood than her husband can drink. She is first in his regard because of beautiful and lighter tresses and because her kin excel with gifts. Their production of so much potent fluid does not, as far as we know, indicate to the headman that his strength is waning but only that his lovely wife's relatives are very rich. The myth does not once refer to her other virtues, if she has any, but literary style may disallow mention of such additional matters. Emphasis upon long hair as one of the most admired of anatomical traits appears also in the myth where the ogress captures Gi'ckux by catching onto his beautiful long hair (34). Flint is ridiculous and fetalized because he has only five little head hairs tied in a knot (18). Another sort of stress upon head hair takes the form of mention of combs and urine shampoos (46).

To a Euroamerican, the striking characteristic of emphases, by many Indian groups of the northwest states, upon beauty in men and women is the selection of long hair as the *sine qua non* among the two or three features listed. Eyes, eyelashes, lips, ears, teeth, chin, and neck—and everything below the neck—are ignored by a Northwest Indian until he is queried about them in so many words. The characterization of Red Hair as the best of the wives because of her hair color and length, and because of her relatives' affluence, is a typical northwest states selection of most valued items.

The anger of the son against the father for wanting to kill him as an infant is avenged by success in acquiring the father's favorite wife. Even a headman's wife seems to be handed about as pure property, without a hint in the present myth that she can speak or make decisions. She is a prop for theater purposes, and she is especially clear in that role because she is described only as beautiful and of wealthy family. Her potential for initiative is nebulous. Citation of her personality features would complicate the plot unnecessarily, from the point of view of a native literary critic—literary style demanded, it would appear, omission of further details about the glamorous wife because the theme dealt with the headman's feelings about his son. Unity and simplicity of plot are not disturbed if the woman's feelings about her incestuous paramour are virtually ignored.

In the light of Clackamas genetics, it is natural that the headman's son who escapes infanticide grows up to be as large and competent as his father. There is literary custom and need to sketch him in just this manner, with certain related details that refer to sexual capacity, and to omit anything else.

The son courageously enters his father's house, as an expression of entrance upon adult genitality. He is able to go undiscovered in and out of the paternal abode for as long a time as he desires, presumably because he is his father's son and therefore has great spirit-power, which here presents him with the capacity to walk without making telltale footprints, notwithstanding oversize feet. He is also superlatively virile. He sleeps repeatedly with Red Hair; in fact, in the cognate Wasco myth recorded by Jeremiah Curtin, raconteurs carry the idea of paternal inheritance and therefore supreme virility to a logical conclusion: the son sleeps with each of the hundred wives, just like his astounding progenitor.[8] The Clackamas son eventually discloses the fact of his entry by making his footprints visible. He does this doubtless at a time when his self-assurance regarding spirit-powers and skills is such that he knows he can protect himself from and then displace his father. Therefore he has passed well over the threshold of manhood.

At no time in the myth is there notation of the particular spirit-powers had by the son, but the raconteur need hardly phrase the obvious to a native audience. Literary convention deters such mention. No premises other than youthful years together with possession of unnamed spirit-powers that are at once as numerous and powerful as his father's, perhaps superior to that worthy's, can account for the son's subsequent victories.

Superficially read, the defection of the slaves sent by the headman is due to the son's persuasiveness. Probably Clackamas would have accounted for their failure to go back to their owner by saying that the son has not only his father's spirit-powers by a kind of inheritance. He has acquired additional spirit-powers. That is why he has become stronger than his father, and that is why he can argue the slaves into desertion and then into submission to his authority. The same explanation might have been the means of accounting for the military defeat of father by son.

In nice Oedipal tradition, father and son shoot directly at each other. But we are not told whether they shoot to kill or to instil fear without any endeavor to aim pointblank. Anyhow, no arrow reaches the target. Both men escape without a wound, unlike the Wasco story in which son kills father. A Freudian inference might be that Clackamas values, unlike Wasco, intervened to prevent a warrior from shooting directly at the heart of his closest kin. By Euroamerican standards the Clackamas father's manner of accepting defeat is dignified, gracious, and realistic; the son's response to victory is tempered and lacks violence. There is no patricidal finale, as in the Wasco version—at least the Clackamas son suppresses a wish, if he has had one, to slay his father. But I can find no special feature of Clackamas culture, or of this drama, which connects with ethical control of his antagonism.

We do not learn that his marriage to Red Hair is with her consent. The question of her freedom of choice need not be raised, for does not any woman prefer a younger and stronger man? She is no extra burden to the value ideals of raconteur and audience because she is, after all, not his mother as in the Greek story. One might plead that the beauteous Red Hair, with a nice passivity or lust which permits her to have a sexual liaison with her husband's son, really stands for mother in his feelings. The recitalist does not even suggest that she enjoys the relationship. She is limned for literary purposes as passive, like a proper wife. If this perchance passionless lady is the glamorous and also most convenient displacement and representative of mother in unconscious depths of his being, as Freudians may suppose, raconteurs have done well in entombing her far below in his psyche and by the capital device of separating his mother into two pieces. One remains unadulterated mother. She is never even suggested as having nice long tresses. In fact, she is colorless physically as well as untouchable. The second piece of mother becomes the mistress whose opulent relatives, superlative tresses, and marriage to the father render her physically enchanting to his son. She lets herself in for iniquitous faithlessness without a murmur because he is so very powerful supernaturally as well as otherwise.

The raconteurs continue to be careful because of their guilt mechanism. They insinuate, What can a luscious mother substitute do when the virile son is irresistible because of his surplus of spirit-power and everything else? Craftsmen and populace who worked over this drama were busily taking care of a puritanical conscience. They split the mother into sexless and sexy segments at the very start of the play, almost before the son had been conceived. Therefore, there never need be a problem of his striking at father by way of biological mother. Then, unlike the robust Wascos, they maximized the appeal of one woman who was a mother surrogate by having him invade only her bed-platform, not the couches of one hundred other damsels who also gratified his father. The youth with the prodigious feet entered the house over the sands, with the help only of heredity, a surplus of spirit-power, and a determination to smite the sire through the choicest of his wives.

Not only does the young man spare the life of his father. Cultural ethics with its strictures against intrafamilial murders seems to have pervaded and determined the treatment of the plot to such an extent that storytellers make no suggestion, and there is also no incontestable evidence of latent content, of desire for patricide. Similarly, the father asks for the return of his slaves. He seems to display no inclination, manifest or latent, to kill his grown-up son, his son's mother, or Red Hair—who he knows has slept with the son. The absence of public evidences of need to kill, by both father and youth, suggests an efficient operation of ethics upon the content of this story, if one rests upon premises of Freudian orthodoxy. Pressure of values, by contrast with Wasco, is such that the son allows all his father's female property, except Red Hair, to decide for themselves what they wish to do. Note, however, that the story permits, without the narrator saying it in so many words, some severity of decision by the son: he does not allow his father to assert or determine which wives he wishes to retain. The son strikes at the father again, but in a very special way.

Although resolutions of drives by way of killings are expressed solely in the old chief's infanticides and in his choice to fight, the myth is actually Oedipal in canonical Freudian terms, just as much so as the Wasco story which is superficially closer to the Greek story in its killing of father by son. Like the Greek dramas which the psychiatric literati have utilized, the Clackamas myth does the essential things, according to Freud, in its representation of intrafamilial feelings. In its own way it sets forth a father's fear of and lethal hostility to the son, the son's need to strike at the father and take his place on the bed-platform of mother or maternal homologue, and her acceptance, whether inert or fervid, of son or son homologue in place of husband. The solution of intrafamilial feelings is notably restrained, unlike Greek and Wasco versions, because of the elimination of effective violence, although noisy threats and warlike twangings of bowstrings heighten the approach to the climax. No epilogue which treats of feelings of guilt need be appended because the son is not in the least aware that the woman whom he marries is his mother. On the surface she is not his mother anyway.

The myth is therefore a drama of intrafamilial relationships, one wherein feelings are revealed only in overt behavior and are not cited as such. That is the typical, the required stylistic way of handling a drama of feelings. The totality of the myth really incloses some latent ambivalence toward two headmen. The one is bad because he murders sons; the other is bad because he is incestuous. Both are good bo cause they are remarkably wealthy, virile, and supernaturally endowed. The father is too polygynous; the son is better because he leans in the direction of monogamy.

The myth lacks specificity of delineation of personalities, although a little is done, quite enough for a Clackamas audience, to dramatize the virility of the two men. But father and son are types rather than individuals. The wife who deserts the chief in order to raise her son, his beloved wife Red Hair, the slaves, and the villagers also represent types and relationships of such folk in a family situation. Feelings which are basic to the relationships are those which any examples of such types would have had. It is apparent, then, that Clackamas must often have been fairly clearly conscious, whether they approved or not, of emotions of actors in an Oedipal net; but they could do little or nothing to portray such feelings because of the traditional demands of literary style. Literary convention permitted only selection and description of some few things which the characters acted out.

The closeness of this Oedipal plot to the standard which is set up in Freudian theory bears comparison with myths which in this collection also contain expressions of Oedipal feelings, although central developments of a few such plots may not be wholly Oedipal. Stories which contain one or another version of an Oedipal theme, or which exhibit expressions of Oedipal feelings, are classed together in Part II.

The Literature as a Whole

INTRODUCTION

THE eight sample analyses of Part I dealt impressionistically with some of the content of each story. Little was said of traits of form and almost nothing was done to corroborate impressions or set them in order by means of controlled procedures. The study of a story in isolation provides no characterization of the literature as a whole, although most features of the literature may be cited if all the myths and tales in it are discussed; therefore, Part II undertakes a comparison of sixty-four stories, both myths and tales, and generalizes about them. The principal method resorted to in its preparation was to fragment the stories, isolate minimal units which I was able to identify, place a notation of each on a file slip or table, and assemble similar items found in the collection. For example, the listing of each occurrence of the "youngest-smartest" motif produced almost twenty items. When this trait appeared several times in one myth (e.g., 40), it was counted as one occurrence. Therefore only fifteen stories, about one-fourth of the collection, exhibited "youngest-smartest." The pattern number five occurred in thirty-two myths—well over half the myths alone—but not one tale had it. The personality of the Grizzly Ogress, an important feature of content, appeared in six stories, that is, an eighth of the myths or a tenth of the whole collection. Traits of the personality or behavior of Blue Jay Man were found in eleven myths. About one-fourth of the myths and tales exhibited a simple type of plot. Only two, both of them myths, were centrally humorous plots (19, 41), although funny items were woven into about half the myths. Enumerations and percentage determinations of such kinds rendered possible many formulations.

The two subdivisions of Part II, content and form, are only vaguely distinct. They amount to opposite ends of a continuum. Content always displays form, and formal features are never wholly extricable from content. Although materials segregated under the two captions overlap and interrelate, the advantage of the classification is that it points to contrasts and stresses.

I have not attempted to perform analytic operations which are best assigned to anthropological specialists in linguistics, music, and dance. A full analysis of the literature would include materials which they prepared. When a raconteur presented a story, he employed formal linguistic features continually, and sometimes he sang or sang and danced. When people discussed a myth, they sang and danced at appropriate parts of it. However, my impression is that few linguistic, musical, or dance forms were peculiar to myths and that none constituted their decisive features. Probably no musical or dance features differed significantly from music and dance which was not a part of folkloristic sessions. Only a relative terseness and staccato manner of speech seems distinctive and important in oral literature style, in Clackamas and in all its neighbors. Phrase structure—perhaps syntax, too—rather than lexicography, phonemics, or morphology marked the literature.

Analysis must be predicated upon an "as if." The assumption is that Mrs. Howard's dictations provided a usable cross-section of Clackamas literature. In formal features I think that they did approach such reliability. In features of content they are not a trustworthy cross-section. The very selection of stories given by a single informant who lived her entire life in a surrounded and moribund culture must have been affected by special conditions. These would include local forms of culture contact and acculturation, special circumstances of sociocultural disintegration, the informant's personal background and idiosyncratic traits, and her feelings about the anthropologist writing in front of her. No doubt most of the stories recorded by Mrs. Howard are pretty accurately representative of the same stories as told in precontact days, if one allows for minor omissions of content, short cuts, and formal infelicities; but it is impossible to determine how many different stories were current in Clackamas villages before Caucasians arrived. Nor is it possible to suggest the frequency with which such stories were recounted in precontact or reservation eras. We shall never find out about the average and variability of audience size or about the percentage of the people who knew stories well enough to recite and theorize effectively about them.

Although I offer an expression of confidence in the significance of frequencies of features of content and style, assurance is needed that the collection is a good random sampling of the precontact literature. Such assurance cannot be given. Analysis is limited by circumstances and factors peculiar to local reservation conditions and to Mrs. Howard as an individual, and evaluation of such determinants is not possible. Since the processes of invention, borrowing, and creative change of the stories were largely shaped by the ways in which precontact village people felt about, discussed, and handled story content, we can hope to provide only scattered suggestions on the dynamic processes in an oral literature.

I wanted to obtain many more stories in text and translation, but Mrs. Howard professed that she had reached the end of her repertoire or at least of her capacity to dictate stories as wholes. She asserted that her people had once told more stories, but she was unable to recall any of them in forms which to her justified similar dictations. I should have asked her if she had heard each of hundreds of motifs which were present in other literatures of the Northwest, so that a fuller picture of motif presences and absences could have been given. When folkloristic research is conducted in a decaying culture, the task is to obtain all possible stories and the components of other stories which an informant cannot dictate or refuses to recite but which he recalls having once heard. Raconteurs of precontact times must have known scores, if not hundreds, of stories in addition to Mrs. Howard's collection.

Vital factors in assessing both the collection and the analysis reside in Mrs. Howard's personality and in the personalities of the two women, her grandmother and mother-in-law, who she asserted were the sources of stories she recalled. As far as I could ascertain, these two women were largely Clackamas in ancestry, but certainly they were products of decades of Caucasian envelopment, not of the earliest contact decades and least of all of unadulterated precontact life. Mrs. Howard, who was partly of Molale ancestry, was a second- or third-generation product of shattering acculturative conditions. Undoubtedly each of these three of a rapidly deteriorating subculture surrounded by Caucasians of pioneer western Oregon enjoyed, remembered, and told Clackamas stories which had remained current and which also suited their individual needs. Each woman may have suppressed or forgotten stories which other women and many men recalled during the nineteenth-century decades of acculturation; I believe that most reservation Clackamas had less interest in tales that were placed in Transition and premodern eras than they had in myths.

This collection may therefore be regarded as a consequence of acculturational selection. There is no certainty that it can stand as a representative sample of precontact Clackamas literature. It may be representative of the stories that reservation women liked and told, and a male informant might have provided a distinctive repertoire partly overlapping with Mrs. Howard's. I believe that men would have dictated more and better stories about Coyote people than did Mrs. Howard and that a collection offered by a man might therefore have had a more east-of-Cascades flavor. The Coyote personality would surely have been identified with more often by men than women. In a sense, Coyote myths are men's stories. However, Coyote stories were so important that Mrs. Howard seemed to feel need to tell them, but my impression during the field work was that in some instances (especially myth 9) she did so without animation or identification with their leading actor. I suspect that she told enough of such stories to satisfy herself that she was "telling everything," and that she avoided guilt by going almost mechanically through the motions of their narration. A few Coyote myths (7, 10) which were patently congenial to her she recounted effectively and I judge with excellent management of style. Possibly this collection is well skewed in the direction of expressing the needs of painfully frustrated females who were humiliatingly surrounded and rejected by their Caucasian neighbors.

Projection, displacement, and other mechanisms exhibited in the literature were probably shared by all members of the community. The individual raconteur's projections or displacements may be minimal in a collection of this kind, although they appear in the particular selection of the stories which she dictated to me. But in general the student of an oral literature has to accept the fact that his subject of study is largely the creative expression of a people, not of a unique individual or of a series of so-called geniuses. Mrs. Howard's stories consequently serve adequately for many—though not all—aspects of analysis. While frequencies of many features of content must be commented upon with caution, and while some may be regarded as revealing little about the Clackamas people, manifestations of literary style in Mrs. Howard's dictations may be thought of as almost purely precontact and cultural. I shall discuss later the important but insoluble question of how closely a Clackamas or any other northwest states narrator hewed to the line of verbatim memorization of stories.

In spite of the attempt in Part II to find minimal units, to count, and to classify where it seems sensible to do so, doubts must remain about how Mrs. Howard's collection had been distilled in her mind from the whole of Clackamas literature and actually from the uncountable thousands of versions which preceded her by not many decades. More oppressive are perplexities about whether the minimal units really are minimal and whether the interpretations of them as units or members of categories are reliable. Today we have imperfect knowledge of how to probe into the body of an oral literature. Reliability of identification of unit items, their placing in types, their interpretation, and the formulation of significant or central characteristics of a literature as a whole rest upon a foundation which is all the more uncertain when dictations have come from a solitary acculturated survivor with whom the anthropologist did not become intimately acquainted. No highways and byways of precise method, no exertions directed toward objectivity, can remove such doubts or go far to repair errors due to ethnocentric interpretation and deduction ventured in a twilight perception of a vanished heritage. A principal obligation becomes then not so much to render deductions more valid by reducing them to seemingly objective tables and enumerations as it is to be alert to everything which has bound the span of comprehension.

A principal handicap in the pursuit of generalizations is paucity of exploration. Sixty really good stories from one semimodernized informant are insufficient. While it may be reasonable to search in an oral literature for evidences of personality traits and structurings,[9] or to locate themes, qualities, and symbols,[10] such studies, like Rorschach tests, are partial if not pursued further. They attain greater reliability if considered as segments of a fuller analysis. On the presumption that a part is more trustworthily formulated if the whole has been explored, I have tried to examine many facets of Clackamas literature as it has been left to us in the Howard dictations. I think that some decades of special and limited kinds of laboratory research in psychology have shown—if an analogous methodology is instructive—that it might have been as well to frame research on psychology within a larger structure of theory which dealt with human nature as a totality. Themes, qualities, symbols, and personality structures are parts which may be defectively limned if spadework has not also been done upon a number of additional facets of a literature. As for Clackamas, major barriers also include our incapability of perceiving the social structure, manner of life, and ideological heritage, and there are the additional basic problems arising from the use of one informant who was long resident among whites, who offered only a few score stories, and who was interviewed by only one anthropological worker.

Processes accepted in psychiatric theory do not explain myths satisfactorily, if used without other hypotheses. Every plot, act, scene, and motif is a mosaic of processes and items of diverse kinds. Some may be historical; others arise from the Clackamas world view or from its specific ideology of supernaturals. Still others arise from the social structure which failed to provide formal or permissible outlets for feelings which were then expressed in precultural actors and happenings. The interactions of processes and materials were always complex. Comprehension of such matters is still so slight that one must regard a venture of the kind exemplified in this book as an exploratory exercise, an experimental model, or a fabric of hypotheses. The attempt is, I think, of especial interest because it proceeded upon an exceptionally small base of ethnographic information, supplemented only slightly by ethnographic deductions made from the literature itself and from the little that is known about peoples who lived nearby. An extremely full ethnographic picture of a people is needed in order to approach a full analysis of their literature. Comparative ethnographic researches upon Northwest peoples would have improved our sensitization to Clackamas society and culture, but the pursuit of such comparative studies would have long delayed an analysis of Clackamas literature. It seemed worthwhile to attempt an exploration of the literature as if it were isolated from other peoples and literatures of the Northwest.

Features of Content

CHAPTER IX

EMPHASES IN CONTENT

A CENTRAL formulation about story content in Mrs. Howard's renditions is the stress on relationships: both direct observation and simple counting show that although actors' personalities, fun, the awful or tragic, ethical lessons, sex, spirit-powers, and foods were important interests, by far the most outstanding interest was in the tensions and releases from tension which arose from identification with actors in their social relationships. Clackamas literature stressed social relationships—so much so that the only story which lacks reference to one is "Coyote Awaited Sleep" (12). In contrast, other interests were omitted from considerable numbers of stories.

In Mrs. Howard's collection I count well over 250 distinct items which point to more than forty kinds of relationships. Quantification of these is extremely difficult, however, partly because they were almost never phrased, but only implied by the narrator. The same difficulty arises in the arithmetical handling of personality traits, but these items seem fewer than those which delineate relationships, even though more than 250 actors crossed the stage. Some other items—traits which stimulated responses of humor, for example—appear to be easier to enumerate, and there are definite emphases on these, although their occurrence is less frequent than that of relationships. Ethical implications, explanatory and origin motifs, references to spirit-powers, and sentiments of tragedy or horror are in this category: frequent but patently in smaller numbers. Only eighteen stories lack a reference to food, but the significant references, for instance, those which connect with relationships or which deal with food anxiety, are not many. Thirty-eight stories lack an overt sexual reference; but a few of these contain an avowed Oedipal situation (e.g., 7, 27), and many others also include latent Oedipal components.

I categorize the more important kinds of content in Table 1 and indicate for each type the approximate number of stories which I believe contain an item of that type. It would be absurdly mechanical and methodologically incorrect to give the actual figures which I counted, because errors of judgment in identification and selection of items must be added to the skewing consequent upon Mrs. Howard's background and upon the choice of stories which she felt warranted dictation. The last story in *Clackamas Chinook Texts* (70) is not included in the count.

Few stories (like 12) contain only one kind of content; most include three or more of the ten important types listed in the table, and longer stories (such as 46) contain items of most of the types. Although two stories (19, 41) are centrally humorous, they include relationships, personalities, the macabre, and other components. In other words, most stories are not primarily or largely characterized by one emphasis. Accordingly, it would not often be correct to say that a story is a relationship play, terror drama, origin myth, or story about sex or religion. Such characterizations are in a majority of instances oversimplifications, or else they point to the effect which the stories may have on a Euroamerican reader. In order to avoid culturally bound reactions, and in the absence of native critics, it is best to take into account the several kinds of content in a story and to be restrained about determining their relative weights. Numerical notations of frequencies of the types must, as elsewhere, be judged cautiously because of the special factors which may everywhere have distorted the findings.

In order to place in perspective the kinds of content which have been noted and which will be discussed presently, and in order to see the ultimate relation of the

TABLE 1

LEADING KINDS OF CONTENT

Content Items	Approximate Number of Stories
Relationships (apart from sex)	62
References to traits of personality	30
Explanatory and origin items	30
(This count excludes the epilogue, which was a required feature of style in each of the forty-nine myths.)	
Humor-generating items	30
Ethical implications	25
Spirit-power references	25
Stimuli to a response of horror or terror	20
Stimuli to a response of tragic feeling	10
References to foods (in most instances only incidental)	45
Overt references to sex	25

literature to the society, it is necessary to comment on types of content which might be expected but which are manifestly absent, infrequently expressed, or disguised by means of displacement or other mechanisms.

Ethnographic researches in various cultures west of the Cascades have always shown that Indians of the region were intensely interested in seasonal rituals, girls' puberty initiations, marriage negotiations, and marital ceremonials. But rituals as such are almost wholly unnoticed in the literature. One might suppose, upon a basis of stories alone, that Clackamas did not have a single ceremonial connected with berries, roots, fish, or hunting. Not one story tells about a girl's puberty ceremonial.

Then, too, every ethnographer who has worked in the region knows that its Indians were extraordinarily fearful of illnesses caused by other persons' spirit-powers, especially deliberate "poisoning" caused by malevolent use of spirit-powers and failure to handle properly one's own spirit-power. One might apply to this common regional fear a caption such as "sickness anxiety" coupled with "death anxiety," or one might use a term for a combined response, for example, "pain and annihilation anxiety." Undoubtedly the chronic concern, whatever name it is given, weighed so heavily upon the people that it is necessary to ask why the only important recurrent stress resembling it in the literature was upon fear of famine due to frigid winter weather and blizzard conditions. It is as if the sustained concern with sickness and death because of supernaturals had been deliberately omitted in literary expression.

One might suggest, as independent corroboration of the hypothesis of deliberate omission, the rarity of citations of shamans doctoring the sick and dying. To be sure, the stories present a few such occurrences: Coyote doctors a girl he has raped (9), and three bird people attempt to revive a drowned woman (25). But these doctorings really have nothing to do with typical or serious sicknesses of the kinds to which Clackamas were subject. In the solitary instance when an actor exhibits a typical illness, Coyote fails to summon even one shaman to provide therapy for the false patient, Skunk (1). Furthermore, Skunk's affliction represents the commonest of ailments but not fears of sickness and death; instead, the situation is manipulated to generate humor around frauds and gullible visitors. Indeed, the infrequency of shamanistic séances in the oral literature indicates either acceptance of the availability and efficiency of shamans or suppression of mention of feared persons who were present at every myth recital.

If ethnographic researches in the Northwest have been well oriented, these and other remarkable absences of vital characteristics of the sociocultural heritage show that its myth screen hardly represents what is known of prevailing feelings in the people. One might then deduce that Clackamas literature avoided mundane facts of Clackamas life. The stories do stress some important and perhaps outstanding tensions—especially those in which spirit-power poisonings and rituals or ceremonials were not involved—but other extremely important tensions were not allowed ventilation in the literature except by means of humor. Fears of destruction of one's self, for example, were often treated with laughter in the stories. People smiled or roared with mirth at Blue Jay's murderousness. And the Grizzlies' hatreds and cannibalism tied in with feelings of distrust and aggression directed toward elders, headmen, and older women. The fascination of spirit-power relationships and the securities which they gave may have distracted attention from basic fears of suffering, mutilation, and annihilation; but these distractions and channelings do not seem sufficient to account for so little literary mention of illnesses and shamans. One might resort to a theory that literature focused attention upon all the principal points of tension in the culture except the most central. One might urge that the literature's very capacity to entertain served, above all, the function of helping everyone to escape the constant dread of pain and death.

On the other hand, I do not think that the problem is resolved by such theorization. I believe that the key to its resolution is as follows: People did speak out and help one another with open, direct, and unrepressed attention to spirit-power and other sicknesses. Everyone, except maybe the younger children, could be present at one after another shamanistic curing session. Therefore, people felt no need for a fantasy screen for certain kinds of fears; pain, death, and shamanism involved public participation and realistic resolution. The society had long since devised the daily means for airing feelings about these things.

The point, then, is that the literature served needs for which the society had not provided public outlets. That which the culture truly repressed was the tension about women, grandparents, some other relatives, and in-laws. Here is the area of tensions where the screen of literature served. This is why poisoning, shamanism, rituals, and girls' puberty rites are so conspicuously absent from the stories. Stresses which were comparatively conscious, incessantly verbalized, and resolved in such completely public and institutionalized procedures as shamanistic curing, winter spirit-power performances, seasonal rituals, girls' puberty initiations, and marriage rites did not need to be projected onto the screen of a Myth Era. It was the suppressed tensions which found their way, as if by subterranean streams, out into the light of literature and which thereupon dominated its expressive content. I think that psychoanalytic writers are essentially right in their conviction that myths are the screen for projecting that which is overtly denied and repressed and, one should add, for whose handling few or no cultural institutions exist. I can find no other means of explaining presences and absences of important cultural content in Clackamas literature.

The study of content in an oral literature accordingly provides an indispensable check upon analysis of the overt, expressed, and institutionalized components of culture: the traditional kinds of ethnographic information as such (those things which native informants display en masse and phrase for the anthropologist and which he, in turn, provides with an analysis of religion, kinship, and social structure). The literature seems to expose what the natives do not express directly or what they never perceive about themselves, and what the social anthropologist is sometimes unable to deduce from other kinds of observations. The natives know only that they enjoy and treasure their literature. All this is another way of saying that a traditional ethnography or social structure analysis can offer only a partial comprehension of a people. One can and should find out much in addition by analyzing the content of their literature.

CHAPTER X

RELATIONSHIPS

C LASSIFICATION, analysis, and manipulation of social relationships in Clackamas literature are much more difficult than treatment of other units of content—personality, for example. In spite of real-life complexities in personality configurations, Clackamas narrators depicted so few features of personalities that analysis was greatly facilitated. But narrators did not select one or two or three facets of a social relationship; they left it with structural complexity, which of course it had in reality. In addition, the feelings connected with every relationship are difficult to reduce to manageable units. Because of the problem of translating emotions into concrete categories, even a simple enumerative approach to studying social relationships is burdened with methodological limitations and almost insuperable involvements.

Nevertheless, in this chapter I have tried to classify and summarize relationships, to suggest how important their types are in the literature, and to show what each tells about the society.

I noted about forty different kinds of social relationships, expressed manifestly or implicitly, and counted the stories which contained a mention of each. Again, if an item occurred twice or more in a story, it was counted as one item in order to prevent imbalanced results due to repetitions within stories.

Sibling relationships of various kinds appeared at least once in each of approximately twenty-five stories. Monogamous marital relationships totaled about the same. No other neatly specific relationship was so frequent. I counted only eighteen stories which contained overt or covert Oedipal situations, although I suppose that this enumeration is an underestimate. Parent-child relationships which may have been covertly Oedipal appeared in another sixteen stories.

In Table 2, I have grouped types of relationships which in structural or external respects seem distinct; I amalgamated those in which actors were likely to have responded with closely related feelings. The result is that the approximately twenty-five citations of sibling relationship lessen in significance, although the figure is sufficiently large to point to an important constellation of feelings. Less tension is suggested, however, than is indicated by the group of citations comprising monogamous marital relationships, polygynous ones, various ones which are Oedipal, manifestly parent-child ones (maybe often Oedipal also), ones involving incest with aunt or grandmother (and therefore Oedipal too), and headman-headwoman roles. That is, approximately eighty situations dealt with marital and a variety of related Oedipal feelings. Because the number of these situations is disproportionately large, I suspect that certain kinds of nuclear and extended family relationships, and feelings generated by them, needed more airing in stories than did feelings about sibling ties or feelings of any other kind.

The concept of the family as it existed among Chinook peoples needs some explication. The response in the literature was a stress upon projections and ventilating devices for the society's feelings about extended families. The core of the social structure was the network of family relationships, conceived from the Northwest

TABLE 2

MAJOR FEELING CONSTELLATIONS IN SOCIAL RELATIONSHIPS

Constellation of Feelings		Number of Stories	Total
About siblings...............	....	25	25
In marital and Oedipal situations...	Monogamous marital	24	79
	Polygynous	4	
	Oedipal	18	
	Overtly incestuous	2	
	Parent-child	16	
	Headmen, headwomen	15	
About pre-adults................	Kidnappings	2	28
	Avunculate	2	
	Children	12	
	Youths	12	
About elders....................	Evil older women	8	35
	Headmen, headwomen	15	
	Older men	7	
	Shamans	5	
About social inferiors.............	Dependents, followers	9	23
	Lower-class persons	8	
	Slaves	6	
Derogatory of women.............	Evil older women	8	24
	Derided or maltreated women	10	
	Women who desert husbands	4	
	Women who trick men	1	
	Women who infantilize children	1	
About non-villagers..............	In-laws	12	28
	Intercommunity relationships	10	
	Games and sports	6	

and west-of-Cascades viewpoint, which included a number of household elders and, to all intents and purposes, the village headman himself in the primary social group. The important thing is not to highlight a nuclear family triangle of father, mother, and offspring—the nuclear family of Western civilization. One must orient one's thinking toward the familial group of close relatives, household elders, and village headmen; this functioned as does the small nuclear group among Euroamericans. To understand the essential familial ties of residents of Clackamas villages, one must regard household elders and headmen as members of the family.

Older men and women were presented in at least half the stories—I include head-men and headwomen here, even though this creates an overlapping with the marital and Oedipal category, because sentiments toward them were like those toward household elders. If one adds to this number of stories the five which make note of shamans, an intensity of feeling about older persons, that is, about persons who possess controls over others, is all the more evident. Since thirty-five stories contain feelings about elders or individuals with some sort of dominance, this becomes the second most important theme. However, the statement of this theme's importance is predicated upon the assumption that it is valid to separate the group of elders from older persons who were a part of a familial relationship.

Youths were cited in twelve stories, children in twelve, kidnapped children in two, and boys with admirable uncles in two. Items of various kinds about young persons of all ages appeared, then, in perhaps less than thirty stories, about elders in definitely more than thirty. Clearly, the feelings of identification, guilt, fear, and anger directed at elders and dominating people are a stronger force in the literature than any constellation of emotions about pre-adults; probably this reflects the fact that Clackamas were less romantic, angry, or anxious about young people than about old ones.

The group of citations which includes references to lower-class persons, dependents of well-to-do households, and slaves totals only twenty-three instances. This is an important inventory, pointing as it does to another social group about whom there were strong feelings; but in comparison with the stress on families, elders, and children, this is not an outstanding theme. Since the literature for the most part expressed the inner life of well-to-do persons, the likelihood is that Clackamas tensions about social inferiors were not as great as those about other people.

Feelings about people of other villages appeared in almost thirty stories, and so another important emotional involvement is indicated; this relates to financial and other connections between in-laws, fears about alien shamans and "poisonings" because of them, competitiveness over the status of headmen, and intervillage sports which were accompanied by betting.

Evidences of antifeminine sentiments can be gleaned with ease and in various quarters. These evidences are impressive no matter what procedure of classification and analysis is employed. In fact, the count of twenty-four stories in which females were depreciated may not indicate the strength of antifeminine feeling. When the constellation of feelings directed toward older women is contrasted with the tepidity of such sentiments about older men, antifeminism in the literature becomes even more striking. However, this contrast is revealed more clearly in the separate analyses of personalities and humor (given in later chapters) than in the citation of relationships as such.

These, then, are the most important types of social relationships included in the content of Clackamas stories. However, the overwhelming importance of the marital and Oedipal situations warrants specific notations of some of the stories which contain Oedipal relationships narrowly conceived.

A patently Oedipal theme appears in many myths, but the one most closely resembling the Greek Oedipal story is that of the virile headman who kills all his sons until one who has been hidden matures, sleeps with his father's favorite wife, battles with his sire, and eventually replaces him as headman (38). This myth is presented in Part I.

At the end of the Orpheus myth, the daughter angrily scolds the meddlesome old woman, her mother, who has caused mortality rather than everlasting life for all people (45). The rage of the daughter is manifestly due to her mother's well-intentioned but improper removal of the daughter's infant from its cradle, but this episode is only a displacement of any daughter's resentment toward her mother. Clackamas recognized the feeling but evaded conscious acceptance of its origin.

In another myth (42) the tongue of Tongue Man can be regarded as a phallic symbol because it is an enormously long organ, like a ribbon of fire, and seeks to eat, that is, to penetrate a girl's body. The stepson of Tongue Man, that is, the ogre's son, collaborates with his mother to kill her husband. Freudians would surely regard this story as an overlaying, with especially archaic fantasies and some displacements, of latent Oedipal feelings. If such an interpretation is correct, the entire myth is actually an Oedipal plot.

In still another myth (7) Coyote rejects his four maturing sons as unworthy. He really does much more. He refuses to participate in spirit-power dances which would build new spirit-powers—that is, life, virility, and well-being—into his sons. At the same time, he responds with ardor to his daughter's acquisition of a new supernatural which is his own. The myth therefore contains the whole of the Oedipal pattern: the initiation of Oedipal feelings in the father's attempt to kill his sons by rejecting their spirit-powers, in other words, their very life, and the seduction of the daughter, expressed only in identification with her father by way of introjection of his spirit-power.

Another Coyote, an aged one, becomes sexually reawakened and rivalrous toward his so-called grandson, whom Clackamas narrators name Panther ("so-called" because grandfather and grandchild signify a relationship corresponding to the father-child bond in Euroamerican society). Coyote steals Panther's wife and flees with her in tow (6). The old man's Oedipal passion spins the entire plot.

Still another Coyote hates his Salmon grandson and, again, envies the younger man's possession of a young female (5). In order to minimize feelings of guilt, the old man recruits vicious Wolves to kill the youth. But his guilt, coupled with terror lest a just vengeance overtake him, is so overwhelming that he maintains hypocritical mourning for years and insists that his comrade Skunk mourn, too. The plot is transparently Oedipal.

Other myths not so closely resembling the Greek play have plots containing Oedipal components. The behavior of a murderer, Flint, who rapes his comrade's wife and eventually cuts him to pieces, includes an obvious Oedipal patterning (18). It is the psychology of Flint, with its strong Oedipal content, upon which hangs the plot. One more Oedipal pattern initiated by a father's feelings (23) suggests the father's disapproval of Hot Weather Wind, the unattractive young husband of his daughter.

Snake Tail Woman uses her five Snake sons, who obviously symbolize phalli, to kill girls who come to marry the sons—in Clackamas literature termed "grandsons" (24). The older woman, who is in terror lest she lose exclusive possession of her five males, must kill any female who comes to deprive her of what she has. Once again, a plot is determined by Oedipal feelings in the elder. So too, Awl Woman (27) kills each girl who comes to challenge her exclusive possession of her grandson. In another myth, a rollicking comedy (25), a lecherous old woman deliberately awakens the sexuality of her grandson, and they have a passionate affair. In still another story, which is a tale, not a myth, a hating father burns a coal through the hand of his son (60).

More citations of Oedipal relationships could be found. In the majority of the twelve stories just listed, Oedipal feelings are initiated by an elder and directed at a child or grandchild, or at the homologue of a child or grandchild, of the same sex. Seven such instances (5, 6, 7, 18, 23, 38, 60) are of older men; three (24, 25, 27) are of older women, and only one of these three (25) starts with love rather than hate. No more than two plays (42, 45) seem to bestow initial feelings of rancor upon the younger person: in one the son kills his murderous stepfather, and in the other the granddaughter scolds her grandmother whose meddling has prevented immortality. The numerical preponderance of Oedipal feelings originating in older persons suggests that Clackamas did not blind themselves to the variety of such feelings. Probably they understood that most intrafamilial tensions originate not in biologically generated sentiments of younger people but in older persons' fears of old age, their threatened dislodgment from controlling positions, their needs to recapture youthful virility, and their simple sexual passions. The multiplicity and variety of Oedipal themes and the stress upon origins in older rather than younger persons constitute evidences of sophistication in the narrators and public who transmitted the literature.

A similar assembling of sibling relationship feelings, and theorization about them, is included in the discussions of "pattern number" and "youngest-smartest" because their treatment is especially stylized.

In fact, the repeated projections of Oedipal and certain other relationships onto the folktale screen, and the very stylization of sibling relationships on it, contrast with the omission, on that screen, of relationships in the most important rituals and economic activities. The explanation is inescapable: Clackamas discussed, projected, and ventilated, in literature, whatever failed to run securely and smoothly for them, or for which they lacked efficient supernatural allies.

CHAPTER XI

PERSONALITIES

THREE interconnected questions arise as one examines the personality traits which the stories make evident in one way or another. The first question is the simple one of how to identify and classify as many personality traits as possible. In this case, their numbers, ascription to one or the other sex, to age level, or to a group within Clackamas society, and other data permit evaluation of the importance of such traits in the culture. The second question is also not difficult to handle. It involves assembling clusters of traits so as to delineate the literature's actors as they appeared in the minds of Clackamas.

The third question—how to assemble clusters of traits so as to sketch personalities of real, not folkloristic, Clackamas people—presents thorny problems. Discussion of this question may be anticipated immediately with the assertion that it is largely insoluble for Clackamas, although it may be pursued with greater returns for oral literatures in other parts of the world. I am convinced that for solution of this question no northwest states oral literature provides materials more usable than Clackamas; their myths, like the other myths of the region, were the product of so many generations of exhaustive community scrutiny, dissection, and reformulation that few myth actors were approximations or replicas of real persons. And we have no means of finding which ones were taken unchanged from community life. To integrate discrete traits of story actors into configurations that depict modern Clackamas people is to vault from well-evidenced fragments to their unevidenced integration. And were one to choose to make such leaps, one would find no possibility of verification. I therefore envisage no means of sketching, with traits harvested from myths, any significant number of persons or types of persons of a Clackamas community. Just as archeological researches do not grant reconstructions of a functioning social system in its complexities, so the fibers of personality structures which a northwest states mythology reveals cannot be woven so as to display whole persons of the post-Myth Era. If there were a much larger number of tales, and if ethnographic observations had been fuller, the task might be pursued. The present collection can supply resources only for study of major and minor personality characteristics apart from their patternings in personalities of the modern period; accordingly, this chapter is confined to answering the first two questions, first for male actors, then for females, then for children.

Northwest states narrators depicted actors, as they did situations, with only a few selected strokes. Where an actor appeared in several stories, each might contain a distinctive additional item of personality characterization: in these cases, one can get a kind of additive knowledge of a single character's personality. Still, a Chinook audience was aware of many details of an actor's personality never explicitly stated in the stories; a non-Chinook can only venture to assemble some characteristics from a collection of stories. Since many stories were never recorded, he cannot be sure that he has approached a listing of most of the personality details. The method available is to summate delineative items in different stories in which the actor was presented and to deduce from all the stories which cited that actor.

No actor seems to be accurately or even approximately a historical figure, except in tales. Because of the manner in which myths constitute a projective screen for proclivities which cannot be expressed in other ways in daily life, and because of generations of community manipulation of story materials, each myth actor must have been only an anthropomorphization or projection of specially channeled feelings and values. Unless specifically noted as a person of the poor class or a slave, each myth actor was of the wealthy class. Only a few important actors lacked names or were referred to teknonymously.

Although most actors appearing in several stories have an essentially unified character, occasionally different myths seem to present either different aspects of an actor's personality or a single characteristic which does not fit with other traits delineated for the same actor. There would seem to be at least two possible explanations for this variance within a character. In a few cases, among which Grizzly Woman seems to constitute the best illustration, unique items of personality characterization may have eventuated from different literary traditions, that is, from earlier borrowings from other Northwest mythologies. These adopted items were in process of fusion. Sometimes differences in delineation of the same actor arose from the Clackamas tradition itself, caused by a need to account for specific plot situations. An outstanding instance of an actor who appeared in wholly different delineations is Hot Weather Wind (22, 23). The identity in name and variance in characteristics, except for the one trait of possession of hot weather wind spirit-power, are explicable on the assumption that two different actors happened to have such a supernatural.

1. MALE PERSONALITY TRAITS

More than 150 males acted in the collection, but only a small percentage were lead actors, appeared in a number of plays, or displayed more than one or two strokes of personality delineation. The inventory of actors who are discussed commences with those of importance who appeared in more than one story and were also named by the narrator.

Coyote.—A Coyote appeared in thirteen myths and no tales; in other words, he was wholly precultural. Clackamas probably had at least five appellations for the different Coyote Men who lived during myth times, but unfortunately Mrs. Howard recalled only three such names, each as untranslatable as John and James.

The ninth myth's description of successive stages of development in a Coyote personality, that is, a sequence from a trickster who is impelled by youthful drives, to a conscience-controlled announcer and transformer, was paralleled even slightly in only two other myths. Myth 3 described essentially the same stage sequence. Myth 10 very briefly suggested it. Ten other stories which included a Coyote actor lacked a developmental plot, but some of these (e.g., 2, 4) probably ascribed the name "Coyote" to an actor who was only a headman, husband, or father. In other words, a distinction must be drawn between stories which were really about a Coyote personality (e.g., 9) and others which may have been at some undetermined point of refashioning and which were changing in the direction of presenting a veritable Coyote. Stories of the latter kind could have been late borrowings or refurbishings of stories once ascribed to another actor.

Myth 1, which was surely one of the older or genuine Coyote stories, cited an incompetent hunter who was selfish, greedy, and dishonest. He pretended competence but duped and exploited his younger brother and did not share food which the brother produced at great pains.

Myth 2 bore no internal evidence of an ancient Coyote plot. It set forth so aberrant a picture of the man that it seems possible that the appellation of "Coyote" was an attachment of recent date. He was a respectable, righteous husband who with utmost severity punished his erring wife. Only his considerable spirit-power, evidenced in skin-shifting and partially successful moon-swallowing actions, seems to have warranted the name "Coyote."

In myth 3 Coyote was in several respects like the Coyote of the ninth myth. He changed from an immature to a mature phase. He started out as an inefficient and ridiculous hunter, a glamorless and blundering nincompoop. He brought home only culturally tabooed and despised fare such as mice and insects, and he lacked the sense of humor of his light-fingered partner, Coon. His strong oral drive appeared when he remained eating ravenously and almost stupidly in the house of dangerous Grizzly Ogresses. He exhibited overweening oral needs, lack of judgment, and hardly any awareness of reality. Only when shocked into appreciation of danger did he surrender his oral preoccupation and respond sensibly and resourcefully. He then engaged in judicious bargaining and presently was displayed in a deity-like role, one of great competence and indicative of tremendous spirit-power.

Like myth 2, myth 4 had the quality of a story in which raconteurs termed the old headman "Coyote" by a process of secondary association because they—and the Clackamas community—conceived any Coyote to be wealthy and supernaturally potent. The story did not describe him in other details.

Myth 5 offered items which appeared in a few other myths. An older man with Oedipal envy of and hostility toward his grandson, Coyote employed Wolves to kill the grandson and take away his wife. Then Coyote's fright and guilt became so great that for years he acted out an elaborate and sham mourning. Although he seems hardly a desirable parent here, headmen and father figures are not necessarily perfect, and the best of people may become involved in difficulties, especially in an ugly Oedipal situation. Therefore characterization of a Coyote father was not inconsistent with the glamorized Coyote of later episodes of myths 3 and 9.

Myth 6 stressed a Coyote's lust, as did myth 9. His sexual excitement was discharged in Oedipal rivalry and hostility to a virile grandson, Panther, after the latter's young wife arrived. Undeterred by the reality of his own advanced age, Coyote became almost insane in the completeness of his identification with the grandson. In spite of repeated failures, his passion for the young woman drove him into ludicrous situations; he was a comical and inept pretender who also briefly escaped punishment by means of trickiness. Clearly he revealed cultural insight into emotional needs of old men, as well as the culture's thinking about their weakening spirit-power resources.

Myth 7 offered little information about a Coyote. He was a blowhard who claimed falsely that he killed Grizzly and then unfairly led followers to attack Mudfish, who had actually killed Grizzly. The play also displayed feelings within an Oedipal situation: Coyote rejected his four sons but showed enthusiastic identification with and love for his youngest child, a daughter, who had acquired his fish fat spirit-power. The myth agreed with myth 6 in its stress upon deficiencies in an older man. On the other hand, myth 8 indicated only Coyote's deity-like nature, when he—or, in another version, Salmon—ordained the name and role of each of the foods.

The many scenes of the important ninth myth commenced with the allegorized form of a conscienceless and tricky youth who satisfied food, sexual, anal, and sadistic urges without a vestige of restraint. He duped Pheasant Woman in order to kill and eat some of her children, copulated with a woman's prepubescent daughter, and released bees to sting a family. Then because he could not distinguish wish from reality, he was deceived by imagery of dancing girls and dashed about seeking nonexistent people who he believed were cooking sturgeon. He acted maturely when he taught a precultural man how to carry fuel and how to copulate. He was still oversexed when he borrowed a long penis, copulated across the river, manipulated genitals of fifteen humiliated females, raped a shrieking girl, and allowed his lust for a Woodpecker to trap him inside a hollow trunk—he had to dismember himself in order to get out of it. He cruelly tricked Snail Woman into giving him her good eyes, tried on Skunk's anus, and enjoyed fellatio. Subsequently he became a fine man of great spirit-power. He saved women from a cannibal stew, killed Grizzly Woman and Earth Swallower, operated on mouthless people and taught them how to eat, instructed terrorized villagers to spear fish, and killed River Swallower. Wherever he served people well and they presented him with wives, he departed unaccompanied in order to continue traveling and doing good works for the sake of additional villages. In short, the myth started with an irresponsible youth and closed with a teacher and benefactor of deific proportions.

In myth 10 Coyote was the father who grieved for all his murdered children instead of rejecting his sons, as he did in myth 7. But he was a bungler whose attempts to commit suicide failed and who went astray in an elaborate endeavor to return his dead children to life. He failed partly because he could not hold anger in check and partly because his intent was selfish. At long last he stepped into his role of mature father and, deity-like, announced the inevitability of permanent death. Suffering and error were succeeded by maturation into an admirable man, a deific figure who defined the tragedy of life and death. The play therefore offered a succinct duplication of the theme of growth and development which dominated myths 3 and 9.

In myth 11 Coyote was a projection of cultural values. He was altruistic and deity-like although his technique was that of a trickster. He succeeded, as he did in the last scenes of myth 9, because he was no blunderer when his motive was to do good for the sake of people to come. In myth 12 he was again a kind of deity, but the play expressed the view that no one, not even Coyote, was really omnipotent or omniscient for all time. In other words, he was only a glamorous transformer and announcer of the future. Myth 30 returned to the theme of uncontrollable urges for food and sex, coupled with trickiness and deceit.

The discrete representations, which doubtless do not include all Clackamas narratives about Coyotes, offered lineaments of a personality which manifested the worst and best in men. Coyote was not so much a cultural hero, trickster, or transformer as he was at one extreme an expression of Clackamas comprehension of the deepest feelings in headmen and, at the other, of their obligations and potential capacities. This was a sophisticated depiction in which such a man's deficiencies were neither underplayed nor rejected; his profoundest needs and most extravagant foibles were set forth.

Plays which portrayed Panther (6, 18) and *Gi'ckux* (34), for example, were less sophisticated, because they were shaped by a Clackamas brand of Puritanism. These two actors were idealized, perfect, one-sided men who were rarely or never found in reality; they were almost unadulterated representations of cultural values. For all the unrealism of the fantasy world of an imagined era of precultural creatures, the total understanding which Clackamas had of Coyote was their closest approach to realistic analysis of the personality structure of an adult man of the upper class, as well as of his development through the years. The best explanation which I have for the retention and multiplicity of Coyote stories is therefore that a Coyote's personality represented better than the actors of any other stories the kind of upper-class man who told and listened to them, the kind of man that Clackamas men wanted to be and in some instances knew that they could be, and the kind they found in some and desired in all headmen. At least one precultural actor was allowed to approach understanding of what upper-class men were like in their many-sided actuality. Men of an audience must have identified with him as with no other precultural actor.

The multiplicity of Coyotes demands explanation. It is possible that Mrs. Howard lacked knowledge of a temporal sequence once ascribed to Coyotes (as in Coos mythology, about two hundred miles distant along the central Oregon coast). If there were multiple Clackamas Coyotes in a time series, I would account for such a concept by suggesting that many generations of discussants and raconteurs among Chinook and other peoples of the northwest states had agreed in the need to account for a Coyote's many experiences and characteristics by dividing him into successive persons. No other personality was presented in so wide a range of situations and traits. Evil actors such as Grizzlies, Cannibals, Thunders, and Wolves also appeared in plural forms; but they were contemporaneous, not sequential, and their numbers apparently served to intensify awfulness.

No Coyote female appeared in northwest states literatures. (Coyotes' daughters were not thought of as feminine Coyotes.) The reason for absence of such an actress seems to be that the main traits of a Coyote's personality were masculine and could not possibly be present in a female of the area. Clackamas women and their literary counterparts did not often display gross sexuality; they did not travel for the sake of adventures; few of them announced the future. For the most part males, not females, were the deity-like fashioners of things to come.

These may be reasons why wives of Coyotes were not themselves named "Coyote." And another important reason may be the custom of patrilocal residence: a woman came from another settlement to her husband's. Therefore, in myth times a Coyote's wife's place of origin would not have had an upper-class Coyote lineage; his wife might, then, be unnamed or be identified with Frog or other minor females of precultural epochs. Furthermore, the circumstance that none of these females were accorded Coyote-like personalities reinforced Chinookan inability to name them "Coyote Women": only if a female shared basic traits found in the male, as in Grizzly, were actors of both sexes depicted as "Grizzly Men" and "Grizzly Women."

Blue Jay.—This important northwest coast actor appeared in fullest detail in myth 26, an obviously coastal play in which, as elsewhere in Clackamas theater, he was only the clown, not a leading actor. He was the only member of Seal Hunter's group who was so inept as to slip and break through ice. When he emerged ingloriously because he was soaking wet, he offered the ridiculous claim that he went underwater deliberately in order to wash off perspiration, thus providing comic relief after a macabre episode. He made claims patently contrary to fact. He volunteered, with seeming bravery, to compete with Snipe Girl in an underwater contest. But he won only by cheating: he came up to breathe, against the rule of the contest, and furtively killed Snipe Girl with a blow of his crest. He brashly offered to represent his side in a contest before the leader had properly named the team's representative, and such ill-mannered presumption was probably more reprehensible to the Clackamas than his bragging, cheating, and murdering.

In a succeeding contest he acted as if lighthearted and confident of winning— amusing the audience because of anticipation that he would win dishonestly—then he adroitly killed his opponent, Sapsucker Girl, and displayed his own agility as another comic touch. In various contests he was by turns frightened and silent, taciturn because of fear, speechless with fright, and hopelessly incompetent; but after his team's victory in every competition only he boasted about his side's abilities, capered about in circus-clown fashion, and with his crest killed five persons of the opposing group. Later, attempting a feckless imitation of Sturgeon Man, Blue

Jay cut his wife's throat gruesomely and with utmost foolishness, butchered her, and roasted her carcass; all he had done was murder his wife and humiliate himself in the eyes of an upper-class guest.

In myth 25 different stresses appear, although there is some consistency with the personality structuring given in myth 26. Blue Jay was paddling along with his younger brother Jay Bird, who saw a hide floating. Although Blue Jay failed to notice the object, he argued, with juvenile impudence, that he had seen the hide first. The brothers employed shamans to resuscitate a nearly drowned old woman in the hide, and their efforts to revive the lascivious old woman were ridiculous because she might as well have been dead from the Clackamas point of view.

Blue Jay's inability to act honestly was expressed in the resale of the refurbished and girlish-looking old woman to her dull-witted and unsuspecting grandson, Wren. The dishonest and burlesque salesmen shrewdly advised her to laugh with her mouth shut lest her new husband discover her toothlessness. In other words, Blue Jay and his brother deliberately sold damaged goods at the profit which undamaged merchandise would net. Their consciences were conspicuously absent. They displayed additional cheek when they added to the overpriced commodity the hide, that is, the wrinkles, of the old woman. The story told that the brothers again tried to revive her when they found her in the river a second time. Presumably their thought was to engage in another dishonest sale, although the second effort at resuscitation was vain. In short, myth 25 stressed cheek and mendacity rather than hyperactivity, exhibitionism, aggression, and cruelty.

In myth 47 Blue Jay perpetrated a dastardly trick by pouring water on the fire in a deserted boy's house, so that the youngster would soon die of cold. Later, Blue Jay was the supreme villain when he spied on the good Crow Women and then leaped inside and snatched a chunk of fish from one of their children. Then he revealed the Crows' secret: they were receiving food from some wealthy man. Clackamas feeling that the meanest people survive was expressed in a final stroke: only the Blue Jay family escaped a storm which capsized others' canoes. But the sons of the wealthy man deservedly drove away the family. Throughout this myth stress was on Blue Jay's heartlessness.

Myth 41 presented another sort of Blue Jay, although he shared some traits with those already denoted. He lived in an end house (that is, the house of a poor man) with his unnamed older sister and her daughter. He was an impenetrably humorless dolt who failed to comprehend oblique references and who performed literally whatever his sister jestingly told him to do. The first episode suggested that as a result of inability to interpret his sister's words, he played sexually with a rotting corpse and even laughed while amusing himself with it. In a second episode he clumsily attempted to make a canoe from a soft and rotten log, because he again misunderstood his sister's instructions. When the craft fell to pieces, he blamed men who were so kind as to make an unpromising attempt to launch it for him. In a third episode he again acted literally upon his sister's words. He hung on to a canoe and threw pulverized fish at the people in it. Then he spied on some widows who were defecating and collected their excrements. The myth accentuated that facet of Blue Jay which was a literal-minded, incompetent, and anally fixated blockhead; he was defective either to the extreme of psychosis or in the direction of feeble-mindedness.

In myth 34 he was a heartless tease who entered the story briefly to annoy and mock a nearly blind man; in myth 46 he was also pitiless, and was an impatient fool. He impersonated a weeping blind boy's long-lost older brother. Neither this blind boy nor the blind man of myth 34 was hoodwinked, but both resented the attempt at deception. When Blue Jay re-entered myth 46, he was the precipitate fool, as well as the villain, who wanted to achieve successful separation of Siamese twins who would have divided naturally and lived had he left them alone. When everyone else wept in mourning for them, he was unable to cry. He was truly a psychopathic personality who could not feel and was unable even to pretend that he could. Accordingly, in order to display a suitable amount of grief, he went to an old woman and purchased a "cry formula" which allowed him to weep. Shortly afterward he stumbled, ostensibly because he was clumsy, and at once forgot the formula for crying.

In myth 43 a group of villagers crossed the river to kill Crawfish Girl and her older sister Seal, because Blue Jay overheard Crawfish yelling. Again Blue Jay was pitiless. He killed Crawfish with a blow of his crest. Gluttony and cruelty led him to extract and eat the tiny one and a half fish hearts in the girl's stomach.

In myth 23 he was only a cheat. He was the one villager who tried to bluff the headman in a test of village men to determine which one had firewood that burned longest and was therefore father of the headman's daughter's child.

In myth 13 Blue Jay's personality was not directly characterized, but he was appropriately a follower of an evil headman. The headman sent Blue Jay to invite two visiting youths to come and gamble, and the younger youth cast a flame which burned Blue Jay's eyes. They became "turned." Later, during gambling, Blue Jay playfully or teasingly offered a moistened finger to the youth's grizzly pup, which at once bit off the finger. Introduction of Blue Jay in this drama seems to have been primarily to allow an explanation of his physical appearance.

In other myths Blue Jay appeared briefly in each instance as a device which served to awaken associations with droll facets of his personality. In such myths cruelty seemed to interest the audience less than blockheadness, fumbling, and disagreeable intruding. In myth 6 he was merely mentioned as a resident of an end house; the indication of low status was degrading and therefore warranted laughter at him. In myth 7 he was the person who was so unamiable as to express displeasure because Crow Woman had been invited to the spirit-power dance. Although his objection to her was reasonable, because she used excrements as a hair pomade, his disapproval was cruel in the light of her excellence as a kindly old person.

In myth 26 the guardian hostess of Seal Hunter hauled in a string to which a feather of Blue Jay was attached at her end. A pull on the string indicated that her departing guests, who included Blue Jay, had navigated safely beneath sky shutters.

The reason for employing Blue Jay's feather was nowhere suggested; the citation may add nothing to knowledge of his personality.

The details which characterized Blue Jay displayed a juvenile. Like Grizzly Woman and Flint Man, he was almost or entirely lacking in conscience; he was at once complex and immature; his intelligence was more often deficient than serviceable. Equally interesting is the manner of describing his drives: since he was warped and youthful, he acted out his urges in culturally disapproved ways. He was never indicated as genitally developed or adult. In other words, he was a composite of various immaturities and deficiencies whose traits were exaggerated so that they were especially amusing. Possibly every auditor had a lurking awareness of his own more controlled predispositions of the same kinds.

Blue Jay probably had a strong oral drive, especially to steal foods, but the present collection does not offer good documentation for this trait. The stories also do not stress a sexual drive in spite of the suggestion in the story where he spied on defecating widows—in this case, stress was on anality and stupidity rather than sexuality. He was not so much unrepressed as he was a clumsy boy of adult age who, because he lacked self-confidence and courage, needed to exhibit prowess. Where he could not flaunt his superiority, he lied and claimed it. After every victory, whether a result of unearned and dishonest winnings of his own or the success of covillagers, he shrieked, bragged raucously, strutted, and claimed falsely that he and his people could do even better; his hyperactivity was given free rein only at the times when it was safest.

Clackamas must have sensed that such a personality included both irrepressible hostility to others and uneasiness about competence. Blue Jay's loyalty was opportunistic gang allegiance which served to protect but not to satisfy him. Although his hostility to outsiders was well documented and although he displayed pugnacity, aggression, and incapacity for affection, he could hurt only non-villagers because he was a cowardly rather than a faithful member of the gang. It was only outside the sphere of his allegiance, when he was unlikely to be hurt, that his aggression took the form of cruelty and murder. In brief, he was a nasty, foolish, incompetent, humorless, affectionless, chronically hostile, dishonest, exhibitionistic, and murderous juvenile of a most hyperactive kind.

One of the interesting features of this depiction of a hoodlum and humbug resides in Clackamas acceptance and enjoyment of him. He was the principal clown of the literature: he served as an effective dramatic device, providing a moment of light relief or distraction in a drama. On the other hand, he rarely played a decisive role. He was a titillating appendage, a minor actor. Perhaps a borrowing from coastal literatures accounts for this manner in which he was added to rather than centered in plots. The type that he represented must have been intriguing because it symbolized chronic hostility and fear of ineptitude or immaturity. His behavior permitted Clackamas to laugh at themselves and to relieve some latent anxieties; that may be why he came to play an important role in the literature as a whole.

Jay Bird.—This actor, who appeared only in myths 25 and 26, represented a man who, as occasion called, co-operated with or scolded his older brother. And the brother was Blue Jay. It is as if the clown were so overpowering an entertainer that in the course of generations of community thinking he had developed a sidekick who played straight man in the comedy, offset his extravagances, and enhanced his outrageousness. The dramatic function of Jay Bird did not clash with his personality; he was a man whose sibling loyalty coincided with freedom to chide. Clackamas knew siblings who were like Jay Bird. Although the story characterizations presented only a few strokes of personality delineation, more were unnecessary because Jay Bird stood only for the sober brother who tried to hold his grotesque kin in check. In myth 25, when he was Blue Jay's companion in youthful rascality, he was the loyal brother; in myth 26 he was the brother who reprimanded. No specific traits of personality can be deduced, only a phrase or two about the sibling relationship that the culture approved. Scoldings which Jay Bird leveled at his ridiculous and irresponsible brother expressed values and sibling duties, on the one hand, and an undercurrent of awareness of minor sibling tension, on the other. In addition, a stylization complicates the picture: Jay Bird was the younger sibling, and the motif of youngest-smartest therefore also pressured a raconteur to present Jay Bird as wiser and more mature.

Skunk.—Although Skunk was a lesser actor, raconteurs offered in him a deft sketching of a distinctive type of personality. In myth 1 his brother Coyote deceived and exploited him in a story which stressed Skunk's weakness, dependency, and subservience to a rascally brother. He was also a feeble hunter who procured nothing more nutritious than the yellowjackets which he shared with Coyote.

In myth 5 he engaged in mock and hypocritical mourning with his fearful and guilty brother, Coyote, who had committed murder. The myth again noted Skunk's dependency and lack of self-identity, although it did not suggest that Coyote exploited him. In myth 9 the characterization was consistent with drawings in myths 1 and 5. With his usual passivity, Skunk agreed to exchange anuses with Coyote.

In myth 19 additional strokes of characterization indicated stupidity and masochism. Skunk's fatuity was exemplified in his misunderstanding the morpheme for "breast meat" so that he pulled out his "teeth" and returned with them in his pack. The leading traits of personality in the several stories in which he appeared were sibling loyalty, weak dependency, inability to hunt like a man, correlated poverty of intellect, and matter-of-fact anality.

Clackamas regarded Skunk as especially funny because of his atrocious odor, which connected with his superlative capacity for aggressive flatus, his habit of living where fallen and therefore largely useless wood was decaying, his feeble talent for hunting, his generally inept actions, and his harmlessness—his gassing caused unconsciousness but was not lethal. The characterization in myth 19, which adds stresses upon suggestibility, stupidity, and masochism, was also funny because such traits in themselves amused Clackamas. A foolish and incompetent person was *ipso facto* funny. In all likelihood the Skunks embodied projections of feelings about lower-class people, followers of headmen, and younger brothers.

No Skunk Woman was mentioned in the collection. In only one myth was Skunk married, and there was no indication of the identity of his mate.

Grizzly.—Depictment of his personality is based upon appearances in seven myths. In myth 6 five Grizzly brothers swam across the river to fight Panther, but only the youngest and most ferocious reached him. They dismembered each other in a lethal duel. The play stressed the anger of male siblings because of loyalty to their blind grandmother and fury at theft of fires which she tended for them. The story also emphasized the fighting ability of a Grizzly. Perhaps, too, the story reinforced religious ideology, whatever it was, about grizzly spirit-powers.

Myth 7 exhibited only a Grizzly's cannibalism. He swallowed and killed a person, thereby representing the feelings of grizzly spirit-powers toward people and of some persons toward others. Later a weak and tiny Mudfish cut Grizzly's heart from within and killed him—poetic justice meted out to a monstrous murderer.

In myth 9 Grizzly ate women whom his wife, also a Grizzly, cooked for him. Subsequently he unwittingly ate his wife after Coyote had pushed her into the oven. The story again emphasized some people's murderous feelings, projected into the cannibalism of Grizzly and his awful wife.

In myth 14, which is interpreted in this book, another man who was represented as a Grizzly gouged out and swallowed his wife's eye, then ate her brothers. That is, some men were cruel to their wives, and unable to hold in leash feelings toward in-laws. Grizzly also really ruined his daughter because, as any daughter might, she introjected her father's viciousness.

Myth 36 exhibited another aspect of men like Grizzly. It showed the unattractiveness and extraordinary gullibility of four Grizzly brothers. Each was tempted by a tiny but smart Greyback Louse Woman to attend a dance and receive women as gifts. Grizzly Men therefore stood for dupes who were driven by sociability and vanity. The youngest Grizzly, who possessed the meanest disposition, was more fortunate than his brothers. He was sufficiently advised by Meadow Lark Woman, whom he encountered quite by chance, so that he alone learned how to dispose of Louse. In this manner Clackamas could explain why the most despicable man sometimes acquired a good spirit-power. Stresses were on some men's sociability, vanity, sexual desire, stupidity, potential anger without cause, and general suspiciousness. In myth 40 the focus was again on cannibalism: five male Grizzlies had vast spirit-power and ate people. As in myth 36, emphasis in myth 49, which noted another five Grizzlies, was on their gullibility and vanity.

The total picture of Grizzly Men therefore included two main facets which may have been originally distinct components that merged. One of them displayed uncontrollable aggression, expressed in rampant cannibalism, and minimal competency and standards; the other showed a less villainous disposition but still much hostility

to people, in a personality which was conscienceless, stupid, conceited, and credulous.

Grizzlies of both sexes top the list of creatures who were feared, hated, and convenient for scapegoating. I suggest that Grizzly actors therefore served as homologues of older persons and headmen. Clackamas displaced onto Grizzlies—both
spirit-powers and precultural actors—their essentially Oedipal feelings about the
elders and wealthy men who controlled their lives. Grizzlies were caricatures of such
dominating villagers.

Coon.—Coon appeared in at least three myths. In myth 3 he was a competent
hunter who lived with and contrasted with the incompetent Coyote who brought
only interdicted food. Coon was also a clever thief who retained what he stole when
his companion knew nothing about it. He was a fraud, with a sense of humor and
enough intelligence to keep the peace with his ineffectual and humorless companion.
In myth 49 he was again thieving and gluttonous. In addition, he lacked remorse;
he enjoyed torturing and killing Grizzly Men. However, his lack of generosity toward such persons is partially mitigated by the fact that his victims were bad people
and deserved such a fate, anyway.

In myth 6, which is analyzed in Part I, initial stress was on Coon's warm, un-
selfish, and resourceful parental behavior, later emphasis on his urge to poach, his
skill in stealing, and his capacity for compromises. But petty thieving and mendacity
were his inner nature more than capacity for fine parental service, and ultimately
he was foolish because he was a chronic marauder and liar. He was a troublemaker
whose impulses led to disaster. Although in myth 49 he was shrewd or brave enough
to torture one Grizzly after another, in myth 6 he lacked courage or endowment to
fight: Panther had to defend him. He was also absurd in his pretense that he could
provide food for Panther's son. But he wept with unfeigned grief when his brother
and nephew left him, and in myth 49 he also cried because of loneliness—maybe
degradation too—when his grandmother departed.

The three myths agreed in the patterning of a personality which possessed several
unfortunate drives: destructiveness, stealing, and lying. But Coon was bright, and
he could act with skill, certainly more so than the younger Coyote. He also had a
sense of humor. His conscience showed strengths in unselfishness with kin, loyalty
to and affection for a brother, and consummate handling of the brother's baby.
From one point of view, his murders of bad people seem unreprehensible, but supplementary torture of them was perhaps a defect, although Clackamas enjoyed vicarious aggression here because it was directed against the most feared creatures.
Clackamas may have meant to evaluate Coon as shrewd and in some fundamental
ways as good. He brought disaster upon himself and his family only because he was
careless and occasionally unable to control selfish and sadistic impulses. Perhaps he
was a projective representation of a kind of talented man whose occasional competence and goodness were admirable but who got himself and kindred into predicaments because of thoughtlessness, narcissism, and dishonesty. One may wonder

about an undisclosed meaning in his inclusion with Grizzly Men in two very different myths, but I cannot suggest an answer. No Coon Woman appeared in the collection.

Crane.—His personality was represented in two myths (16, 46) as one of the most attractive of precultural men. In a third story (9) he was merely one of the large and noisy birds who contributed to the din of audience singers during a doctoring séance. In that myth he was only a theater device, but in the two other myths he was a kindly and clever parent homologue, maybe also a projection of an ideal headman or well-to-do man who offered food, shelter, and safety from attack. He confounded villains by pitching them neatly into a river to drown. He was cool, courageous, confident, firm, mature, and hospitable. He encouraged no weakness, dependency, or immaturity. Those whom he assisted had to rely upon their own resources. His personality was so integrated and sturdy that he was unruffled by insults, and he had a fine sense of humor. He was so imbued with correct principles that he was relentless and punishing toward evildoers. He was the finest of hosts and the leading protector of young fugitives and orphans. It is this admired parental and headman-like role which characterized Crane in many other Northwest literatures, too. Perhaps no other personality except Coyote was drawn with so little change or showed so little remodeling by raconteurs from group to group in an extended area of the northwest states. The collection offered no Crane Woman, nor did it suggest that Crane was married.

Beaver.—The comparative picture of Beaver's personality may be suggested in the light of items in the two myths where a Beaver acted. In myth 26, Beavers were loyal comrades or followers of a headman who went on a canoe expedition to the Oregon coast. They were faithful handymen who dug holes, plugged a leak in a canoe, and cut through stout ropes. One courageous Beaver even offered himself as a living target for opponents to shoot at. In this myth Beavers were, to be sure, only supporting actors. Conceivably they were representations of loyal adherents of a well-to-do man.

But in myth 48 a Beaver, although a leading actor, played a stereotyped role of a pathetic older man whose spirit-power, if he had one, was inadequate to overcome an enemy. Later he became a devoted parent or grandparent homologue and so gave his spirit-power, that is himself, to the youth he reared. The narrator's verbalized design of a personality was meager, but the impression left is that of a kindly, loyal, and courageous person, an excellent father homologue, and a man who had a few special skills and some spirit-power. These traits were desirable in followers of headmen, and in any men. Possibly Clackamas had additional myths in which Beavers appeared, and if so a Beaver type of personality might have been deduced in more detail. No myth presented a Beaver Woman.

Panther.—Like Beaver, he appeared in only two myths (6, 18). In both he was the ideal well-to-do gentleman and the admirable lover and husband. His principal occupation was hunting. If two stories were sufficient evidence, his role highlighted the tragic fate which befalls the best of men because their relatives are less than perfect. He was a means, almost a stylized plot expediter, by which Clackamas expressed concern about the demerits of kin. To the food, affectional, security, and sex needs which psychoanalytic writers have underlined may be added, for Chinook peoples, a particularized security need for devoted, well-to-do, and competent relatives. Panther was not so much an individual Clackamas man as a symbol of an ideal man whose course through life was troubled by kin who were not what they ought to be. The depiction of familial situations was realistic; the sketching of the man was idealistic, without specific lineaments of the kind found in an everyday world.

No Panther Women were present in the collection, although Panther, unlike Beaver and Coon, was a married gentleman. He was much too masculine for some woman actor to have been accorded the name of Panther by a process of secondary association. Panther also had sons in the two myths, but no additional characterizations of Panther personality can be deduced from them. In this context, it is of interest that Coyote—who was as masculine, in his very different way, as Panther —had daughters.

Thunder.—Two myths spoke of male Thunders, none of females. In myth 30 a Thunder orally impregnated a well-to-do girl by urinating (that is, raining) upon her strips of basketry material. His son, Thunder Boy, grew with miraculous speed, and when he traveled away from his mother, as Clackamas youths did, he displayed his flint-eating mink spirit-power which killed Grizzly Women's grizzly-dogs. The story really told how a powerful shaman vanquished supernaturals of other great shamans. It ascribed shamanistic power to Thunder Boy with utmost exaggeration in order to dramatize his greatness, although he was a mere youth on his first solo journey. Later, when he acquired a two-faced Grizzly Ogress' head and hide as spirit-power paraphernalia and traveled with a Coyote, the story expressed a wishful fantasy. An auditor identified with a shaman of outstanding spirit-power who gave various demonstrations of supernaturals to his traveling companion.

In myth 40 five Thunders of progressively greater power were so defeated by Ku'šaydi at the entrances of their bearlike dens that lightning would not burn Indians later on.

The two stories were not contradictory, because they presented allegorically a segment of the ideology of spirit-power. The stories showed a portion of a shaman's notion of his identification with and abilities acquired from especially potent supernaturals. Possibly no other myths point so effectively to the projection mechanisms and kind of wishful identification which distinguished a shaman's personality, to such a person's need to have power which could kill other persons (that is, destroy their spirit-powers), and to the manner in which a shaman's value-ideals were woven into his self-identity and fantasy system. A shaman could be at once safe—because he was able to murder competitors—and compassionate to a dishonest but harmless man—in this case, Coyote. A shaman was therefore an admirable person who was capable of both murder and the utmost of mercy.

Although the stories disclose something of the way in which a shaman's self was constructed, since shamans were only an extreme in a continuum of persons, the stories also indicate everyone's aspirations and the mechanisms in supernaturally well-endowed people. The stories really divulge community discussions about the kind of person which a shaman might be, and they thereby point to needs, wishes, and processes in all the people. Of course everyone wanted to have relationships with supernaturals which would permit the accomplishment of wonderful things. Men wanted to travel with impunity. Any person would have liked to live in a marvelous home like Thunder's one in the sky, visit mother whenever he wanted to, and protect and feed dishonest but entertaining old men like Coyote.

Salmon.—Clackamas culture resembled in many respects both coastal and interior or Plateau cultures. Along the ocean front Tillamooks, for example, regarded Salmon as an outstanding precultural actor. The ideology of interior peoples was extremely different, but dependence upon salmon was considerable too, in spite of the lack of an important Salmon actor. Therefore it is not surprising that the two Clackamas myths in which a Salmon is presented have no apparent common denominator of personality traits for Salmon. In fact, myth 5 itself is difficult to explain because of unclear and terse depictions of Salmons. Wolves murdered Salmon at the behest of his grandfather, Coyote. Salmon's son, who may be identified as Steelhead, was raised by Crow Women, who were of lower class. Because he was a Salmon too, he took vengeance upon Coyote, then married his murdered father's widow. She was disguised, in an easily perceived defense mechanism, as his stepmother. Salmons, father and son, Coyote, and the widow seem to have been no more than the personnel of a transparent Oedipal theme. The main traits of personality that can be deduced are the universal feelings found in a familial triangle, and Clackamas seem to have been as prone as any peoples to allegorize the participants. The story shows how Clackamas, who identified with young Salmon or Steelhead, regarded a father, acted by Coyote, and what they felt about these two actors: a father would kill his son, fake feelings of grief, and relate to various liegemen in order to maintain inner security; as for the son, the younger Salmon, he would shake every bone out of such a father, marry his mother, cause all her other lovers—represented by Wolves—to be nearly parched to death with thirst, and drown them in water underneath his mother's very genitals. Then because of her relationships to all these parent homologues, he would punish her by hurling her upon a bluff to die in the hot sun and threaten her with filthy Crows who would gouge out her eyes to eat them; after so gratifying himself because of his anger, he would float her down upon the wings of magnificent birds, heal her with curing water, and wind up by marrying her. In brief, young Salmon was any man who struck back at the parent of same sex.

In myth 8 Salmon, or Coyote in another version, represented a very different personality. He was a deity-like headman who made fundamental decisions. These were significantly about foods, and they supplied answers to intellectual and anxious inquiry concerning the food resources upon which the people's security depended. The myth really discloses wishful feelings which Clackamas had about headmen and fathers who took primary responsibility for procurement of food. The vengeful Salmon son exploded in wrath against his father; his fury against his maternal consort of Wolves was relieved after he struck out against her; but his feelings were not necessarily contradictory with the sentiments ascribed to the headman-like father, the older Salmon, who planned foods which would save apprehensive persons' lives in successive seasons. Important men were also human.

Sturgeon.—This minor actor appeared in three myths. Nothing which may have represented a feature of personality seems present in myth 8. In myth 9, however, Sturgeon offered his body as delicious food for Coyote, who there represented any man of the village as well as one of the preculturals who did important things for the people. In myth 26 Sturgeon again offered food, not his own body but his wife's baked carcass. In another scene which seems not to connect with the preceding repast, he was a thief who absconded with artifacts belonging to an unsuspecting woman. One may query whether the various elements in the three Sturgeon scenes pieced together. There is nothing that can be cited to controvert the reasonableness, to Clackamas, of a man who bilked a woman, was a burglar, and participated in basic food production for the village. A man could be despicable and still be a recipient of the most wanted supernaturals. Elements that feel contradictory in Western civilization were fused in normal Chinook personalities. The most essential thing about Sturgeon is that, like headmen, he stood for one of the providers of food. His treatment of women is also of interest in its support of other evidences of the low regard for females.

Dog.—Attitudes toward dogs in the region around Chinooks were, as in Clackamas, that dogs, whether male or female, constituted exceedingly inferior supernaturals, conferred little spirit-power, and were filthy although useful allies. They were associated with excrements, contact with which was humiliating. Five stories, four myths and a tale, mentioned a dog. In myth 16 a dog, whose sex was irrelevant to the narrative, was not a person but the loyal pet which misdirected Grizzly so as to allow Bear Boys more time in flight from her. She kicked the dog viciously, in a manner which probably did not horrify Clackamas as much as it would Euroamericans. In myth 28 a dog was again not a person but an animal which a well-to-do girl substituted for herself as a bride. She did it in order to shame the man who should have been her husband because he purchased her in marriage.

Reference to dogs was entirely different in myth 30. Thunder Boy's supernatural was a mink which he metamorphosed into a dog named Chews Flints. It was so powerful that it killed Grizzly Woman's five mighty grizzly-dogs. In myth 32 an angry father killed and served a dog to his returning married daughter in order to express utter rejection of her. The dog was her pet, but her meal of dog was the most extreme indignity she could be made to suffer. Tale 65 was again of another kind. It was about a Clackamas girl who ill-advisedly related to her pet as if it were a person.

I deduce from the stories and sundry ethnographic observations on Clackamas and adjacent peoples that an intensity of response to excrements was decisive, not dogs as such or their sex. The problem, regarding which I can offer no useful suggestion, is to account for horror and shame about contact with excrements. An answer might be given if sufficient ethnographic materials had been obtained and if there were reports of Clackamas handling of and feelings about dogs.

Elk.—In myth 1 Elk was a helpful visitor who felt badly that Skunk was ill. Elk's ridiculous credulity caused his own death. Myth 6 accounted for his acquisition of antlers and offered no more about him. Myth 25 displayed Elk as a ponderous victim of little Wren, who easily penetrated body apertures and chewed Elk's heart fat. Since myth data on Elk are spare not only for Chinooks but for most northwest states peoples, and since ethnographic information about feelings toward elk is almost entirely absent, one wonders if Elk represented not only a desired food and source of leather but also a dull and unsuspicious person who was easily killed, perhaps by use of lethal spirit-power which, like Wren (25), entered the body and ate upon vital organs.

The minor roles which Deer and Elk played in the region's literatures and spirit-power ideology contrast with the strategic economic position of deer and elk. One therefore wonders why such basic food and artifact resources were allegorized so palely, and why various unnamed myth actors did not in course of time have the names "Deer" and "Elk" ascribed to them. On the other hand, the unimportant roles of deer and elk in Clackamas literature are consonant with the minor parts played by Salmon and Sturgeon, also important foods. Camas and berries, which were major foods too, were virtually ignored as actors in the literature. In short, one might deduce that important foods either were not anthropomorphized at all or were allowed negligible dramatic roles. Major actors such as Coyote, the Grizzlies, Skunk, and Coon were either untouched as foods or of small economic import.

Flea.—Flea persons acted in two myths, although fleas were cited as mere vermin in other stories. In myth 9 people sent Flea through matting in order to spy on Coyote. The sole point is that a Flea was appropriate because he was tiny, fast, and addicted to close body contact. In myth 46 the hero met Flea Men, killed them, and announced their future harmlessness. The two stories tell almost nothing beyond the presence of the familiar process of anthropomorphization of creatures and their relegation as persons to a precultural epoch. Fleas may have been competent or dangerous then because early peoples lacked the knowledge and skills of moderns. I cannot find a plausible answer to the question why other vermin were feminine and fleas masculine, except for the thought that fleas were exceptionally mobile.

Many male actors who were on the stage in only one story can be bypassed in this book's discussions in order to allow the reader to observe the essentials of the method of analysis without burdening him with its details. I shall therefore withhold, perhaps until a later publication which is specifically on Chinook and is directed to specialists in Northwest anthropology, mention of the personality lineaments of gullible people named Doe, Buck, and Horned Buck (1); several Coyotes' grandsons (2, 4); hill folk named Mountain Cannibals (4); Rabbit, a shaman (7); a poor person, Fuel Carrier, who lacked sense (9); a man who had an enormously long penis (9); and a great many others. But a few male actors who, like Flint (18), are present in only a single story disclose such important information about personality traits that they ought to be commented upon. Flint, a striking male actor, has been discussed in Part I. Wren (25) can be selected from the long list of actors in single stories now.

Wren.—He was a boy whose stages of development from childish pranks to adult genitality and conscience were symbolized by sadistic treatment of animal persons: playful killing of the stupid Elk, almost conscienceless observation of his lecherous grandmother's sexuality with Elk's organ, and awakening of genital interest which was quickly expressed in a wish for a slave girl. He became so absorbed in sex that he accepted his grandmother's offer to satisfy him. As soon as people discovered his incestuous escapade with her, he developed awareness of his people's values and tossed her away. In nearly conventional fashion he shortly bought what he supposed was a young wife and then divested himself of her, again with societal values in mind, when he discovered that he had been tricked into purchasing his grandmother. The two central themes were the levels of sexual development in a youth and his acquiring of standards in sex and marriage. Drives which operated in these two important facets of personality were of central interest for a native audience, not depiction of a youth's personality as a whole. On the other hand, Wren was a useful caricature of emotional growth in any young fellow. His immaturity, development of affect, and increasing interest in being respectable were neatly stressed in the play.

Canoemaker and Seal Hunter.—Canoemaker represented a sibling who used spirit-powers to try to kill his younger brother, Seal Hunter, in a nice demonstration of sibling tension (26). The younger brother, as often in a society which glamorized the younger sibling on its fantasy screen, was the brave man who survived murderous hatred because of his spirit-power and his followers' loyalty. Neither sibling was really delineated, only the roles they acted out, although a trait or two of the younger man of wealth comes through in the course of his adventures. For example, he responded like any Clackamas man in his acceptance of a woman's offer of sexual hospitality.

The recitalist was interested not in the personalities of Seal Hunter's liegemen but in their loyal relationship to him; absence of mention of feelings of such a leader toward his followers implies either that etiquette or cultural restraint impeded phrasings about such matters or that headmen took followers' services and attachment for granted and felt secure in such adherence. Nothing in the literature points to suspicions or uncertainties in headmen toward dependents or villagers. As far as overt evidence goes, the sentiments of security of a headman such as Seal Hunter were threatened by polygynous wives, sons, kin, other headmen, in-laws, spirit-powers, or people of other villages, not by male household retinue or by male covillagers outside the household.

Two hunters.—These unnamed actors represented lonely unmarried men who acquired spirit-powers because they expressed desire for companionship (27, 29). A significant item may be the one hunter's (27) securing a female supernatural. She was a bad person because she murdered his potential wives; but the other desolate hunter's (29) new spirit-power was good because it was a male who was responsible for bringing his wife to him. However, two such instances do not necessarily point to lesser desirability of female supernaturals, since an example of an excellent feminine spirit-power, Seal Hunter's guardian hostess, can be cited (26). Paranoid-like anxiety, suspicion, and spying on the intruder marked each hunter's initial responses to the supernatural person who had come to him, but such behavior may not have been foreign in a society of hunters, some few of whom occasionally lived apart from settlements. Cautious observation of strangers by lonely men points to aloneness, not psychological aberrancy: suspicion dissipated when the new arrival was no longer strange. Nor was concern about the new supernatural unrealistically intruded by a psychologically naïve storyteller. Since a supernatural was an expression of one's needs and wishes, suspicion of that supernatural must have developed frequently because of criticism by the Superego, to use the shortcut terminology of Freudians. Storytellers treated psychological mechanisms in their own way, but they were essentially sound in what they stressed.

Cock Robin.—He was so stupid a youth that he baked his sister's infant daughter, but he was smart enough to steal salmon left on a beach by fishermen and to eat it without sharing it with his sister (31). Traits implied include many that appeared in Blue Jay. The emphases in Cock Robin were on stupidity, cupidity, heartlessness, failure to share food, incorrect relationship to a sibling, excessive orality or gluttony, and absence of conscience. These were Clackamas indications of immaturity, in a culture which, I think, placed greater value upon maturity than does Western civilization and which fashioned a number of Myth Era projections to show for us its concern about its many unsatisfactory youths. It laughed at such nuisances to relieve its concern about individuals who were really dangerous when they were not merely irritating.

Gi'ckux *and his older brother.*—Two exceptionally full portraits of personalities are found in these men (34). *Gi'ckux* was a loyal sibling, a devoted father homologue to his brother's children, a man of invariable courage, generosity, and compassion. His older brother at first suffered paralysis of will due to fear of his Grizzly wife and concern for his sons by his first wife. Later, when the first wife had been killed by her co-wife, Grizzly—and with the help of still another spouse, his third—he was enabled to take initiative and do what was necessary to vanquish the Grizzly wife. He transformed into a good and firm husband. His life presented a first stage of weakness and a second of adequacy and strength, influenced by his fine third wife.

Ku'šaydi and his older brother.—These siblings offer two of the best depictions of the collection (40). *Ku'šaydi* was a pregenital youth, a conscienceless narcissist of indomitable spunk, with boundless drive to kill everyone except the older brother whom he threatened, insulted, and used mercilessly. The youngster also exhibited excessive oral needs, that is, immaturity of another kind. The older brother typified an important value, sibling loyalty and devotion. He was steadfast no matter how criminally intolerable the younger brother's acts or how extreme the maltreatment to which he was subjected. He accompanied the horrible young daredevil until the latter's death.

Tongue.—He represented a murderer (42), like Flint and *Ku'šaydi*. But, like Grizzly people, he was cannibalistic or primarily orally fixated, unlike Flint and *Ku'šaydi*, who killed in other ways. His explosive anger was touched off by an oral mutilation, *Ku'šaydi*'s by any person of authority or strength, Flint's by a slight or rejection. Tongue, *Ku'šaydi*, and any Grizzly shared hatred and need to kill. They seem to have been projections consequent upon a general anxiety about waylayings and murders by non-villagers, lethal hatreds sensed in some persons of one's own community, and awareness that shamans poisoned people. Competitiveness and hatreds were intense in this slave-owning and wealth-seeking society whose members gained by destroying others with a technique of humiliation and use of supernaturals. The society held together because of a machinery of headmen who utilized dependents, levied fines, and offered effective father-like protection and sustenance in time of need. Destructiveness was thereby minimized, angry persons held in check, and everyone's security cushioned.

Tongue's stepson.—This unnamed actor represented a youth whom the judicious and correctly opportunistic mother reared properly in order that he might acquire supernaturals who would permit her to resolve her intolerable bond with Tongue. Her son was not really delineated. He was the heroic youth who was shocked by murders of his mother's people and who patiently accumulated and nurtured supernaturals that would allow him to right wrongs against his kin and to eliminate his paternal homologue, Tongue. His response when people humiliated him by unfair accusations was culturally standard, in all likelihood. He simply left such bad people. The delineation also indicated his stages of growth from childhood to hunting skills and then to adult acquisition of supernaturals. Clackamas literature expressed in various biographic sketchings a strong evaluation upon maturation out of an untutored childhood when one had not yet "found" a supernatural.

The youth who traveled in the sky country.—In a long myth (46) the unnamed hero was presented chronologically in stages of development from babyhood to parenthood. Culturally regular wanderings of youths became, in him, fabulous adventures with a Basket Ogress, Crane Man, Vermin people, Sky Cannibals, and so on. He typified a normal upper-class young male who obtained spirit-powers as such young gentlemen would and should. He did the right things as a child, youth, and married man and was undistinctive in personality. But as every male wished, he had extraordinary experiences before his return with spirit-powers, wife, and children. In the myth he came back to his parents' settlement. He was always normal, colorless, and correct, but no male in other stories of the collection had so many remarkable chapters in his life.

A Clackamas hero, that is, a most admired and supernaturally fortunate upper-class man, was never exceptional in the ways a hero was supposed to be in Western civilization. He was the most approved of headmen, or he was a chief's fine son and supernaturally well-endowed successor to the chieftainship. Lack of a projective concept of a deity connected, I think, with a number of factors in family and social life, and not least with the absence of conceptualization of a European-like hero. Since only the wealthy and proper man was idealized, no heroic projective figure of another kind could have greater desirability. The sketch of Coyote was more realistic than that of the traveling youth, in spite of fanciful escapades and ogres, because it contained more insights into a youth's and young man's feelings, and it went on to scenes from an older man's life. Treatment of the peripatetic youth of myth 46 was fuller only in childhood items. Its spareness in details of emotional experiences suggests that it may have been a novelette more recently worked over and elaborated by discussants and narrators. They could also have theorized upon it without a barrage of stimulation by contiguous peoples, all of whom possessed closely related acts and scenes of the Coyote comedy-drama (9).

Sky Cannibal.—The Sky Cannibal Hunter of one myth (46) was not as strikingly characterized as his daughters, but he may have been pregenital and pre-anal—as suggested by his girls' lack of excretory orifices. Sky Cannibals were oral and filthy, and the father was in addition a murderer. Hill or upriver peoples of poorer economy and the Clackamas anxieties about such groups no doubt reinforced the image of a Cannibal in precultural eras. One might suggest that that concept had to do with a fairly manifest feeling that, since the Sky Cannibal must have contained excrements which he could not void, he was so unclean within that he could not relate to a good spirit-power. Therefore he must have lacked proper supernaturals to aid him. He acted with especial aggression, as people would who were dirty, deficient in supernatural relatives, humiliated, and frustrated. Chinooks must have known how deeply angry a person was if he lacked a single spirit-power. A Chinook in such a predicament was probably a crushed and dependent person of low class. In the Myth Age such a person did what Chinooks supposed he really wanted to do: murder, eat people, and use their anatomical parts.

It seems to me that the fantasy of Sky Cannibals could have evolved in a kind of vicious circle of consciously phrased premises, one of which tended to develop and reinforce the other and all of which were bolstered by latent feelings of great intensity. I think that we can indicate some of these. There was fear of and hostility to uphill and upriver villages whose small bands lacked wealth and rich headmen. Such peoples were therefore of low class. That is, they were dirty. They were hardly able to fish and hunt deer and elk. They could not do things well. Their status, from the Chinooks' ethnocentric point of view, connected with excrements—as witnessed in depictions of Crow Women in several myths. But some interior or upriver peoples were so much more filthy than Crow Women that they must have retained excrements inside them. Therefore they lacked the needed excretory orifice. Like modern Snake Indians east of the Cascades, Sky Cannibals killed travelers. It follows that probably they ate, dismembered, and flayed Chinooks. And in northwest states Indian logic, whatever probably happened certainly transpired. They must have done it. Therefore they definitely did it. Because they were low-class and incompetent hunters, lacking in supernaturals and perpetually humiliated with retention of excrements, they must be unceasingly angry at good people like us.

I do not urge that these were even many of the items, much less the very sequence of notions and feelings, in the life history of a concept and attitude. We cannot reconstruct its evolution. But I hope that I have given some exemplification of the pyramiding and buttressing of factors which eventuated in the Sky Cannibal. When he was presented by a narrator, only a few delineative strokes had to be employed, because audience imagery and feelings about such a creature were replete with supporting materials on various levels of awareness. His pregenitality and fixation at an oral sadistic level may have been the least consciously articulated of all the things about him. One cannot doubt that community theorization about him continued uninterruptedly through the decades and was bolstered by the anxieties and sundry attitudes toward Indian bands in backwoods country and in districts east of the Cascades.

The mean boy.—A deserted mean boy (47) exemplifies a fantasy construct or literary category of disagreeable or difficult children of either sex. Mountain Cannibal Girl (4), Crawfish Girl (43), Grizzly Boy and Half Grizzly Foot Girl (14), Wren (25), Flint Boys (18), Sky Cannibal Girls (46), *Ku'šaydi* (40), two disobedient youths who were murdered (35), and a number of children in tales (55, 56, 66) also point to feelings of annoyance with troublesome children. In the characteristic manner of the recital style, many traits of the mean boy (47) were not listed by the evening's storyteller. It is significant that the trait singled out for mention was oral aggression. The boy ate the "lunches" of his playmates. A traumatic desertion by parents, kin, and villagers, and the boy's resultant pitiable situation, generated courageous and resourceful responses in him. He acquired a supernatural and presently became a wealthy husband and father. He was generous to poor persons who had been kind to him when he was an unattractive child, but he was merciless toward all those who had left him to die. He was a male Cinderella who also illustrated the developmental stages motif.

Profile.—The Profile ogre (48) seems to have constituted a caricature of a cripple like the sketch of the Flint dwarf (18). A one-legged, one-armed person might be a chronic hater and thoroughgoing sadist. Nor was stress only on oral sadism: Profile took almost all the trout obtained by the good man, Beaver. Emphasis was on other kinds of sadism, too; the ogre resorted to violent corporal punishment when he belabored Beaver and nearly drowned him, and he also caused a flood by his voluminous urination. It was terrifying in its association with death because it was blood red and because he ducked Beaver repeatedly in the bloody waters. Profile's frenzy therefore also included destructive and punishing use of urine and death threats. Such anger was especially scary because Profile's motive to act against so decent a gentleman as Beaver was not suggested. He seems to have been any cripple who lashed out at anyone. Clackamas must have known horrible people like Profile and sensed that some persons felt like that toward everyone.

2. FEMALE PERSONALITY TRAITS

Over a hundred female actors crossed the stage; they ranged from named to unnamed, from those few who were provided a number of strokes of delineation to the many—such as slave women—who appeared briefly without a single characteristic to distinguish them from a type. Not one actor in a myth bears the mark of representing a historical, or remembered, person. Most female actors, like males, were upper class, and the narrator remarked when an actor was poor or slave. Although some notable female actors had names such as Basket Ogress, Bear, Grizzly, Seal, Meadow Lark, and Water Bug, a number of almost equally striking actors who appeared in only one myth lacked names. As with male actors, one wonders if unnamed ones correlated with relatively recently devised or borrowed myths, named actors with myths possessed over a longer time. Miss Sally Snyder has remarked to me that her initial determinations of provenience and tentative comparisons of myths from both sides of the Cascades in northern Washington indicate that names of fauna known only east of the mountains did not adhere to actors when myths about them were narrated in groups who lived west of the range. Long ago Professor Franz Boas also commented upon this simple phenomenon. The causes for presence or absence of some Clackamas actors' names might be revealed if we had adequate story collections from contiguous districts with different ecologies.

In the following assembly of personality traits in female actors, the first cited are named actors who appeared in more than one myth.

Grizzly.—The male actors who appeared most frequently, Blue Jay and Coyote, were a clown and a somewhat realistic portrait of a well-to-do man. Female actors whom narrators spoke of most frequently (if Mrs. Howard was representative of narrators) were a wholly bad type of person named *Ki'cimani*, which I cannot translate but which was the personal name of every precultural female identified with Grizzly people. Assuredly each *Ki'cimani* represented not a known person or type but the culture's judgments and sentiments about certain kinds of women. Just as

"Uncle Sam" and "John Bull" are caricatures of a type, so *Ki'cimani* or "Grizzly" was a caricature, or rather a horrible parody of what Clackamas perceived in many wives and maternal figures. She functioned as a scapegoat who permitted winter-long public ventilations of feelings toward purchased female commodities and maternal surrogates.

Only adult females were real Grizzlies. One girl (14) had the potential to become a Grizzly but did not arrive at that fearsome estate until long after her marriage. This fact fits well with what the literature clearly shows about Clackamas depreciation and distrust of older women. A relative neutrality in sentiments about younger married women and mothers is not sharply indicated, but Clackamas regard for prepubescent females is strikingly shown by the sketching of little Water Bug (17) and is evinced in other stories, too. It is safe to say that, in general, the older the female, the less she was liked.

Just as a Sky Cannibal concept was compounded of and supported by a variety of feelings, so feelings about older women should not be left explained as a simple response to Oedipal factors. I believe that whatever was primary in attitudes toward such women was supported or complicated by residence customs which were very likely patrilocal in most instances of their actualization, by the status of the feminine sex, and by disciplinary assignments which women carried out. In addition, many older women lived in their husbands' villages, where, because they were residents in a network of aliens and in-laws, not of their kin, they acted out their insecurities in sundry and special ways. They felt distrust and antagonism toward the in-laws and reacted accordingly.

Women's feelings were represented in the literature by a variety of feminine actors, but the repetitions of unattractive females such as Grizzly Women indicate an emphasis in the culture. Patrilocal residence supported Oedipal patterns, feminine lower status, and other factors in maintaining the literature's prevailing treatment of some older females, among whom Grizzly Women were outstanding. The more favorable depictions of younger females may reflect, among other variables, residence in their home village and anxieties that had not yet been quickened. Young women had not yet gone to live with their husbands' strange people; they were not yet objects of suspicion, nor were they controlling still younger persons who were only half theirs.

For the scholar whose curiosities lead him in the direction of historical reconstruction or evolution, the possibility arises that Clackamas were for some time in process of merging historically different Grizzly Woman actors. These may have been consolidated to such an extent that in the modern period a single personality type was intended for creatures termed "Grizzly Women," although treatment of them varied.

In spite of the fact that in myth 3 the narrator employed actors whom she called "Grizzly Women," they were no more than plot expediters. They were bad only because they hoarded water creatures and prevented them from dwelling in rivers. That is, older women kept important things from people. There was a latent stress on oral needs and on the interest which certain women had in controlling such matters. In one scene of myth 9 a Grizzly who was married to a cannibal Grizzly Man killed human women whom she had forced to collect the greens needed for the oven in which she cooked them. Again emphasis was on orality.

In myth 14 raconteurs sketched the development of a girl's personality which at the start was apparently human. A Grizzly-like drive to kill was kept under control because of early identification with a weak but principled mother; the killer component, which was due to early identification with a Grizzly father and brother, burst through at long last when the girl's two sons reached puberty. Stress was therefore on gradual development of dominance of drive, that is, spirit-power and inner need, to kill people. Clackamas would have rationalized about the nature and power of such a force by asserting that it was determined by the girl's early contiguity to an elder—here her father—who had such a supernatural or was that kind of person. Actually, Clackamas were saying in this myth that women get more Grizzly-like as they get older.

The statement of a Grizzly personality in myth 16 was analytic rather than developmental. It was really a projection of feelings about many women. Grizzly was psychotic. She had intense maternal feeling, which Clackamas accepted as characteristic of females, even the worst of them. But this Grizzly had no affection toward persons other than her offspring. She was not merely a bundle of dangerous drives with constant need to kill; she lusted ravenously for human and other foods; she was so stupid, like many older women, that her drives sometimes got under way slowly; and her orgies of murder and voracity were supplemented by scheming and sadism to an extreme of madness. Furthermore, she was vain about her appearance. She was so disgusting, stupid, and insane that she used her menstrual flow as facial paint. In other words, her awareness of reality was capricious. Although devoid of ideals, she determined the future of each kind of tree, in a final episode of deity-like work which might be assigned to anyone who had an effective spirit-power. She did it arbitrarily and by subjective whim because her reactions were emotional responses to flattery or lack of it.

A similar structuring of an ogress was implicit in myth 17. Again she was a murderous psychotic under a mask of wifely pretense. In addition the myth suggested, with notable insight, a special sort of communication of feelings between her and a little girl whom she feared and hated.

Myth 30 added several descriptive concepts. Grizzly unfairly accused the youth she met of wanting sexual intercourse with her at once. In other words, like the Clackamas stereotype of women, she projected her sexual wish onto a male. The myth also presented a fifth Grizzly as a doubly terrifying psychotic because she had two faces, one in front and the other in back. Again derogation of women was represented, and here with especial exaggeration. No male actor had two faces.

The inventory of traits in myth 31 was brief and repeated other stories. Grizzly was a mother with a baby, but she was also a killer. Again she believed that males wanted her for immediate sexual intercourse. In my opinion, the Grizzly concept

applied primarily or originally to somewhat older women, but unnumbered generations of discussants had allowed an extension of the stereotype to cover any married women. Since women are nubile from the teens to the forties or later, one must
not suppose that citation of a Grizzly with a baby necessarily meant a very young
woman.

Treatment of a Grizzly personality in myth 34 was comparatively detailed and
subtle. She symbolized a polygynous second wife who displayed wild jealousy and
murderous fury toward her husband's first wife; because of her need to identify herself as that wife, she flayed and wore the skin of the murdered woman. This is the
only story in the literature which pointed strongly to preference for the position of
first wife in a polygynous household, or to feelings of resentment solely because of
having been sold in marriage to become a second or third wife. In this myth Grizzly
may also have represented a homicidally jealous younger sister. She sadistically
employed her husband's kind younger brother as her anus-wiper. In short, she was
a psychotic killer who used sex, marriage, family ties, and slavery in order to humiliate and hurt men. Women she merely killed. Narcissistic, suggestible, anally compulsive, anally sadistic, and orally sadistic, as elsewhere she lacked adult genitality.

Myth 40 adds no details of significance. Each of five Grizzlies accused a traveler
of coming for sexual favors, but his spirit-power was so great that he killed them by
turning their strength against themselves.

Mrs. Howard added comments on Grizzlies in three short ethnographic texts
(134, 143, 144). Text 143 offers visual imagery, especially of pendulous and unattractive breasts thrown over shoulders; Grizzly Women were also hairy and had
long sharp claws because they were really grizzlies. The descriptive items again suggest feelings about older women.

Seal.—Seal Women were actors in three myths, although no Seal Men appeared in
the collection. A Seal hauled Seal Hunter and his followers to the coast and attempted
to kill them (26). I deduce that she was the spirit-power of Seal Hunter's malevolent
brother, Canoemaker, and carried out his bidding as supernaturals would. Other
Seals (37, 43) were entirely different people. They did not play roles of evil persons.

One of these Seals (37) was a woman who followed etiquette in being so circum-
spect and uncomprehending about perils in an in-law relationship that she did not
act in time to save the life of her younger brother, whose wife decapitated him. The
delineation was of a well-mannered and weak or frightened woman.

The other Seal (43) was a bullied older sister and maternal homologue whose
capacity to accept a nagging girl had limits. When sibling toleration reached a point
of unendurance, she escaped, unlike *Ku'šaydi*'s brother (40). But one may not
deduce, without more evidence, that it was feminine to decamp and masculine to
endure.

Little can be achieved by comparing the Seals of the three plays. Perhaps these
plots—and surely myth 26—were borrowed from coastal sources and had not yet
received integration. If the three are pieced together, we have to reconcile a mur-

derous female who did the bidding of a disapproved man, a woman who was so cautious about in-laws' feelings that she failed to act in time to save her brother's life, and a maternal person who at length got away from a vexatious sibling. The stresses were not necessarily contradictory because they were on different kinds of behavior that occurred in the society, but they do not allow a meaningful formulation about a personality. My feeling is that Seals were a wide category of minor women, some of whom were good and others bad. Probably a variety of undistinctive women who had been added to the literature were automatically put into the category and termed "Seals." Comparisons with contiguous literatures might reveal the merit, if any, of this suggestion.

Bear.—A Bear was presented and briefly characterized in only two myths, but unrecorded myths might have included her, too. Like Seal, she was offered in a delineation (16) which demonstrated the relative helplessness of a good woman in a familial situation which was affected by the viciousness and great spirit-power of another woman. Bear was an industrious, co-operative, and attractive person whose fate pointed up another type of woman (Grizzly) who was wholly bad. In fact, although Bear was hardly more than a plot expediter in the myth, she illustrated an ideal mother and sister who did very well what she could, although her situation was beyond hope and she knew that it was so. She reacted in the sole way remaining for a fine mother: she prepared her boys for her inevitable death.

The only other Bear actor (15) emphasized admirable maternal feeling, but in a different manner. She grieved so deeply for her deceased child that she could not eat until her feelings were released by means of a wrathful explosion against salmonberries. This myth highlighted any mournful mother's feelings. Ascription of the name "Bear" suggests that Bear constituted a symbol of a good mother. The latent depreciatory feeling about women is shown by the paucity of female Bears and the multiplicity of Grizzlies. Bears were admired but tragic; Grizzlies were terrifying and bad.

Meadow Lark.—Appearing in four myths (14, 24, 27, 36), she represented a spirit-power whose special ability was to know what was currently happening. Like most other supernaturals, she enunciated no values; she never spoke for the society. She emitted only impeccable information and predictions in return for relationship with a human being. A slight distinctiveness of treatment appeared solely in the myth (27) where she also accompanied the girl to whom she gave advice. In that story she sat on the girl's shoulder as she went along with her, nudging and prompting from time to time.

A personality sketching of Meadow Lark was never suggested because of her completely automatic *deus ex machina* and spirit-power functions. Her mechanical and neutral services warrant queries. Did she reflect not merely a spirit-power but also an idealized person? Was she a projection consequent upon the wish for absolutely sound information and advice in a society where people were never certain about what was going on or what was going to happen? Did she also represent or resemble in some respects a shaman who long before had acquired a spirit-power giving the capacity to observe contemporary events and to perceive in people deficiencies or vulnerable spots which might prove their undoing? Lark did not see into the future. Her unique ability, which some shamans were believed to possess, was in awareness of contemporary events. She knew reality so exactly that action taken in the light of knowledge which she offered permitted a person to succeed in a perilous situation.

Why was a helper of this kind feminine among Clackamas and Sahaptins to their east? Lark stories do not reveal that she was married. Does that circumstance connect with a possible fact that unmarried older women were often shamans? Did an older and apparently unmarried woman grant especial security because she lacked kinship or community ties? Could she therefore give impartial assistance to all? Although answers to such questions await surveys of the region's shamanism and its literary treatments of such a precultural functionary, the Clackamas Lark bears the mark of having constituted or having been reinforced by a projection arising from the quest for definitive steps that could be taken in crises. The literature contains only one similar spirit-power informant, two in fact, in Coyote's pair of voluble excrements which functioned for him alone. It is evident that Lark, whatever cultural items and psychological processes account for her presence in the literature, functioned as a plot expediter—like the broken bow, broken root-digger, feather signal, and arrow ladder motifs. If she also represented strands in the personality structures of some real Clackamas people, they were in features evidenced by native conviction that a few persons, such as shamans with certain kinds of spirit-powers, were able to analyze present situations fraught with peril and to resolve them safely. Such shamans were probably often, if not always, older persons.

Crow.—Crow Women were never leading actors, but they were presented in five myths (5, 7, 16, 47, 49); no Crow Man is found in the collection. Two Crows (5) reared young Salmon or Steelhead Man with fine grandmotherly regard, and they were also kindly toward an imperiled widow who lived with them after her rescue. Stress was thus upon the protective and maternal facet of older women, who were often if not always poor. Their omnivorousness, indicated by their proposals to eat the eyes and cheeks of a human being, may suggest not only the fitness of their characterization as crows but also awareness of strong oral needs in older persons. Although this delineation implies no marked hostility toward them, it includes a comical component of depreciation of their orality.

Calumniatory feelings about older women come out forthrightly in the myth (7) where a Crow was vain and evil-smelling because she used the most intolerable substance, excrement, for pomade. Elsewhere Crows (16) were more like scavenger birds than persons. They were plot expediters introduced in order to have the filthiest creatures pick at Grizzly's vulva till it bled. Two poor, aged, and reeking Crows were the sole villagers sympathetic to a deserted boy (47); their kind effort saved him from cold, hunger, and death. The myth was really saying that the poorest old women, dirty as they may be, can show more mercy than kin or the well-to-do.

Nothing of value was added to knowledge of a Crow in another myth (49). Again she was a plot expediter briefly introduced in order to allow Coon's grandmother to be informed about his foraging. The implication I find is of a generous villager of poor class telling another older woman about petty thieving that was going on. Even if she was as smelly as a crow, an older woman of low class was helpful, not antipathetic. She was especially observant about foods.

In the literature, then, Crows represented as no other preculturals older women of poorer families. Never young or attractive like Woodpeckers, all Crows reinforced a stereotype of poor older women: they stank shamefully, even intolerably, but they were large-hearted, amusing, and very much oriented toward comestibles; not once were they misanthropic. This characterization becomes the more reasonable when one realizes that the literature was principally modeled in the light of feelings and values of the well-to-do, maybe largely at their hands. Lower-class people may have identified so completely with well-to-do ones that everyone regarded the poor as at once shameful, pitiable, and ludicrous; probably the poor felt that way about themselves.

Precultural Crows therefore constituted a projection of feelings about lower-class persons, especially about grandmothers of that stratum of society. The aura of excrements about them, an unsurpassedly humiliating trait, was a defense against identification with or overt sympathy for such women. It permitted the stereotype to contain a central judgment that poor women were kindly, because it allowed the well-to-do to look upon such creatures as disgracefully filthy. The literature offers no comparable stereotype of poor filthy males, possibly because no one felt as much guilt about them. Actually, the culture's feelings about freemen of lower class remain largely hidden from us, and since the connection between low class, excrements, and dogs was region-wide, we are unable to account fully for the dearth of Clackamas expressions of such feelings.

The genial Defecators (13) were minor actors in a sixth myth which I believe also referred to Crows, although they were not so named. Since they appear to have been regarded in exactly the same way as Crows, I am confident that they were only another pair of hospitable and sympathetic Crows who were accorded a special personal name on account of their exhibitionistic wrestling and diverting anal resolution of defeat.

Robin.—The two myths in which she appeared present only one or two strokes of personality. Her age and marital status were not mentioned. She exhibited a sibling's intense feeling of loss and aloneness when her younger sister died (44). Men reacted in the same manner, as in the scene in which a blind boy wept for his lost older brother (46), and in the one where the older brother was sad when his merciless sibling died (40). The woman who felt cold in warm weather and warm in cold weather was either a Duck or Robin (21), but this story adds no knowledge about women, although it may indicate minor feelings about some women.

Yellowhammer.—In the tenth scene of myth 9 a Yellowhammer, probably young, unmarried, and attractive, tried to peck a hole in vain, whereupon the self-imprisoned Coyote had to summon a stronger woodpecker person. In another myth (29) Yellowhammer was her community's best wrestler who was defeated by Hazel Gambler. Later she became his older brother's devoted and energetic wife and bore him two sons. She represented a fine wife and mother who before marriage had been athletic, probably an occasional phenomenon in Clackamas villages.

Sapsucker.—This young person resembled Yellowhammer in her vain effort to peck a hole for Coyote (9) and in her athleticism. Blue Jay defeated and killed her in a pole-climbing contest (26). Unlike Yellowhammer, who was also an exemplary wife, we have no further information about Sapsucker. The interesting feature of these athletic woodpecker women is that they were young, unlike Meadow Lark and the Crows, and their attractiveness was stressed.

Trout.—Either Coyote or Salmon announced her future name and service in the one ritual-like myth (8). In another myth (6) Trout was a thoroughly human actor. She traveled to Panther's house to become his wife. Her typically feminine helplessness or defenselessness at the hands of Old Man Coyote did not absolve her from guilt which was wholly consequent upon Coyote's lust; she paid with her life because, like any woman, she was unable to resist a relative's improper advances. The delineation was a stereotype which applied to even the most personable wife. Since trout was the most delicious fish, Trout was the name which befitted a desirable wife, a youthful person who did what she could. But in this instance she was trapped by an older man's covetousness and desire to be young. No woman had means of self-defense, except persuasion, against such a man. Their offense was the more iniquitous because it was incestuous.

Greyback Louse.—This woman crossed the stage in three myths. The first (34) was not explicit; it only pointed to a Greyback Louse married pair who were not well-to-do and who therefore lived in an end house and infrequently partook of fresh venison. The same feelings which resulted in ascribing ludicrous orality and anality to Crows produced a characterization of these Greybacks' vanity and undignified expression of pleasure when presented with a gift. Such reactions were amusing to Clackamas. In a second myth (36) a lone Greyback Woman who was presumably of lower class and living alone shrewdly tricked and drowned, in nothing bigger than a mussel shell, four gullible and vain Grizzly Men. The story was really saying that a woman of low status, unable to act through a man because she was unmarried and lacked a grown son, might muster her tiny artifact resources and with cunning vanquish powerful persons because she comprehended men's foibles.

It might also have been saying that a woman of low class had an especial need to use supernaturals so as to hurt people. One may guess that the little tune Greyback hummed and her diminutive canoe represented a spirit-power or powers of a destructive kind.

On the other hand, if Clackamas felt this way about her and about low-class women, they covered their feeling by showing that her song was as silly as a song could be, and that her victims were such bad men as to deserve drowning. Perhaps the veiling of Greyback's mischievousness, by portraying her as trapping and attacking scoundrels, was a defense against admission and open statement that poor people could resort only to villainous and undercover means of acting upon the hostility they felt. I think too that in northwest states societies older persons who lived alone, even though they stayed "in an end house" and had wealthier kin nearby, generated uneasiness among the people. Such nervousness was then displaced onto the malign spirit-powers which solitary elders were supposed to have.

Just as benevolence and ingenuity among the poor were separate traits of Crows and Greyback Women, no upper-class female actor displayed both generosity and craftiness. To be sure, upper-class women of the literature were usually excellent people, but their merits were those of what we may regard as a Northwest variety of Victorianism: women were supposed to be loyal to kin, and they were expected to be guileless bores in a man's world—at least before the menopause, for there was no restraining them after that. Clackamas values, sanctions, and controls did not go so far as to guarantee such qualities in any women, and certainly not in those of lower class; the society only verbalized and represented itself as standing for Victorian-like values. In their literature Clackamas preferred to think of opposite characteristics in women—ungenerousness, suspicion of non-kin and non-villagers, artlessness, opportunistic management, and sexual license, especially in older women.

The third myth reference to Greybacks (46) is of interest solely because these creatures were again both feminine and vermin. The myth adds little to knowledge of the Greyback actors in the other myths (34, 36), although it is worth mentioning that vermin were like excrements in their connotation of shamefulness and that the very name "Greyback" therefore reinforced the stereotype of lower-class women.

Sun.—Female Suns occurred in three stories. In one of them Sun was a good upper-class wife (13), the mother of a boy, and the stepmother of his half-brother; elsewhere she was also an exemplary wife and again served as a mother to two boys (46). In a tale (61) she was not characterized because she was merely a discussant, with Moon Woman, in a "contest of wills" motif. She averred that she proffered light to persons who in summertime were cleaning and repairing their money beads. These estimable labors, along with her characterization in the two myths, clearly suggest that Sun was a symbol of an admired upper-class wife and ideal mother. Her behavior was not presented in sufficient detail to allow a sketch of a personality, although we read, for example (46), of her wifely delousing of her husband and her restoration of eyesight, with healing water, to her husband's parents and their slaves. In other words, the perfect wife and mother performed labors which were expected of a close relative. Otherwise she need not be shown to have feelings.

Moon.—She appeared only twice and seems to have contrasted with Sun as a symbol of the opposite of feminine rectitude. Her class status was not indicated, nor do we learn that she was married or had children. In a tale (61) Sun told Moon that her pale light was good only for fornication and defecation, uncommendable kinds of behavior. In a myth (2) Moon was swallowed by Bull Frog Woman in order to make a dark night in which young women might have illicit affairs. No further trait of personality was set forth for Moon. The two references probably do not include all in Clackamas literature, in view of the many Moon stories of peoples immediately north of Clackamas, but the only traits that can be deduced from these two trifling mentions are femininity and connection with unrespected behavior. In contrast to the femininity of both Moon and Sun, the stars, referred to only in passing, were persons of either sex or of any social level.

Frog.—Bull Frog (2) was the upper-class monogamous wife who abetted other married women's sexual affairs and accordingly suffered the frightful punishment she deserved—her husband flayed her. She was really a symbol of a woman who was bad because she assisted frustrated feminine victims of polygyny and thereby threatened upper-class society. In the only other mention of Frog females (33) she had five daughters. The recitalist gave no details about her personality, and no Frog male stepped forward in the stories.

There are no other feminine actors who were present in two or more plays. Again, I shall attempt to avoid swamping the reader with comments about the many females, some of whom Mrs. Howard named, who appeared in only one play, although a list of such minor female actors and their characteristics of personality is as methodologically necessary for full documentation as is a list of all the one-play male actors.

Dupes.—A succession of females were duped by the conscienceless young Coyote (9). They included Pheasant, a pubescent girl whom Coyote raped, another with whom he copulated several times, fifteen whose genitals he manipulated, and Snail, whose eyes he appropriated after she foolishly believed his fib. He saved a number of despairing females from a cannibal stew. One mother deliberately sent her daughter to be violated by him. This largest myth of the collection lacks a single female who, excepting Grizzly, stood for either a thoroughly hateful or admired person. A vital theme in the myth is that of feminine paralysis, and Clackamas reaction to such a theme was uproarious laughter.

An evil daughter.—In one myth (13) an unnamed mother spoke for the culture in admonishing her errant daughter. The older woman was pitiable because her daughter responded with brutality. The drawing was of any mother who was correct and ethical. Dramatic considerations alone warranted her presence in the lines, in order to intensify the daughter's evilness. Depiction of the daughter was of a type, not an individual. In order to justify polygyny, Clackamas apparently needed to sketch her as a second wife who deserted her polygynous husband and child and as a cruel person who wanted to deny her motherhood, lash out at her own mother, and live with her brother, whom she wanted to kill her husband.

Village women.—The successive groups of village women who followed a Grizzly Woman to a root patch were among the few instances of mass rather than individual characterization (17). The women of that myth were responsible workers who liked to go to the root patch together and to sing and camp there for a day or two away from home, in a manner that must have been culturally standard. In the myth they passively and trustingly followed an upper-class woman who directed them to the best patch and led their singing around the evening campfire. They became distrustful and fearful if they sensed danger—here the possibility that someone possessed a malevolent supernatural. One is tempted to deduce mass feminine dependency, helplessness, and general anxiety when away from the men at home; but men may have been as paralyzed as women by what they feared was certain doom. For example, the headman himself was as demoralized as the village women when his frightful Grizzly wife approached.

Additional cases of mass characterization were the groups duped by Coyote (9), the people whom he saved from Grizzly's stew, and village populations which he rescued from ogres or to which he offered instruction. All these groups (9) represented average people of a village.

Water Bug.—A number of females received delineation in the myth which I regard as the outstanding "woman's story" of the collection (17), and the actor named "Water Bug" provided one of the best sketchings in the literature. In addition to the youngest-smartest role, she exemplified the capacity, which was more than region-wide, to respect initiative and discernment in a child. In addition, the story pointed to the girl's unique susceptibility to the motives and likely behavior of a psychotic. She was so crafty that she alone could foil a monomaniac. Emphasis was not on the child's goodness but on perceptivity, adroitness, and fearlessness. Males of the literature were as glamorous, but in each instance a supernatural lent them aid. Water Bug was so smart that, as far as we know, she operated without a supernatural. She exemplifies Clackamas approval of early maturation.

A headman's daughter.—A headman's daughter who was orally impregnated by the loathsome Hot Weather Wind Boy (23) was noble because of her toleration of the companionship of so horrible a youngster: that was the way an upper-class person should behave toward the poor and pitiable. She was not a person but a stereotype of a proper upper-class maiden. When the youth was revealed as the father of her child, she became his wife without a murmur of dissent from her father's decision. If her mother did any deciding the myth version did not suggest so. The unmarried young mother symbolized only the faultless maiden, obedient daughter of an authoritarian upper-class man, and impeccable wife of upper-class membership.

Oedipal elders.—Snake Tail (24) and Awl (27) may be discussed together as examples of Oedipal older women who killed their grandsons' prospective brides. They point to awareness of older women's competitiveness with and hostility to young women, desire to maintain a husband-wife relationship with a young man, and need to regain youthful wifely attractiveness. Young women whom they killed represented the young woman who was respectful to the older female in-laws of her husband's household.

Wren's grandmother (25) was an Oedipal type of a related kind. The difference of stress was in her lechery and incestuous relationship with her grandson, not on a desire to kill younger rivals. She did not have to commit murder to get to her grandson. Her assumption of a young girl's "skin" also displayed an older woman's need to recapture youthful appearance and attractiveness.

Girls who compete with older women.—The fifth and last girl, who in two different myths was proceeding to the doom which her four older predecessors had met (24, 27), was enabled to take action which saved her. She could do so only because she encountered Meadow Lark. The evident meaning was that if a female acquired an appropriate spirit-power, she could resolve a crisis without assistance of a male. In these two myths Meadow Lark represented such a supernatural; in the society a shaman probably constituted a recourse. The two dramas offered no delineation of any of the ten girls. Such maidens were devices to show what menaced or happened to nubile females when an older woman attempted to compete with them for a relationship with a young man. The stories told almost nothing about feelings generated in the girls.

A wealthy woman who rejects suitors.—In one myth the depiction of a well-to-do young woman's personality contained distinctive features. She was intolerably aberrant. Contrary to standards, she alone decided about her marital destiny. She mocked and humiliated in an extreme manner the well-to-do man who should have been living with her as her husband. Of her free will she remained ostensibly unmarried, although legally she belonged to him. His oral impregnation of her, so that she died in a labor which produced snakes, symbolized the torture and degradation a woman deserved for presumption, arrogance, and shameful treatment of a fine man. The myth pointed a moral about an upper-class woman's proper status and prescribed inertness. It said little about the personality of a wealthy woman who defied rules and limitations which the upper stratum of society accepted as proper. The literature provides not a hint about younger women of lower-class families.

Cock Robin's sister.—She deserted him only when he failed to share food with her, not when he killed her baby. The implication was that she was a bad mother. Something was awry in her values. She lacked ordinary feelings. But she metamorphosed into a good woman in all respects after her marriage to Fish Spear Pole. The story may not have been integrated, but if it was a unified account rather than an unsuccessful piecing together of disparate stories, it means that Clackamas understood that a female could progress from premarital lack of affect to womanly feeling and virtue after marriage to a fine man. The myth may have been, like some other narratives, a terse or overly compact depiction of a personality in several stages of development.

I need to comment upon the trait of feminine immobilization which the society emphasized as of great value and which was projected into a number of actors, especially the following.

An unmarried and unnamed headwoman (4) unwittingly clubbed and injured Coyote's headman-grandson when he furtively came to her bed-platform. Her insulting aggression upon the person of a wealthy man justified his killing her. But when Mountain Cannibal Men, that is, filthy persons of low status, revived her she had to live with them. She reared her children in their household until her son was old enough to help in killing the Mountain Cannibal family. After the initial clubbing of the wealthy young man her deportment was good, as a passive wife's should be.

The wife of Tongue (42) was similarly good because she too reared offspring under adversity and at length with her son's aid eliminated the ogre. Both women were models of wives who did their best in a horrifying situation caused by bad husbands whom they could not leave. Only the spirit-powers of sons made possible a proper resolution of such an impasse.

Salmon's widow (5) expressed the same theme of feminine immobilization. She was forced to live with Wolves who helped to kill her husband. Escape was impossible until her murdered husband's son arrived.

Panther's wife, Trout (6), endured a generally similar fate at the hands of Old Man Coyote. She had to endure the creature as best she could, although her destiny was death inflicted, because of the crime of incest, by her inflexibly upright husband. Again, a lady had no physical defense against a predatory man. If he was her kin, her sin was incest, which meant that she must die. One can only wonder how such a woman felt or what Clackamas would have said about her feelings.

In the Flint myth (18) the humiliation suffered by Panther's unnamed candidate for his hand in marriage was like that of the other Panther's woman (6). Flint expressed the wish—or ability—of a man to have his will of any woman resident of the house. She had to accept maltreatment even if it meant being raped twice daily by an outrageous dwarf. For fear of reprisal she did not dare reveal what he was doing to her; she could only scheme to let her presence be known. A woman's policy, again, was not so much to be passive as to be judicious, overtly unaggressive, and to survive. She must be realistic, bide her time, and await favorable opportunity to hit back, but always by having a male do it for her.

The impressive number of eight different women followed a sensible and culturally idealized opportunism. They included, in summary, the following: the former
headwoman who was forced to live almost polyandrously with Mountain Cannibals (4); the wife of Tongue (42); Salmon's widow, who lived in seeming polyandry
with Wolves (5); Panther's woman who had to tolerate Coyote's demands (6) and
his woman who had to accede to Flint (18); Grizzly's wife, who stayed with him
after he gouged out her eye (14); the second wife of Gi'ckux's older brother (34);
and the wife who deserted "Oedipus" in order to save her son (38). The wife who
married a dead person (45) endured her lot, but no man resolved her predicament.

I think that it is improper in a single case to caption such required feminine
behavior as simple passivity. Stress was on sitting it out, being vigilant, having
acumen, and bracing up a male who could take over. It was aggression by indirection, anticipatory design, and tactful arranging for a man to complete the plan.
Therefore Clackamas allowed no virtue in true passivity. Women took positive and
even vengeful action, but in a Clackamas manner. In most instances they worked
through men. And there are a few striking cases of precultural women who acted
without men where they had to, because there was no man. The unnamed huntress
(34) who married the older brother of Gi'ckux is an illustration, as is little Water
Bug (17) until the completion of the flight back to the village, when the men there
could start shooting at the ogress. These examples support the generalization that
a woman expected to act through men if men in the correct social relationship were
present. Further support is given in the drama (28) of the wealthy girl who determined her marriage and struck directly. She was accorded a most dire punishment
for non-male-supported aggression. Finally, ogresses acted without men; that is,
older woman, except such filthy lower-class women as Crows, were really ogresses.

Another trait in women's personalities comes out in the instances of the unmarried female actors who stole children in order to bolster their feminine self-regard
and to hit at nubile married females. Such kidnapers appear to have been interested
in both male and female infants. The two Gophers displayed (20) only slight competitiveness with each other over the little girl whom they reared. They were murderously vindictive to the child's mother and to the child when she left them, as a
child would when it learned who its rightful parent was. The Basket Ogress (46)
stole a male infant and forthwith infantilized him, so great was her maternal need
for a perennial infant rather than for a growing boy who would shortly become a
man. Personality traits indicated in these instances are not all clear. Possibly an
important component of the sketchings arises not from the culture's involvement in
characteristics of kidnapers but from anxiety over slave-raiding and loss of children.
An audience was being reminded not about needs and personality features of kidnapers but about fears of mothers lest they lose their children, and about stories
contrived for children's consumption: stay close to home lest someone steal you!
Actually, the slave-raiding customs of the area generated realistic fears. Many
northwest states stories duplicated the Clackamas motif of a proscribed direction
(13, 20, 35, 46), which did not include a fear of kidnapping but contained the same

underlying worry of loss of a child because of the animosity and cupidity of another Indian group of the region.

Apart from mothers' fears for their youngsters, if wifely quietism, patience, and virtue in sheer survival were found in only one myth, it would be significant. But a number of very different narratives contained the motif of captivities or impasses which were featured by an unflinching maintenance of standards and personal dignity until a supernaturally well-endowed young gentleman rescued the lady. One may question whether such a theme connected both with feeling about slave status and with more repressed sentiments about the fates of young women sold in marriage to such repugnant men of means as elderly shamans. A narrator, and surely all other Clackamas, was much more interested in the ethical point than in citing a single feeling of indomitably patient women. We can deduce that some women were game to the backbone, whatever may be guessed about their feelings.

Although we can perceive something of the later-developed features of personality in all Clackamas women, arising in expectations and requirements that they be purchased in marriage without freedom of choice, that they go to live in their husbands' communities, and that they always maneuver through men, the variety of women in the myths shows that Clackamas did not oversimplify the woman question. For example, a number of female actors, besides the Grizzly Women, showed violent aggression. Beetle Woman (26) castrated men, and Seal Woman towed Seal Hunter's party for many miles. Both women appear to have expressed deep hostility to men. Snake Tail (24) and Awl (27) shared rancor against young women. Snipe and Sapsucker symbolized athletic ability in some young women (26). Water Bug showed how crafty even a girl could be. These and other citations of traits found in women actors contrast impressively with a central characteristic of Clackamas women: they were prevailingly docile, defenseless, and helpless unless they were alone or aged.

3. CHILDREN

Prepubescent males numbered various traits: display of miraculous growth in the instances of Thunder Boy (30) and young Salmon (5), craftiness in Badger's sons (10), paternal wisdom in the oldest Bear Boy (16), compassion in Beaver's young helper (48), unusual spirit-powers in *Ku'šaydi* (40) and both Hot Weather Winds (22, 23) and Fire's great-grandsons (13), nasty hyperactivity in the Flint Boys (18), childish forgetfulness and errors in Frog's children (33), noisy quarrelsomeness in both girl and boy (66), disobedience such as travel in a prohibited direction (35, 55, 56), general excellence in Panther's son (18), identification with paternal uncle Hazel (29), torture of a grandmother (49), sadistic play with animals (25), killer drive and extreme narcissism in *Ku'šaydi* (40), stealing of other boys' lunches and intolerable unsociability (47), teasing of an older woman (31), infantilization by an older woman (46), and grief because of an older brother's supposed death (46).

The fewer prepubescent females displayed various traits: athleticism in Coyote's daughter (10); miraculous growth, hyperactivity, horrible food habits, insufferable rivalry toward a younger brother and humiliation of him in the Mountain Cannibal

Girl (4); extraordinary insight and leadership in Water Bug (17); a healthy attitude held by a stolen girl toward her own mother (20); unendurable nagging by Crawfish of her older sister (43); and Seal's daughter's perspicacity about her homosexual "aunt" (37).

Disobedience in the form of wandering off in a forbidden area was noted for boys, not girls. No girls stole. None were infantilized. None were in mourning. Both sexes were crafty, but no boy exhibited the precocious insight of Water Bug or Seal's daughter. No boy was singled out as athletic.

An important feature of literary style which related to feelings about female inferiority, children's immaturity, and the great value of maturation was the motif of biographical developmental stages which has been mentioned earlier. But only males advanced through stages to fine adulthood. The notable instance of a female life history, Half Grizzly Foot Girl's (14), showed a development in reverse; a good girl deteriorated into a wild murderess. The change in Robin's sister (31) from an early unconcern about her brother's baking of her child to a subsequent career as a normal wife may be an example of a developmental pattern, but it may also amount to a recent threading-together of discrete stories; and the development did not commence with her childhood. Males who progressed from childhood inadequacy, immaturity, or consciencelessness to maturity and total goodness included Coyote, Wren (25), *Gi'ckux*'s older brother (34), Tongue's stepson (42), and the youth who traveled in the sky country (46).

Another important feature of the literature which connected with contrasts in attitudes toward males and females, and with feelings toward children, was the stress upon adult females resolving situations by acting through males. Reflection upon this emphasis leads to ethnographical questions. One asks, Did Clackamas disapprove of immaturity in youths? Did they condone dependency and immaturity in married women? Was there therefore permissive infantilization of prepubescent girls but not of boys? The story of Water Bug (17) indicated the culture's approval of early maturation in a girl, and Crawfish's disapproved immaturity suggested the same. But the youngest-smartest motif allowed a fifth and youngest girl the opportunity to act maturely only when Lark provided information, that is, when a supernatural was "found" by the girl. On the other hand, various young male actors, such as Thunder Boy (30), the oldest Bear Boy (16), and Fire's great-grandsons (13), were well regarded because they acted maturely. I think that the collection contains too few instances to warrant definitive answers to the questions, and the ethnographic notes are too spare to provide the slightest assistance.

Nastiness, quarrelsomeness, hyperactivity, and other disliked traits (e.g., Flint Boys, 18; the children who quarreled noisily, tale 66; Wren, 49) which were cited for boys and which were either disapproved or amusing point strongly to an absence of regard for infantilized young males. The meager data on young females are more difficult to interpret, but there may have been a sharply restricted area of approved infantilization which took mainly the form of acting in important issues only through males and accepting others' decisions about marital choice and purchase. However, each sex was expected to become competent in skills assigned to it and to relate to spirit-powers at or following puberty.

Obedience to parents' and household elders' orders was stressed for the years preceding puberty and for certain kinds of behavior in early adolescence before marriage. A splintered Oedipal relationship seems to have characterized childhood upbringing because of the number of myth actors who were remarkably parental in feeling and deportment from the viewpoint of Western civilization, yet who were uncles and grandparents. The consequence seems to have been intensity of feelings of belongingness to and identification with close kin of such kinds rather than excessive dependency or infantilization.

4. SUMMARY: PERSONALITY

Comparisons of a few similarities and differences in literary personalities of the two sexes are of limited significance due to imprecise trait definition, subjective factors of selection and identification, and numerically small returns. The purpose here is not to offer a definitive quantification of personality items but to point to a possibility of devising or improving upon a method by which deductions of some utility may be obtained under more favorable conditions (such as observation of a living literature, discussions with many informants who are not adversely affected by acculturation, and employment of a number of analysts who work apart from each other). One problem in considering a method of this kind concerns the value of existent trait inventories developed for analysis of personality profiles in Western civilization. Could such trait lists have been applied to the literature actors of a non-Western people? My decision was to bypass such devices and operate inductively. I tried to list only traits whose presence I sensed or identified in Clackamas stories, in other to point up contrasts between men and women in the society.

Each trait in Table 3 is noted with the number of adult actors who exhibited it, not the number of times the trait was exemplified. Since male and female actors each numbered well over one hundred, the frequencies in the table may be significant if other aspects of the analysis are not skewed beyond propriety.

The table offers reinforcement, if such were needed, for the deduction that females were held in ill regard. Superior worth accorded males is shown in the larger number of male actors who are indicated as industrious, expressing benevolent feelings, co-operating with siblings, doing household chores in old age, exhibiting bravery, pitiable because of their mutilations or bodily deficiencies, admirably tricky or crafty, and hostile to the opposite sex. Such merits in Clackamas culture are countered by evidences that more male actors were cannibalistic, stupid, suggestible, vain about their sexuality, conscienceless, immature or pregenital, murderous, or generally suspicious. Characteristics found in more female than male actors include docility, living as a good married partner, intense Oedipal feeling toward offspring, judiciousness in frightful predicaments, a distaste for polygyny, and vanity about personal appearance.

The pro-male slant of the culture is probably also displayed in the larger number of male actors who were sketched in developmental stages. Lives of males may have had greater audience interest than lives of females. Another emphasis is witnessed in the considerable number of motifs symbolizing security and strength in spirit-power acquired by males; fewer females secured supernaturals. Males who obtained a supernatural of one or another kind include Coyote's sons (7), Fire's great-grand-sons (13), Awl's grandson (27), Hazel Gambler's older brother (29), Thunder Boy (30), the son of "Oedipus" (38), Tongue's stepson (42), the deserted mean boy (47),

TABLE 3

Contrasts between Men and Women

Trait	Number of Male Actors	Number of Female Actors
Anality	4	4
Athleticism	4	4
Cannibalism	6	3
Steals a child	1	2
Compassion	17	4
Conscienceless	9	6
Co-operative with sibling	10	3
Courageous	17	0
Dirty	2	3
Docile or helpless	4	9
Duped	7	9
Pregenital but of adult age	6	2
Good husband or wife	7	11
Grandparent figure does chores	4	1
Hostile to opposite sex	8	3
Humiliates a headman	1	2
Deserts mate	1	2
Immature	7	0
Procrastinates fatally	0	2
Paralysis of will due to fright	3	2
Industrious	5	3
Kills mate	9	1
Kills everyone	8	2
Kills villain	9	4
Suffers mutilation	16	2
Oedipal elder	7	9
Correctly opportunistic in predicament	5	10
Hoards	2	1
Threatens polygyny	1	3
Stupid	7	1
Tricky	6	3
Vain about appearance	1	3
Vain about sexual capacity	2	0
Suggestible	6	3
Shows developmental stages in personality	7	3
Generally suspicious	4	0
Acts without aid of mate	many	3
Rivalrous toward sibling	2	2
Defends polygyny	3	0
Parent who protects son	2	3

and Beaver's youthful companion (48). Females who obtained spirit-powers included Coyote's daughter (7) and Milt's wife (39).

Aside from contrasts of male and female, analysis of an oral literature such as Clackamas allows little more than gleanings of items and lists of components of personality. The narrator presented few distinctive personalities as such, and only fragmentarily, because actors whom she set forth were for the most part means by which she sketched situations of stress, upper-class roles, and upper-class values. Clackamas therefore emphasized, discussed, and enjoyed upper-class relationships rather than character sketches; any attempt to describe the average features or variabilities in the modern communities' male and female personalities, or in children, would be ill-founded. Although the personality structurings of a Clackamas settlement cannot be indicated, I have tried to show that analysis of stories may help to salvage evidences of many strands within those personalities.

Some of these components may amount to the kind of personality feature which Drs. Ralph Linton and Abram Kardiner had in mind as important for a concept of basic personality structure. If a mass of ethnographic data had been obtained, story items would support formulations based upon ethnographic materials. Unfortunately, the story actors set forth value ideals, disapproved traits, and stereotypes more than they permit warranted deductions as to average characteristics of Clackamas, whether child or adult, male or female. The majority of Clackamas personalities seem to have had little interest for discussants and narrators. The literature focused upon the most well-to-do to such a degree that it left almost a blank for other well-to-do, poor persons, and slaves, whose percentages and roles in communities cannot, for the most part, even be guessed. Knowledge of Clackamas personality therefore remains about as unsatisfactory or fragmentary as information about village economics, artifacts, social institutions, religion, or art forms except literature and music.

Nevertheless, a few summary deductions about the personalities of many Clackamas women seem to me to be so important for comprehension of some of the Northwest's literatures and societies, so supported by everything which we know from ethnographic data, and so evidenced by the depictions on the myth screen that they should be emphasized here.

Upper-class married women had self-identities which suffered confinement, compression, or blocked action before the menopause and were no longer held in bounds after that period. One might employ a metaphor of valuable work horses, long in harness, who in old age are released to graze and roam freely. Buried resentments which connected with inferior status as a nubile wife and overtly passive behavior which featured maneuvering solely with the aid of men were later allowed metamorphosis. Women looked forward, for their years past the age of nubility, to unrestricted action, freedom of choice and movement, and permissible expressions of hostility—especially by way of supernaturalism. They could look ahead to years of higher status and to creative aesthetic expression. Self-identity and feelings of worth could be magnified.

In Western civilization older women have had little that is ego-enhancing to anticipate after the climacteric. Their secondary status drops still further, and often they resolve intensifying frustrations and sentiments about their decreasing worth by turning aggression inward, in infantile or depressive behavior. Their contributions in art and community life decrease. They feel less and not more wanted. But older Clackamas women could become progressively freer. Now they could do exactly what older men were able to do. Few needed to strike at themselves, because various external targets and forms of expression were more available than before. Now they could have romantic liaisons with youths, behave as if they were young and physically attractive, travel alone, further develop their artistic potentials, and be unaffected by the tasks, restraints, and sanctions which imprisoned nubile females.

Furthermore, the myths are examples of a beloved art form which almost literally belonged to fulfilled upper-class elders, women and men both. Myth plots and actors often expressed what these elders would have liked to have done in their earlier years; feelings long since suppressed could be re-created and drawn on the myth screen. Although older persons were the transmitters of literature and the seminal minds, the absence of subcultures of the youth and younger married folk, and the extraordinary identification of younger people with elders, meant that the youth could also participate to the full in enjoyment of art products which were emotional outlets for respected older people. Youthful genius has often created magnificently in poetry and other literary forms in Euroamerican culture. I suggest that it did so infrequently if at all in Chinook and nearby literatures.

CHAPTER XII

HUMOR

CLACKAMAS literature generated both laughter and sadness, but smiles are everywhere more easily identifiable than reactions of sorrow. An anthropologist's observations, field notes, and memories allow him to select with much more confidence instances which were funny. Only a few occurrences of a tragic kind of audience sentiment can be identified, and these are only the extremely sorrowful; therefore, an attempt to arrange Clackamas responses on a continuum from laughter to responses of a dolorous nature would probably fail. Nevertheless, I think that an effort to classify humorous responses alone is worthwhile and that the results are helpful for comprehension of the society and its carriers.

In fact, it seems to me that humor is a facet of life which has been almost irresponsibly neglected in anthropological research. It is a part of literatures which folklorists have studied for other components. Its importance for understanding a people and their literature may be no less than the importance of traditionally studied topics such as social structure and religion. At the least, analyses of humor, whether inclosed in an oral literature or expressed in conversation, provide needed corroboration of deductions made from other field data. Possibilities in quantification of humor materials should also be intriguing to workers in the behavioral sciences. I have tried to work out and display a method of analysis which allows a many-sided study of a part of life about which the behavioral sciences know little.[11]

Accordingly, I enumerated 130 instances in the Clackamas collection where I was certain that an audience at a folkloristic recital responded with smiles or laughter. I recognized at least one such reaction in each of thirty myths and three tales. That is, 60 per cent of the myths contained fun, but only 20 per cent of the tales. This difference between myths and tales is significant. A Euroamerican might suppose that myths would contain less humor than tales, but the opposite is true.

To Clackamas, myths offered trenchant and unquestioned evidences of prehistory, while tales spoke piquantly and equally validly of recent times. Myths may be regarded as remainders of long periods of village discussions and commentary. Tales were relatively recent acquisitions, not cultural heirlooms like myths. I suppose that the greater elaboration of humor in myths therefore reflects a longer time during which they were possessed, contemplated, theorized upon, and worked over. Their truth was not lessened nor their worth tarnished by embellishments of humor. Absence of a concept of the sacred also made it possible, and even preferable, to treat accounts of the past with a light touch. No community of the northwest states brooded over narratives of ancient times and people. The long ago and the long since dead were laughed at more comfortably than the present and the recently deceased. The one was far less threatening than the other. Likely reasons for the lower percentage of humorous items in tales are, then, that myths were not so close to the anxieties of today, that most myths were much older than tales, and that myths had therefore received more processing in a culture which did not set fun apart from value ideals.

I took each of the 130 fun situations and attempted to pinpoint each fun-generating factor or stimulus to humor which I believe to have been present in them. I counted 914 such stimuli. Every one of the 130 instances of humor was patently determined by a cluster of stimuli, few or none of which a Clackamas verbalized as such. The average number of stimuli which I identified and estimated in each instance of fun was at least seven. But I am confident that I underestimated, oversimplified, and missed many stimuli which were there. The actual average must have been significantly higher.

I arranged the 914 stimuli in sixteen types, some of which overlap. I feel no vested interest in these types. It would be foolish to claim that they give the best arrangement possible. Indeed, several incongruous polarities which are set apart in the classification might be handled in other ways. Nevertheless, the types which I present have some value: they display differences in the fun-generating factors; for purposes of analysis of humor as a whole, they are to be regarded as meaningful units; they permit the student to avoid oversimplification; and they facilitate studies of humor in its relationship to the society and in other oral literatures of the Northwest, if not elsewhere.

The 914 stimuli include totals from only the first fourteen types because I was unable to conduct arithmetical operations upon types 15 and 16. Table 4 displays, with catchwords, the kinds of stimuli which I have assembled to constitute a type. Types 2, 3, and 4 were so varied in content that further subdivisions of each were meaningful and therefore necessary. These subdivisions are presented in Tables 5, 6, and 7, respectively. Type 14 contrasts with types 1 to 13 by being quantitative as well as qualitative.

Instances of type 15, pantomime, mimicry, and vocal mannerisms, were so infrequently noted in field research that they could not be quantified. Occurrences of type 16, which comprises onomatopoetic, diminutive, and augmentative linguistic devices, could be ascertained only following full analysis of the language.

The sixteen categories of fun stimuli, frequencies of items in each of them, and omissions of categories which appear in humor expressed in other societies should receive discussion for whatever light they shed on Clackamas social structure, cultural heritage, and personalities. In the following comments I discuss each type of humor stimulus in the order in which it appears in Table 4.

Type 1, which stresses physical expression, appears to be a common human kind of stimulus to laughter. A notable aspect of fun situations and actors in the literature is that Grizzly people were the prominent ones deliberately and aggressively subjected to slapstick by other actors. For example, a son of Fish Spear Pole Man

TABLE 4

TYPES OF HUMOR STIMULUS

Type	Instances	Approximate Percentage of Total
1. Trick, transformation, practical joke, slapstick	94	.10
2. Anatomical reference; regressive behavior (see Table 5)	173	.19
3. Trickiness, cleverness, resourcefulness in relationship (see Table 6)	51	.056
4. Female; older person (see Table 7)	81	.089
5. Pomposity, vanity; foolishness, naïveté, gullibility, stupidity, ignorance, incompetence; childishness, immaturity; lack of skill; timidity; lower class	91	.10
6. Eccentricity; incorrect behavior, the forbidden; incongruity; narcissism, greed, penuriousness	95	.10
7. Insanity due to spirit-power relationship	14	.015
8. Humiliation	58	.06
9. Evildoer comes to grief	59	.06
10. Irony, satire, sarcasm; understatement, exaggeration	41	.04
11. Victory, release from anxiety or tension	44	.05
12. Dishonesty	50	.055
13. Language error, misunderstanding of a verbal form	4	.004
14. Repetition, progression, saturation	59	.06
15. Pantomime, mimicry; vocal mannerism	not noted	
16. Onomatopoeia; diminutive, augmentative verbal form	not noted	
Total	914	app. 1.00

TABLE 5

REFERENCES TO ANATOMY AND REGRESSIVE BEHAVIOR (TYPE 2)

Subtype	Instances	Approximate Percentage of Total
a. Sex	38	.04
b. Anality	27	.03
c. Mutilation, maiming, physical pathology	32	.03
d. Orality	34	.03
e. Physical unattractiveness	16	.016
f. Becoming unconscious, falling asleep	6	.005
g. Fear of great height	3	not significant
h. Burning	1	not significant
i. Drowning	7	.005
j. Diminutiveness	7	.005
k. Death	2	not significant

TABLE 6

RESOURCEFULNESS IN RELATIONSHIPS (TYPE 3)

Subtype	Instances	Approximate Percentage of Total
a. Men	34	.03
b. Children	16	.016
c. Women	1	not significant

TABLE 7

FEMALES AND OLDER PERSONS (TYPE 4)

Subtype	Instances	Approximate Percentage of Total
a. Females neither children nor aged	56	.058
b. Older women	13	.015
c. Older men	12	.015

transformed into a feather (text 31) and floated about in order to tease a Grizzly Woman who tried in vain to catch him. His older brother turned into a snake, and she could not catch him either. Water Bug infuriated and frustrated Grizzly Woman by keeping the fire burning brightly all night long (17).

Coon and Coyote appear to have been the outstanding employers of physical sadism. Coon tortured a succession of Grizzly Men by putting black powder and urine into chisel cuts he made in them (49). Coon teased Coyote with fake magic which seemed to draw food from under a pillow (3). The younger Coyote (9) played tricks on a succession of people, mostly females. Principal cultural factors ensconced in items such as these, and which everyone the world over may find amusing, were the specific kinds of personalities which Grizzly, Coon, and Coyote people stood for. In the literature Grizzlies often represented unlovely older persons, and Coon and the younger Coyote perpetrated deviltries to which many or most pre-adult persons inclined. Besides, slapstick tended to occur at the expense of feminine actors. Along with a deep feeling of incongruity, slapstick appears to substitute for fear of violence and destruction. It replaces fear of real damage to the self with a resolution where no such damage is done or, in oral literature, with hurt to a projection figure who is so poorly regarded that the audience does not identify with him.

The virtual 20 per cent of all stimuli found in type 2 comprised an interplay of two set of factors and an especial importance of one. The common human factor in type 2 consisted of evaluations and therefore learned attitudes, whatever they were in the Northwest, toward anal, oral, and genital behavior and the physical wholeness of the body. Very likely all peoples have laughed at pre-adult physical excesses and at some mutilations suffered by other persons.

The second group of factors in type 2 was much more cultural and local. The collection exhibits laughter at burning once, at seven drownings—a small number for a people who navigated much on waterways—and at two other deaths. The weighty feature about type 2 is its thirty-eight instances of sex stimulus, twenty-seven with an anal reference, thirty-four with an oral stress, and thirty-two captioned as mutilations. The culture was severe in its demands about a premenopausal woman's restricted sphere of activity, the breaking of taboos, children's disobedience, and gentle prolonged sexual foreplay. But it lacked inhibitions about verbal mention of orifice pleasures and showed no evidence of repressing the citation of mutilations. Anal quips connected in some way with the feeling that soiling with excrements was uniquely humiliating. But laughter at urine is never found, and contact with urine was not at all degrading. Probably every house had a wooden urine bowl or box, and people therefore found no more occasion for laughter about it than we do about our bathtubs. Laughter at anal references, in a society which repaired to the brush or woods nearby to defecate, therefore connected with feelings that excrements were debasing. In the same way, sexuality outside the marriage bed was disgraceful. Laughter at sexuality was always, then, at sexual acts committed outside a marital relationship. Laughter at orality appears to have eventuated in another way and to have had a connection with food anxieties in a region where seasonal uncertainties about food production or reserves were substantial.

Type 3 includes pleasurable responses to resourcefulness, skill, and trickiness. Such responses may be universal, but in Clackamas literature only men and children displayed such abilities. Most significantly, the literature presented few female actors who possessed such admired traits after the childhood years. The culture's low regard for the worth of females from puberty to old age is therefore neatly expressed in the figures for humor stimuli of this kind.

Type 4 includes, I think, only regionally circumscribed cultural stimuli. Hostile feelings toward females at and past puberty and toward older men, headmen too, were relieved in laughter at them. Further significance may be found in the fact that of eighty-one stimuli of this type, sixty-nine were leveled at females. People laughed much more frequently at adult females than at men, even headmen. Types 3 and 4 show very well the core of antifeminine sentiment in the Clackamas heritage.

Pleasure at competency, denoted as type 3, is paralleled by relieving laughter at incompetency, which is placed under type 5. The concept of incompetency extended to immaturity of children and to any other childlike or immature behavior. It also covered freemen of poor families. Slaves were not laughed at, at least in the literature, and I do not know why. An interesting spread of the concept of ineptitude was into the area of pretense that was not fully justified. Vanity and pomposity were funny, but evidence is insufficient to demonstrate that a pretentious headman was laughed at. At the same time, headmen were patently subjects of gibes in literature sessions, as is shown by the narrator's handling of upper-class gentry like Coyote. One may find, in a shared feature of types 4 and 5, a decisive process in Chinook humor. It arises in the discomforts and pains felt because of power, controls, and authority possessed by shamans, elders, the rich, and—not least—headmen. Relief is felt when such people are cut down to size, shown to be fallible, or lampooned. Thus the individuals manifestly idealized are rendered bearable by changing them into less than ideal figures. Persons who are incessantly referred to as worthy, good, right, or competent are metamorphosed into actors who are naughty, wrong, prone to error, unreliable, capricious, or enjoying the very satisfactions which they do not permit others to have.

Type 6 is probably, in its central aspect of incongruity, one of the basic characteristics of many jocund responses the world over. But incongruity differs from culture to culture, and one may make an excellent case for its relativity. In Clackamas literature incongruity applied to greed, penuriousness, extreme self-love, and eccentric ways of the kinds stressed in Northwest societies. In addition, one changes into enjoyment feelings of disappointment, self-pity, fear of self-destruction, or any feelings of unpleasantness or pain. One defends against feelings which are responses to direct contact with unwanted reality by transforming such contact into something which generates a feeling of amusement. Responses to fun include the incongruity of a shift from painful to pleasant feeling, where the former is real and the latter a substitute. There is a contrasting, subliminally, of opposites, at the same time that such opposites are sensed as not opposites but the same. As Martha Wolfenstein has suggested in her *Children's Humor*, there seems to be an unconscious fusing of opposites and a concomitant suggestion of the absurdity of such fusing. And there is a postponement or release from feared stress.

Type 7, insanity, probably connected in native feeling with types 3 and 6, that is, with resourcefulness and eccentricity. In any case, it infrequently set off laughter. But insanity, even of kinds which Western culture regards as extreme, may have been thought of, in most communities the world over as in the Northwest, as manifestations of relationship with special supernaturals and therefore as relatively "normal" behavior. The few instances of what may be identified as insanity in Clackamas literature accordingly were determined by the manner of their identification by the culture.

Type 8, humiliation, may have been tragic in one setting and comic in another constellation of factors. Humiliation ties in with Northwest aspirations to rise to or maintain social level or acceptance as a worthy person. Constant tension about maintenance of status was drained in laughter at those who demeaned themselves. The literature presented instances which show that the concept of humiliation extended to contact with excrements and relationships with dogs as if they were humans.

Type 9, the evildoer who comes to grief, seems universal and perhaps displays no specific Northwest cultural factors of importance except in the special ways in which a villain was humbled or eliminated.

Type 10—irony, understatement, exaggeration, and the like—which connects especially with the factor of incongruity in type 6, is very likely universal too. These devices were not often employed in Clackamas literature except on a linguistic level. For example, Chinook possessed consonantal shifts which expressed diminutive or augmentative nuances. Occasional employment of such devices for the purpose of incongruous connotations provoked amusement.

Type 11, release from tension, is probably universal and may not contain specific Northwest cultural manifestations except for the devices which alleviated tension.

Type 12, dishonesty, is very likely a product of Northwest values which gave approval to success no matter how trickily or even cruelly attained.

Type 13, language mistakes or misunderstandings, may be common to all human beings. I find nothing distinctively Northwest in hue in this type of stimulus to laughter.

Type 14, repetition, progression, and saturation, must also be universal, although their manifestations in Northwest literatures were in terms of local stylizations. Clackamas used the pattern number five and the "youngest-smartest" motif among specific stimuli of this quantitative kind.

One of the most important and recurrent elements in humor in Western cultures is the factor of surprise, or the sudden and unexpected turn. Clackamas humor in myths and tales lacked such a component, no doubt because the literature was a community possession. Apart from children, auditors were familiar with most or all of the stories of Clackamas provenience and participated actively in year-round discussions of their content.

Another aspect of humor which is found in Western cultures but not in Clackamas is the stylized form which the West calls a "joke." Clackamas probably joked interminably. But they seem to have had no concept of or word for a joke. Their literature displays no evidence of the structured entity which we term "joke" incorporated in stories. They expressed themselves humorously in the day's chitchat and in story recitals. Fun functioned integrally with the rest of conversation and literature; it embellished and lightened all forms of speech even though there was no identifiable joke category. All that we can do, accordingly, is to attempt to spot situations whose components produced a response of the comic. Not a single factor in humor, whether of content or structuring (except for mimicry and vocal mannerisms), was peculiar to fun situations. Only the weight and patterning of several interwoven factors tipped the balance toward laughter.

In order to exemplify the kind of analysis of humor situations which has been suggested, I have selected a portion of the myth of Coon and his father's mother (49), and a part of the short myth of the married Skunk (19). Myth 49 commences as follows, in translation: "They lived there. I do not know how long a time after, he said to her, 'Grandma! I am hungry. Grandma! (I am) hungry.' 'What then will you eat?' She showed him something or other (to eat). 'Hm. No!' She showed him something else. 'Hm. Oh oh no!' (She showed him) everything (available). She said to him, 'What then (do you want)? Go to our storage pit, bring acorns. We shall wash them.' 'Yes yes grandma! That is what I want.' He dashed away, he got to that place, he opened their storage pit (one of the five she had). He ate acorns (and the best ones only). The ones that were wormy he piled elsewhere. He ate them all (only the good ones). He moved on to another one of their storage pits, again he did like that, he piled aside the wormy ones. He ate them (the good ones only) all up (in the second pit). Then he went on again to another of their storage pits. . . ."

Coon's first words about being hungry are at once funny, I think, because of a complex net of factors which I suggest with appended numbers that refer to stimuli listed in the tables. Coon speaks and acts like a child (5), but he does so because he is really tricky and dishonest (3, 12). He uses his immaturity in order to get the old woman's food (1, 2d). He is a greedy (6) little fellow. Whatever he does to his grandmother is funny because Clackamas laugh at an older woman merely because she is an older woman (4b). An audience probably felt that while Coon might be hungry he was even more motivated to play a mean trick (1) on his grandmother (4b).

Her query, "What then will you eat?" is amusing because the audience knows what the child (5) wants—both food (2d) and an opportunity to be dishonest (12) and to play a mean trick (1, 3) on his grandmother (4b). Her question is also funny because it implies that she is now and always foolishly gullible (5) about the callow youth. "She showed him something or other" continues the stress on an older woman's (4b) naïveté (5).

Coon's reply "Hm. No!" compactly refers, first, to his clever (3) but dishonest (12) initial response of "Hm!" It implies that he is really pondering about her offer of something other than acorns. The audience knows that he wants only those products of her industry. He lets her think that he might accept her offer and at once lets her down with a rebuff expressed in his curt "No!"

The same factors recur (14) in her second offer: "She showed him something else." Further repetition (14) appears in his second reply, "Hm. Oh oh no!" which is funnier than the first because he intensifies his rejection. She is thereby made to appear even more foolish.

Either the storyteller recites four offers by the grandmother and four progressively more definitive rejections (14), or the audience responds as if they were cited, because a Northwest audience always reacts automatically as if there were so many questions and answers.

Upon the fifth offer of acorns Coon "dashed away." The verb "dash" is funny because only a greedy (6) youngster (5) with a hardly repressed oral need (2d) would run rather than walk to the food. Running may also be incongruous (6), for there is no implication that Coon is starving.

In the next sentences Coon rejects edible but wormy acorns and greedily (6) devours (2d) all the good nuts in his grandmother's cache. He really destroys (1) the old woman's (4b) valuable property. He does it without heed (6) for her order to bring the acorns to the house where they can be washed. Without once returning, he ransacks all of her acorn storage pits (14), in each place gorging (2d) on the best nuts.

It is not necessary to continue with the myth to show in greater detail the techniques of repetition and saturation (14). They are pointed at Coon's practical jokes (1), trickiness (3), and orality (2d) at the expense of the gullible (5) old woman (4b), and there is a steady undercurrent of incongruity (6) arising from her loyalty and devotion to a youth who has no generosity toward her. My suggestions of fun stimuli undoubtedly do not include all the factors which render the scene funny to Clackamas. For example, a raconteur doubtless used mimicry and vocal mannerisms (15) and in some instances linguistic devices (16).

Additional exemplification of the complexity of the fabric of factors in a fun situation is provided by a glance at a very different story (text 19), no more than a joke which has been relegated in native theory to a precultural age.

A devoted wife pleads with her husband Skunk, who is in fact a hopelessly incompetent hunter, to go out to the woods and bring home a deer with nice fatty breast meat. When he returns the next day, his face is bandaged. His pack contains not a single slice of meat, only his teeth, which are wrapped in ferns. He has not hunted at all. It turns out that he misunderstood the morpheme for "breast meat" and perceived it as the homonymous morpheme for "tooth." His wife can do no more than throw away his teeth.

Stimuli to laughter in this skit seem to include at least the following: slapstick (1), several anatomical factors such as mutilation (2c) and physical unattractiveness from the loss of teeth (2e), the humiliation a wife suffers because of her ridiculous husband (4a, 8), his incompetence as a hunter and therefore his own humiliating situation (5, 8), the incongruity of going to hunt for good food and returning without it but with one's teeth pulled (6), a verbal misunderstanding (13), and probably pantomime of Skunk's pain and bandaged face (15). These and assuredly other factors which I have failed to perceive apply to the skit as a whole. The phrases and words of the dictation supply a number of additional fun stimuli whose citation would add to the analysis. One might suggest, however, much as in the example above for Coon and his grandmother, that a background of humiliation and pain due to feelings of identification with both the wife and Skunk is so burdensome as to call for relief. An escape from sadness by way of laughter may be an important ingredient of the little play.

Essentially, a response of amusement arises because of the weaving of a special kind of fabric which contains many strands: laughter is consequent upon multiple factors. Some are consciously employed by the narrator and obvious to the audience, but most are subliminal.

Maybe, too, the response is a needed ventilation; one's feeling of identification with the mistreated old woman who is Coon's grandmother might result in sadness and hurt if enough factors that stimulate laughter were not brought in to tip the balance so as to effect an overt response of humor. The extent to which some comedy constitutes for the audience a kind of airing of feeling which offers relief from sadness or pain, owing to identification with a person who is degraded or hurt, has been a moot question among students of humor. Illustrations of humor from the Clackamas collection do not controvert a theory that humor often includes a factor of unpleasantness from which there is need to distract or relieve. Furthermore, the spinning of the web of factors, which balance out to produce smiles or laughter, is not wholly or even largely a matter of sharply conscious manipulation. Most of the components are hidden from both jokester and auditors, and these factors are in large numbers in almost every fun situation. If my attempt to inventory components of Clackamas literary humor is not far off the mark, they rarely number less than six or seven for each such situation. Identification of them, and of a broad factor of relief from disphoria, must remain hypothetical in instances like those in Clackamas humor because of the passing of native informants. However, in the next years the survivors of adjacent peoples could be employed as partial checks should students wish to engage in such a follow-up.

In summary, central tasks in comprehension of humor in an exotic society include the listing of probable items in an inventory of fun-producing factors, attempts to locate the common human and sociocultural origins of each, and indications of their likely psychological dynamics. Since at present rather little is known about any of these, it seemed useful to commence with definitions of some of the problems, to display a possible methodology of analysis of essential factors in humor situations, and to warn that laughter responses always constitute very complex reactions to many quickly woven-together stimuli, most of which are far below the surface of verbal awareness.

CHAPTER XIII

THE GOOD

T HE stories offer only spotty indications of the ethical system of the people; the collection is too small to provide full coverage of this facet of the culture, so as to show the background of values and ideals which would further illumine narrators' motives and audiences' feelings. Ethical formulas were not often explicit in the stories or the all too few ethnographic comments, although, when Mrs. Howard and other informants of Northwest groups were queried directly, they were frequently able to formulate ethical principles. The many principles which were well phrased in direct instruction given to children and youths, and which must have also enjoyed frank discussion by adults, were not often—if ever—offered in stories. I think that this paucity of direct expressions of principles in stories indicates that Chinook society had efficient procedures for inculcation of ethics.

The following inventory is based, then, upon manifest and latent story content, actors' personality structuring (which was in every instance also deduced), and my judgment regarding ethical standards which constituted factors in shaping story content. A narrator virtually never said that an action or actor was good or bad, because everyone automatically responded with evaluations or feelings and took them so for granted that during a story recital nothing about ethics was put into words. Like other peoples of the Northwest, Clackamas elders preached to individual youngsters, especially around puberty, and at such a time were articulate about right and wrong. Ethnographic details about the content of such special pedagogical sessions, with their core of sermonizing, have never been successfully noted.

The literature's evidences for an inventory of major values for men included membership in a family and lineage of well-to-do persons; early maturation and competency at puberty; acquisition during adolescence, by quest or infectious inheritance, of strong spirit-powers; polygynous marriages to girls bought at a high bride price because they too were of well-to-do families; industry and high competency at hunting; bounteous generosity; giving of feasts and dances; loyalty to siblings, kin, and covillagers; sturdy responsibility for everyone's welfare; shrewdness, resourcefulness, and even ruthlessness for the sake of the villagers; willingness to accept sons' maturation and acquisitions of spirit-powers; functioning as an ungrudging son-in-law and a gentle and patient lover in marriage. The mature stage of Coyote (e.g., 9) even stressed the excellence of good works achieved by trickery if all the people, not just a single village populace, were benefited. But in general the principles of ethics must have emphasized good behavior within a village or a small cluster of contiguous villages rather than a larger region.

Ethical principles for men appear to have emphasized hunting more than fishing. Seal Hunter was a man's name (26), and he speared a seal in the story, but no ethical statement can be deduced about fishing. Since a number of myths displayed notable approval of the good hunter (e.g., 1, 3, 18, 19, 34), the stress upon boys' learning to hunt pointed to a greater value placed upon hunting than upon other skills assigned to men. The worth of men's ability to make artifacts was hardly more than implied in the personal name "Canoemaker" (26) and in artifacts which Coyote made for villagers (9) and for ogresses (3). Flint's tarweed-collecting was woman's work which he did, as the older man must, in the absence of a woman in the household (18).

A man, that is, a well-to-do man, was supposed to be sharp of tongue in some situations, but he also had to control himself, be even-tempered, and avoid explosive behavior (10). He had to protect allies and aid those who were friendly and helpful, especially poorer persons who had been generous (13). He deceived and killed such evildoers as murderesses (16) and was allowed to torture men whom he regarded as villains. He was not supposed to engage in unfair tactics or cheating in games (26), although cleverness and resourcefulness in them were good (26, 29). Gullibility and stupidity were preposterous (1, 9, 41). One was expected to respond with verbal bite to a competitor or foe (9, 40). Since the blind were tragic figures, they were not to be treated cruelly (46). Attempts at suicide seem to have been pitiable but absurd (10). An outstanding ideal was that one must never desert kin (47), except in very special kinds of situations such as those presented by boys who endangered the community (55, 56).

Older men were expected to carry packs while younger men who traveled ahead walked unencumbered (30). Men of any age assisted covillagers, as in launching a newly finished canoe (41). Flint's and Panther's carrying-in of fuel may have been an obligation when an in-law visited his wife's family (6, 18), because the likelihood is that collection of fuel was normally woman's work.

Ideal traits which the literature expressed for women included membership in a well-to-do lineage, although a woman did not choose her husband-to-be. She or those who acted for her had to accept the highest bride price offered. She was supposed to resolve crises only with the help of men. Ideally, she was intelligent, mature, and generous to poorer villagers. Her daughter was not to be interfered with when she took care of and raised the grandchildren. A woman was not to try to be young when no longer youthful. She was expected to be competent, responsible, and industrious at feminine tasks like root-digging, and if left alone she was supposed to be able to carry on temporarily without a man's help. Her mourning for a deceased husband was relatively long.

A number of myths offer cumulative evidence of the importance of feminine duties, and the enjoyment of visits, at root sites (e.g., 3, 14, 16, 17, 31, 46). Root-digging was more often cited than berry-picking or other feminine work assignments, but the only overt ethical compulsion connected with a woman's absence at root-digging was to return home if she learned of trouble or danger there. The core of

the obligation was that she not be indecisive or procrastinate and fail to return quickly because of feeling that she ought to get as much food as possible (14). That is, her
kin were more important than her production and storage of food.

The same value which men respected in their serving plenty of food to visitors
and graciously giving meat to poorer villagers applied to women (23, 26, 34). The
stress upon women's distinctive relationships to foods is of interest. Women were
expected to produce efficiently foods such as berries (16); they were expected to
pick up salmon, if they had need for them, when the fish were left on the beach by
fishermen (31, 39).

It is remarkable that the collection provided no pattern of desired traits in
shamans, whether male or female. Apparently distrust of such indispensable gentry
was so great that ideal traits of well-to-do persons were set apart from whatever was
regarded as good in shamans. One might suppose that they were looked upon as
necessary evils, used but feared, although documentation for such a characterization
is lacking in the stories.

Standards for prepubescents, that is, pre-adults, cannot be given in age levels.
Reference is only to children in general. Dangerous beings were more likely to turn
up after dusk, so children were admonished to get into the houses by twilight (18)
and not leave again until sunrise. Neither boys (56) nor girls (43) were supposed to
nag. They were not to chatter or quarrel through the night and disturb the sleep of
others (66). A boy could not maltreat other children (47) or speak angrily to excrements (55). An older brother was expected to share food with his younger brother
(1) and sister (31) and be loyal to a brother no matter how bad the latter's behavior
(40) or how socially intolerable (6). Probably any child rightly acted out a stylized
depression, lying down and neither speaking nor eating if humiliated, mocked, or
maltreated (20). A child rightly maintained ownership of personal effects or pets
given to it (34). These comprise a handful of standards which the collection makes
more or less explicit for children.

Another group of values contains aspects of a single theme: children, especially
boys, were supposed to mature and be ready at puberty to act in an adult manner.
A prepubescent had to become so courageous, skilful, resourceful, and industrious
that if necessary he could support himself and live alone (47). He was expected to
be protective and parental toward younger siblings (16). Infantilization of a prepubescent was bad, indeed (30, 46). The boy was to learn to hunt, usually in his
father's company (4, 30, 46). Feeling that a boy ought early to be identifying with
his father may have had several props, including the promasculine and patrilocal
features of the heritage, but stress on early maturation in terms of work participation may have been an even more important factor in support of the principle that
a boy remained with his father if his parents separated (30). In spite of emphasis
upon early personal independence, a realistic concern about boys' inexperience and
the actual danger to visitors in some villages—in addition to the severe demand for
obedience and loyalty to male authority—may have been at the base of the dictum
that youths mind admonishments about travel in interdicted directions (35).

No one story highlights so well the value placed on perspicacity, bravery, and resourcefulness in children as the myth of the young girl, Water Bug, who revealed and confounded an ogress (17). However, the literature did not urge the theme of early maturation as sharply for girls as for boys. Special concerns for purchasable maidens were barely indicated except for the tale of the girl who, during her first menstruation, should have split a wild celery stalk before eating it (59).

Clackamas stories implied adherence to additional values concerned with children. Such principles connected with some stories which showed how a child was raised with utmost self-sacrifice and devotion (6, 11, 13, 15, 20, 34, et al.). The interesting thing here is that stories lacked any indication of adult expectation or demand that children return an equal amount of love and devotion to parents, apart from dramas wherein a child almost automatically recognized its biological parent of male sex (6, 20, 23). Maybe Clackamas took it for granted that everyone had a romantic kind of love for all consanguineal relatives and only a special sense of belongingness to parents.

If we turn to persons of headman class, we observe that a chief was expected to provide food for his village people when rations were low (8), and at such a time people were to follow his detailed advice about use of food, lest they die (57). Well-to-do people and, of course, persons of headman rank presented gifts of food to the poor in a gracious manner (23). Their wives gave presents of fresh meat to poorer villagers (34). Well-to-do men and headmen were supposed to serve food to visitors (34) without parsimony (31). The literature highlighted the values of the well-to-do and headmen. Presumably slaves and the poor had much the same values, but it is frustrating to find them largely ignored in the literature, so that one cannot deduce distinctive features of their values or anything else about them.

Standards which the literature suggested for husband-wife relationships dealt with matters of separations and extramarital adventurings as much as any other subject. An outstanding formulation is that while the literature did not specify one married man who had an affair with another woman, it treated of a number of wives who had extramarital liaisons. Emphasis was on the importance of a wife's loyalty to her polygynous husband. Extramarital affairs of co-wives were not condoned (2), nor was the behavior of any other woman, such as Bull Frog (2), who abetted them. The principle is explicit that clandestine affairs at dances were disallowed (2). One myth cited a woman who took another's husband. Chinooks must have deprecated such behavior (39), but the blame seems to have been on the female rather than the errant husband.

A husband could kill his wife's inamorato (6). He was allowed to kill her too if the affair was incestuous—apparently a more serious offense. A man whose wife had merely left his household might not always punish her. He could courageously attempt to get her to come back to him (13), and indeed only a brave man put his head into a den of lions, which might constitute in-laws, metaphorically speaking. But a husband could punish his wife severely, even kill her, if her desertion indicated to everyone rejection of his worth (32). The important thing was that he not be made to feel shame. The father of a woman who deserted her husband humiliated her rightly (32), because she shamed him also when she showed her inability to maintain the status of an adult who cared above all for family and home. In deserting her husband, she shamed her father.

Humiliation and incest were patently more serious offenses than extramarital sexuality as such. An analysis of values must retain distinctions between these three, although they interconnected in many situations. There seems to have been an especially unspecific standard that foolish maltreatment of a wife was bad. It might result in her death (14). She could be maltreated, but the treatment ought not to be lethal!

Males who suffered by death for sexuality outside of marriage included unmarried youths who committed incest, knowingly or unknowingly (6, 13). Sexual contact with a menstruating female was probably strongly disapproved, but the literature omitted indication of punishment (13). Accepted as humorous were the accounts of an unmarried youth's mischievousness, sadism, or other acts at the expense of women (9) and of a male shaman's sexual untrustworthiness when he doctored younger women (9).

The proper expression of genitality, whether verbal or physical, was probably always in private, except for humor. A man who enunciated publicly his positive feeling for his wife was ridiculous (18, 19). A sexual climax correctly followed a prolonged period of gentle foreplay, as symbolized in several myths by the supernatural joining of five days and nights. A quick sexual act was bestial (18).

It is difficult to see feelings about right and wrong in the various precultural women who came to marry men, especially headmen. Perhaps the meaning of these incidents is that well-to-do men ought to be unusually cautious about their potential mates because the women could have vicious spirit-powers. Everyone had to keep a watchful eye on a headman's wife on the assumption that she might have an extremely dangerous supernatural. I think that the feeling here is a displacement of anxiety about the wealth and power of headmen's in-laws. The principle also appears that when a wife turned out to be a murderess, a good husband was right to kill her (16, 17).

Feelings and standards about relationships with kin other than husband or wife were often indicated in stories, but not enough to warrant more than tentative generalizations.

The ethical standard of acceptance of children's worth took specific forms. Like anyone else, a parent was supposed to respect a child's words, advice, and insights (14, 17, 37), to a degree perhaps never found in Western civilization.

Training of children in relation to toilet habits is more than obscure. There is only a hint that persons normally did not defecate in one another's presence (30) and another hint that urination may have been more public because of the universal household urine container and its employment for shampooing.

A man's respect for children continued into respect for the beginning adulthood of his sons. He was not to fear sons as growing competitors, as an Oedipus-like headman did (38). Later he would surely be humbled. A father ought to accept his son's adulthood, as symbolized in the son's first spirit-power relationship (7, 60). In fact, a man was supposed to help sons or grandsons acquire supernaturals, even if they took his own spirit-powers (13). A father was expected to inform his sons of all weighty matters after the youngsters passed through puberty (42).

A youth expressed approaching maturation by journeying, having a variety of experiences en route, and bravely seeking spirit-power kin with the aid of his father (13, 46, 48, 60). That was the time when a son could plan to avenge his father's murder (5, 13). Perhaps he had been raised by his father's brother, for a good uncle took tender and unremitting care of an orphaned nephew (6, 29); he also took the same interest in and care of the boy while the boy's father was living. In fact, brothers functioned as paternal teammates toward their sons. A young man was expected to avenge his father's murder (5) and could do so by mutilating, torturing, or killing the offender. He might correctly slaughter the entire village populace whose headman had killed his father (13). The literature did not suggest rights in the case of a mother's murder.

Parents and other adult kin rigorously controlled and suppressed expressions of grief or fear before children who had not yet reached puberty, lest the child identify feelings which no child was sufficiently mature to handle (13). Adolescent youths who were already seeking supernaturals were probably still so lacking in such allies, or in increments of strength from them, that they were to be cautioned about journeying in a direction where there might be danger (35). Youths had to obey such admonishment.

Standards in kin relationships from the feminine viewpoint included some distinctive emphases and omissions. The stories indicated truly romantic uncle-nephew ties but lacked mention of aunt-niece bonds. One myth treated of two bad sisters who kidnapped a girl (20). In another an older sister at length deserted her younger sister who was an inexhaustible nag (43), whereas the older brother of another myth remained admirably faithful to his younger brother in spite of great irritation and provocation (40). Female siblings were cited in other situations: sororal polygyny appeared symbolically in the several accounts of five girls who came to a man's abode (e.g., 24, 27).

The majority of ethical principles expressed for women in the literature had to do with their roles as wives and mothers. If a girl had an illegitimate infant, she hid her pregnancy, delivered the baby unobserved by villagers and maybe all alone (30), and had to accept marriage to the man who was found to have impregnated her (23). An unmarried girl, even a headwoman, could not reject the suitor who offered an adequate sum for her in marriage (4, 28) lest he be humiliated by her refusal. Parents who greedily held out for an exorbitant bride price for their daughter were not well regarded (45).

A widow had to raise her orphaned son (4, 18). Like any good mother, she would put valuables on her child so that he could be justified in pride for his parents (20). A woman could never leave her nursing infant for an extended time even if she was wealthy and had slaves (46), nor could she desert him or her polygynous husband (13). If he left her, she must patiently wait and go back to him when return was possible (4, 18). She also assisted her husband in final preparations of the body of his other wife (34).

The lower status of females was pointed up by additional special standards for women. A female probably used an elegant name when she addressed an upper-class man (33). Poor women, not poor men, were cited as the ones who exhibited notable hospitality to visitors to a village (13). While various stories indicated that murderesses were to be killed, murderers were less often cited. Little was said about distrust of alien men, while explicit mentions were made of the importance of suspicion of the advice (17), motivations, and dangerous supernaturals (14, 17) of alien women, especially those who had married into the village.

No story suggested that an older man of the household became too dominating, although he might lust for a son's or grandson's wife. But several stories expressed dramatically the principle that one could properly disapprove of the behavior and motives of an older woman who would be likely to want to maintain her control and position in a son's or grandson's house after the young man married. She ought to accept his young wives, surrender management to them (24, 27), and reconcile herself to second place in his feelings.

There was no intimation that a man was supposed to side-step hostility directed at him, but a female was supposed to deflect or skilfully avoid anger and jealousy directed at her by another woman (27) unless the other was her co-wife. Then a good fight was in order (34), and people stood by anxiously or amusedly to watch it. Although brutality in a husband may have had to be borne with some resignation (14), a woman could not humiliate a fine headman (28); she was outwardly loyal to him no matter how awful his village or kin (45). Her status was nowhere so effectively indicated as in stories which depicted a woman who endured a frightful situation for years. She resolved it only with the assistance of her son at the time when he entered adolescence and effected relationships with supernaturals. Therefore a woman did what she had to and took aggressive action only through men and with their help and approval (e.g., 6, 38, 42).

A woman was not to infantilize a child (30, 46), but nothing was said about a man doing that. A girl could not speak to her dog as if it were human (65), but no story of the collection referred to a man who addressed his dog in such a manner. A headwoman's daughter was expected to be gracious even to the poorest and most unattractive boy of her village (23), when nothing was said of a headman's sons' obligation toward the poor. No principle was found which applied to a man's behavior toward his former wife, but a woman who attended a dance given by the man from whom she had separated was in bad taste at the least (46), and probably she subjected herself to public shame. A man was quickly freed from mourning restrictions, but a widow had to wait many months before she was allowed to go about as before (69). Although a man could be spunky, clever, tricky if for the welfare of the people, and courageous even when in mortal danger (9, 10, 11, 40), a woman was expected to sit it out with poise, if not equanimity, until her son or another man could render assistance. Nonetheless, to speak of an ideal of feminine passivity is to oversimplify. Women were by no means passive in a majority of situations, but we do not have sufficient evidences to show how or when they were relatively passive, except for the few kinds of predicaments mentioned.

For both sexes credulousness, timorousness, and lack of skill must have been laughable and shameful, possibly more so for men (9). In addition, a man was expected to keep his word (23), and there is nothing to warrant a thought that such a standard did not hold equally for women.

These distressingly short inventories of values may be regarded as representative of those stresses in sociocultural life which, for reasons that are not clear, received ventilation and affirmation in literature. The whole picture of value ideals remains to be filled in, by means of comparative ethnographic studies. Such research may add to literary indications that the transmitters of Clackamas oral literature had no important values or aspirations beyond high social status, wealth, absence of humiliations or slights, and need for the utmost feeling of security in ties with kin, foods, and animistic supernaturals. Emphases seem to have been also on maturity, intelligence, shrewdness, and courage. The opposite of the good was to be poor, stupid, immature, humiliated, and lacking in the ties indicated.

Implicit and explicit components in the philosophy of ethics which would, if known, have efficiently presented the whole background of values held by narrators and audience are most unsatisfactorily evidenced in the tiny lists of almost wholly upper-class values that have been cited. If this chapter has merit, it is as an example of deduction of ethical principles from a small body of stories, when ethnographic procedures had to be relinquished. A rounded comprehension of a literature and its multiple determinants is impossible without possession of the people's value ideals and depiction of the various functions of those ideals in the sociocultural system. Since only a few ideals have been harvested, and their roots in the social system are obscure in many instances, an important part of a full literary analysis remains unexplored. Too, a number of ethical factors which supported borrowings of story content, and which pressured choices of what to include and what to omit, can never be ascertained for Clackamas literature.

CHAPTER XIV

WORLD VIEW

I F KNOWLEDGE of Clackamas ethics is a thing of shreds and patches, the yield of data on their world view is even less satisfactory. The few findings and deductions should nevertheless be assembled in order to display something of the ideological frame which bounded stories.

Peoples of the Washington-Oregon area undoubtedly had myths which described ultimate world origins. Villagers who polemicized informally about myth situations and actors surely did not block at every point when basic ideological matters were questioned, but Indians with whom anthropologists have worked in the northwest states patently had retained little interest in matters of theory which conflicted in most respects with the Christians' orientation. Either collections such as Mrs. Howard's lack cosmological content, or origin legends dictated have reached a degree of attenuation or compression which does not permit clear deductions.

Whatever the detailed structure and history of the Clackamas universe had once been, narrators in many groups of western Oregon agreed that the Indian world view had been presented in a developmental or historical frame. Mrs. Howard was definite about three stages of evolution: a long precultural era, the Myth Age, in which often extraordinary events succeeded one another; a later and probably much shorter transitional era; and a brief modern period whose actors and events were of kinds which modern people experienced. Her collection contains no myths describing significant features of the modern world structure or the physical aspects of precultural times. One myth cited a few details of a land of dead persons, another of a land in the sky. Mrs. Howard probably failed to recall other myths which would have added to our knowledge of Clackamas cosmology.

A few features of the Myth Era can be gleaned. There was an earth, with precultural hamlets and peoples, in various conditions of incompleteness and with many things and creatures which were like humans, but no recorded myth shows how that earth and its inhabitants and things came to be. Some precultural people lacked mouths; others lacked such basic artifacts of food production as fish traps and spears. Men did not know how to pack fuel or copulate. Oral impregnation occurred. Some people were ridiculously immature or ignorant. Dangerous beings such as the Earth and Water Swallowers imperiled everyone. Dangerous animals like grizzlies were in larger numbers than now. Vermin were killers. Fauna which now dwell in the waters, on land, and in the air were both human-like and animal. Certain rocks were at one time precultural creatures. Seasons had different durations. Winter was colder than in later eras. Some few people like *Ku'šaydi* (40) and the adult Coyote had vastly greater spirit-powers than a modern ever acquired. Things were in general very different. But stress was on incompleteness, immaturity, incompetency, and greater dangers.

In various writings on Pacific Northwest folklore, Professor Franz Boas employed the terms "trickster" and "transformer" for some of the most important Myth Era actors. These terms cannot be applied aptly as designations for Clackamas actors of that epoch. Although the younger and impulse-driven Coyote (9) was tricky, emphasis was upon his unrepressed acting-out of needs for food, sex, and killing. He lacked cultural restraints because he was still immature. Blue Jay was a juvenile of another kind and, unlike Coyote, never outgrew immaturity. Both young men were unmarried. Even the older Coyote, when unmarried, showed continuity with his youth. He was tortured by impulses which youngsters had, and like them he could not hold such drives in check. He then represented many older men.

I shall later consider the stylization which I term "announcer." Its discussion may be anticipated with the observation that Boas' term "transformer" emphasized overt efforts of Coyote and a few other deific actors of great spirit-power. "Announcer" is a more apt designation of such Clackamas actors, although some also transformed specific features of the inchoate precultural world. They asserted that certain characteristics of the future would presently take form, or they also effectively decided upon such forms. But in only a rare instance or two did a more or less altruistic actor shape with his own hands some feature of the modern world, as Coyote did when he made fish spears and cut the faces of mouthless people (9).

The Clackamas world view included among the many actors of Myth Times a small group of unrepressed juveniles, such as the early Coyote and the clownish Blue Jay, and a larger group of announcers of the future (the latter included the mature Coyote, who had value ideals). But only a few such announcers were altruistically motivated. Most of them no more than proclaimed what was going to happen, in some one respect, when the world changed in later myth times or during transitional times. The Chinooks' Sahaptin neighbors' stress that a tricky "Coyote changed everything" possibly was weak or lacking among the Clackamas. Announcements devoid of deity-like transforming were a clearly defined kind of precultural behavior and were central in the Clackamas conception of the myth period. Actors who were not at all tricksters announced. All preculturals, in fact, might announce, but some also transformed creatures and things—among them a number of persons who announced their own transformation. Portentous consequences developed from mere errors made by a few precultural actors, or from actions which were due to their human-like feelings. For example, because Coyote (10) was unable to control his fury at a Centipede, no one could return from death and no one could live for all time. In other words, transformations or determinations which decided the future more frequently flowed automatically from situations in which preculturals were the actors than from deliberations or choices by those personages.

The line between a mere announcement and a deliberate and effective manipulation of the future, after the fashion of a deity, remains unclear. Coyote was the sole actor who did both (9). Apart from him, those actors who transformed things or persons included the following: *Ku'šaydi* (40) ordained the future for the Thunders and for the creek which flooded over. Cock Robin's older sister (31) ordained his subsequent behavior. Her two sons transformed themselves into a snake and a feather, perhaps for all time to come. The stepson of Tongue Man (42) did deific work when he transformed things into people and canoes. Thunder Boy (30) also did transforming.

A much larger number of persons, who include even the insane Grizzly Woman (16), did announcing only. The number of announcers was at least twice the number of precultural persons who did transforming, although transformations and announcements were assigned to both sexes and to young and old.

Although Clackamas literature glamorized or set upon a pinnacle only three males, each of whom had great spirit-powers, two of the three, Coyote and *Ku'šaydi*, transformed things. Panther did not. Cock Robin's sister, her two sons, Tongue's stepson, the insane Grizzly Ogress, and Thunder Boy were not as memorable as Panther; but they transformed things, while he never did so. The point is that minor as well as major actors transformed features of early times. Minor actors as well as major actors were also announcers. And any actors might be tricky.

One myth (8) exemplified an exceptionally formal announcer and showed that he was truly a projection of an altruistic headman. Other announcers, as already noted, were anything but altruistic or representative of headmen.

More important for comprehension of the Clackamas world view than ultimate origins, cosmology, supernaturally potent juveniles, and announcers was the ideology of relationships of people and kin, major artifacts, foods, and spirit-powers. These linked like a chain welded by intense feelings of mutual belonging. People, artifacts, foods, and animistic supernaturals needed, wanted, and upon occasion effected helpful relationships with each other. But the role of individual people—their initiative, courage, potential for maturity, and cleanliness—was the decisive factor in bringing about such relationships. Self-identity and props to feeling of personal worth and security were not located in cosmology, least of all in a deity or pantheon of great supernaturals. Clackamas probably had no elaborate universe which extended far into space. The sky country was at no enormous distance.

Nor were Clackamas monistically inclined. Their reality was not a universe but a pluriverse. It lacked a mana-like basis or ultimate substance. The world was a patterning of interpersonal relationships forged by adults. The components of the pattern included a large number of variably potent entities—some were located not far away from the settlements, others at a fair distance. It is as if modern reality comprised village headmen, consanguineal kin, distrusted affinal kin, anxiety-provoking distant villages and peoples, and innumerable helpful entities which were basic artifacts, foods, and spirit-powers, some of which were relatives. This was a concrete world of kin, kin in the broadest sense, in a big chain or pattern. All these kin needed, wanted, and often obtained each other's help, and spirit-powers were only a degree less tangible or visible than the others. Every person constituted a link in the chain of relationships, but only during a lifetime, for upon death a tragic and irremediable severance occurred. His spirit-power kin left him; his abilities in use of artifacts had diminished some time before; and his soul-ghost went to dwell far away in the land of dead persons for a short period of years, then vanished forever. A living person had only tepid feelings for entities, structures, and lands far beyond in past or future. Clackamas lived in the present, and in the present they had all these different kinds of kin.

The collection does not answer important questions such as the life span of spirit-powers and their relationships to each other apart from ties that they wanted with humans. Present knowledge of other northwest states groups suggests—and the notion is not contradicted in Mrs. Howard's materials—that two or more Clackamas might acquire almost identical spirit-power kin, because each type of spirit-power was represented by many individual spirit-power beings. That is, there were many supernatural coyotes, many male grizzlies, many female grizzlies, and so on. Each spirit-individual was a potential relative of an individual Clackamas. Probably, therefore, many a winter spirit-power dance witnessed a person singing and dancing to express his relationship to his supernatural, while another member of the audience thrilled with utmost identification because he too related to such a spirit-power.

Unhappily, there is no Clackamas evidence regarding the feelings toward one another of persons who shared spirit-powers of similar kind. Nor is there evidence as to whether so-called inheritance of a supernatural, because of the kind of close contiguity exemplified by Fire's great-grandsons (13) or Hazel Drumstick's nephews (29), involved joint possession of the same supernatural or a kind of introduction to another supernatural of the same class. In addition, there is no information about the abode or nearness of a spirit-power which a person acquired away from the village, and where it went when that person aged and later died. The question concerning its life span or immortality is insoluble, too. Probably it returned to its haunts in the waters or hills where it had lived years before, and rested in loneliness again or slept until another suppliant approached it.

Interests in and therefore theorization about spirit-powers, the land from which babies came, the land of the dead, and ghost-souls were evidently considerable. On the other hand, either curiosity regarding sun, moon, stars, sky, storms, the development and structuring of the universe, and other cosmological matters was slight, or the content of this collection does almost nothing to point to Clackamas preoccupations with such subjects. The explanation of differing intensities of interest seems to be that personal security and death anxieties were resolved by spirit-powers and by notions of the beyond, that is, the lands of babies and dead persons. No one suffered as much anxiety about the nature of heavenly bodies, the origin and layering of the universe, or storms except blizzards. Blizzards were, in fact, cited a number of times in this collection. Again, the world view focused upon the near at hand, in the forms of relationships of various kinds, not upon the far and distant, in the forms of cosmological theory.

The special role of Coyotes in the totality of primarily mundane components of the Clackamas world view strengthens curiosity about the causes for their retention and maintenance. Why were Myth Era personalities like the Coyotes conspicuously earthly? They are quite unlike some of the Near Eastern supernaturals. Even in

Thunder Man there is only a trace of the celestial. The speculation which I have to offer contains these suggestions: Incessant public discussions around myths, myth actors, lands beyond view or travel, and people's spirit-powers tended to align with innermost anxieties and needs of "good" or well-to-do persons and lineages rather than with poorer lineages or slaves. Lineages of "good" people made up a large percentage, although no one knows approximately how much, of village populations. Ratiocinations by such dominant gentry about the qualities and adventures of the most pleasing personalities of yore—that is, Coyote people, Panther people, and the like—sustained a constellation of traits which "good" people sanctioned and desired in themselves. If a body of priestly specialists rather than lay shamans had been needed and supported, that group might presently have set forth and elaborated supernatural constructs of other kinds to bolster its self-esteem and social role.

In the absence of philosopher-priests the Coyote and Panther projections persevered as myth screen representations of the principal custodians of familial, lineage, and community security. There was no social base for projection of potencies which resided in austere father figures. In addition, there was no concept of lives which endured, following mortals' deaths, in lands ruled by deific persons. Protectors were actualized efficiently in headmen, lineages, communities, food beings, artifact beings, and spirit-powers. Only headmen and their well-off associates, not shamans, were the articulate creators, sources, and perpetuators of the world view of all the people. They spoke for the people in more ways than one. Since priestlike groups were entirely absent in all northwest states Indian societies, the type of philosophizing or structuring of a special security system, which such men might offer, could not be present. The cosmology of a well-to-do and all-controlling rank and file of the kind found in a Clackamas village, with its disrespect for its land of the dead, was unlikely to depart as far from reality as the fantasy world of a group of philosopher-priests.

Any effort to deduce Ruth Benedict's type of culture pattern, upon a basis of stresses, feelings, and value ideals expressed in the oral literature, would oversimplify the picture of the Clackamas world view. One doubts whether any people's world view can be well characterized by an isolated utilization of those projections and other kinds of content which the folklore displays. If a number of so-called culture themes, as suggested by Morris Opler for a whole sociocultural heritage, were deduced from the folklore alone, their value would also have to be regarded cautiously. Folkloristic source materials require an adequate supporting ethnography to give the entire range of evidences for culture pattern and culture theme presentations. On the other hand, statements about themes seen in the folklore, as in the chapter on principal emphases of content, serve as tentative hypotheses pointing to prime features of other northwest states cultures where some of these features had not earlier been sensed by anthropologists and where informants could still give evidence. An anthropologist can and should use an oral literature in many ways, and some of the insights which he extracts from it may be seminal. But he must connect and strengthen them with what he draws out of other facets of the people's behavior.

CHAPTER XV

SONGS

A N ANALYSIS of an oral literature would be incomplete without inclusion of songs, dances, and other dramatic forms of expression like the mimicry to which a narrator and discussants resorted. In a dying culture the recording of some of these aspects of the literature may be difficult or impossible, but in their sessions with a visiting anthropologist, even the last surviving northwest states raconteurs have given excellent evidence that their literatures were punctuated by songs of various kinds—spirit-power melodies, feud songs, and lullabies. Some of them were only the musical facet of a song-and-dance whole, as in a spirit-power performance or in pre- and post-fighting song-dances. The dance facet of a literature must almost always be omitted from consideration, not because of lesser importance or aesthetic worth, but because the twentieth-century narrator recalled only the melody, sat when dictating, as did Mrs. Howard, or was sometimes unable, as Mrs. Howard was because of her heart condition, to illustrate the dance of a myth actor. Such an actor, like modern Clackamas, frequently used song and dance forms, and these features of stylization are no less deserving of consideration in study of an oral literature than are the verbal expressions which constitute the major portion of an anthropologist's field records.

Mrs. Howard did not remember a large number of songs which were integral with myths. The small inventory of melodies which she recalled she sang onto Ediphone cylinders, and others (songs 19 to 26) I did not, at the time, appreciate the importance of obtaining on a mechanical record, or I neglected to check whether I had recorded them.

Mrs. Howard mentioned no songs which were part of the tales. One may therefore infer that the longer periods during which myths had been discussed by the community were responsible for musical additions and embellishments to literature. Tales, with their shorter life span, had as yet failed to receive ornamenting with musical or music-dance forms.

Because of the rarity of anthropological musicologists, neither myth nor other songs which Mrs. Howard recorded on Ediphone cylinders (copies of which are in my possession) have been analyzed. This section accordingly is limited to brief citations of myth songs, without discussion of their musical features or correlation of such characteristics with the content and style of the rest of the literature. *Clackamas Chinook Texts* also presents citations of myth songs.

Each of the birds and animals, whether modern or precultural, had one or more spirit-power songs, just as well-to-do people did; and the words of such songs were often similar in content, whether ascribed to myth actors or to modern birds or animals. Frequently the creature selected one or two distinctive characteristics of himself, as in Rabbit's and Owl's songs below, and these salient features of self-identity were accorded expression in the song words. The words made statements of the tersest kind about his appearance and habits, never about his supernatural strength.

I have numbered myth songs from 1 to 26 in this section, in order to expedite referral, and I have placed this section under the larger heading of features of content only because data which I possess and statements which I am able to make are fuller for items of content than of form. Like everything else in a cultural heritage, songs display both content and form, but the line between them can never be drawn with razor sharpness, and musicological analysis must be ventured before a broader sketching of formal aspects of myth music can be offered.

1. Rabbit Shaman's spirit-power song (myth 7, Ediphone cylinder song 14524*b*, tape 6) was possibly sung with percussion accompaniment on a skin drum, during a recital of olden times. Mrs. Howard did not own a drum. A free and uncertain translation of the words is:

> I am standing and sneaking around (in the woods).
> I stand (sit) up on my haunches in the underbrush.

Mrs. Howard sang it faster as she repeated it, perhaps thereby illustrating Rabbit's —and any shaman's—crescendo of intensity and effort to employ his spirit-power at full strength. The words of Chipmunk's spirit-power song (14537*d*, tape 9) may be compared because, although not presented in a myth, its verbal content was like that of Rabbit's song. Chipmunk said in the words of his melody:

> Only in the fog.
> That is when I stand on my haunches.

2. Owl Shaman's spirit-power song (myth 7, song 14524*c*, tape 6) was sung by the narrator in the same context in the same myth as the one which presented Rabbit Shaman. A free translation of the words is:

> This is how his little bill goes—it is noisy.
> My legs are covered with feathers.
> My eyes are yellow-green.

3. In myth 7 the spirit-power of Coyote's fifth, youngest, and favorite child was of fatty things and perhaps specifically referred to a sturgeon which she acquired, as her spirit-power kin, while she was going beside a lake. It flapped onto the gravel and presently became her supernatural. The words of the girl's spirit-power song (14537*e*, tape 9), sung by the storyteller in the manner in which a person sang his own spirit-power song at a winter dance for renewal of supernaturals' strengths and relationships, are in free translation:

> While (I was) going beside the lake,
> a fish flapped ashore right here (by me).
> A fatty one, a fatty one.

Significantly, a myth actor, like a singer at a spirit-power dance, did not name her new supernatural. She cited only a characteristic or two of her new relative—here, that it came from the water and was fat and oily. Mrs. Howard supposed that it was a sturgeon, although that fish is not ordinarily landlocked.

4. The spirit-power song (myth 25, song 14540*a*, tape 10) of Wildcherry Tree Shaman, a woman hired by Blue Jay and Jay Bird to doctor Wren's drowned grandmother, resembled other songs of myth actors in its selection of one of her own traits:

> Drum drum drum drum.
> They use me for sewing canoes.

5. The same statement holds for the comical spirit-power song (14540*b*, tape 10) of Diarrhea Shaman Man in the same myth (25):

> Thickly I flow.
> Very very thickly I flow.
> Thinly (like water) I flow.

The expressive content amusingly contrasted three consistencies and perhaps was the funnier because the thinnest was third and last.

6. The third shaman employed in this myth (25) was some kind of bird person; she was not remembered or identified by Mrs. Howard, apparently because the words of her song (14540*c*, tape 10) did not denote anything about her. They expressed instead her effort to resuscitate the drowned grandmother, with these wishful statements:

> I wish my younger sister would move.
> I wish my younger sister would turn on her side.
> I wish my younger sister would sit up.

One wonders if the word for "younger sister" suggests that a shaman might thereby say, in his song to a sick or dying aged woman, that she was not so old that she should be dying.

7. The content of most Myth Age spirit-power songs, with their selection of a salient characteristic of the actor represented as singing, was repeated in the hand-game song of Hazel Drumstick Gambler (myth 29, song 14540*d*, tape 10). He pointedly identified himself in his three song words, repeating interminably as he played with the hand-game sticks:

> Hazel drumstick gambler.

The narrator sang these words with variations in word order, syllable stress, vowel lengthenings, and perhaps other variations, permissible and typical of all the music.

8. Another stress in content is found in the mocking song (myth 28, song 14542*a*, tape 10) of the well-to-do girl who sang these words as she paddled past the village where her deceived purchaser dwelt with her dog as his wife:

> He thought it must be me.
> But I deceived him with my dog.

9. Still another emphasis appears in the words of the lullaby sung to little Thunder Boy by his mother (myth 30, song 14542*f*, tape 10). Mrs. Howard beat time lightly, but a narrator did not use a drum for the song. Mrs. Howard's baby boy had this lullaby sung to him by her father's aunt, and other people also used the melody when they held and rocked male—but not female—infants. Although the adult sang to the child, the words suggested that the infant sang and spoke, and they expressed Thunder Boy's capacity to grow with uncanny rapidity:

> Only one year,
> only one year.
> The second year,
> then I'll take care of myself.
> Then I'll take care of myself.

10. Another kind of song content is found in the musical expression of pleasure, surprise, and flattery felt by the lower-class people, Greyback Lice, when the headman's second wife, Grizzly Woman, made them a gift of venison (myth 34, song 14543*a*, tape 10). The Lice sang and danced gaily, using words which were approximately these:

> Whenever before had they given us victuals?
> (Now) they give us food!

The astonished Lice were really saying "Surprise! For the first time we have been presented with fresh meat!" One wonders whether the song and dance satirized the generosity of headmen's wives and whether its words thereby suggested that only an error would result in a poor person being given truly fine food.

11. In myth 5 Coyote indulged in unceasing mock mourning for his Salmon grandson, whom he had murdered (14543*c*, tape 10). The words of his endlessly repeated song of mourning expressed his wish to show that he would continue to mourn for ten years and that he would feel great grief for this extraordinary period. His singing was designed to give evidence that he was confused and half-crazy with grief. The words "one side they are heaped" refer, I presume, to the bones, that is, the body of the grandson buried nearby. The words about being poisoned for five years may indicate that for the first of two five-year periods he would be, he deceitfully claimed, sick with grief, unable to eat anything, and mourning especially intensely because of the close kin who was dead. During the first period he would also be doing "nothing the right way"; he would be chronically hostile and irritable, "kind of fighting all the time." He "kind of cries and howls" in his song, according to Mrs. Howard. A free translation is:

> I shall mourn for ten years.
> They (his bones) are heaped to one side here,
> they are heaped to one side here.
> I shall remain poisoned for five years.
> They are piled on one side,
> they are piled on one side.

12. In the same myth (5) the vicious Wolf Men sang, over and over, words which expressed their preternatural awareness that Coyote's great-grandson, Steelhead, had dried up the springs to which they usually resorted for drinking water upon their return home (14543d, tape 10). The song words indicated that although a person might not be manifestly aware of what was transpiring, his spirit-power expressed latent knowledge and evidenced it in the song. The Wolves did not suspect Steelhead's presence or intent, but the words they sang revealed that their supernaturals knew about their destiny and its cause:

> Steelhead! Steelhead!
> His (Salmon's) son! His son!
> He has dried up
> our water, our water.

13. Trout's outraged husband, Panther, expressed his feelings about Coyote's attempt to take Trout (myth 6, song 14543e, tape 10) in three words which, freely translated, are:

> We have only one wife,
> the rascal and I.

14. Coon acted as a father to Panther's baby boy (6) and, when feeding the motherless infant with marrow spread on a burl, sang a sentimental lullaby (14543f, tape 10):

> The tiny nipples, the tiny nipples,
> they make him grow, they make him grow.
> My brother's son! my brother's son!

The romantic feelings of the paternal Coon toward the infant were enhanced by the morpheme for "nipple": it is apparently a rare instance, among Northwest languages, of a special morpheme of the kind known in languages of the West as baby talk.

15. Milt Man's first wife sang and danced hostilely in front of the second wife (myth 39, song 14544b, tape 11). The words of her jeering song, which from the Clackamas viewpoint expressed the essence of what had transpired, were:

> She deceived herself with milt.

This phrase was repeated many times.

16. The mournful Bear Woman, grieving for her infant who had just died, expressed her feeling about her child. She redirected her intense grief into anger at the ripe, edible, and tempting salmonberries which were falling on her and which, she supposed in her paranoid-like depression, were dropping deliberately on her. She sang over and over (myth 15, song 14547a, tape 11):

> Keep away! salmonberries!
> My child is dead! salmonberries!

One may conjecture that a modern person who was grieving for a recently deceased close kin also expressed himself spontaneously in song form, seizing upon immediacies which intensified sad or angry feelings and ventilating his hurt in the song.

17. Coyote called out—he really hallooed in a kind of song recitative—to each of five animal people to come help him with his dying brother Skunk (myth 1, song 14547d, tape 11). The song was sung supposedly five times to each animal person summoned. Freely rendered, the words are:

> Who will come?
> Our older brother is going to (might) die because of his stomach.

18. Frogs sang a recitative or song in the presence of Lizard Man (myth 33, songs 14548a, b, tape 39). Freely rendered, the words say:

> FROG: Now we are (on our lake) sitting on our croak,
>   now we are sitting on our croak.
> LIZARD: Croak croak.

Later the Frogs sang without Lizard present:

> Where will Snake's son (Lizard) come from?
> Now we are sitting on our croak croak.

Although frogs and lizards were projected into anthropomorphic actors of Myth Times, they were unimportant to Clackamas because their ability to confer supernatural power was slight. The poetry of the song words was a romantic expression of some minor naturalist biology.

19. Rabbit Shaman sang one of his spirit-power songs during a dance for Coyote's daughter, who had just evidenced her relationship to a new supernatural (7). This song of Rabbit is unfortunately not on an Ediphone record. All I have are field notes giving the text and translation of song words, which, approximately rendered, may be:

> Where it breaks, where it breaks,
> it will shake and loosen the crossbeam of the roof.
> Where it breaks, where it breaks,
> it will shake and loosen the crossbeam of the roof.

The connotations are not certain to me, but I offer the suggestion that Rabbit was boasting that his spirit-power was so great that he could shake a crossbeam loose. To be sure, the beam fell, but no one in the myth audience was injured. Rabbit sang a recorded song (number 1, above) following his unrecorded roof beam song.

20. Unhappily, the spirit-power song of Pheasant Woman, in the first scene of myth 9, was also not recorded on a cylinder. Only the single Clackamas word which was used in the song is given in the field notes, and without translation. This word was repeated interminably, with the stylized variants of stress and lengthening which characterized musical style. Mrs. Howard did not know what the spirit-power of the Myth Age Pheasant Woman was. Curiously, the only song in this long Coyote myth was in the initial scene, but one must allow for the possibility that another storyteller might have offered a version with additional musical content.

21. During the rendition of myth 20, which told of the girl who was kidnapped by two Gopher Women, a narrator always sang a song at the point where the child became a toddler and thereby made her mother especially happy. The song represented the Gophers' singing and the way they made the child dance at this time of transition in the youngster's life. If a modern Clackamas mother failed to sing and to make her child dance in like fashion when it reached this stage of its growth, it might weep, become ill, and return to the land of babies because it felt unappreciated and rejected in the land of the Clackamas. Unfortunately, although Mrs. Howard knew all this, she was unable to recall either music or words of the Gophers' song. She only knew that there was such a melody. Obviously Clackamas were sentimental about little children's stages of growth and were deeply anxious that their care of children, and manifestations of affection and concern, were such that the children would realize how much they were wanted. Lullabies were therefore supplemented by songs marking the stages following infancy in arms and cradle.

22. Snake Tail Woman's hallooing to her Snake grandsons (24) may have constituted a song recitative of the type exemplified (in myth 1, song 1, above) where Coyote summoned animal people to help him with his supposedly dying brother. The words uttered by Snake Tail in her song-call to a Snake grandson were:

> Son's son!
> Snake Tail (is speaking)!
> Some person has come to me!

Regrettably, I did not make an Ediphone recording of this call, probably because at the time of field research I failed to regard it as in a category of songs. My hunch is that it was in a monotone.

23. Another song, sung by a lone Greyback Louse Woman (36), was a song and dance expression of glee after she tricked and drowned a Grizzly Man. Her song words, doubtfully translated, were perhaps:

> I killed the timbers' paddle.
> I am Greyback Louse.
> I am Greyback Louse.

Again, I have no Ediphone rendering of the song. It was funny because it expressed the incongruity of so tiny a female, vermin and a lower-class person to boot, killing so large and dangerous a male.

24. The only humming which I noted in the literature was by the same actor, Greyback Louse Woman (36). The melody, indicated in *Clackamas Chinook Texts* (see note 286), was funny, both musically and because it represented wordlessly the sardonic intent of a small and lower-class female actor to ensnare and kill a vain male monster, Grizzly Man. Sometimes Mrs. Howard varied her humming of the melody by singing it with "nonsense" syllables. I believe that modern Indians used the fetching little melodic theme in appropriate situations which also contained a reference to malicious and sadistic behavior.

25. Coon's grandmother (49) felt so upset, after she beat him and he left, that she

wept and sang a song of regret as she went along seeking him. Her songlike crying said:

> Grandson! my grandson!
> He went to get a (small spotted) doe for me
> my grandson.

These evasive words were means of saying that he should return to her in spite of her having whipped him. She wanted to say that she had not meant to whip him. She said, with poetic indirection and sentimental emphasis upon the presumed love of a grandson for his grandmother, that he had gone only to seek a doe for her. I did not obtain an Ediphone record of this song.

26. In his turn, Coon (49) went along, purged of his former need to be vindictive against his grandmother and burdened with self-pity because he was alone. Now he was a kind of orphan. So he, too, wept. When he passed by a house and its occupants sociably invited him to come to play at a gambling game with them, he cried out in a songlike recitative which said:

> Oh no!
> My grandmother whipped me.
> She broke my tail.

Coon's grandmother had not literally broken his tail, but she had marked his body —or his coat of fur—for all time. Therefore he selected this striking feature of his appearance as evidence of the woman's maltreatment and rejection of him, and in order to receive the pity of all the people. He felt too lonesome and unwanted to enter the company of persons who were playing happily, and each group he passed responded to his crying and singing by laughing at him and saying that he deserved his stripes because he had been stealing after the fashion of raccoons. I neglected to ask Mrs. Howard to make an Ediphone recording of this song of complaint, but I might add that a similar song, for a comparable scene, was in Tillamook Salish literature which Elizabeth D. Jacobs recorded on the northern coast of Oregon.

Although my field notes about the twenty-six Clackamas myth songs were fragmentary and Ediphone recordings made of only eighteen, a few statements can be offered about the poetry of song words, in addition to observations which accompany the citations above.

Songs certainly exhibited some distinctive verbal features of a stylized kind, apart from purely linguistic characteristics. Most notable is the repetition of a word or phrase of at most two or three words, while the entire song was almost always sung five or more times. In other words, the culture's five-pattern applied only to song wholes. Other structural features were applied, one might say internally, within songs. The "double repeat" structuring is found in myth songs numbered 1, 3, 9, 11, 12, 14, 16, 18, 19, 23, and 25. Perhaps it was present in others, too. It also characterized a number of non-myth spirit-power songs and probably songs of additional kinds. Word or phrase repetition was superseded by a threefold form where repetition, saturation, or progression needed emphasis: In the fifth song, a triple repetition of "flow thickly" intensified the comic aspect of the content, and another triple form in the sixth song indicated progressive stages of resuscitation.

Again, the many distinctive linguistic and musical devices in songs are not treated here because special approaches are demanded for their detection and analysis. It is sufficient to remark, regarding linguistic traits, that among them it is obvious that morphemes, especially their sonorous segments, were often greatly lengthened. Non-phonemic vowels frequently replaced junctures between consonants.

I perceive no regularities in frequencies or occurrences of songs in myths, other than their likely but not habitual presence when myth personages were acting out their spirit-powers. For example, occasions in the long journey of Coyote (9) when actors sang and danced or resorted to a spirit-power performance were definitely in the scene with Pheasant Woman, and probably also in the scenes with the dancing girls across the river and with Coyote's doctoring of a sick girl. But Mrs. Howard sang only in the episode when Pheasant practiced singing and dancing. The tending of an infant actor was sometimes but not necessarily accompanied by a lullaby, and a scene of precultural fighting was only occasionally punctuated by pre- and post-fighting singing and dancing. Again, my feeling is that the longer a myth had been possessed, the greater the likelihood that song and dance components had been added to it; however, proof of this suggestion may not easily be given because of the insurmountable obstacles that preclude time-dating in folklore.

Finally, songs presented in oral literature recitals or in village discussions of stories functioned as entertainment, as art forms in themselves, and as reinforcement of beliefs and customs. In the last instances, songs most often expressed and validated convictions about supernaturals to whom people were related.

Features of Style

CHAPTER XVI

VARIABILITY IN PLAY STRUCTURES

FOLKLORE has long been regarded as the collection, comparison, and study of orally transmitted stories, with emphasis upon the word "stories." Since anthropological folklorists have rarely recorded in field situations which were living folklore sessions, and since they have stressed plots, themes, dramatis personae, and tale types, the impression has remained that folklore is everywhere storytelling which resembles the written short story or novel of Euroamerican culture. But if folktales are interpreted in the light of native usage, manner of recital, audience behavior, content, and design, they are often found to resemble the theater of Western civilization rather than its short story or novel. It may therefore be fitting to employ for folktales captions such as "skit," "one-act play," "two-act play," "comedy," "tragedy," and the like. If such captions are not taken literally, they serve usefully for Clackamas and other folktales of the northwest states.

Clackamas narrators seem to have performed in the manner in which an actor of Western civilization gives solo readings of plays. I would add that a play-reading in the presence of an audience is to be regarded, for Clackamas, as a specially stylized and dramatic summarization of a story. Its full details are not recited. The audience projects into the recital its knowledge of such details.

In the study of Clackamas literature, one use of captions borrowed from Western theater arises from the need to describe the range of dramatic forms, from small to large and from comedy to tragedy. But it is hardly possible to classify them sharply in types; the forms intergrade. An oral literature may contain brief scenes at one extreme exemplified in the tiny Clackamas myth "Duck Was a Married Woman" (21) to multi-act dramas like those of Fire's grandson (13), *Gi'ckux* (34), and *Ku'šaydı* (40). Furthermore, some myths, such as the ones in which Awl Woman (27) and Hazel Gambler (29) are actors, display exceptional integration and an unusually well-contrived manipulation of elements of design. The framing of such plays contrasts, at one end of the continuum, with the sprawling formlessness, at the other end, of so effective a comedy-drama as "Fire and His Son's Son" (13) or a lengthy drama like that of the adventures of *Gi'ckux* (34).

Only the shorter Clackamas plays showed an obviously consciously fashioned unity and integration which held throughout. Longer plays were generally about as devoid of temporal or other unity as a historical novel which lacks a main actor or central location. On the other hand, some short plays were almost formless, and a long play, exemplified by the story of *Ku'šaydı* (40), sometimes had a remarkable degree of design.

Even without specialization of literary or theater personnel such as may develop in a society of wealth and social stratification, a Northwest oral literature displayed many kinds of aesthetic designs. Since in Clackamas literature it was usually the short plays that were painstakingly modeled, a reasonable deduction is that re-working of longer plays so as to produce integrated designs was more difficult for the non-specialists of a food-gathering society. In such a milieu everyone discussed and participated to the full in the literary heritage. Therefore creative addition, insertions, and subtractions must have been more numerous for longer than for shorter plays. Shorter ones were less likely to be subjected to refashioning. They remained more rigidly designed because such forms could be more easily managed and contained less content for the community to discuss. Longer plays with more features of content remained relatively amorphous except for a few quite deliberately contrived structurings within segments, which could be easily accorded frames of the kind had by short plays. The subject of process of folkloristic change must be approached with the premise that a community subjected the content of long plays to discussions which allowed more recital alternatives than could be given to short plays. However, researches are needed to give proof or disproof for the premise that because there was less stylization in longer plays they witnessed more penetrating and rapid changes than shorter plays.

The presence of a few unstructured short plays (such as the moralizing tragedy which is myth 35) among many others that were short and well designed suggests two possibilities, neither of which seems subject to checking. One is that such a play was recently borrowed and had not yet been remodeled. Another is that Clackamas borrowed, on the one hand, from contiguous peoples whose myths were frequently neatly designed and, on the other, from adjoining peoples whose myths were, in some instances, as amorphous or simply chronological as myths 34 and 35.

Questions as to which plays were composites—welded or alloyed from short plays that were native or borrowed—and which plays were segments that had been dis-sected out of longer plays—probably often plays that had been borrowed—cannot be answered without comparative studies of cognates in neighboring groups.

Since plot content was decisive for community and narrator, formal features were those which the raconteur could insert or frame without injury to chronological or developmental presentation of events. Clackamas indulged their feeling for form and frame by employing structural and ornamental features which neither intruded upon nor distorted the content. They employed a traditional design or frame whenever they could. When they could not, they permitted description or chronology to take its course. Additional traits of design are seen in various motifs, each of which was applied to several plots.

Consciously applied stylization appeared in formal introductory sentences which were not so much prologues as curtain-raising devices. It is as if someone advanced to the front of the stage before theater footlights and uttered a sentence or two which pointed up what was going to happen, with the audience filling in a great amount of detail about the setting of the play which was about to start. Stylization also is shown in closing paragraphs, which were really epilogues. These were more detailed than introductions and were followed by a brief phrase which ended the performance. Stylization is exemplified by a variety of devices that expedited the plot. These included the pattern number five, which framed siblings and organized repetitive actions and sequences. The youngest-smartest motif is another example of design. Less consciously applied stylization is evident, principally in some of the shorter myths, in integration by means of unity of time and place; it is also apparent in some sequences of acts and some scenes within acts in longer myths. It appears in the genetic stages which expressed the development of a personality, as exemplified by Coyote in the long myth 9. It appears in progressive saturation with humor, or in intensification of frightfulness. The narrator never permitted a flashback— not once did a story pause to revert in time to an earlier situation.

Traits of design were applied with conscious manipulation to short myths or to single acts within extended narrative plots. Storytellers could design segments of plots, that is, short plays within larger ones; they were less able to apply canons of unity and consistency to lengthier plots. It was easy to proceed from one to another event, and often this was done without a special device to signal transition. An important feature of such chronological succession was the omission of matters—such as comments on journeys—which Euroamerican literature finds necessary to mention. Since Western drama might omit the very connections which Clackamas folklore ignored, a theatrical rather than novelistic quality of the latter is felt by us.

The components of gross structure in a short play or within a segment of a large play, and the very points of separation which I have regarded as spaces between scenes and acts, were marked by transitions which have never been carefully examined in field recording situations. These transitions took many forms. For example, a morpheme translated as "and now then, then next" could be employed, and was so employed in every northwest states language as far as I know. Again, there might be only an especially pointed pause with silence. If neither device appeared, only plot content itself effected transition to a succeeding portion of plot, or to the next scene or act. It is my impression that the stylization of such kinds of transitions is found over a wide area of the Northwest and is in no respect distinctive in Clackamas.

When field research has been conducted directly in English, that is, when the informant has translated mentally and dictated in English, pauses and transition points are not quite as evident as in dictations offered in the native language. Therefore an analysis into plot segments, whether termed "introductions," "acts," "scenes," or "epilogues," is sometimes not feasible for recordings made in English. For example, Ballard's and Adamson's folktales from western Washington Salish peoples, recorded directly in English, are in few instances such close translations that it is possible to analyze individual stories into segments which may be termed "acts" and "scenes."[12] Not all texts are superior to dictated translations, but text dictations tend to be closer to original recital design. For practical purposes most folktales dictated and written in English cannot be used for design analysis.

An exception is Elizabeth D. Jacobs' field recording of Nehalem Tillamook tales from the Oregon coast. Her informant adhered with such unexampled fidelity to the original phrases and words in Salish that a stylistic study of the versions which she dictated in English might be comparable in validity to the better text dictations.[13] English recording of such exactitude is rare. Mrs. Howard's texts, also, were fortunately so well dictated, as far as I can judge, that a design analysis which identifies acts and scenes is also possible.

The principal factors that permit valid analysis of gross design are, in the first place, degree of acculturative deterioration and conscientiousness of the informant, whether he dictated in his native language or translated directly into English, and, in the second place, quality of relationship between informant and anthropologist. Nowadays use of a tape recorder might minimize factors of relationship with the anthropologist who is present and might tend to encourage more responsible dictations in either the original language or English.

Emphases in the methodology of field text dictations, when the recording was with pen or pencil rather than a more impersonal tape machine, have long been such that plot content and linguistic features have been the central interests of research workers. I know of no anthropological folklorist or linguist who, in field research, made careful note of or even attempted to ascertain points of segmentation within a connected narrative which he was recording. Usually he later supplied paragraphing, sentencing, commas, and periods, where he judged them apt for purposes of an acceptable-looking publication. It is difficult to determine the spots for partitioning within narrations, because the raconteur usually proceeded without audible evidences of transition points other than the natural pauses that set apart successive situations and the connective morphemes which the language possessed. In other words, the story itself had its segments, evident to both narrator and audience, but the separations between segments were likely to be very brief periods of silence, not other kinds of signals.

Western civilization has much the same style of oral storytelling. When a Euroamerican tells a joke which contains several parts, he does not say, "End of the first part," and later, "End of the second." No matter how dramatically rendered, a monologue is unlikely to be offered with audible or easily recognized punctuation. Nevertheless, stories told by non-literate peoples may have their special punctuation which sets apart segments of content. In my judgment such markers, whatever they are, need to be indicated not by use of new symbols for markers as such but by showing content sequences like acts and scenes or by traditional paragraphing. The task is to determine the segments rather than to clutter the presentation with unsightly symbols, and to ascertain whether the segments add up to a more or less deliberate design.

I suggest that whatever they are, separations of content into acts and scenes in Clackamas literature functioned like phonemic or other junctures which scientific linguists have lately been noting. It is of interest that such linguists long failed to perceive or make formulations about the very presence or functions of junctures. If

linguists, who have been in relatively considerable numbers, were deaf to the phenomena of juncturing, it is not surprising that the tiny fraternity of scientifically
oriented folklorists, with their pen and pencil tools and their preoccupation with
plot and motif analysis, paid no attention to implied pauses or plot transition
points. Plot junctures were very likely evident to storyteller and audience, were
manipulated by the storyteller, and framed plot content in gross segments. Resultant structuring should be described. In addition to the more familiar because more
patently stylized introductions, epilogues, and endings, numbers, frequencies, and
weights of plot segments (such as acts and scenes) should be noted where possible.
If points of plot segmentation are assumed, the Clackamas stories can be shown to
separate out into acts and scenes as well as introductory and closing formulas.

Informants should usually not be asked to develop awareness of features of transition in plot presentation. Junctures which set acts and scenes apart should not be
noted with an informant's help, at any rate not in the course of a dictation. Instead,
the narrators should be allowed to adhere as closely as possible to natural recital
style, lest they be distracted or self-conscious about items for which earlier they had
only subliminal sensitization. Since melodic line, pause, connection, or other indication of discourse segments may be either lacking or too varied to permit easy partitioning of a story, its plot movement is likely to offer the principal or sole means for
plot segment analysis. I have used plot content alone for the following sample analyses, because I lacked other means of identifying plot segments.

Although I have attempted to analyze all the stories into acts and scenes, I present only a few analyses because this kind of dissection is sufficiently revealing. The
stories used here were selected to show contrasted extremes of story length and
structuring. There are stories of intermediate length, and in fact the continuum
ranges from very short to long.

An example of a long story which is unique in its structure is Coyote's journey
(9). This comedy-drama contains twenty more or less equal segments, each of which
may be regarded as a scene, but the scenes do not group into acts. I have briefly
characterized each scene so as to permit easy identification of the sequence.

> Introduction
> scene 1: Pheasant Woman.
>   2: Coyote deflowers a girl.
>   3: Coyote releases bees.
>   4: Coyote is unable to reach dancing girls.
>   5: Sturgeon's body scrapings.
>   6: *a*. Back-somersaulting Fuel Carrier.
>   *b*. His wife's pregnancy and Coyote's lesson.
>   7: Coyote rapes a girl across the river.
>   8: Fifteen females transport Coyote.
>   9: Coyote doctors a girl.
>   10: Coyote is inside a tree and summons Woodpeckers.
>   11: Coyote dismembers himself.
>   12: Coyote visits Snail and steals her eyes.
>   13: Coyote borrows Skunk's noisy anus.

14: Coyote enjoys fellatio.
15: Coyote makes a cascade and berry sites nearby.
16: Coyote kills Grizzly in her oven.
17: Coyote defeats Land Swallower.
18: Coyote cuts mouths.
19: Coyote instructs in the use of salmon.
20: Coyote defeats River Swallower.

The first fourteen scenes represent the younger Coyote and are largely humorous; the last six depict the deific Coyote and are less funny. His development from immature to mature is itself a stylization. Moreover, five-patterns are inclosed within scene 1, where the actors perform spirit-power song-dances five times; scene 8, where Coyote is carried by three successive groups of five females each; and scene 9, where doctoring songs, which are repeated five times, are only implied. The play's structure is amorphous apart from its series of equally weighted scenes, five-patterns, introduction, ending, and chronological succession of actions in one upriver direction. Coyote's development from pre-adult to adult is the only remaining important feature of gross structuring.

No other play resembles this one at all closely in design. Although some longer plays have about as many scenes, these group into acts. The ritual myth (8), which is as uniquely structured in its way as is the Coyote journey, has as many discrete scenes; and in that myth each is quite like the others in content, expression, and design. Only two of the scenes of the Coyote epic are alike, those of the Land and Water Swallowers. Scene 6 is distinctive because of its halves.

The next example of act and scene structuring is the Bear-Grizzly drama (14), which was a kind of novel in its range of content.

Act I, scene 1: Bear and Grizzly capture two girls.
              2: Bear kills his wife.

Act II, scene 1: Grizzly swallows his wife's eye.
               2: She bears a son.
               3: Work at the root patch.
               4: Work at the root patch.
               5: Work at the root patch.
               6: Work at the root patch.
               7: Work at the root patch.
               8: The females incinerate the male Grizzlies.

Act III, scene 1: Daughter hurls mother onto a rock bluff.
                2: Girl throws an old woman into the fire.
                3: Girl in a headman's house.
                4: Girl throws an old woman into the fire.
                5: Girl in a headman's house.
                6: Girl throws an old woman into the fire.
                7: Girl in a headman's house.
                8: Girl throws an old woman into the fire.
                9: Girl in a headman's house.
               10: Girl encounters Meadow Lark Woman.
               11: Girl kills her mother.

Act IV, scene 1: Girl marries a headman, raises two sons.
               2: She metamorphoses into a Grizzly.
               3: She devours inhabitants of five villages.

Five-patterns give special frames to Act II, scenes 3 to 7; to scenes 4 to 11 in Act III; and to scene 3 in Act IV. The patterning in Act III is unique in the collection because of the alternation of two five-patterns—the breakdown of Mrs. Howard's dictation only apparently, not actually, misses perfection of design by omitting one scene of each of these five-patterns. Scenes 10 and 11 really complete each five-pattern. The play also contains a developmental feature; the girl goes through three stages: immaturity, marriage and raising of sons, and dominance of hate and killing after the sons mature.

A third example is of one of the most effective dramas, that of Grizzly and Water Bug (17). Except for two five-patterns, its design is about as sprawled and shapeless as any. The first five-pattern occupies scenes 2 to 6 in Act I. There is an especially long and climactic fifth episode, in scene 6. The second five-pattern is the headman's stylized shooting of five arrows at his Grizzly wife in scene 2 of Act II.

Act I, scene 1: Grizzly marries a headman.
              2: Grizzly murders a group of women.
              3: Grizzly murders a group of women.
              4: Grizzly murders a group of women.
              5: Grizzly murders a group of women.
              6: Water Bug accompanies the fifth group.
              7: Water Bug finds paddles and corpses.
              8: Water Bug and Grizzly jockey all night.
              9: Women flee homeward.

Act II, scene 1: Grizzly pursues fugitives.
              2: Fugitives reach village and headman shoots Grizzly.
              3: People bring corpses back to the village.

A fourth example of the prevailing kind of chronologically presented plot in a goodly number of scenes, within some of which are five-patterns, is the Wren comedy (25). Progressive saturation with the obscene and incongruous was perhaps the principal means employed for audience effect, and the five-patterns were minor devices. The play seems to have been excellently designed because of its piling-up of incongruities which were ludicrous. It may be segmented as follows.

Act I, scene 1: Wren insults five animals.
              2: Wren enters and leaves Elk five times.

Act II, scene 1: Grandmother will carry a hind quarter only.
              2: Grandmother uses a fragile packstrap while
                   Wren journeys five times with heavy packs.
              3: Wren finds his grandmother masturbating.
              4: Wren sleeps with his grandmother.
              5: Wren throws her away.
              6: Blue Jay and Jay Bird haul her from the
                   river.

Act II, scene 7: Three shamans try to revive her.
　　　　　　　8: Blue Jay and Jay Bird sell her to Wren.
　　　　　　　9: Wren plays with her, throws her away again.
　　　　　　10: Blue Jay and Jay Bird cannot revive her.

Each of the first four scenes is a five-pattern. A unique three-pattern appears in scene 7 of Act II. The story's impact was consequent upon pyramidings of burlesque situations until the climax in scenes 9 and 10.

A medium-length play which lacks a five-pattern, but whose aesthetic effect was largely a consequence of straight chronology leading to a climax of violence and tragedy, is the dog-wife myth (28). It seems to be framed in two acts and six scenes, as follows:

Act I, scene 1: Wealthy girl marries her dog to a suitor.
　　　　　　　2: He smells excrements about his bride.
　　　　　　　3: Girl paddles past his village.
　　　　　　　4: He shoots his dog bride.

Act II, scene 1: He puts snakes into maple bark which the girl
　　　　　　　　　flavors.
　　　　　　　2: She gives birth to snakes and dies.

There are two climaxes, one at the end of Act I, the other and terrible end in the final lines of Act II. The effect depended principally upon plot content, with a build-up to a frightful resolution and Draconian justice.

Chronological presentations exemplified in the preceding, with their slight framing and dependency upon plot for aesthetic effect, resemble many other comedies and dramas of varying lengths. These contrast with the much more structured horror drama of Awl Woman (27), which is of medium length.

Act I, scene 1: A hunter turns his awl into Awl Woman.
　　　　　　　2: She hides, works for him, is confronted by him.

Act II, scene 1: Girl comes, Awl terrorizes then kills her.
　　　　　　　2: Girl comes, Awl terrorizes then kills her.
　　　　　　　3: Girl comes, Awl terrorizes then kills her.
　　　　　　　4: Girl comes, Awl terrorizes then kills her.
　　　　　　　5: Youngest girl comes, is helped by Meadow Lark
　　　　　　　　　Woman.
　　　　　　　6: Girl kills Awl.

Act III, scene 1: Hunter rushes home when his bow breaks.
　　　　　　　　2: He arrives, buries four corpses, explains Awl to
　　　　　　　　　　girl, marries her.

This drama has unity of time and place, and presents few actors. It engages in no digressions. Act II is a five-pattern, with youngest-smartest and Lark plot expediter devices. Perhaps scene 2 of Act I had a five-pattern too, if five days passed before the hunter confronted Awl. Myths 1, 24, and 36 exhibited the same over-all design. These four stories exemplify a distinct type of play in which the frame itself pleased,

I think, to a greater degree than in most other stories of the collection, but the four also had content which dominated the effect, as in amorphous plays.

Several very short myths are formless single-scene dramas. Examples are Coyote's waiting for Sleep (12), Bear's mourning (15), and Robin's weeping for her younger sister (44). These three have only one actor each, and unity of time and place. They are like one-stanza poems whose compactness and sheer simplicity produced an effect of pleasure in form like that stirred by the four myths cited above (1, 24, 27, 36).

A few plays contained a scene which was an entr'acte. The myth of Panther, Coyote, and Trout (6) has five acts, with two or more scenes in all acts but the first. Act IV contains, in scene 1, an explanatory side excursion in which antlers are tried on various animals. Another excursion in scene 6 accounts for snowbirds. Both scenes relieved tension, did some explaining, and contributed nothing to the main plot. They certainly went far from the central line of the story. A similar entr'acte appears in the comedy interlude of Blue Jay's slipping through ice in Act I, scene 5, of the Canoemaker-Seal Hunter myth (26). Act III of that myth is an entr'acte too, which distracted from tension maintained in the remainder of the drama. In general, however, these digressions were rare in the literature. They were not present in comedies. They bear earmarks of being secondary additions inserted in bygone times in order to alleviate tension or mounting audience feelings; they were asides that were entertaining or instructive or both. Reflection upon ways in which community discussions may have resulted in changes in story content warrants the observation that, all in all, the infrequency of entr'actes points to a strength of feeling for uninterrupted plot continuity. This is a feeling for form.

Although most plays lack perfect designs as wholes, apart from a straight plot line and climaxes, many or most stories contain one or more especially well designed scenes or an act which is a succession of scenes in a five-pattern. In other words, Clackamas could provide a perfect story frame if the recital occupied a short space of time. People were disinclined to work toward such perfection or to force plots in order to effect it in longer narrations. The ever-present feeling for design might be taken care of by the stylized short introduction, longer epilogue, formal ending, succinct style of speech, stylized selections and very limited numbers of descriptive items, chronological succession of plot situations, and some other traits that characterized story recitals.

Structures of tales are to a degree distinct from myths. Six tales are formless anecdotes, each in a single scene; the eight remaining tales have two or more scenes, but only one (which is in two versions, in texts 57 and 58) has as many as six. And every tale is relatively feeble in design. Neither youngest-smartest motif nor five-pattern appears. My deduction is that tales had not been subjected to long periods of community discussion and creative treatment, so that they lacked the introductions, epilogues, and endings which were minimal requirements in myth recitals and which granted such occasions a special luster.

CHAPTER XVII

STYLIZED DEVICES AND MOTIFS

TUDENTS of sculpture, pottery, basketry, and textiles produced by non-Western peoples have long recognized the presence of inventories of formalized expressive items, items of a non-expressive decorative kind, and items of framing, from which a native artist selected. Some of all these he was required to employ when fashioning tangible products which the community accepted as worthy. Students of folklore have been so absorbed in tale-type, plot, and actor content that, unlike students of plastic and graphic arts, they have infrequently directed their attention to stylizations and frames. Such aspects of an oral literature, which are of prime importance to its native discussants, critics, and recitalists, can be interpreted to and enjoyed by non-natives. I classify features of Clackamas literary style or recurrent form in nine or more types, from (1) to (9).

Following discussions of stylization of (1) introductions, (2) epilogues, (3) story endings, and (4) the pervasive phenomena of pattern number, the analysis goes on to a hitherto little appreciated but very large group of formalized folkloristic features. They are treated in three intergrading subdivisions. The first of these lists (5) stylized features of distance or location. Devices of this kind offered few increments of meaning. The second type (6) is of devices which formally date actions. Some of these features are difficult to distinguish from the type of motif listed in the third subdivision (7), whose many motifs were frames or expediters for the plot, in some instances cutting corners in order to allow action to move speedily to the next episode, as one could in precultural eras. Without a plot device or expediter of this kind, a story might stall on the hard rocks of reality.

I have supplied captions for features of types (5) and (6), but I have resorted to motif titles which are familiar to folklorists in order to designate many features of the third type (7). Because of special Northwest characteristics which motifs exhibited, the rubrics which I have given for them are not always apt for the purposes of folklore study in other parts of the world. Such titles may work satisfactorily only for motifs peculiar to Northwest folklores, although comparative researches may be facilitated by employing familiar captions when these are available. A large number of motifs have not been cited because they occurred only once in the collection. Discussions of (8) explanatory elements, (9) stylization of story titles, and other matters are added at the end of this chapter.

1. INTRODUCTIONS, 2. EPILOGUES, AND 3. ENDINGS

The narrator of a Clackamas myth commenced his recital with a phrase which in effect said, in a most automatic way, that a person or persons lived in a house or village. He concluded his narration with two other prescribed formulas. One, in penultimate position, metamorphosed precultural actors into animals, fish, or birds, and assigned them their future habitats and habits. I call this feature of style an "epilogue." The other device closed the myth. It was a simple announcement, "Myth myth." Although these three essentials of design for beginnings and endings of myths tended to weaken under acculturative conditions (a number of versions by Mrs. Howard lacked them), the simplest of the three devices, the ending formula, survived longest the ravages of a way of life where Caucasians had surrounded and greatly outnumbered the people.

Apart from "Myth myth," whose durability under acculturation may have occurred partly because it was a form that lacked variants, devices which a narrator employed when he recited a myth were analogous to phonemes which are actualized phonetically in allophones. That is, they were variable in form, and they permitted, in the case of stylistic matters, choices within narrow limits. They are not likely to be well displayed in all their variability when myths are recorded initially in an English approximation. They appear more reliably in text dictations because pressures of style were greater when the native language was employed and context and manner of utterance felt more natural to the storyteller.

Forty-seven of the forty-nine myths had one or another variant of a simply structured introductory phrase (1). It can be generalized as "He (or she or they two or they plural) lived there." The subject of the verb "live" was determined by the first actors to appear in the play. Or the subject of "live" represented people who lived in a village. That is, in one stroke the narrator presented a village setting or a house in which people dwelt. He described neither the house nor its residents because the context of the story, known as it was by almost everyone in the audience, supplied such delineative details. The requirement of style was to make simple and succinct mention of a village or a house and the actors therein. No one was ever introduced, at the beginning of a myth, out on a trail or in a boat or far away in the hills. In most instances one or more leading actors, the subject of "live," were named in the introduction. Or they were referred to by kinship terms. Or both named actors and kinship terms appeared. No myth introduction which referred to scenery or the weather or heavens was possible. One commenced with a house or village and with one or more persons there.

In three myths (17, 18, 46) the initial phrase, with its reporting of persons who "lived there," was followed by an item which affirmed that the headman's house was in the center of the village. Since a Clackamas headman's house was probably in a central location, the affirmation very likely served solely a stylistic function.

In five myths (23, 34, 40, 41, 47) the initial phrase was followed by an item which reported that the house of the actor just mentioned was at the end of the village; that is, he was not well-to-do. Again, since the audience knew the story and therefore had no doubts about the actor's poverty, the item was really stylistic.

In six stories (5, 27, 29, 37, 49, tale 58) a second, third, or fourth phrase said, "I do not know how long a time. . . ." It is of interest that a tale shared this stylistic feature with myths even though it lacked other features that characterized myths; maybe the tale is an example of an early stage of stylization of a story which after some generations might have become accepted as a myth.

The forty-nine myths of Clackamas origin exhibited only two introductions of unusual kinds. One, "They would say," appears in the peculiarly ritual myth (8). The other, "Coyote thought," preceded the unique myth which was the long developmental narrative of Coyote and his travels (9). I suppose that in these two exceptional myths, which were also distinctive in content and other features of form, introductions of specially designed kinds had long before developed and alternatives had become disallowed. All other introductions were specific and permissible variants of three or four designs. Each variant was consequent upon the narrator's small range of permitted choices and upon circumstances and personnel of the play's opening scene.

Mrs. Howard employed either Clackamas style or an identical Molale style, if it was identical, for introductions to five myths of Molale provenience. These stories are in *Clackamas Chinook Texts* (50 to 54). Dr. Leo J. Frachtenberg's Bureau of American Ethnology manuscript of Molale myth texts, obtained from a Molale named Stevens Savage, may not be authoritative for Molale introductions, and so we cannot be certain about the identity of Clackamas and Molale stylistic features of this kind. An introduction to a Molale story of transitional times was rendered by Mrs. Howard in her Clackamas style (64).

Each Clackamas myth and tale of transitional times (55 to 62) was dictated with an introduction, as was each Molale myth which Mrs. Howard dictated in Clackamas to me (50 to 54). A "They used to say" introduction to the ritual myth (8) was also used in minor variants in three Clackamas tales of transitional times (59, 60, 62). But only one of the six Clackamas tales of pre-white times had an introduction. It is typical. One of the two Molale tales (63, 64) of transitional times, dictated by Mrs. Howard in Clackamas, had an introduction. She obviously felt less stylistic pressure when she recounted stories which were not of precultural eras. But there was evidently great strength in the stylistic demand that there be a formal beginning phrase or phrases in myth recitals, and it spread into the five Molale myths and eight Clackamas tales of transitional times.

Epilogues, which were the most stylized of explanatory elements, preceded the terse formal endings. Every epilogue told where the myth's actors went—whether to the streams, mountains, or air—and whether they became water dwellers, mountain dwellers, or birds. An epilogue drove home the thought that precultural actors metamorphosed and that the land then became as it was during the modern period. Probably any correctly recited myth had an epilogue, then an ending, but in Mrs. Howard's versions of myths more or less formalized epilogues appeared in only nine of the forty-nine she dictated (2, 10, 24, 34, 40, 42, 45, 46, 47). The reason why she felt that she should give utterance to epilogues at the close of just these myths and no others is unclear. I am convinced that she was acculturated to such an extent that she felt burdened or bored by repetition of epilogues whose range of variability was small. To her, the concept of transformation of precultural creatures into their modern garb was obvious. Besides, the change of emphasis from meticulously correct presentation for a wholly native audience to informing the outsider about a story which he had never heard tied in with acculturative disintegration. The presence of an anthropologist with his notebook and pen was so unprecedented that it is not surprising that almost forty myths were given without a ponderously repetitious epilogue which from Mrs. Howard's point of view added nothing to content. Her task with me was to tell a story, not to tell it with all its trappings. Undoubtedly she felt much the same when she recounted stories to her very acculturated family —it was hardly better informed about Indians than was the anthropologist. In Mrs. Howard's time, stories were stories rather than plays which everyone present also knew.

At the end of one myth in *Clackamas Chinook Texts* I appended a short statement which Mrs. Howard dictated in text some time after she gave the myth dictation (17). Her words were, "When they were finished with everything (i.e., when the narrator had completed his recital) then they (storytellers) would say, 'Now let us (we Myth Age actors) separate (and go to the rivers or mountains or into the air).' And they would do just that then. Some of them would become birds, some of them animals of the forests, some of them (the creatures) in the rivers, some of them (including the larger animals) in the mountains, all sorts of things (they would become)." Single quotes are translations of actual words of every raconteur; after such words he probably followed with a final "Story story," or more accurately, "Myth myth." It appears therefore that the preferred if not invariable ending of a myth consigned each actor to his post–Myth Age water, mountain, or air habitat. After each actor was explicitly told where he would go and in some instances how he would be living in the future, the narrator halted the recital with a final "Myth myth" or "Now then myth myth."

The brevity, simplicity of design, and comparative monotony of introductions to myth recitals and the few permissible variants of standard introductory formulas contrast with the variety in epilogues and endings. The specific epilogues and endings given by Mrs. Howard must be supplemented by her clear and strong statement above about the manner of their stylization. Her endings of myth dictations were inconsistent. Unlike formal introductory phrases and epilogues, her stylization of endings was obviously disturbed by several factors. The principal cause of disturbance appears at the end of no less than twenty (1, 5, 7, 8, 9, 14, 15, 16, 18, 19, 21, 30, 31, 32, 33, 35, 37, 38, 39, 40) of the forty-nine Clackamas myths, when in each instance she indicated that she might have forgotten portions or additional scenes of the myth. Because she lacked conviction that what she had just dictated was precisely right in the telling, she completed the myth in a mildly unhappy and frustrated mood. She omitted a formal ending of any kind in seven other myths (10, 11, 12, 41, 43, 44, 45), although she did not assert that she had forgotten parts of them. The discomfort she felt at the end of a recital-dictation that had failed to satisfy her may be set against the fact that all forty-nine Clackamas myths commenced with a proper introduction.

The five Molale myths which are in *Clackamas Chinook Texts* were each presented with an ending. Five Clackamas tales and one of the Molale tales of transitional times had endings. Three Clackamas and one Molale lacked them. The six Clackamas tales of pre-white times lacked stylized endings, except perhaps for one which had the frequently found "I recall only that much of it."

Sometimes Mrs. Howard made an attempt to provide a proper closing phrase in spite of her apparent dissatisfaction with her rendition. For example, in one myth (14) she said "That is all now," following an expression of lack of knowledge about the subsequent destination of the last actor; then in final position she appended the probably correct closing phrase, "Myth myth." She did almost the same at the close of another myth (16). But in a third myth (15) she said, "Then she went on to I do not know where she lived. Now that is as much as I recall of it. All done." The "all done" was either an alternative formal closing or a comment to the anthropologist so that he could recognize the completion of dictation.

4. PATTERN NUMBER

When a Euroamerican reads a translation of a northwest states folklore, perhaps no feature of its style is as apparent to him as the stylized repetitions—whether four or five—of acts and actors. I shall describe this important recurrent phenomenon of pattern number in the Clackamas collection, and then I shall suggest why it was maintained by generations of discussants and raconteurs. The principal stylized repetition in Clackamas folklore is five and, accordingly, I shall adopt the term "five-pattern" to refer to it.

All five-patterns in Clackamas literature were apparently deliberate framings. Community and narrators applied them wherever a concept of plural persons, beings, or events was consistent with plot, sometimes using a sequence of five to create progressive intensification or saturation toward a climax. The entire frame of four (1, 24, 27, 36) of the forty-nine Clackamas myths was a five-pattern. These were stories of medium length. Twenty-eight (3, 4, 5, 6, 7, 9, 10, 13, 14, 16, 17, 18, 22, 25, 26, 29, 30, 31, 32, 33, 34, 38, 40, 43, 45, 46, 48, 49) of the remaining forty-five Clackamas myths contained five-patterns of similar or different kinds. Seventeen stories lacked any five-pattern. Some stories included only one; others contained two or more.

Two-patterns were probably not contrived. They may have been fortuitously determined by plot content, or in some instances they may indicate recent adoption of a story; they never served to build toward a climax like a series of five actors or events. Although at least fifteen stories possessed two-patterns, it looks as if most or all instances were not consciously fashioned as a matter of preference for two rather than some other number. In story 5 there were two Crow Women, two Buzzards, two Black Vultures, and other pairs of large birds; in 9, two dancing girls; in 11, 22, and 56, a contest of wills between two antagonists; in 13, two boys and two Defecators; in 14, two girls and the two men who were Bear and Grizzly; in 16, the Bear and Grizzly Women; in 20, two Gopher Women; 25, Blue Jay Man and Jay Bird Man; 29, 31, and 35, two sons; 40, two brothers; 47, two Crows and two sons.

Each such citation indicates a pair whose presence was consistent with the plot. In only a few instances, such as that of the two dancing girls (9), three or more might not have clashed with the plot or diminished plausibility.

Again, this stylistically accepted, even congenial, feature of a pair of persons seems to have been largely or completely a product of plot appropriateness which may, to a degree, reflect a tendency against absolute aloneness in residence or travel and in some cases a need to offer contrasted opposites. A special instance of contrast combines a five-form and a two-form: the five Badger children and Coyote's five children (10). While not a single instance of a pair seems to have eventuated from stylistic manipulation, the twenty-eight occurrences of an encapsulated five-pattern and the four plots which were wholly five-patterns appear to have been an arrangement long since imposed by the community and its storytellers.

A three-pattern occurred only once in the entire collection, in the myth of Wren and his lecherous grandmother, who was doctored by only three shamans, the third of whom resuscitated her (25). The rarity of a triad form suggests an accidental factor, not design. Or Mrs. Howard may have forgotten two members of a five-pattern. The play would certainly have had a more familiar design if five shamans had been put to work on the patient.

Stories numbered 55 to 69 were Transitional Era or pre-white tales. Since not one exhibited a five-pattern, the likely deduction is that they were relatively recently accepted and that myths which included five-patterns were of longer standing in the repertoire. Plays with five-patterns had been remodeled and framed with designs that were possible in a kind of theater where stress was upon chronological presentation of episodes and the essentials of situations and personalities. Plots permitted additions of stylistic features which did not alter content and which, in many instances, permitted both symbolic and seemingly realistic presentation.

As far as I know, theoreticians have not ventured to account for processes which created, maintained, and spread pattern number motifs in the northwest states. In order to solve similar problems, folklorists have sometimes used an essentially descriptive—not explanatory—geographical distribution procedure which is an application of the diffusion method long characteristic of social anthropological studies in the United States. Although such diffusionism exposed fallacies in evolutionist or stage-level arrangements of data, it fell short of constituting a broadly useful theoretical system. It had little utility in guiding research toward decisive causes or processes, toward the discovery of factors reinforcing a phenomenon, or toward factors that effected spreads. Five-patterns undoubtedly spread in bygone eras, but diffusionism never seemed to be able to tell why. Among Americanist folklorists there has been almost a studied evasion of hypotheses which might suggest origin, reason for maintenance, function, and causes of diffusion of the five-pattern.

I am persuaded that so stylized a feature is neither pure form nor esoteric content. I believe that we are not dealing with something that is wholly a matter of rigorous, monotonous, and largely inexplicable recapitulation of an ancient feature of style which was forever reinforced by the circumstance that most or all neighboring groups had it, too. So oft repeated a trait is not at all times unaccompanied by special feelings on the part of raconteur or audience. I therefore propose that in Northwest literatures such as Clackamas a stylized succession of ever smarter, meaner, or more suspicious siblings who were entirely of one or the other sex, and who numbered four or five, was retained by untold generations because it felt right in terms of their feelings about real human relationships. It felt right in purely formal respects too, if pure form can be abstracted from relationship feelings, and it was also supported by factors that may be designated as purely psychological. In other words, this recurrent phenomenon in Northwest literatures had sufficient causes in addition to factors of design present in immediately neighboring literatures. The phenomenon had multiple causation; it witnessed actively supporting or reinforcing factors within each culture that had a five-pattern.

Although employment of a pattern number in rites, songs, and dances was undoubtedly a strong cultural factor supporting its conservation in the oral literature, the hypothesis which I suggest as a principal factor in maintenance of the Chinook, Sahaptin, Kalapuya, and other five-patterns, the northern Puget Sound Salish four-pattern, and the intriguing Tillamook Salish combination of five for males and four for females is based upon the familiar observation that, as in Euroamerican culture, rivalrous feelings developed between siblings. Younger siblings must often have resented the favored status of older ones in societies such as those of the northwest states, where older children may have been in a more advantageous position. Evidences of such pique are apparent in many societies the world over and are inescapably visible in Clackamas literature.

Each younger Grizzly in the Louse myth (36) says, for example—and with a little hostility—that he is better looking than his older brother. Louse herself appears to cater shrewdly to his vexation and need for self-esteem by tempting him with one woman more than his older brother supposedly received. She also counters his greater suspicion by resorting to a larger amount of feminine bait. I believe that this myth and others of similar framing therefore support the theory of Clackamas sensibility for the psychological appropriateness, in stories, of progressive increments of suspicion, rancor, and allurement. Would not Clackamas have observed in their little settlements and intense familial relationships evidences of sibling feelings that coincided to a degree with a feature of stylization in many myths? Would not literary convention, as unpliant as it may have been, therefore be reinforced in many narrations? Would it ever be challenged in community discussions of myth content?

But if Clackamas social relationships, particularly sibling relationships, help to account for the multiple patterns, they still do not explain the attachment to particular pattern numbers. Possibly the use of five and four and the absence of three as major pattern numbers in Oregon and Washington groups connects with the strength of multiple kin ties in these societies and the somewhat lesser fervor about the nuclear family triangle that appears in Euroamerican society. That triangular relationship was extremely strong in Northwest groups, but Northwest Indians'

Oedipal responses were not so largely inclosed within the nuclear triangle alone. Societal relationships supported any numeral larger than three as much as they bolstered a three-form.

Therefore the pattern numeral itself may be regarded, I think, as just a numeral, a relatively pure trait of style without social or psychological reinforcement in intra-familial relationships. The central problem is not whether the northwest states pattern numbers were four or five; the problem is why a pattern number was so important and effective a feature of literary style. Still, it would seem to be possible to account for the numbers themselves. A proper starting procedure to account for five rather than three, four, six, or seven would be to commence with the distributional method of diffusionist workers, because the selection of and maintenance of one or the other numeral may have been due partly to pressures of neighboring literary and ceremonial patternings. But once such influence has been shown and measured, other factors must be sought. These are located principally in features of the social system itself. I urge, although I cannot prove, that the latter factors are decisive.

Nor is utilization of a numeral such as five ever the entirety of the literary phenomenon. Much more needs to be explained. We find five brothers or five sisters, five successively from oldest to youngest, five successively from brightest to most stupid, gullible to least credulous, mean to meanest, and so on. Only rarely does Clackamas literature imply mentally or emotionally identical siblings and then only when the storyteller is not building to a climax. Stylistic matters of kinds mentioned here connect patently with psychological concomitants of social structure, that is, with culturally patterned feeling responses in members of families. In order to determine what such responses may have been, one may borrow current theorems, preferably the simplest and best documented in clinical and sociological studies, and apply them in order to ascertain their relevance to and consistency with everything else in the ethnographic and folkloristic materials.

One may query why the younger of two siblings displays greater meanness, as with Brown Bear and her murderous younger sister Grizzly (16). Why does the youngest of five siblings of same sex always exhibit greater intensity of some trait, such as shrewdness, than the other four? Why (vide 17) is the youngest person of the community the only one capable of resolution of a tragic situation? Why are five siblings most often of one sex, not both? Apart from a chance that the region's cultures did contain special or local characteristics that acted as reinforcing factors for stylized literary expressions, societies the world over include families where differential treatment of siblings occurs. Sometimes the younger sibling has to be brighter or meaner in order to maintain self-esteem. Sometimes, as in northwest coast communities, a younger male sibling was harder pressed for wherewithal to purchase a bride. Sometimes, as in the Northwest again, mild avoidance occurred between siblings of opposite sex when they neared adolescence, and so myths somehow reflect single-sex groups that grew up together and for a time kept apart from the other sex. Since few opportunities remain for direct field observation of households and villages in the Northwest, one must conclude unhappily that if anthropologists had done sensitive ethnographic research at an earlier time, they would have uncovered intrafamilial and intracommunity relationships that connected with Northwest literary stylizations.

The reverse side of the coin is that if connections of stylized literary features and factors of cultural reinforcement are denied, few means may be left for explaining a region's particular ways of utilizing a succession of siblings of the same sex, in plot after plot. Again, the number five or four is not the point in question. The issue is the problem of accounting for the succession from oldest to youngest sibling of the same sex, and of explaining the special place that the literature accords to the youngest child. Discussion of the related motif, youngest-smartest, is offered below.

The sequence of episodes in a five-form is never characterized by a carbon copy duplication of every word of the first episode, or by every feature of sentence melody. The raconteur always omits and adds words and changes tonal features in the second, third, and fourth repeats. These variations warrant intensive study, where it is possible to conduct such examination. In other groups of the Northwest where there are still a number of well-informed survivors, one should compare alternate versions offered by different informants. Repeated recitals by the same informant should also be compared.

Psychiatric theoreticians would no doubt argue that the several factors which reinforce the four- and five-patterns of the Northwest include a defense mechanism of multiplication of instances, where excessive or incongruous repetition of the stimulus tends to diminish intensity of feeling, to reduce painful emotion, and sometimes to permit feeling of the comic. The limitation in this or any wholly psychological hypothesis, apart from the difficulty in finding ethnographic or other direct evidences to support it, is that it supplies no means of clarifying problems such as the presence of a prevailing five-form in some literatures, a four-form in others, and a five-form for male actors conjointly with a four-form for females in the northwestern Oregon Tillamook villages adjacent to Chinooks.

5. DEVICES WHICH EXPRESS DISTANCE OR LOCATION

Enter an end house.—When a narrator brought a visitor to a myth village, he might have the newcomer encounter children playing near the settlement and inquire of them the direction to the headman's house. Without such an approach the visitor entered the village directly, going into an end house—which probably was denoted as one of poor people. The feature of style here was the raconteur's unneeded mention of the fact of entrance in an end house. Custom probably demanded that a newcomer do so; therefore auditors took for granted such a manner of entry into a village. The stylistic trait served as means of bringing a traveler into a community.

Dwell in an end house.—A stylized way of designating that a resident of a village was aged, feminine, and therefore presumably of lower status was to say simply that she lived in a house at the end of the village. No story cites an unmarried older man as a resident of such a house. Where an older couple lived in one, the understanding was that they were of the poorer class. Among examples of end-house dwellers are the Defecators (13) and Hot Weather Wind's grandmother (23), who continued to live apart in an end house even after her grandson metamorphosed into the wealthiest man of the community.

Village seen from above.—When a narrator took an actor toward a village, he very often if not invariably signaled its proximity and visibility by saying, in varied wordings that were permissible, that the actor looked down below, saw the village from the trail above, and saw many persons there. The stylistic trait functioned as a means of noting the visitor's nearness to a village that he would enter presently. But the words said that he looked down from above and observed many people. Not one story recorded that he perceived only a few persons, although in instances of massacre the narrator said that the actor saw no one.

Headman's house in middle of village.—A storyteller did not often say, in so many words, that a person entered the headman's house. The narrator usually indicated this fact, in one or another way, with a phrase which said that the headman's house was in the center of the village; in most instances it probably was. The stylistic trait involved utterance of a statement which must have been trite.

Five villages.—The five-pattern penetrated various categories of stylized devices and motifs. For example, when Half Grizzly Foot Girl paused at each of a number of villages in which her mother's relatives dwelt, the narrator suggested the multiplicity of visits formally by asserting that the girl paused at five villages (14). Such stylization connoted a goodly number of communities, not necessarily the number in the formula. As in some other contexts, the morpheme "five" must be translated "many," with the understanding that a number between three and ten was implied.

Five mountains. The fifth mountain.—When a storyteller spoke of a long journey afoot by trail through mountainous country, he was likely to say formally, in order to point to the fact of coverage of a great distance, "over five mountains" or "at the fifth mountain," depending on the context. For example, Coyote's grandson halted "at the fifth mountain" in order to wait for the woman who was following him (4). The intent was to point up the great distance he had made her walk before he deigned to turn and recognize her.

Drag corpse aside.—If an ogre killed a person, the narrator usually added a phrase which said that the villain took or dragged the corpse to the side or back of the house, or if not at a village, he dragged it beside a spring. In many if not all northwest states groups there was a cultural factor in bringing a corpse outside a house, for dying persons had to be taken out so as to save people from need for incinerating the structure. But the stylization resided in overt mention of removal of the corpse from within. Even an ogre automatically and always explicitly did so, partly in order to hide evidence of a nefarious act. Coyote's grandson, a severe gentleman and no ogre whatever, dragged his wife, whom he had just executed not in a village but in the mountains, to a spring and placed her personal effects beside her (4). The storyteller must have felt the usual compulsion to cite explicitly the location where the deceased was deposited, in a context where every auditor already knew where her body would be left.

6. DEVICES WHICH DATE

(a) *The next day.* . . . (b) *After a while then.* . . . or *Presently.* . . . (c) *I do not know.* . . . —These three very frequently recurring features are outstanding characteristics of the literary style. Hundreds of illustrations may be found in the texts. Hardly one myth lacked these forms, and sometimes all three were present many times in a story. Their most common occurrence was directly following introductory words like "They were living there." The narrator at once proceeded with something such as "The next day" or "I do not know how long a time after that, and then" or "Presently."

Of the three distinctive basic forms, (a) was simple; (b) and (c) occurred in variants—especially (c), which exhibited, for example, "I do not know what . . . did," "I do not know where . . . went," "I do not know how many times," "I do not know how long a time after, and then." There is a question whether Mrs. Howard's kind of employment of these features of design represented the style of all Clackamas narrators, but means of answering the query can no longer be found.

That is the way. . . . —This base actualized in variants such as "That is what . . . was continually doing," "That is how . . . was living," "That is the way . . . was." The form was really the opposite of the "I do not know" form and, although less frequent, is evidenced in scores of instances. Probably it occurred less often because Mrs. Howard's acculturation, feeling of aesthetic responsibility, and awareness of limitations in her knowledge of the literature obliged her to reiterate the "I do not know" form. An older Clackamas' confidence in his knowledge and control of the literature would have minimized the need to say "I do not know" and would have provided, in his dictations, a larger number of "That is the way" forms.

Five times.—This stylistic feature is of overruling importance throughout the northwest states except for Tillamook groups and peoples of northwestern Washington. The five-pattern was, as has been remarked, a characteristic frame for songs, dances, and rites. Probably it was employed in everyday speech as a means of expressing plural number or more than three.

So many times.—When a storyteller did not choose to say explicitly that something was done five times, she might say "so many times" or "that many times" in order to designate an undetermined number that was more than three. The form was frequent in myths.

For so long a time.—This idiom meant an unspecific but long duration—days, weeks, or years. Context supplied whatever connotation was understood. For example, *Ku'šaydi's* older brother said that *Ku'šaydi* had supposed that he would live "for so long a time" (40). That is, in the context of the myth, for a long period of years. The storyteller rarely employed numerical expressions for months or years, nearly always for days and short-term actions, and then in almost all instances five were specified. One rarely said "five years," "five seasons," or "five moons," that is, months. Apart from one or two exceptional instances, the longest time units enumerated were five or ten days. A longer period might be phrased "for so long a time," and a very long time in terms of years would be expressed without stylization by a word such as "long, long ago."

All day long. All the time.—These were variants of a form which exaggerated duration or repetitive actions. For example, Coyote was represented as crying audibly and continually in mock mourning for his actually unlamented grandson (5). While it is unlikely that a person's wails would be continued all through the day, both conversational and literary style were characterized by this expression of unremitting continuity. Northwest states Indians, not only Clackamas, preferably said that a person did such and such "all the time," not that he did so a great deal, occasionally, or intermittently. They said the former when they meant the latter.

It was a long time before. . . . —This phrase contrasted with "shortly" and "after a while then." It referred to a relatively longer interval, in our terms to most of an hour or to a number of hours. For example, Crane forced Grizzly Woman to wait for a time which we can only guess at but which may have been a good part of an hour or more than an hour, while he coolly ignored her pleas that he extend his leg bridge for her to cross over (16).

Now . . . got ready. Now then . . . made preparations.—A raconteur infrequently reported what a person did when preparing to take action or go on a trip. Auditors' knowledge of customary ways rendered detailed description of preparations superfluous. The common expressions here were variants on a base form "prepare." Often a phrase which followed was "the next day," as exemplified in "They got ready. Then the next day they went, they arrived there, they went ashore" (17).

The illustration shows the preferred and formal selections, in the literature, of aspects of an action which was a departure, journey, and arrival at a destination. The first item a storyteller selected was usually a variant of the "prepare, make preparations" form. The second item was usually "the next day." I have failed to note a single instance of departure designated as "at once," or "the same day." In a northwest states literature one almost always departed "the next day." The third item was likely to be a variant of a base form "go," or "proceed along," which implied travel either by canoe or afoot. The narrator rarely designated which. The fourth item was frequently a variant of a base form "arrive." But if the trip had been by canoe, a fifth form was likely to express "go ashore." Auditors had not yet learned that the journey was by canoe, and only now was the fact phrased. If the trip had been by trail, a fifth form was often a variant on a concept of entry into a village, more frequently into a house, or specifically into an end house. A narrator was unlikely to detail other aspects of a journey. One may search in vain through northwest states literatures for comments about weather, scenery, canoeing through rapids, condition of the trail, cutting through brambles, stepping on a snake, seeing a porcupine, passing by and observing a village or villages, or encountering others going in the same or opposite direction. Happenings or observations of any kind while en route were absent unless indispensable for the plot. On the other hand, a sequence of three, four, or five abstracted features of journey action had to be selected, and these constituted a prevailing pattern of travel description. It was a clear-cut and endlessly recurrent stylization, bleakly undescriptive from a Euroamerican viewpoint. When one cited the fact of a departure, travel, and arrival, this was the way it had to be presented. It must have been a rather old pattern if its areal spread correlates with antiquity.

The people (Indians) are close by now.—Like Clackamas, many northwest states literatures had a standard phrase of this kind, employed almost always by a precultural actor in the course of his utterance of an announcement of things to come. The phrase was inextricable from the announcer motif. During the several sentences of proclamation of the future name, location, role, or manner of living of the metamorphosing creature, the actor-protagonist uttered this pat phrase. It might be initial, medial, or final. A random example, among scores which could be given, is Grizzly Woman's announcement of Wildcherry's future: "You shall be good for burning (as fuel). They (Indians) shall make various things of you. Our (Indian) people are close by now (and when they enter our countryside they shall make use of you)" (16). Words in parentheses are added to clarify; they are not translations of words uttered.

7. PLOT DEVICES

The various motifs grouped in this section I characterize as features of style because all of them had a literary function which was stylistic, even if not primarily so. The announcer motif, an especially recurrent and stylized one, was comprised of situations which folklorists have called "transforming." I employ the term "announcer" because it is more appropriate for Clackamas literature. The six motifs which follow —youngest-smartest, bride comes, bow or root-digger breaks, excrement as adviser, bird adviser, and stylized anger or depression—are essentially like the announcer motif as stylized plot devices. The order in which they are presented is without significance.

Announcers.—Various precultural actors, sometimes during but more often at ends of myths, announced the future role of other actors; the collection contains about seventy such announcements. A notable aspect of announcing, found in a small number of instances (about fifteen), was the decreeing of an actor's lesser harmfulness or his entire harmlessness. A second aspect of importance was the frequent specification of his future use as food. Sometimes the future name of the actor was pronounced, sometimes the eventual habitat, sometimes the creature's manner of employment by Indians who were "close by," that is, who were soon to enter the land. However, direction of such entry was never phrased, and there is not a hint of the ultimate origin of the entrants.

The ritual myth (8) was a series of about twenty decisions and announcements, by a Coyote or Salmon, of bird, fish, and berry foods. The myth is unique because the promulgations in it were not incidental or secondary items, as announcements were in other myths; these announcements were the heart of the myth.

Skunk was subjected to multiple announcements. An unnamed animal actor who may have been a Grizzly Man told a Coyote's companion, Skunk, that his flatus would never again be lethal, that he would have a bad odor, and that he would live where there was rotten wood (1). Salmon limited pronouncement to the assertion that Skunk would live near rotten wood (5). A Coyote, who in one myth was Skunk's comrade (1), decreed that a skunk would not enjoy continuously repetitive flatus but would live around rotten wood, where occasionally he would discharge musk at a person (9).

The fifth, youngest, and meanest of the vain Grizzly Men announced the prospective harmlessness of lice and by cracking Greyback Louse Woman gave a sample demonstration of how people would kill these vermin (36). An unmarried young traveler encountered a group of Greyback Lice Women and decreed virtually the same thing (46).

In two myths Sun Woman announced that she and her sons, who were to be stars, would present signs of deaths of well-to-do or poorer persons (13, 46). In one of these myths Sun was Fire's grandson's wife and addressed no one in particular (13), but in the other account Sun was a traveling youth's wife and addressed her husband (46). The myths had wholly different plots except for a seemingly tagged-on ascription of the name of Sun to a wife who had two sons and symbolized feminine excellence. It would appear that audience and raconteur theorization resulted in identifying female actors of disparate myths as one precultural personage. The two women made identical announcements, although they displayed a minor feature of difference in persons to whom they spoke.

Although one of the Grizzly Women was regarded as especially arbitrary and insane, she was still permitted to decree, to a dozen trees and bushes, their future use by Indians (16). The ritualistic succession of twelve episodes in which a madwoman enunciated the future values of flora contrasted with the wise pronouncements of Salmon or Coyote (8); thus the two myths highlighted the point that announcing assignments ranged from feared and horrible to godlike precultural actors.

A special sequence of announcements appeared in an epilogue (43). Seal Woman told the nagging Crawfish Girl that she, Seal, would henceforth live in the river and Crawfish in creeks. Crawfish wept, entered a creek, and in her turn announced,

"Sick people will eat me." The point is that both actors, a harassed maternal figure and a vexatious younger sibling, spoke authoritatively. No outside functionary had to step before the curtain to speak in their stead.

Epilogues were announcements too, and the epilogue feature of style was so like the announcement in meaningful content and function that in a few instances the two features merged. For example, in a typical epilogue the sister-in-law of *Gi'ckux* announced that she would become a water being and that *Gi'ckux* and her husband's two sons would become mountain dwellers. Then her husband asserted that he would go by himself, although he did not say where (34).

It is apparent that almost any Myth Age actor might be assigned announcements, without an evident indication that he had a special mission or unique spirit-power for the occasion. Whoever happened to be on the spot said what needed to be said. Announcing, then, was a feature on a largely stylistic plane, not a characteristic of redoubtable gentry who transformed the precultural world for the sake of the Indians who were soon to enter the land. Clackamas did not conceive of demigods for any era, past or present. Individuals were deity-like—some, like Panther, were almost perfect men—but their powers had limits, and death overtook all of them. Nevertheless, they said what was right and true, for no higher being existed who could speak about reality. For the purpose of an announcement, which was a prime means of explaining reality, Clackamas made use of any precultural actor who was on the stage at the moment. There was no factotum or offstage actor, a *deus ex machina* to whom explanations were assigned.

When the great killer *Ku'šaydi* died, the unnamed older brother who survived him stepped forward to attest that no one would ever be indestructible (40). Who else could speak forth if that brother was the sole actor on the stage in the myth? For all we know, no Clackamas went on to inquire how this nameless actor knew about the future. The diffuseness and impersonality of authority about cosmology and the seeming failure of the Clackamas mind to pinpoint the source of judgments and adjudications about the course of history are comprehensible in the light of the social function of the announcer motif. What it did for Clackamas was to provide, in a stylized and hence rather rigid and authoritative manner, a certainty and assurance about reality and the direction of past events which only people, kin, and a father-like village headman could grant in a society whose cosmology was devoid of a deity. In other words, announcer motifs provided an underpinning of zoölogical and related certainties. Their source was the people, just as certainties in the modern village arose from decisions and securities granted by the headman.

One may then query why Coyote, in Clackamas, Sahaptin, and other groups near Chinooks, gave utterance to more announcements than other preculturals. I can offer only one explanation of his prominence among many announcers of both sexes and all ages. I believe that the reasons for his eminence are simply that he represented the wishes of younger and older men as no other precultural actor did and that he traveled more than any other actor. Therefore he went to more places and had more experiences. Had the cold-blooded *Ku'šaydi*, who traveled with an older brother, been represented in more than one myth (40), additional announcements would have been attributed to him.

The multiplicity of actors who made announcements is reflected to some degree in various superficially contradictory decrees: three different persons announce Skunk's future, two announce decisions about Greyback Lice, and Sun Woman makes the same pronouncement in two different myths. One may ask how Clackamas reconciled such independent decisions or announcements. I suggest that upon such a query a Clackamas might have responded in words like, "Oh, they merely said that and that is the way it was then," or, "Maybe those were different Skunks or Greyback Lice." The probable point is that in Clackamas cosmogony no one precultural actor decided final actions; the stress was on promulgation of a fact of the future, not its manipulation. Things continued to happen in a certain way, and the announcer's decree only foreshadowed what was inevitably to come. The fate of Greyback Lice Women, for example, was heralded in two myths but not definitively brought about by a myth actor. Therefore the two accounts did not clash. They did not need to be accommodated to each other.

In the case of identical pronouncements appearing in two or more contexts, the repetition may have expressed the importance of such pontifical utterances, their function of establishing unquestioning comprehension of things as they were, and the strength of community conviction and agreement about such matters. It is as if each time one said something, its truth and rightness were reinforced. Repetition in a new context generated no feelings of inconsistency or doubt as to which of several declarations was correct or authoritative. Each was connected with and sanctioned by absolute truth: the decisiveness of all that had happened in the precultural world and the certainty about it which flowed from its transmitters, the supernaturally equipped elders who narrated myths. Who had said something was important, but it was well that it had been said two or three times, and it was of utmost importance that it had been said before the precultural world changed into the modern world.

Although most announcements were directed, to all appearances, to a single actor, they were really addressed to all precultural people. No better illustration of this could be offered than the ostensible contradiction in stories where in one case Sun Woman spoke to everyone (13) and in another to her husband alone (46). Furthermore, in some stories announcements were not directed toward a single precultural auditor. In the most ritual-like myth (8) Coyote's or Salmon's decisions were made in the presence of the precultural village populace. The fifth girl of the Snake Tail myth (24), Ku'šaydi's older brother (40), and Crawfish Girl (43) spoke to no one person. In three myths Coyote spoke as if to himself (9, 10, 12), and Gi'ckux's sister-in-law and older brother seem to have discoursed to themselves rather than to anyone else (34). These pronouncements were offered in no different vein than those spoken to a fellow actor.

These seeming peculiarities of announcements can be partially explained by their very nature. Announcements were supplementations of myths and never appeared in tales. They bear every sign of being secondary additions to plots, and their content was in each instance a consequence of community philosophizing about causes of things. To a Euroamerican a striking feature of omission is the failure even once to invoke a wholly deific actor; any precultural, feared or respected, adult or immature, prophesied on occasion. But any actor of myth times could serve as a mouthpiece for the community philosophy of causation. The very process of causation interested Clackamas little by contrast with their fixation on what some person— it mattered little who—had said long, long ago.

Youngest-smartest.—Since this notable motif has been partly discussed along with the five-pattern, it is sufficient to cite examples and to weigh the device against the very few instances where an older person was abler. Coon deceived his older brother (3). The youngest of five Mountain Cannibals acquired a wife (4). The younger the Wolf, the more vicious, and the fifth was the worst (5). The youngest of five Grizzly Men succeeded in swimming across a stream and he fought Panther (6). A Coyote's youngest child, a girl, was more fleet of foot than her four brothers (10). A younger brother acquired more spirit-power than his older sibling (13). Half Grizzly Foot realized better than her mother the peril at home (14). Little Water Bug was superior to all the women of the village in her comprehension of the murderess, Grizzly (17). A Hot Weather Wind made it possible for his three older brothers to travel east (22). The youngest girl killed Snake Tail Woman, thanks to the bird adviser, Meadow Lark (24). The fifth and youngest girl killed Awl Woman, again because of Meadow Lark (27). A younger brother warned his older sibling that an ogress was dangerous (31). *Gi'ckux* was more perspicacious than his older brother (34). The youngest Grizzly Man killed Greyback Louse, with the aid of Meadow Lark (36). *Ku'šaydi* had more spirit-power than his older brother and surpassed the latter in other ways, too (40). The youngest Thunder, youngest Grizzly, and youngest Grizzly Woman were more vicious and powerful than their older siblings (40). The youngest Sky Cannibal Girl and youngest human girl, Sun, consorted sexually with a traveling youth (46). The youngest hunter was taken by Beaver (48). The fifth and youngest Grizzly Man escaped Coon's lethal beautifying (49).

Most instances were in a five-pattern, and therefore the two traits of style, youngest-smartest and five-pattern, could merge. Some instances of youngest-smartest depended on Meadow Lark's propitious intervention and in a sense consolidated with that bird adviser motif. Some examples exhibited greater spirit-power or viciousness than smartness in the youngest and last of the five to appear.

The few cases of emphasis upon greater capacity in an older sibling should be mentioned in order to show the comparatively great strength of the youngest-smartest motif and to highlight its stylistic function. Skunk was weak, subservient, almost a simpleton, by contrast with his scheming and controlling older brother Coyote (1). But the relationship between the two was not really a sibling bond in spite of the myth's use of the terms "younger brother" and "older brother" for Skunk and Coyote. These were etiquette, not biologically connotative terms, in this myth. Skunk really represented, I think, any villager or follower of a headman, and Coyote stood for a well-to-do man at all times. The older Grizzly sister warned her younger sister that "Coyote is beating you" (3). The story offered the sole instance of an older female sibling who had more sense than her junior. The oldest Bear Boy acted paternally toward his four younger siblings, but he was so represented in order to intensify pity for the youngest child, who was only a baby and who whimpered when he smelled his mother's roasting flesh (16). These three stories were the only instances of plots where an older sibling was more competent, and except for the two Grizzly sisters (3) they did not really constitute opposites of the youngest-smartest motif.

Bride comes.—One of the prominent devices of Clackamas mythology was the stylized handling of a concept of an unmarried young female who, unlike the girl in a modern social system sold in marriage by male relatives, took initiative to go to a marriageable man's house. She collected her personal effects and money beads, traveled alone on the trail with them, and entered his abode without the slightest awareness on his part that a woman was coming to him. She sat on his bed-platform at once so as to symbolize her wish that she might decide upon and institute a marital relationship which neither he nor her male kin had determined or even anticipated. Without indication in the myth of monetary payment or in-law lineage exchanges of presents, she presently functioned as his wife. In fact, she slept with him the night of her arrival. One gets the impression that Clackamas had not the slightest doubt that a precultural man who was descended upon in this culturally most improper manner suffered from paralysis of the vocal cords and everything else except his sexuality. Clackamas obviously supposed that that one segment of his psychological machinery performed its expected function.

I recall only one myth (31) which suggested that a precultural man rejected, or could reject, a precultural female who walked in on him in this stylized way—which as far as the anthropologist can learn had not the slightest resemblance to occurrences among modern Clackamas except in their wishes, jokes, and oral literature sessions. I should add parenthetically a suggestion that in modern villages postmenopause widows may have invaded the couches of youths, and therefore the myth motif may reflect something of modern custom, if it was custom. In the myths examples of bridal invasions by young and virginal creatures included Trout Girl (6), Half Grizzly Foot (14), Grizzly Woman (17), the youngest of five unnamed sisters (18), five unnamed girls (24), another five girls (27), another Grizzly Woman (34), and an unnamed woman (37). While some instances were of wholly unlovely females, others like Trout were felicitous. I think there was less pressure to use myths as a fantasy screen for wishes about older women, because the society allowed them the right to take sexual initiative and leave relatives financially uninvolved.

One wonders if anthropologists received information so exclusively on upper-class marriages that they failed to discern a marital initiative which was permissible among lower-class belles. I believe that I always inquired about such matters but never received a cue which would warrant deduction that a few girls found husbands without familial participation.

An ancillary feature of style which attached to a number of instances of "bride comes" was the hiding of the newly arrived female by an older male who happened to be in the house when she arrived but was not her husband-to-be. Examples were a Coyote's secreting of Trout (6) and Flint's hiding of an unnamed girl (18).

Bow or root-digger breaks.—Means by which precultural people who were far from their village learned of an important change or tragedy at home were, for a female, breaking of her major artifact, the root-digger; for a male, snapping of his most important artifact, the bow. When the cherished implement broke, its owner recognized an incontrovertible indication and returned rapidly to the village. For example, when the idiotic Cock Robin (31) baked his older sister's infant, her root-digger broke and she rushed home. When Coon stole a Grizzly Man's fire (6), Panther's bow broke and he returned at once.

Excrement as adviser. Magic object answers fugitive.—Where a magic object, as folklorists have termed it, was excrement, the two traditional motifs merged. Coyote's excrement, which Clackamas regarded as two spirit-powers, proffered information to him on several occasions when he was nonplussed (9). Excrement which said only "woo woo" to a deserted boy (47) apparently suffered from a limited command of language compared to Coyote's loquacious advisers of identical composition. When a Grizzly Woman (16) spoke to excrement that had been placed on the limb of a tree, it only fell down upon her. It could not utter a word. Fuller comment on the motif, a substitute title for which might be "excrement as agent," may be found in the discussion of myth 34, to be published elsewhere. Very likely all northwest states peoples had an intense anal preoccupation, the causes and significance of which need not be examined here. It is enough to point out that the engrossment in anality had become such as to receive stylized expression in oral literature.

Bird adviser (Meadow Lark Woman).—This motif has been discussed above in the chapter on personality.

Stylized anger or depression.—A number of myths contained citations of an actor, young or old, who acted out in a stylized way feelings of anger or depression which he was unable to resolve. Such a person reclined on his bed-platform if at home and refused to eat, speak, or go anywhere. Examples were Half Grizzly Foot, who was furious at her irresolute mother (14); the girl who was angry at her Gopher kidnapers (20); and Beaver's adopted son, who was depressed and perhaps angry because of the cruelty which Beaver had to endure (48). A narrator never asserted anything about a person's feelings but reported one or two externals of behavior: the person lay idle, remained uncommunicative, and did not eat. Although the myths stressed only a manner of response, which was probably identical with an accepted resolution of emotions in the modern society, it is likely that the behavior, which was region-wide in myths, was stylized for several forms of intense feeling. For example, it is possible that Clackamas reacted with this kind of behavior, as other northwest states Indians did, to an initial awareness of a spirit-power relationship. The behavior seems to have functioned as a publicly recognized means of permitting a person unable to handle his feelings to enjoy a time interval during which he could work them through without interference or prying by others.

The preceding six motifs intergraded, in degree of stylization, with motifs which follow. The number of the latter was large, but the stylization which adhered to them would be easier to characterize if a larger collection of stories had been obtained. I have not listed many familiar motifs of world or Northwest folklore which were found once or twice in the collection because their stylization was either so slight or difficult to evaluate, and their functions as content so salient, that it is unsuitable to enumerate them here. Omitted motifs of this kind include, for example, minuscule packs (46), spider sky rope (46), tests of son-in-law (18), telltale hair in stew (18), impossible tasks (18), leaping mountains (or journey with magic speed) (6), and smoker coughs when looked at (6).

Ogre defeated by overeating.—A stylized way of vanquishing a dangerous being was to force him to overeat so that he became torpid, fell asleep, and could then be killed. Examples were Tongue Man (42), Grizzly Woman (34), and Mountain Cannibals (4).

Roof spy.—Precultural actors who suffered from superabundant curiosity and needed to be secretive about it did only one thing. They pretended that they were going far away, circled back toward the house, climbed onto the roof, and peered inside through the smoke vent. The architecture of a northwest states house allowed this recurrent device by which a person descried unobserved what was going on inside. Examples were found in four myths (27, 29, 40, 47).

Seduction with magic vermin.—In several myths an unmarried person who was enamored of a lone overnight guest sent fleas which caused the visitor to decamp from the bed-platform assigned him. The only bed-platform which was not ridden with fleas was the host's. Examples of perpetrators of such seduction, in each case successful and respectable from the precultural viewpoint, were a huntress (34) and Fish Spear Pole (31).

Monster killed from within.—Five myths exhibited variants of this motif. Coyote cut the hanging heart of the Land Swallower and later, in identical manner, the heart of the River Swallower (9). These ogres in their last convulsions disgorged recent victims of their maws. Mudfish entered a Grizzly Man, cut at his heart, and so killed him (7). Wren ate Elk's heart fat, and presently Elk succumbed (25). Flints attached to *Gi'ckux's* bald head cut up into and killed the Grizzly Woman who had been using him as her anus wiper (34). The Coyote, Mudfish, and Wren feats stressed the conquest of a big creature by a tiny antagonist. The pitiable *Gi'ckux* in his turn was the adversary of a being of great power, although difference in stature was not involved. The motif expressed the same feeling that was central in the David and Goliath theme.

Cremation to insure enduring death.—In several myths cremation was sufficient to kill an ogre. Profile (48), Tongue (42), Mountain Cannibals (4), and Grizzly Man (6) were merely incinerated to guarantee that they would not return to life. But an equally thoroughly burned Grizzly Woman was resuscitated after some time. Male ogres could be done away with in the flames, but the appalling female of precultural eras needed additional treatment to make certain that she would never come back to plague people. Two myths documented the point that her cremated corpse must also be ground and the ashes and powder blown away (17, 34). These auxiliary procedures seem to have permitted further ventilations of aggression against horrible older women who preyed upon good folk. An ancillary motif was Half Grizzly Foot's discovery, with Meadow Lark's advice, that her mother's hat, the projection of conscience, must be burned to forestall its reappearance (14).

Mysterious housekeeper.—Two myths offered the motif of unseen persons who had come to a lonely person's house when a wish was expressed for a companion (27, 29). Plots in which the motif was present centered upon spirit-power and familial relationship problems. The invisible housekeepers represented both spirit-powers and relatives who lived in the house, and the situations generated feelings which Clackamas had toward the most vital props in their security system.

Years thought days.—This catchword from Old World folklore took the form, in two myths, of "joining" of five days and nights in order to express intensity, quality, and duration of newlywed love (18, 34).

Magic storm.—In several myths an actor burned cottonwood bark and blew the ashes into the air, and a wind and snowstorm developed (32, 47). Cold snaps and snowstorms were directly caused by children breaking taboos or disobeying in tales (55, 56), or sometimes by an unindicated cause (57, 58). Awl Woman produced darkness and a rainstorm in some unexplained way (27). The folkloristic caption of "magic storm" therefore applies to three or more motifs in Clackamas literature.

Proscribed direction.—A recurrent motif was a parent figure's interdiction of travel in an indicated direction. The youngster disobeyed, went in the forbidden direction, and in some instances suffered punishment. Examples were a Basket Ogress' warning to a captive youth (46), two disobedient boys who died (35), the Gophers' stepdaughter who found her mother (20), and *Ku'šaydi* and the lake (40).

Cannibalism.—As far as is known, human flesh was never engorged by a people of the northwest states, but Clackamas myths employed the concept of cannibals in order to intensify the awfulness of two distinct kinds of people. One, exemplified by Grizzlies and Tongue Man, lived in Clackamas villages. The other, represented by Mountain and Sky Cannibal people, lived at a distance; in other words, they were depreciated rustics whose diet and very persons were loathsome in the eyes of well-to-do Chinooks. Grizzly Man and Woman were the literature's outstanding cannibals. She cooked almost mesmerized women for her husband (9). Grizzly Man and Boy ate the elder's brothers-in-law, and years later the daughter devoured all her mother's kin (14). A Grizzly Woman swallowed every villager in another myth (34). After an unsuccessful effort at necrophagy, Tongue Man gulped all the inhabitants of a village (46). The horror of necrophagy, cannibalism, or both was exhibited not only in characterizations of various omnivorous actors. It came out in another form when *Ku'šaydi* unwittingly ate the mashed bones of dead persons and shortly suffered agonizing pains and died (40).

Immaculate conception.—Three instances of oral impregnation contrasted with one of self-pregnancy on the little finger (9). There was no other kind of immaculate conception. Two of the three orally induced pregnancies were consequent upon drawing basketry fibers through the lips. A woman's fibers were moistened by Thunder's urine, that is, by rain (30). A boy furtively placed his semen on basketry fibers (23). Another oral impregnation was distinctive: an infuriated husband caused his haughty wife to imbibe maple juice which had been metamorphosed into snakes' semen, so that later she gave birth to snakes and died (28).

Dirty boy as hero. Loathly bridegroom. Male Cinderella.—These captions apply to a single concept which was developed in entirely different ways in two myths. A Hot Weather Wind was poor and physically loathsome (23). Later, after he orally impregnated the headman's daughter and became her husband, his nasal mucus and open sores metamorphosed into valuable shells and beads. He became wealthy. The other account was of a deserted boy who acquired a wealthy water-dwelling supernatural as his wife (47). His tiny house transformed into a wonderful abode stocked with food; his wife's many blankets and hides were of finest quality. The core of feeling which was expressed in the two dramas had to do with unattractive persons who related successfully to wealth-granting spirit-powers, a bond profoundly wished by the region's peoples.

Miraculous growth.—This concept, which was a projection of a universal wish, was developed in three myths in wholly different ways. A Mountain Cannibal girl quickly grew, with five tossings directly after her birth, into a little girl who walked and talked but was revolting because of her incapacity for affectional and accepting relationship (6). A flame-throwing youth who sought dire vengeance on the torturers of his father transformed fourteen grizzly hairs into grizzly puppies which burgeoned in a few moments into adult grizzlies and ate the ill-fated villagers (13). The impeccable Thunder Boy spoke as soon as he was born and grew so rapidly that he could care for himself within a year. Shortly he could hunt like an adult (30). The two instances of Mountain Cannibal Girl and Thunder Boy are not sufficient documentation to support an idea that a quick maturation in a girl produces horrible results, while the same speed in a boy does precisely the opposite. Nevertheless, our total knowledge of Clackamas culture does not controvert the suggestion.

Inappropriate action from misunderstanding.—Three myths exhibited distinctive developments of this motif. Skunk misunderstood his wife's request for breast meat and instead pulled out his teeth, the morpheme for which was homonymous (19). Not very different was the travesty in which Cock Robin, trying to follow his sister's instructions, baked her infant (31). The common thread of stupid literal-mindedness, in Clackamas ways of concretizing this theme, was continued in Blue Jay's humorless and absurd responses to his sister's remarks (41).

Relative's flesh unwittingly eaten.—The omnivorousness of cannibals was turned against them by employment of this motif in two myths. Grizzly Man ate his wife (9), and Grizzly Woman, her sons (16).

External heart. Achilles heel.—These familiar motifs of world folklore combined in Clackamas. A half-grizzly girl's human mother had a heart in her hat (14), symbolizing primarily the indestructibility of values. One Grizzly Woman's heart was on her little finger, and it thereby accounted for her invulnerability and tied in with her terrific spirit-power (17). In each of these myths a woman was almost impossible to kill because her heart was not in the usual place. But so few instances of external hearts in women are insufficient to warrant a deduction that such externality and concomitant indestructibility connected with femininity, especially since the one woman was good, the other bad. Probably the concept of invulnerability because of anatomical aberrancy was worked out in still other ways in myths which were not dictated by Mrs. Howard. In fact, Flint was difficult to kill because of his body of flint (18), and *Ku'šaydi* returned from death presumably because he had spirit-power which made him able to resuscitate himself (40).

Rotten wood.—The world-wide notion of magic objects took the form in Clackamas of rotten wood, although the collection lacked the variety of examples which probably would have appeared if a larger number of stories had been dictated. Four myths illustrate three ways in which the notion was developed. Rotten wood metamorphosed into deer (34, 42) and lungs (6) and was placed in a cradle to simulate a stolen infant (46). In the last instance it may have been resorted to solely because it was so soft that it could be shaped, and it really did nothing. I cite it because rotten wood spoke in other literatures of the Northwest, and Clackamas use of it in a cradle was definitely a cognate. In fact, an ordinary hard stick of wood uttered a single phrase, as the Clackamas form of the "Magic object talks" motif, in the myth in which Coyote ordered a stick to say to Grizzly Man, "He is eating his wife" (9).

Caesarean.—In a few myths children were brought into the world with especial dispatch in order to speed action and permit expression of violent rage against females. No Northwest peoples, as far as is known, attempted to perform a Caesarean operation. But a Panther tore open Trout's abdomen, drowned her four Coyote babies, and saved a Panther infant (6). Raiders cut open a Seal Woman's abdomen, removed fresh fish from her stomach, and she died. Blue Jay in the same myth ate fish hearts which he removed from Crawfish Girl (43). The hostility component of the motif was central, the surgical technique secondary, and other drives may be speculated upon as one wishes. At a deep level related developments were the entry of snakes which burst nubile girls (24) and the concept of giving birth to snakes, with the consequent agonizing death of a woman (28).

Arrow ladder.—A familiar northwest states motif of ascent to the sky country was found in only one Clackamas myth. A person shot arrows at the sky, they joined, and precultural people ascended on the ladder. The variant supplied by Mrs. Howard (46) seems truncated or weakened, and components may have been dropped out in the course of community handling of the notion. The traveling youth in her rendition only joined bow and arrows, without indication of how he did it. He proceeded from the top of a tall fir to climb on his ladder into the sky country.

Local winter.—Three tales reported a local winter in which a village population starved while communities nearby enjoyed summer (55, 56, 57–58). Expressions of this motif were certainly pressured by food and winter weather anxieties.

Crane bridge.—In northwest states literatures Crane Man acted so consistently in a helpful parent role in the succoring of fugitives, and so often used his leg as proxy for a foot-log bridge, that he amounted to a feature of style. However, he extended his leg as a bridge in only one Clackamas myth (16).

Origin of death.—The concept that people might have enjoyed everlasting lives had not certain specific situations turned out as they did in precultural eras was probably present in every northwest states literature. In Clackamas the working-out of the notion took two forms which were very likely historically independent. A grandmother's uncovering of an infant that had been born in the land of dead people resulted in eventual death for all persons (45). Coyote's inability to control his fury at a centipede resulted in failure of persons who had died to return to life later (10). Perhaps the two notions were not irreconcilable to Clackamas, for the reason indicated above: wholly different causes of the same thing only reinforced feeling that each explanation of cause was true.

Resuscitation by arrangement of members.—Sahaptins' recurrent and nicely stylized motif of revivification by stepping over bones seems to have been absent. A related concept with an entirely different device for resuscitation was evidenced in Coyote's vain carrying of his children's corpses in a pack basket lined with fresh greens (10). Panther's unexplained return to life, after parts of his body severed by Flint were buried, may have been a similar if not cognate notion (18). Panther's reassembling after the bloody fight with Grizzly Man was perhaps another cognate of a sort, although the storyteller did not say that he had been really dead when his parts fell to the ground (6). When Coyote dismembered himself in a hollow tree, he lost his eyes before he began to piece himself together. Again he was not thought of, in so many words, as having died (9). In short, resuscitations recurred but were developed so distinctively in each case that to term resuscitation devices a feature of style would be to find style in items of content that shared only one notion. Sturgeon's wife's return as a whole person after her organs had been thrown into a stream was very likely an idea of another kind, related to the northwest states belief that fish came again if parts of them were cast into the river (26). The means by which Seal and Crawfish returned to life after their bodies were slashed open was left unclear (43).

Disintegration. Dismemberment.—The other side of the coin, and one which brought up the same question whether recurrent notions meant presence of a feature of style, appeared in the concept of chopping or separation of body parts. Coyote took his body apart, piece by piece (9). Beaver Man hacked away at Profile Man, in a fatal dismemberment (48). Flint cut Panther to pieces fatally too, at any rate for a while (18). Panther's falling parts exemplified a non-lethal dismemberment (6), as did the case of Sturgeon's wife (26), who returned hale and hearty from her severed internal organs.

Water of life.—Healing water restored sight or health or both to Steelhead's stepmother-wife (5), to Fire's nearly dead grandson (13), to the blind *Gi'ckux* (34), and to many blind persons (46). This world-wide motif appeared in a small number of instances in this collection. It was patently a device which could be employed to provide a dramatically speedy and happy resolution of the tragic predicament of an incapacitated or dying person. Clackamas use of the motif seems to have stressed water as a quick cure for blindness, although water also restored a debilitated person to health.

Flood.—I suggest only a possibility of some little stylization in the various deluge and flood motifs which were frequent in myths of northwest states peoples. As elsewhere, the Clackamas collection contained a number of examples of engulfing waters which were confined to a small district. A local deluge caused the drowning of *Ku'šaydi* (40), vindictive Gopher Women caused another local deluge which drowned a girl and her mother (20), and Profile Man's bloody urination raised the level of a stream (48). I find it hard to believe that Clackamas lacked the great flood motif, with some precultural water dweller like Muskrat diving below for the earth. Contiguous peoples had this motif, and doubtless Clackamas heard it occasionally.

The explanation can be only that Mrs. Howard restricted dictations to narratives which she controlled to her satisfaction.

Giant.—If developments of this notion can be termed a feature of style, Clackamas literature was characterized by repudiation of any kind of giantism. Great spirit-power was unconnected with giantism. A person who had such power was not physically large, nor was the supernatural who conferred it. It is significant that the one kind of unreserved bigness in the literature was in trees: Flint tottered under gigantic Douglas firs (18), and who can gainsay that they are tremendous in the Northwest? An Oedipal headman (38) was represented as gigantic, but querying revealed that Chinooks actually thought of him as maybe eight or ten feet tall! The instance seems to reinforce the deduction that Chinooks adapted negatively to the notion of gigantic creatures and things. They were really unable to conceive it. The reason for their incapacity resided, I think, in their ideology of spirit-powers, co-villagers, and kin, all of them as potent helpers as one needed and all able to aid to the full.

Instances of true giantism may be claimed for the cavernous Land and Water Swallowers which Coyote entered and killed (9) although, to be sure, there is no reason to suppose that their mouths were larger than necessary to engorge a war canoe. Their protests were not uttered in thunderous tones. Their last throes of agony in dying disgorged merely a handful of canoes. And their interiors seem to have been modest-sized caves. Coyote did not have to erect a scaffold to slash at their hanging hearts. When little Mudfish went inside Elk he entered a normal-sized animal (7). Undoubtedly Tongue's member, which was necrophagously oriented toward a deceased headwoman, was enormously long. But its possessor was later represented as a most ordinary appearing man with a vulgarly omnivorous and prodigious appetite (42). To all intents and purposes his formerly extraordinary tongue had disappeared. The *membrum virile* which Coyote borrowed was as long as the Columbia River is wide (9), but since the organ's diameter was only normal, the notion does not seem a telling instance of a concept of giantism. Grizzly Woman ate large numbers of persons, but not once was she represented as bigger than any other woman except for breasts so elongated that she threw them over her shoulders when she ran downhill, in order to keep from tripping on them (143). The interesting thing about her was that she could eat so many persons and retain a torso no more bulky than anyone's. Again, I think, she corroborated the deduction about Clackamas inability, at the cost of illogic, to conceive of examples of giantism. I think that if a Clackamas had been asked to explain a normal-sized precultural actor who could engorge so many persons during a cannibal rampage, he would have responded blandly in words to the effect that that was the way she was, she was a terrible person, and they were awfully afraid of her!

In summary, trees, food needs, cannibalism, and sex organs but no creatures took on characteristics of bigness.

Dwarf.—Although a notion of a gigantic precultural being was alien or lacked anything in the culture to nurture it, diminutiveness was congenial and also feared, in all likelihood. Nevertheless, the collection supplied few illustrations. Minuscule packs appeared as a plot expediting device in a traveling youth's return to the land below (46). The sole instance of an exceptionally small person was Flint, and he was really representative not of dwarf size but of a man of fetalized, congenitally deformed, and generally preposterous appearance (18). He was frightfully dangerous. Beliefs in normal-appearing people of the woods, two to four feet tall and some supposed to be magnificent wrestlers, have been reported by western Oregon groups apart from Clackamas. Absence of Clackamas notation of such "dangerous" people is uninstructive in the light of the scarcity of data on the culture.

Relationships.—I use this caption in order to include familial and other relationships. Primarily these constituted features of content, but they were also features of style because they framed recurrent tensions and solutions of tensions. The caption covers bondings of siblings of same and of opposite sex, husband-wife relationships, Oedipal and non-Oedipal relationships of elders to younger people, relationships of headmen to villagers, in-law relationships, and perhaps others.

Child picks out unknown father.—Several myths presented a motif of this kind. Examples were of diverse content and actually unrelated. A girl stolen by Gophers found her mother (20). A boy brought up among Mountain Cannibals encountered his father, who revealed himself (4). And the child of the uncomely Hot Weather Wind selected him (23). The common thread in these stories was a stress upon a child's intense feeling of belonging to its biological parent.

Life token. Feather signal.—Seal Hunter's spirit-power hauled in a string which had a blue jay feather attached at her end, to learn that her former guests had navigated successfully under dangerous sky shutters (26). A bleeding feather connoted mortal danger which beset the absent grandson of Fire (13). A sign of death also included peals of thunder (30) and one or two stars visible beside the sun (13, 46). The stylization was the presence of various kinds of signals when the plot needed them.

Injured therefore never eats.—Several precultural actors lived without eating because they had been injured. The notion was exemplified in two myths, by Awl Woman (27) and Hazel Gambler (29). The motif of stylized anger and depression which was characterized by refusal of food may share something with this motif, with loss of interest in food consequent upon hurt feelings and injured bodies.

Many additional motifs may have had stylistic functions like the ones that have been listed to this point, but the collection of myths and tales is so small and the single occurrences of motifs of these kinds so unindicative of stylistic services that only comparative studies of literatures of the region may offer important assistance in studies of such matters.

8. EXPLANATORY ELEMENTS

Explanatory elements of a pointed and stylized kind were not numerous, except for epilogues which closed myths and characterized an inescapable feature of the style of every myth. Only epilogues explained the origins of both major and some minor fauna. Other and incidentally inserted explanatory elements bore marks of being secondary additions consequent upon community and raconteur thought, often about petty anatomical and other minor features of the world. Few myths seem to have had a course of development largely determined by their explanatory function, that is, by need to have a severely rational historical explanation of some aspect of the external world; most were explanatory in the broad sense of telling about the whole background of prehistory and the earlier appearances and forms of land, fauna, flora, people, and customs of the era.

The following paragraphs cite some, not all, of the specifically interposed explanatory elements where they constituted devices of a somewhat stylized kind and were manipulated as such. Epilogues are excluded from consideration because of their treatment above.

In myth 6 a largely explanatory scene or entr'acte was a play within a drama. While the play ostensibly accounted for an elk's antlers and interested an audience because it did explain antlers, it functioned as a device to lessen tension before the drama's plot resumed. The scene distracted while it instructed.

In one scene the cut-up rocks at West Linn, Oregon, were ascribed to Mudfish, who broke into them in order to escape the arrows of Coyote's followers (7). But the central interest in the scene was the fate of poor Mudfish and his rejection by unfair persons, not the reason for the appearance of rocks which in all probability were unimportant to villagers at West Linn; the notion of the split rocks seems an afterthought. Significantly, the collection nowhere else accounted for rocks that are structured or cut—rather than merely located—in the entire Clackamas or adjoining regions.

From one point of view all of the ritual myth (8) was explanatory. But the overruling service of this myth may long have been a satisfying expression of relationships to food beings, since the account granted feelings of security in basic relationships. A rational explanatory facet of each episode makes impact upon a non-Chinook, not the feelings toward food beings which were, I believe, Chinooks' main responses to the episodes. Chinooks had no need to have the obvious items of explanation of this myth witnessed annually, but everyone needed and enjoyed repetitions of sentiments of association and assurance about relationships, although these were accompanied by simple explanations of anatomical and other matters which everyone knew anyway.

The Coyote journey contained a number of obvious adjuncts of an explanatory kind, none of which conceivably motivated or shaped the plot significantly in its spreadings, retention, and manipulation (9). In scene 1 Coyote announced various features of pheasants; in scene 2, the correct position in sexual intercourse; scene 4, the reason for the presence of two rocks at a certain point in the Columbia River; scene 5, some matters about sturgeons; scene 6 gave a reason for the conviction that Wishram Chinooks were sexually lax—the cause adduced was amusing, at the expense of outsiders, and bolstered satisfaction in one's greater virtue; scene 12 gave reasons for snails' eyesight, slowness, and shells—in a culture which was indifferent to such creatures; and scene 13, why skunks are found about rotten wood and why they discharge musk. The same explanatory feature about skunks appeared elsewhere (1) and therefore showed nicely the secondary role of an explanatory element. Scene 15 contained an explanation of the origin of a cascade and items about customary activities of people at a certain Chinook village. The reason why the literature accounted for a number of things about this village, and omitted reference to scores of other villages, may reside in the fact that explanatory elements were asides and breaks, not basic items, in literature. Only in scene 18 were traits of another village—the Wishrams again—explained, and the items singled out for mention were minor. However, Mrs. Howard's collection may lack many myths and tales that accounted for some of the hundreds of villages in the world around Clackamas and in the Chinook group itself.

Myth 13 included incidental and appended explanations of a chub's mouth, a blue jay's eyes, and a trait or two in a crawfish. It also explained why certain stars were close to the sun. Since the star item also appeared in the Sky Cannibal myth (46), one deduces that the explanation was at one time tacked on to the different plots which made note of a Sun Woman and her two sons. The explanation connected with death anxiety, and so one can understand why it became attached to at least two myths. There would have been less feeling, for example, about West Linn's rocks (7), which may be why there was a reference in only one myth to their origin.

The Seal Hunter myth (26) contained a scene which was perhaps basically explanatory in its citation of characteristics of a sturgeon's head bones. But the manner in which it became inserted in the plot can be suggested only after the myth's comparison with cognates in the Northwest.

Myth 31 included an incidental explanation of a robin's red breast and his food habits. Myth 11, which briefly accounted for the duration of seasons, could have functioned primarily as a typical Northwest expression of a struggle between competing well-to-do men. Myth 12, also a short story of disputants, accounted for the daily recurrence of sleep. The two stories were undoubtedly unusually strongly motivated by need to explain phenomena as important as seasons and sleep, but studies of their distributions and functions in other Northwest groups are needed before evaluation of their explanatory components. Like myths 8, 11, and 12, myth 33 may have been allegorically explanatory. It dealt with characteristics of frogs. Actually no more than these four myths, and a few scenes such as the motif of sturgeon head bones (26), displayed internal indications of primary rather than tagged-on features due to needs to satisfy rational queries about aspects of reality.

The *Ku'šaydi* myth (40), with its passing notations of matters about thunder, grizzlies, and grizzly ogresses, exhibited clearly the primary literary interest in relationships and personalities and the secondary function of explanatory elements. Myth 49 contained a passing explanation of raccoon markings—his whipping by his grandmother—which was widespread in northwest states literatures. The myth added other items about raccoons' behavior.

It is possible that twentieth-century Indians who were acculturated like Mrs. Howard tended to retain and preferred to dictate to anthropologists stories which were most highly regarded because of functions in confirming the worth of the cultural heritage and system of values. That is, stories about people and relationships may have survived better than stories which centered in formal explanatory elements about things, cited villages which had vanished in the early nineteenth century, or explained sites which were never again visited or used. Their characteristics could have had slight interest for people like Mrs. Howard. Many stories, especially shorter ones which were primarily explanatory of artifacts, geography, fauna, and flora, may also have been sooner dropped in the decades of destructive cultural envelopment by Caucasians. Such narratives did less to buttress the more than bruised security system of reservation Indians.

The discussion of personality characterizations showed that major actors were not identified with principal food resources such as salmon, deer, elk, roots, and berries. These acted in the mythology infrequently. Their roles were minor except for Salmon's possible importance as an announcer, especially in myths which I fear Mrs. Howard failed to dictate. Since there is a chance that she did not maintain interest in and memory of the more authoritative cosmological myths of the kind exemplified by myth 8, explanatory features which could be surveyed came out of myths whose actors were not anthropomorphizations of major resources. That may be why explanatory devices answered, by and large, questions about incidental matters.

One wonders about what appears to have been a capricious choice of so few explanatory elements apart from epilogues. One questions how many matters were formally explained, and how explanations were made apart from the documentation of various kinds provided in the mythology. Obviously, Clackamas literature was not maintained in order to offer voluminous or extensive explanations of nature, people, and customs. Stylized inserted explanations were surprisingly infrequent and in this collection were prevailingly of inconsequential things. In most instances they were patently filigree, not essential, strands of stories. If an ethnographer employed formal explanatory elements as such, or the whole mass of the literature, as a base for a Clackamas ethnography, he would offer a depiction so bare, unrevealing, and unstructured as to be absurd. The important facet of culture termed "technology" was an almost complete blank on containers, garments, house construction, and water craftsmanship. All that was on a geological level was the marking of rocks at West Linn (7), some few rocks among the thousands in the Columbia and Willamette rivers (9), and one cascade (9). The solitary food mentioned in an explanatory element was sturgeon, a fish of minor importance (8, 9). Explanatory elements were inserted for duration of seasons (11), daily sleep (12), omen meanings of sun and stars (13, 46), and the harmlessness of thunder (40). Animal habits and anatomical characteristics predominated in the inventory of explanatory elements, but most possible items were left unexplained.

The function of explanatory elements, including epilogues, tended therefore to be on a stylistic level rather than primarily to satisfy curiosity and make people feel at home in their world. Explanatory elements were, in general, digressions of pleasant and mildly reassuring content; and, like comforting remarks offered to a perfectly well person, there was no special time or place for them. As in other regions, they must have been largely local additions which came out of theorization within a small area or group of villages.

Apart from the relatively formal explanatory elements, which explained so very little, the literature did account for important segments of reality. For example, Coyote's journey (9) showed the reasons for absence rather than presence of ogres. Personalities of actors accounted for many characteristics of modern spirit-powers. Although the whole of the modern world was the end result of earlier times and although in this one respect the literature pointed to processes of evolution of that world, the phenomena of stylized explanations were a special feature of literature, and items so stylized provided little background of a historical kind. Intriguing digressions did not constitute fundamental kinds of explanations.

9. TITLES

Study of story titles dictated and translated, at my request, by Mrs. Howard reveals the fact that a comparatively inconspicuous and simple art form characterized titles and that it must be presented in proper perspective as a segment of the whole literary phenomenon.[14] As far as I know, an aesthetic design of this kind has not been described for other oral literatures because collectors of folktales have almost never consistently elicited the exact manner in which narrators and citizenry referred to or entitled stories. Most folkloristic publications contain story titles which Euroamerican authors devised and which therefore reflect non-native criteria for selection of significant content. Collectors have given the impression that they presumed that native storytellers did not possess canons determining the manner of formal or informal reference to stories, but Clackamas story titles show that there were selected kinds of story content that were included and other kinds that were omitted in titles. In addition, native designs in titles displayed a kind of syntax.

Like other Indians of western Oregon groups, Mrs. Howard usually responded with comfort or alacrity to a request for a habitually applied title of a story. I asked for a customary heading following, not preceding, a dictation and its translation. In a few instances she, like other informants, remarked that she did not know the conventional manner of reference but would fashion one that would serve; remembered and volunteered titles had the same formal characteristics. Occasionally she offered a well-memorized caption before a dictation, when she had become accustomed to questions about titles. Often she repeated a title, without change of a word or morpheme, after completion of a translation; and in a very few instances she offered a similar but alternative title. Multiple headings—and there must have been such—do not diminish the significance of the art form of titles or lessen the need to study its causation, functions, content, and regularities.

In this chapter I include fifty-nine Clackamas myth and tale titles. I have added titles that Mrs. Howard gave in Clackamas words for five Molale myths, two Molale stories of the Transitional Era, and three purely ethnographic narratives. I added Molale headings because they represent Clackamas, not Molale, canons for titles and because they supplement and corroborate formulations based upon headings for Clackamas myths and tales.

Unfortunately I lack field notations on the ways in which Clackamas employed story titles in conversational or recital situations. I do not know whether titles were used solely outside the recital, only as formal introductions to stories during winter evenings, or in both settings. My impression is that titles were most often cited, using one of several permissible alternatives, during conversations when references were made to whole stories rather than to scenes from stories. I suppose that stories were referred to by quotations or other excerpts with greater frequency than they were cited by title. Certainly conversations were punctuated with illustrative extracts and analogies from stories. The literature functioned in a formalized way during winter months and in another way, in allusions and fragmented citations, the year round. Some stories may have been captioned tersely and in much the same manner by everyone, while other stories never had generally accepted headings.

Clackamas titles were of five kinds. The first, exemplified in eight instances, displayed only one name, that of a leading actor such as Beaver (40) or Tongue (42). The second type, exemplified in nine cases, displayed a succinct expression of a relatively external or manifest facet of plot, without the supplementation of an actor, as in "She Fooled Him with Her Dog" (28). The third type, illustrated in twenty-two cases, exhibited one or two names of leading actors, followed by an external or manifest facet of plot, as in "Coyote Made Everything Good" (8). The fourth type, shown in six instances, displayed one or two names of or references to leading actors, followed by a characterization of the state or condition of the actor or actors, as in "Seal and Her Younger Brother Dwelt There" (37). The fifth and last type, for which there are twenty-four examples, was characterized by one or two names of leading actors, followed by one or more kinship terms that referred to closely related but unnamed persons, for example, "Blue Jay and His Older Sister" (41).

The first two types were formally simple because each title contained only one referent, either a name or a terse statement of plot action. The other three types were almost as succinct, but they were symmetrical. Each title contained at least two referents, the first of which was a leading actor. Manifest content which was included in a title was always so sparely indicated that only a native who recalled the story could perceive the reference.

It is impossible to determine and futile to suggest the number of titles which were accompanied by equally acceptable or current alternate titles; in many instances probably one title was preferred to its alternants. I believe that many Clackamas titles had alternants in addition to the very few, mentioned below, which Mrs. Howard dictated. At the time of the research in the field I sensed the need to record alternative titles, but I now feel that I did not follow through sufficiently.

Each type of title is now presented with discussions which suggest why I classified and characterized as I did, and why Clackamas worded a title as they did. I include a translation of the sex prefix as "Man" or "Woman" because it was an identifying factor in titles.

The following eight titles were of type 1 and were characterized by a single personal name.

"*Beaver Man*" (48).—Although five unnamed brothers were first on the stage, Beaver Man was selected for the title because he entered the action presently, was the leading actor, and was a principal in no other myth. His grandson might have been added to the title by some persons, but the name of Beaver was sufficient for identification. One might speculate that "Beaver Man and His Grandson" was an alternative.

"*Tongue Man*" (42).—The leading actor whose behavior determined much of the plot and who appeared in the first scene was the ogre named Tongue. He occurred in no other story. His lack of kin may have constituted a factor in the omission of a second item, a kinship term, from the title, but no additional referent was needed for identification of the myth.

"*Idya'bixʷašxʷaš*" (38).—The main actors were the headman whose untranslated masculine name was the title, his son, and two of the headman's wives. The headman's personal name, which was not mentioned elsewhere in the collection, was sufficient for reference to the myth; therefore his unnamed son, the second leading actor, did not need to be pointed to in the title. I think it possible that "and his son" might have been an addition so as to have constituted, with the name in the first position, an accepted alternant.

"*Greyback Louse Woman*" (36).—The title noted the first and leading actor and ignored the overt themes and other important actors, who were five Grizzly Men. Although other myths presented Greyback Louse actors in minor roles, the title was efficient because no other myth introduced a lone Greyback Woman who was also a leading actor. Omission of reference to the Grizzly Men in the title may have been partly consequent upon their lack of relationship by kinship to Greyback Louse.

"*Hot Weather Wind Man*" (23).—His name constituted the title because he was the first actor to appear and the leading one. The myth entitled "Hot Weather Wind and His Older Brothers" (22) was neatly distinguished by the siblings referred to by a kinship term in the title.

"*Sturgeon Man*" (68).—This was the personal name of the actor of the tale. Sturgeon Men appeared as minor actors or in later acts in several myths which had other titles.

"*The Two Gopher Women*" (20).—The title identified the first two actors. Since a pair of Gopher Women acted in no other story of the collection, recognition was probably automatic. Possibly a lone Gopher Man or Gopher Woman appeared in a story which was absent from the collection, but if there were such a narrative, its title would have been distinctive because of sex and numeral prefixes.

"*The Two Grass Widows.*"—The title was only one Clackamas word. Mrs. Howard applied it to a Clackamas dictation of a Molale tale (63) which she placed in the Transitional Era. Although I did not determine whether her heading was a translation of a Molale caption, my feeling is that she offered headings that were stylized according to Clackamas canons even when dictation content was of Molale provenience. The widows were the sole actors in the tale. Their characterization as grass widows of dual number provided precise identification.

The next nine titles were of type 2, which was characterized by a laconic statement of one overt feature of the action in the plot.

"*She Deceived Him with Her Dog*" (28).—The title offered a designation of the early overt behavior of the unnamed female who was the leading actor. The heading was efficient because in no other myth did a dog impersonate a woman. The action title was also appropriate because the plot dealt with relationships, not particularized or named personalities.

"*She Deceived Herself with Milt*" (39).—The purely topical title expressed only one manifest facet of a theme of female rivalry. The title appropriately referred to the second woman who entered the plot, because she, not the first woman, was deceived. In most other instances an actor who appeared initially was referred to in the title. Could it be that the title came from the words of the song in this story?

"*They Deserted the Mean Boy*" (47).—Perhaps this title could be subsumed under the third type, if Clackamas regarded "the mean boy" as a name. However, statement of an overtly causal feature of the action, without distinctive identification of an actor, may warrant categorization in the second type. The desertion transpired early in the narration.

"*They Died of Hunger*" (57). "K'ašxə′kšix *Is the Name of the Place Where They Died of Hunger*" (58).—Mrs. Howard's two versions of this tale were given these alternative titles. No other title contained a place name, although some tales that referred to sites may have been noted in the manner of the second title. Addition of the village name permitted precise identification, since there were other stories of famine due to cold weather (55, 56), and their titles were of type 3. Selection of "they died of hunger" in both titles of this tale indicates the extent to which Clackamas memorized titles and utilized only one overt aspect which had been long since selected and standardized for purposes of a caption.

"She Ate Wild Celery. A Snake Was inside It There" (59).—This was one title in two phrases, a symmetrical statement which was uncommon in titles of this collection (1, 32). I believe that it lacked special stylistic significance because it is to be regarded as the manner in which Chinook speech handled utterance sequences which in many languages are treated by grammatical subordination. The title selected, as always, certain items of what happened overtly in the plot.

"Four Girls Took Away the Girl."—This was a Clackamas designation of a Molale myth (52), but I did not ascertain whether the title was a translation of a Molale title. Although the caption referred to four girls who did not appear initially in the myth, they were leading actors. Their number, without specific mention of who they were, served as partial identification of the story in conjunction with a central although not an initial feature of the plot, their carrying away the girl.

"She Wished for Meat in the Nighttime."—This was a Clackamas dictation of the heading of a short Molale story, placed in the Transitional Era (64) and indicating the dire consequence of transgressing a taboo. The title was a Clackamas way of summarizing interdicted behavior which began the story, and reference to such behavior provided identification.

"They Were Going To Bury the Old Woman Who Was Not Yet Dead."—A more literal translation of this improvised title is "the old woman they were going to bury her, she was not dead." The text was an ethnographic kind of dictation of a relatively recent occurrence in the Molale group, but Mrs. Howard, as usual, described the event in her Clackamas language (98). It is unlikely that the story was old enough to have taken on a title that was generally employed, and I believe that Mrs. Howard spontaneously devised the heading in terms of Clackamas patterning for that form. That is, she selected the initial situation, and its noting provided the identification.

The third type was characterized by one or two names of leading actors, almost always those who appeared in the first scene. Then the title added a terse statement of an overt feature of plot action which usually referred to the first scene. Twenty-two titles of this kind follow.

"Coyote and Skunk. He Tied His Musk Sac" (1).—This was a single title, split according to Clackamas syntax. The segments are approximated in the translation.

The title presented only the two leading actors and an appended manifest feature of the plot, although the intent also seems to have been to point up an intensely amusing anal reference. But naming the two leading actors was sufficient citation, and one may query whether some persons did not limit the heading in that way.

"Coon and Coyote Went and Stole" (3).—The title cited both actors of the first act and a surface manifestation of its plot, the departure in order to steal. No content or actor of the important second act needed to be cited because the reference was sufficient identification.

"Coyote Made a Dance for His Daughter" (7).—The title of this two-act drama noted the two principal actors and referred to the most important scene. Although leading actors appeared in the play before mention of the daughter, she was chosen for inclusion in the title because the plot focused upon Coyote's special feeling for her, indicated by the statement that he gave a spirit-power dance for her. The style permitted only the statement of the manifest behavior which expressed his sentiment.

"Coyote Awaited Sleep" (12).—The title added to the names of the two actors a verb which expressed an overt feature of the plot. One might suggest that some Clackamas employed an alternative title of the fourth type, "Coyote and Sleep."

"Coyote Made Everything Good" (8).—After the personal name of one of the pre-cultural Coyotes, the title noted obliquely that he changed things of basic importance for the people. It named the sole actor who continued throughout the plot and added a summarization of manifest content which was recognizable by anyone who knew the myth. Possibly no other story referred to this one Coyote. His name alone therefore may have been adequate as a title and could have constituted an alternative heading. If the story had been ascribed to Salmon, as it was in some Chinookan groups, his name would have been substituted for Coyote's.

"Coyote Went around the Land" (9).—The title was much like that of the preceding myth; it gave the personal name of the principal player and generalized about his manifest behavior by saying simply that he traveled the length of the land. This Coyote was very likely the one who was referred to in most of the Coyote myths, but indication that he went around the land established the myth because it described, for Clackamas, the essence of the plot. The title ignored various important themes in the plot and selected the external fact of the great man's memorable journey.

"Bear Woman Ate Salmonberries" (15).—The title gave only the name of the one actor and an external aspect of her behavior when in mourning. Without that additional reference her name would have been insufficient; with it the identity of the story was unmistakably established.

"Grizzly Man and Bear Man Ran Away with the Two Girls" (14).—The title noted the four actors who appeared in the first scene. Although the naming of Grizzly and Bear might have been sufficient identification, addition of a single outward aspect of the first scene pinpointed the myth.

"Grizzly Woman Killed People" (17).—The title appears to have needed an item of plot content. The name of Grizzly, even though her personal name *Ki'cimani* was used, might have been insufficient identification. Addition of mention of the second leading actor, little Water Bug, might have jarred stylistic canons because she did not appear in the first scenes. The narrator therefore added to Grizzly's intimate name a note of a relatively external feature of plot action. In other myths she killed people, too, but the title seems to have been sufficiently distinctive with its two components to have established identity of the myth to Clackamas who knew the several Grizzly Woman narratives.

"Seal Woman Took Them to the Ocean" (26).—The title was unusual in its selection of an actor who was not one of the first to appear in the plot. The symmetrical placing of Seal's name with a statement of one manifest facet of plot action resulted in omission in the title of the various themes of the myth. The title gave a precise reference to the myth not because Seal appeared solely in this narrative but because there was an added descriptive item about her hauling people out to the coast. She did not do this in other stories.

"The Old Man and His Daughter-in-law. Her Fingers Stuck Together" (32).—The title noted the two actors who were mentioned first. Although the leading actor was the daughter-in-law, a reason for the failure to mention her before her father-in-law may be that Clackamas felt that in a title a male should be noted before a female. The selected and added item of initial and external behavior, that of her fingers sticking together, was an oblique way of indicating steady consumption of old fish, therefore a famine situation in which the wife was preparing such food continually.

"Dead Persons Came To Purchase the Unmarried Girl" (45).—Although this title was like type 5 structurally, it may have approached type 3 more closely from a Clackamas viewpoint because the subject of the statement of action was not a pronoun. It was a specific reference like "boy," "stars," "slave," and "widow." Designation of a journey for the purpose of purchase of a bride offered an overt feature of the early part of the plot, so that the combination of a name, dead persons, and their action, a bride purchase trip which occurred in the first act, served as perfect identification of the myth.

"The Basket Ogress Took the Child" (46).—Over a dozen important actors appeared in this long drama, and the ogress did not enter the narrative immediately. But she triggered the entire story, and so the title was based aptly upon her per-

sonal name, with the addition of an indication that she stole a male child. This was one of several long myths where a selection of overt behavior which occurred early or initiated the development of the entire plot had been made for the sake of devising a title. The title was in the pattern that consisted of the name of a leading actor who appeared early, with supplementary citation of that actor's initial overt behavior. Mention of the name of the ogress might have sufficed because she appeared in no other story collected.

"*A Boy Made Bad Weather*" (55, 56).—There seem to be at least two possible reasons for identical titles in two wholly different tales. First, since neither story was a myth, the heritage of memorized titles and title alternants had not yet enveloped these two tales. Second, the boys' covert behavior and the community's various responses were so nearly the same, in the light of a Clackamas' orientation, that the stories might be captioned similarly. Possibly Mrs. Howard devised the words of the titles, although she adhered to canons of patterning. Perhaps the titles can also be categorized in type 5, if a "boy" was as unspecific in its reference as, for example, the "mean boy." The first of the two tales (55) contained only one actor. The reference to bad weather was a selection of the initial and overt cause of plot action. The second tale differed in its addition of a second actor.

"*The Girl and Her Dog Sought a Dry Place*" (65).—This title named the two actors and only an overt part of their initial behavior.

"*The Two Children Became Owls*" (66).—The title named the leading actors and, as an exception to the rule, a final rather than an initial feature of overt action.

"*The Slave Stole the Valuables*" (67).—The heading of this historical narrative noted the leading actor and what she did at the beginning of the story. The title was therefore exactly like any myth or tale heading.

"*A Widow Mourns*" (69).—The title noted the leading actor and an overt facet of her behavior, exactly as if the narrative were a myth or tale.

"*Shaman Coyote Doctored.*"—This heading, which was dictated in Clackamas words, referred to a Molale myth (50). The story had only one actor and described his attempt to bring a burned person back to life. Undoubtedly Molales, who lived adjacent to various Chinook and Sahaptin peoples, shared the long myth of Coyote's travels which included an episode in which Coyote pretended to be a shaman. But the present short Molale myth was about a Coyote whom the title indicated as possessed of genuine shamanistic spirit-power; therefore the heading seems to have provided an unmistakable reference to this myth rather than to the long myth of Coyote's journey in which he proceeded through a scene describing bogus therapy. I am persuaded that an alternative title may have omitted the word "shaman."

"I Was Ill and Then Du'šdaq *Doctored Me."*—This is the translation of Clackamas words which applied to an ethnographic dictation of Mrs. Howard about an illness which she had had (114). For the title she selected the initial event, her illness, and that which followed, the shamanistic work on her by the named man. Her heading was therefore clear and pointed, but she gave it a distinctive form. It was really a sequence of two sentence-phrases, with the connective which may be translated "and then, and now next, after that, subsequently." Probably she could have omitted the connective and thereby have supplied a title which in form was like the symmetrical title "She Ate Wild Celery. A Snake Was inside It There."

"Grizzly Woman Pursued Him."—Literally the dictation read "she pursued him Grizzly Woman," but word order was not rigid in a language like Chinook, where prefixed pronominal morphemes functioned syntactically. I do not doubt that there could have been an alternant and possibly a preferred title with the two words in reversed positions. The story referred to was an ethnographic narrative which described a recent event (134), and Mrs. Howard obviously devised the title on the spur of the moment. Probably that is why its form was slightly atypical. Its content, as usual, selected a leading actor and the inception of the story.

The fourth type, exemplified in six titles, like the third presented one or two names of leading actors but appended a verb which indicated their state or condition, not what they did.

"Duck Was a Married Woman" (21).—She was the sole actor. The assertion that she was married seems irrelevant because the myth itself gave no indication that her marriage had anything to do with the content. Her name alone might have been sufficient identification. But there may have been a long-established precedent or other need to indicate that she was married, rather than that she was warm or cold, in order to distinguish the myth from another story of Duck Woman which is missing from the collection.

"Seal Woman and Her Younger Brother Dwelt There" (37).—The title selected two of the three actors who entered the plot at the beginning of the drama. A fourth actor was no less important. The title was, then, determined only by need for an unmistakable identification. The name of Seal was insufficient because she was an actor in other myths. Since she lacked a younger brother in them, the added mention of him permitted identification. The reason for the supplementation of a verb which, in approximate translation, meant "they dwelt there," is unclear. Possibly inclusion of such a verb was a resort to an occasionally employed alternate heading. A title which said only "Seal and Her Younger Brother" might have been equally apt and stylistically correct.

"Sun Woman and Moon Woman Lived There" (61).—Both actors were mentioned, with what was possibly again an optional addition of a verb indicating that they

lived at the same place. If the verb had been omitted, the title would probably have given an equally definitive reference because no other story of this collection presented both women. The content of the tale referred to feelings about sexual matters, defecation, and money, not at all centrally to the contiguity of two women.

"Badger and Coyote Were Neighbors" (10).—The title named only the two leading actors, ignoring their children and an important actor who was a centipede. The heading added to the actors' names only a reference to their close association. Recognition would have followed utterance of the title merely because of juxtaposition of Badger and Coyote. These personages appeared together in no other plot. The additional item about their neighborliness may have been unnecessary; therefore an alternative, "Badger and Coyote," may have been current.

"Coyote and East Wind Had Their House" (11).—The title presented the two actors and added, like the preceding title, a minor item of plot content, a note that the actors lived in amicable contiguity. The names of the actors were sufficient for recognition. One may wonder whether Clackamas resorted to an equally efficient alternant, "Coyote and East Wind."

"Skunk Was a Married Man" (19).—The title named the leading actor and obliquely noted his wife, the other actor. Although it ignored the plot themes, its mention of Skunk may alone have given adequate identification. But recognition was improved by the added observation about his married state, because he had a wife in no other myth that has been recorded among Clackamas.

In the fifth type, which contains twenty-five examples—three more than the third type—each title contained one or two names of leading actors followed by a kinship term for a close relative of a person so named. Three examples each contained two kinship terms.

"Coyote and His Son's Son and Their Wives" (2).—The title, which said nothing about the plot and its moralistic theme, merely referred to all the actors and thereby pointed neatly to this and no other myth. Three additional titles also cited Coyote and his grandson, but the present title entailed no confusing reference because it added mention of the men's wives.

"Cock Robin, His Older Sister, and His Sister's Daughter" (31).—The leading actor was Robin's sister, and only she continued through the several acts. The title noted solely the three actors of the first act and named Robin first perhaps for no other reason than the fact that he possessed a distinctive name, although there may have been pressure to name a man before a woman. However, the principal factor in the name order was probably the circumstance that Robin was cited with a name and his sister was not. Robin's name alone virtually identified the myth, but since Robins appeared in a few other myths, the added citations of his sister and her

daughter gave absolute identification. A named person was always first in order in a title, and references to unnamed kin followed.

"Thunder and His Mother" (30).—Because he was the leading actor and appeared early, although not immediately, in the narrative, and because he was male and had a name, Thunder was named in the title in first position. His mother was mentioned, too, because without added reference to her there might have been confusion with the *Ku'šaydi* (40) myth in which Thunder Men also appeared. A Thunder had a mother in no other myth.

"Crawfish and Her Older Sister" (43).—These leading actors entered the play at its start. Since the plot revolved about the childish misbehavior of Crawfish, and since she was a leading actor in no other recorded myth, her name alone might have identified the story. But the preferred stylization of headings and the circumstance that the sister of Crawfish was also a leading actor resulted in the familiar patterning characterized by a named actor and her relative. Other interesting features of the title include the fact that the sister, Seal, was cited by a kinship term rather than by the word for Seal. Her name was employed in some other titles (26, 37).

"Coon and His Father's Mother" (49).—The title employed the two leading actors who appeared at once in the first act. Coon was an important actor in two other myths, but the identification was precise because of addition of the grandmother in the title. Since she was not named during the comedy, a kinship term sufficed for her.

"Ku'šaydi and His Older Brother" (40).—The title referred to the two leading actors, who also appeared at the start of the drama. Since the hero appeared in no other myth, his personal name was perfect identification of the story. The supplementary citation of his brother was another example of the vogue in headings, with its patterned symmetry and inclusion of a reference to a second leading actor who was unnamed but a close kin of the first actor.

"Blue Jay and His Older Sister" (41).—The title referred to the two leading actors, who appeared at the start of the comedy. Although Blue Jay acted in many stories, this was the only one in the collection which named him in the title. Perhaps that fact alone identified the myth. However, the added reference to his sister offered reinforcement because elsewhere he lacked such kin. Again, citation of her also effected a preferred kind of title, composed of a named person who was a leading actor and a kinship term for a second leading actor.

"Wren and His Father's Mother" (25).—The actors named in the title were the first to appear, and they were also the leading actors. Satisfactory identification of the myth perhaps would have been made by means of mention of Wren alone. Although the collection contained eight titles which were single names, there was,

as already remarked, a numerical preponderance and therefore undoubtedly a preference for titles with names or notations of two or more actors, the second of which was expressed by a kinship term which stood for a person who was closely related to the first, the named, actor. Such an option may have been only one among several reasons for the added notation of the grandmother. She was perhaps the more important of the two leading players and therefore an especial feeling of fitness accrued to mention of her. But she was unnamed and feminine, therefore the named and masculine actor was referred to in first position.

"Snake Tail and Her Son's Sons" (24).—The title noted only the first actors. Probably there was no other Snake Tail Woman in the literature, and so a mention of her name might have sufficed for a title. The possible lack of necessity for citation of her grandsons suggests a conceivable alternant, "Snake Tail Woman."

"Hot Weather Wind and His Older Brothers" (22).—These were the actors who introduced the myth, and it was the leading actor whose personal name was given. If the title had noted only Hot Weather Wind, it would have been impossible to distinguish it from the story whose heading was simply "Hot Weather Wind Man." Since the latter actor lacked siblings it was efficient to add mention of brothers in the first title, shape it in a manner that was favored, and with the same brushstroke furnish a precise identification.

"Tga'matgma and His Son's Two Sons" (35).—Although the mother of the two sons was at once mentioned in the play, together with her sons and their named grandfather, the title omitted her. The reason is not clear, but one might suggest that there was a factor of preference for designation of male rather than female when a story had many actors, or that the adventure of the two sons was the manifest plot component of outstanding interest. The personal name of the grandfather, which I cannot translate (note that the letter *g* in the name is a velar consonant), may have been enough to identify the myth, since he acted in no other story of the collection. He was also a figurehead rather than an actor in this myth. The added reference to his grandsons, who were unnamed, may have been pressured by their importance in the plot and by the vogue in titles which favored a symmetrical citation of two or more actors rather than one, even though one possessed a unique personal name.

"The Frogs and Their Mother" (33).—An important actor, Lizard Man, was not named in the title, perhaps because he did not enter at the start of the play. A notation of Frogs might have been sufficient for identification if no other myths referred to Frog Girls. The supplementary mention of their mother appears to have made the reference unmistakable and to have supplied the symmetry preferred in headings. Apparently Lizard's masculinity was insufficient to bring him into the title, because of his later entry.

"Gi'ckux and His Older Brother" (34).—The name of *Gi'ckux* should have been sufficient as a title because he appeared, in all probability, in no other myth. The added citation of his brother, who appeared at the start, too, satisfied the liking for two references in the title and took care of the older brother's important role in the drama.

"Stick Drum Gambler and His Older Brother" (29).—The title named the leading actors who appeared in the first scene. Mention of the older brother was perhaps unnecessary, although it could have been pressured both by his importance in the drama and by the balancing of two or more names which characterize the formal symmetry of a preferred kind of title. The notation of one name, Stick Drum Gambler, might have given an unmistakable identification of the myth. Again one may wonder whether many of the titles of the present type did not also occur in an alternate form characterized by omitting notation of a second actor. Field rechecking could have revealed the possibility and frequency of such alternants had an analysis of titles highlighted the problems before the demise of the last informed Clackamas.

"Awl and Her Son's Son" (27).—The title selected the two leading actors, who also appeared in the first scene. Since no other myth of the collection had an Awl Woman, her name might have been sufficient as a title and conceivably was an alternative heading.

"Flint and His Son's Son" (18).—Presumably the title needed to name only Flint Man because this myth may have been the only one in which he appeared. The title added an oblique mention of his grandson, not the actual identity of the actor, who, to be sure, was Panther and who appeared with Flint in the first scene. In this manner the title stressed the leading actor, Flint, added a second and important actor who also appeared at the beginning of the myth, referred only to his etiquette relationship, and so adhered to the more desired kind of patterning of titles. Maybe "Flint" was an alternant.

"Black Bear Woman and Grizzly Woman and Their Sons" (16).—Although the title offered only the leading actors who appeared initially, mention of them identified the drama. The reference to sons was a stylistic supplementation which was in line with the title patterning of choice. Sons seem to have been unnecessary for the identification because no other myth of the collection started with the two women, but if the title had been simply "Bear Woman and Grizzly Woman," its content might not have been shown so pointedly. Mrs Howard volunteered an alternate, "Grizzly Woman and Bear Woman and Their Children." The reversing of actors indicates both that the order of naming lacked significance in this title and that there was a preferred addition of mention of close kin of the named actors.

"Fire and His Son's Son" (13).—The title utilized only the first pair of leading actors, Fire and his grandson, although the latter's two sons were no less outstand-

ing in the drama. The notation of Fire himself appears to have sufficed if the unneeded but stylistically desired supplement of a grandson had been omitted. Unfortunately, the occurrence of an alternate heading such as "Fire" cannot be shown.

"Coyote and His Son's Son Panther" (6).—The title referred solely to the two first actors to appear. The juxtaposition of Coyote and Panther undoubtedly identified the myth. In the Flint myth (18) Panther's name could have been omitted from the title because the name of Flint alone identified the play; in this title Panther's name could not be omitted because of the multiplicity of Coyote stories and the fact that several among them included an actor who was either a real grandson or in a relationship that was equivalent. It is clear from the title of the next myth referred to that "son's son" may have been safely omitted in this myth, while "Panther" was not, so that a hypothetical alternant such as "Coyote and Panther" must be allowed.

"Coyote and His Son's Son" (5).—As in other titles, this one merely noted the two actors who appeared first. Since the unnamed grandson was actually Salmon, a possible alternant was "Coyote and His Son's Son Salmon." One may also query whether the style permitted omission of the kinship term and another alternant such as "Coyote and Salmon." Although the title was almost identical with some others, it seems to have sufficed because in the heading of the next myth (4) Coyote's personal name was specified, and in the myth immediately preceding (6) the grandson was named. The three very similar captions probably were clear designations to Clackamas.

"Coyote (Sasa'ylaxam) *and His Son's Son"* (4).—The title selected only the first two actors and omitted mention of the central theme. The Coyote who acted in this drama was referred to not by the word for a coyote but by a special personal name which appeared in no other myth of the collection and doubtless granted recognition of this myth. But the additional mention of the unnamed grandson substantiates, in the first place, a deduction that the style of captions preferred an indication of the first two or three leading actors to appear, irrespective of their rank in the plot. In the second place, the title obliquely suggested a greater importance of this second actor because of the very inclusion of reference to him. Third, a factor of balance or symmetry, exemplified by many titles, may have operated to favor addition of a kinship term to represent a second leading actor related to the first actor cited in the title. Although the grandson's wife was a principal actor, her later appearance in the story resulted in her omission from the heading.

"The Old Woman Had Five Sons and One Daughter of Her Son."—The literal translation is "the-old-woman five her-sons feminine-one her-son's daughter." The title, dictated in Clackamas, was applied to a Molale myth (51). I did not learn whether the Clackamas wording of the title was a translation of a Molale heading. The content of the myth treated of a Profile Ogre who ate the brains of the old

woman, but the title made note only of the first actors: Profile entered the narrative later. The distinctive trait of the title was the mention of the five sons. Such a notation served by contrast with the title of the next myth.

"The Old Woman and Her Son's Daughter."—This title was phrased for a Molale myth (54) describing an ogre who sucked the blood from the hearts of both actors mentioned in the heading. The old woman of the myth probably also had five sons, but their omission from the caption may have provided the contrast that distinguished this myth from its predecessor. Again the title noted the first actors, not the chief one, the ogre.

"Woodrat and His Father's Mother."—This was the Clackamas title for another Molale myth (53). Children, Crawfishes, and Owls were minor actors, but personages cited in the heading were both the principals and the first actors to make an appearance. The combination of Woodrat and his grandmother appears to have sufficed for identification without mention of content or other actors.

"My Older Cousin and I."—This was a designation which Mrs. Howard phrased spontaneously in order to supply a heading for a story about an event in her own life (130). Literally, however, she dictated "I and my-feminine-older-cousin," perhaps because the principal actor was intended to be herself, and certainly because a kinship term was necessarily placed in second rather than initial position in a caption.

Stylistic features which connected with linguistic factors in titles should be mentioned. In the first place, the translations of titles of types 3, 4, and 5 included an "and." A connective morpheme $k^wali'wi$, "and," was present but infrequently so and in only six titles. In ordinary utterances which were succinct it might not appear. We find, for example, in terms of morphemes which had to be expressed, "masculine-Beaver his-grandson," where a close English translation "Beaver his grandson" is less desirable than "Beaver and his grandson." "Masculine-Coyote masculine-Skunk" is a literal rendering of morphemes of a title which is preferably translated "Coyote and Skunk." "Coon and Coyote Went and Stole" might have been "masculine-Coon masculine-Coyote they-two-went they-two-stole." Again, the significant linguistic feature of the style, from the English speaker's point of view, is the usual omission of a connective morpheme. Its absence effected a desired compactness.

Six titles were exceptional because they displayed a connective morpheme. "Coon and Coyote Went and Stole" actually contained the morpheme "and" between Coon and Coyote. I believe that an alternative was equally accepted, that it omitted "and," and that it was otherwise identical. Since English style of speech demands "and," the slight difference between two such alternants would not appear in their English translations. So, too, "Coyote and East Wind Had Their House" included the connective morpheme "and." I suggest again that an alternate might have omitted this connective. A third title which presented the same morpheme "and" is "Black Bear and Grizzly Bear and Their Sons"; "and" connected Bear and Grizzly. I am confident that a permissible alternant lacked "and." A fourth heading that contained "and" was "Thunder and His Mother"; again a probably allowed alternate might have lacked the connective. A fifth title with a dictated but almost certainly dispensable "and" was "Crawfish and Her Older Sister." A sixth example is in the heading which Mrs. Howard improvised for an ethnographic dictation about herself. Literally it was "I and My Older Counsin."

A second stylistic feature on a linguistic level was the use or omission of a word which may be translated by "had" or "was." The title "Skunk Was a Married Man" was literally "masculine-Skunk masculine-married-person." But the title "Duck Was a Married Woman" was literally "feminine-Duck feminine-married-person feminine-subject-was." A likely alternate would have been simply "Duck Married-Woman," without "was."

The title "I Was Ill and *Du'šdaq* Doctored Me" is distinctive because it contained the statement connective, *aga* (*g* is a velar consonant), which may be translated "then next, and so then." The title was an improvisation, but it combined terseness and the type 3 form with the stylized manner, in running speech, by which phrases and sentences were connected.

Finally, it is evident that Clackamas referred to stories of their oral literature, and perhaps also to narratives of recent devising, in stylized ways. One informant's data were so definitively structured as to prove that Clackamas culture granted her that structure. The five types exhibited in her dictations of titles may not exhaust all the types present in the heritage; but Mrs. Howard's dictated titles permit the deduction that canons for titles allowed alternates and variations, within no longer ascertainable limits.

CHAPTER XVIII

TERSE DELINEATION AND SPEEDY ACTION

STORY dictations in a native language, and renderings in English by bilingual informants, display throughout the northwest states compactness and brevity, especially so in groups where acculturational processes operated with unusual destructiveness upon the cultural heritage and where the collector of stories arrived on the scene several generations after Caucasian entry. In addition, the precontact narrators' selections of facets of action, and the very phrasings applied, exhibited notable similarities in the approximately sixty language groups of Washington, Idaho, and Oregon, and in peoples in contiguous states and southern British Columbia. By contrast with written literatures of the Western world, and oral literatures of some other non-literate peoples, northwest states raconteurs transmitted myths and tales in terms of a distinctive frame of stylizations which effected a Puritanical parsimony in expression of feelings and descriptive ideas.

By terseness or succinctness I mean selection of very few aspects of a situation or action and omission of aspects which another culture's literature might express. But it is not enough to characterize Clackamas and other Northwest literatures in an all-embracing way as terse, staccato, or rapidly moving. One should point to specific traits as well as to general characteristics of style. One should point to the various kinds of items which were especially often selected for expression or which had to be said. Such recurring entities should be highlighted by showing what might have been uttered in a literature with another kind of stylization, one more verbose and needful of visual and emotional documentation. However, since every page of the Howard dictations illustrates this pre-eminent characteristic of style and since it has been treated in Part I, especially in the discussion of myth 1, it is unnecessary to offer further exemplification.

The only trait of style which is the opposite of succinct is the five-pattern, discussed above (chap. xvii). A depiction of a situation was repeated, with only minute alterations in wording, five times for each of five men, five girls, or five siblings who acted in it. For a discussion of stylistic features which were themselves compressed expressions of content, the reader may refer to chapter xvii and its inventory of devices, which include "enter an end house," "village seen from above," "five villages," "five mountains," "the next day," "presently," "that is the way," "so many times," "all the time," "and now . . . made preparations," and some others.

Terse delineation of actors and situations, a characteristic which is most striking to the student of Euroamerican origin and which is responsible for major difficulties in his analysis of content, was probably never consciously designed by a Northwest storyteller. He was succinct because he had learned no other way of expressing himself. The few choices of things which could be expressed were items that had to be articulated with utmost brevity. Such a blanket characteristic of literary style must have been maintained during long eras because of several factors, including the exhaustive familiarity with actors, plots, and stylizations which adult villagers shared. Therefore story content was not repeated *ad nauseam* during formal recitals. Each person's acquaintanceship with literature because of formal recitals was heavily reinforced by year-round chitchat about and discussions of stories.

These conversations were stimulated not only by psychological needs rooted in the cultural and social heritage but by challengingly different versions and treatments of plots given by in-laws, visitors, and alien peoples. The very manner of performance and the limited time available during an evening encouraged compactness. As far as we know, among lower Columbia River peoples the longest myths could be segmented into two- and three-night presentations, but there may have been aesthetic feeling that wherever possible a story ought to be completed before too many auditors were snoring. Such a factor favored some compression if not tight condensation of content, and it counteracted whatever pleasure there was in devising embellishments.

The freedom of choice permitted a precontact narrator is an open question, and I think it can never be solved for any northwest states literature. Alternate versions which a twentieth-century anthropologist recorded were in many instances either versions of several villages or of different village clusters, not of raconteurs within one village. Our collections are also cluttered with truncated and errorful versions by acculturated survivors who never approached mastery of their literature. I believe that relative uniformity and standardization, approaching verbatim memorization, characterized some of the stories possessed by a group of contiguous villages, but at the same time a contrary tendency toward variety was created and supported by social interaction with other groups of villages. Since the patterns of village and lineage relationships were shattered in the earliest years of envelopment by Caucasians, processes of this kind in a northwest states literature can never be witnessed.

But the reason for my proposal regarding near word-for-word uniformity in some stories arises not from observation of a functioning aboriginal community nor from comparison of diverse versions of a single story but from deductions that I made when I watched a few of my oldest informants in nearby groups. For example, when my principal Klikitat Sahaptin informant, the shaman Joe Hunt, dictated to me, his very aged wife often anticipated a short phrase or corrected his words. I therefore inferred that long ago older auditors made word and phrase corrections during myth recitals. Mrs. Hunt certainly exhibited intense involvement in every morpheme of her husband's dictations. She repeatedly corrected him by showing preference for—I should rather say obstinate insistence upon—certain forms or words. If he left out an episode, she was always on the alert with the correct starting words so that he could proceed as she thought he should. He accepted her corrections, which often interrupted his dictation, without manifest irritation. I do not know whether other storytellers would have displayed a like impassivity when they were corrected, but many aged Indians showed the same sort of identification with a narrator who was dictating to me. Some also interjected comments in order to correct words, phrases, or content sequences. The older I supposed a myth might be, the more I felt that in precontact days it had been transmitted with something close to phrase and sentence memorization in some if not all episodes. On the other hand, the informant who displayed the greatest freedom in elaborations and embellishments was a Sahaptin who was an adherent of the acculturated Shaker faith of the late nineteenth century.

But I register only impressions. I cannot support them with better evidence. My feeling is that in precontact eras intermarriages, visits, and unflagging discussions about alternative and contradictory presentations were outstanding factors in producing changes of content and form. Creativity was almost required, to be sure, because of glaring contradictions and differences in plot treatments. But there is no means of indicating the extent or pace of creative changes, nor can we weigh the ultimate factors that made for creativity. I urge only that we resort to theories of genius and creative artists when we lack other means of accounting for literary change, or that we include a genius theory with other formulations of process. Changes of a creative kind certainly occurred constantly, in spite of what I believe was a prevailing need for permanence in features of storytelling.

Although I am inclined to suppose that the behavior of Mrs. Hunt when her husband dictated represented a phenomenon which was region-wide, it is necessary to record the possibility that Clackamas processes of literature transmission and change, whatever they were, were distinctive in significant respects. For Clackamas were wealthier and very likely had a larger populational concentration than any Sahaptin groups, were probably tenser about well-to-do persons and headmen, and differed from all their neighbors in many other aspects of culture. Unlike Mr. and Mrs. Hunt, who were usually together when one or the other dictated in Sahaptin, no aged Clackamas was an auditor when Mrs. Howard sat with me. Therefore I cannot at any point be certain about matters of relative fixity of words, phrases, and other traits of Clackamas literature except for Mrs. Howard's consistency with her other dictations.

Speed of action cannot be regarded apart from terseness. The two were facets of a single characteristic, and a Clackamas could not perceive a distinction between them. Since everything was depicted in one or two or three quick strokes, the action moved rapidly; one could not delineate so compactly and at the same time advance slowly through a plot. Every story illustrates this point. It is, however, important to emphasize the impact of speed as a central feature of style, to suggest its causation, and to show that such causation really means manner of maintenance of the trait, not its origin. Speed of action arose from the circumstance that all adults were more or less participant in the transmission of literature and that they knew it thoroughly. Therefore they felt no need to present stories in recitals with many descriptive details of the context. They responded aesthetically to their raconteurs' dexterous selection of items which effected abstractness, starkness, and speed of movement. The fewer such items, the better the effect. Newly borrowed stories could be placed only in the same kind of skeleton of presentation. The recital of such a story in its turn allowed the audience to fill in with new associations, new but again unphrased descriptive matter. The audience in its subsequent discussions created the context and helped to formulate the content expressed in later recitals of the new stories. Speed of plot action was therefore not so much caused as it was a stylistic characteristic indefinitely maintained by a traditional manner of recital and the concomitant fulness of community discussions of plot content.

Stress in recitals was, on the one hand, on a storyteller's skilful selection from the small kit of things that could be said and, on the other hand, on the community members' maximal range of responses, such as visual and feeling associations, empathy, and identification. Such responses were not in isolated individuals sitting passively at a recital. These individuals presently interacted and changed one another's responses. In the society men did many things together and women did many things together, chatting, joking, carping, and theorizing ceaselessly. The two sexes sat about in the houses and discussed stories with each other again. When myth-telling time came around, during the damp and cooler months, the people who had been conversing about stories during the dry, warm months sat together at night, but with youngsters beside them, to hear the stories intoned in a more formal way, without interruptions for fantasying and theorizing, and with utmost identification with the narrator who set forth in precise phrases what everyone loved to hear. It was true because it had been said so many times, and by those who knew best.

CHAPTER XIX

CONCLUSION

A SEGMENT of a non-Western people's sociocultural heritage can be studied with profit before the most fundamental characteristics of the society have been ascertained. In fact, anthropology, folklore, and linguistics have long taken for granted that they could perform certain operations upon parts of a society before they knew much about the whole. In a society whose structure and functionings are virtually unknown, we can turn the spotlight advantageously upon its literary expressions of relationships, personality traits of story actors, features of humor, premises regarding values and world view, and stylistic items of many kinds.

A criterion that should determine a choice of what to study—for example, a social structure or that structure's and its people's projective expressions—is the manageability of the descriptive material at hand. That is, where a facet of a way of life is composed of a relatively small number of items falling into relatively few types, we can move in quickly and discern a good deal of what goes on. Obvious examples are numeral systems, color constructs, scale patterns and rhythms in music, and the syntax of story titles. Each such segment of a sociocultural system also ties in with many other facets of that configuration. It serves no purpose to delay analysis of a numeral system or a color terminology on the grounds that we should first examine and formulate the social structure. We can make worthwhile statements about numeral or color systems long before we have exposed the design and operations of the social system which they express in their special ways. When something is known about the content and structuring of another segment of culture, such as myth actors' personality traits, it is useful to suggest their connections with the sociocultural system which generated or maintained them, if for no other reason than to reinforce with additional evidences statements about the social system which traditional methods of ethnographic research supply.

The units and classes of units in the religious ceremonies, governmental machinery, dance repertoire, world view, and ethics of Clackamas are at the best meagerly revealed in their folklore. I suggest that the reason for this is that Clackamas institutions and relationships took such adequate care of these portions of the heritage that there was little or no pressure to express them in the oral literature. On the other hand, the heritage evidently creaked and clanked so as to proliferate expressions in that literature of various troublesome social relationships, behavioral or temperamental traits in actors' personalities, incongruities exposed to view in humor, and aspirations projected into supernaturals. These could be listed from the literature materials, arranged, and connected with trouble spots in the functioning society. Although the numbers of such expressive items were considerable, they were fortunately not prodigal to the point of bewilderment. Stylistic characteristics of the literature were also in numbers and types which allowed easy handling.

Preoccupations which scholars versed in psychiatry and written literatures, and interested in folklores, have had in constructs such as archetypal plot, symbol, and texture seem to me to offer no means for exploring the range, functional significance, or causation of folkloristic phenomena among Clackamas or other Northwest Indians. Employment of such concepts, appeals to causation by genius, or resorts to impressionistic criticism impede study of important questions and obstruct thinking which can advance field or analytic methodology. The archetype construct which has fascinated a generation of literary critics is too cumbersome, if not too irrelevant, to assist in revealing the various contents, forms, and dynamics of a folklore. The concepts and approaches of those who work with archetypes and symbols must in general be shelved, as a matter of immediate policy in folkloristic analysis, to be replaced by the sensitivity and strategy which a mature science exemplifies in its judicious selection and weighting of fundamental and minor units, its taxonomy of the classes of such units, and its systematic theorization about their multiple causation.

Our venture at analysis of segments of literary content and traits of style should be regarded as an exploration in the application of scientific method rather than as an excursion leading rapidly toward a theoretical system. That which is theoretical for the wide field of folklore in this book is almost entirely appropriated from scientific method and from psychological hypotheses. The method followed in the book is original only in its specific manner of application to a folklore. It is an effort to select, identify, and arrange some of the principal classes of content and style components in an oral literature and to suggest, without oversimplification, their more likely causes.

The book also contains incidental theoretical inferences about the Clackamas and other Indians of the northwest states. These locally limited deductions comprise the beginnings of a system of theory about the society and culture of one region. They will stand if supported by evidence from other analyses of Northwest materials.

The results indicate, I think, that henceforth we must work in new ways in folkloristic science and field researches. Principal emphases in the latter enterprises used to be to collect whole folktales, and in as many variants as there was time for. In future field research, story-collecting should be accorded only second priority, other things equal. First priority in field method should go to ascertaining from informants their associations and feelings about each unit and type of literary content and style. Speculations of kinds which characterized parts of the Clackamas analysis should be minimized or replaced, wherever possible, by specific responses from many native informants. Such returns should compose the larger portion of the field notes and at a later time should receive a central place in publication of the research.

The study displays the need to present oral literatures not solely in bare reportings of recitalists' words, motifs, and plots but also in their types of units and the contextual associations which societies have for such features. Such full write-ups will do three things. They will permit far greater appreciation and enjoyment of exotic literatures than folklorists ever made possible for readers of their publications or even for other folklorists. Fully annotated write-ups will effect utilization of oral literatures for many and new scientific purposes in sociocultural anthropology. And they will provide means by which folklore itself can emerge from its larval stage of collecting and comparing motifs and plots to press forward toward a mature stage of scientific workmanship.

NOTES

1. Franz Boas, *Chinook Texts* (Bureau of American Ethnology, Bulletin 20 [Washington, 1894]). He published a second Chinook volume of the same kind, *Kathlamet Texts* (Bureau of American Ethnology, Bulletin 26), in 1901, and *Tsimshian Texts* (Bulletin 27), in 1902.

2. Morris Weitz, *Philosophy of the Arts* (Cambridge: Harvard University Press, 1950), esp. chap. iii.

3. Franz Boas, *Tsimshian Mythology* (Annual Report of the Bureau of American Ethnology, No. 31 [Washington, 1916]). Gladys A. Reichard, *Coeur d'Alene Myths* ("Memoirs of the American Folklore Society," No. 41 [Philadelphia, 1947]).

4. A number in parentheses refers to a story so numbered in *Clackamas Chinook Texts*.

5. Edward Sapir, *Wishram Texts* ("Publications of the American Ethnological Society," No. 2 [Leyden, 1909]), p. 149.

6. Franz Boas, *Kathlamet Texts*, p. 79.

7. Verne F. Ray, *Lower Chinook Ethnographic Notes* ("University of Washington Publications in Anthropology," Vol. VII, No. 2 [Seattle, 1938]), pp. 54, 73.

8. Edward Sapir, *Wishram Texts*, p. 249.

9. Margaret Lantis, *Nunivak Eskimo Personality As Revealed in the Mythology* ("Anthropological Papers of the University of Alaska," Vol. II, No. 1 [College, Alaska, 1953]), pp. 109–74.

10. Victor Barnouw, "A Psychological Interpretation of a Chippewa Origin Legend," *Journal of American Folklore*, LXVIII, Nos. 267, 268, 269 (1955), 73–85, 211–23, 341–55.

11. The present chapter parallels several unpublished papers of mine.

12. Arthur C. Ballard, *Mythology of Southern Puget Sound* ("University of Washington Publications in Anthropology," Vol. III, No. 2 [Seattle, 1929]). Thelma Adamson, *Folk-tales of the Coast Salish* ("Memoirs of the American Folklore Society," No. 27 [New York, 1934]).

13. Elizabeth D. Jacobs, *Nehalem Tillamook Tales*, ed. Melville Jacobs. In press, University of Oregon. This collection, dictated by a Nehalem woman to Mrs. Jacobs in 1933 at Garibaldi, Oregon, lacks interpretive comments.

14. This chapter parallels my article on titles in the April, 1957, issue of the *Journal of American Folklore*.

Index

INDEX